THE MODERN HOTEL IN BRITAIN

Bruce Peter

THE MODERN
HOTEL
IN BRITAIN

Front cover: The Hotel Piccadilly in central Manchester when newly completed in 1965.
Rear cover: Clockwise from top left: the Art Deco ballroom entrance of the Park Lane Hotel in London, a vestibule in the Cumberland Hotel in London, the early-1960s Ariel Hotel at London Airport and a mid-1960s view of a bedroom in the Albany Hotel, Birmingham.
Title page upper: The Birmingham Airport Hotel as it appeared in the early-1950s. Designed in the late-1930s, it was completed after the war.
Title page lower: A late-1950s view of the Hotel Leofric in Coventry, which opened in 1955.

Lily
Publications

Published by and copyright © 2017 Bruce Peter.
All rights reserved.
ISBN 978-1-911177-23-4
Exclusively distributed by Lily Publications (IOM) Ltd.
www.lilypublications.co.uk

Contents

Foreword

Opposite: The London Hilton at the foot of Park Lane as it appeared shortly after opening in 1963.

The Modern Hotel in Britain represents my attempt to fill what I consider to be a gaping hole in the historical record of modern architecture. Hotels, it seems to me, are culturally important buildings, reflecting changing social, cultural, technological and aesthetic conditions – yet I could find very little about them in existing publications on British architectural history. Although large and prominent, they seemed to be a building type hiding in plain sight.

My interest in commercial buildings began in student days, while studying at The Glasgow School of Art in the first half of the 1990s. At that time, architecture lecturers there sought to inspire students to aim high by exposing them only to canonical works by great names. I, however, became intrigued by a grotty old bingo hall that had once been a cinema in the city's East End, finding its quirky façade, ugly rear quarters and exotic interior to be much richer and more curious than the 'masterworks' I was taught to admire. This initial interest led to a major study of cinema architecture and subsequently to a PhD examining modernism and the architecture of pleasure in the inter-war era. At the same time, my life-long interest in the design of modern merchant ships led me to investigate passenger liners, cruise ships and car ferries in terms of design history.

The idea for this book first occurred in 2008 when I was working on a history of the Cunard trans-Atlantic liner *Queen Elizabeth 2* and, as part of the research, I interviewed the architect and interior designer, Brian Beardsmore, who had been employed by Dennis Lennon's practice. In addition to designing large parts of *QE2*, I found that Lennon's firm had produced interiors for a series of Albany hotels for J. Lyons, projects for which Beardsmore had been responsible. The photographs he showed me revealed them to have

A recent view of the Dorchester in London's Park Lane; completed in 1931, the hotel's reinforced concrete construction enabled open planning and corner windows. Verandas lend an air of continental levity, unusual for a major building of the era in the capital.

been decoratively very similar to the liner. During the subsequent eight years, I carried out research in archives, conducted interviews with other retired architects and interior designers and examined architecture, construction and catering journals. In these endeavours, I received indefatigable help from The Glasgow School of Art's Senior Librarians, David Buri and Duncan Chappell and their assistant, Rebecca Olivia. The staff of the GSA's Research Office were also immensely generous in assisting me – particularly Ken Neil, Alison Hay and Julie Ramage – as were my own department colleagues, especially Nicholas Oddy and Sarah Smith. Above all, my wife, Elspeth Hough, and my parents, Ann Glen and John Peter, have been very supportive. Outwith work and family circles, I am especially grateful to Elain Harwood of Historic England – who probably knows more about British buildings of the mid-twentieth century than anyone else – for acting as a 'critical friend' in reading the manuscript, commenting upon it and making numerous helpful suggestions. In addition, other knowledgeable friends, including Anthony Cooke, Robert Proctor, David Trevor-Jones, and Thom Gorst have helped me with specific aspects of the research. I have received great assistance from the General Services Department of the Mitchell Library in Glasgow, the British Architectural Library, the Design Archives at the University of Brighton and from local archives throughout the British Isles. All errors are mine alone.

Many present-day hotel operators and managers allowed me access to their premises with great patience and courtesy. In comparison with past research projects, during which my interest was sometimes treated with suspicion, I have received only very warm welcomes from hoteliers and their staff; I am grateful to all of them and I earnestly hope that readers will enjoy this book.

Bruce Peter
Glasgow, December 2016

Introduction

'A reading of press reports on recent hotel projects makes it clear that hotels arouse feelings in a way that one would more normally expect from projected race tracks, abattoirs and amusement parks. It is obvious that to a small, but highly articulate, section of the public hotels retain the stigma of theatrical raffishness… Experienced hotel operators know that, like turtles, they should keep their unhatched children underground until the last possible moment.'[1]

*

From grand edifices for social elites to repetitive 'machines' accommodating the masses in transit, British hotels of the mid-twentieth century are a controversial and, hitherto, critically under-scrutinised architectural genre. In addition, they were an early and prominent building type to exemplify various forms of architectural modernism.

Providing temporary shelter and recuperation, hotels are cosmopolitan environments rich in opportunities for the experience and performance of modernity through up-to-date planning, technology, design, décor, hospitality, catering and social activity. Their appeal perhaps arises from their sense of purposefulness in combination with their potential for being utopian spaces in which most human needs may be met or exceeded. From automatic sliding entrance doors to elevator lobbies, cocktail bars and *en suite* bedrooms, the typical characteristics of the modern hotel have become a metropolitan global ideal and, consequently, such tropes of *hotel-ness* have spread to other building types, including private apartments. Yet, although hotel advertising invariably promises guests an aura of glamour and escapism, this assurance is tempered by operators' needs to maximise profitability by carefully regulating the amount of expenditure on buildings and their interiors and the level of hospitality provided.

This study seeks to examine and evaluate the diversity of British hotels displaying characteristics of the Modern Movement and its decorative and commercial derivations. The timespan begins in the mid-1920s in the wake of the *Exposition Internationale des*

The Midland Hotel in Morecambe, opened in 1933, was among the earliest examples of seaside modern architecture to which the public had ready access. The landscaped environs enabled the building's design to be appreciated.

Arts Décoratifs et Industriels Modernes – a great exhibition of art, design, architecture and *haute couture*, staged in central Paris in 1925 – and ends in the mid-1970s when the Oil Crisis brought an abrupt but temporary halt to hotel development in Britain. It will investigate the circumstances that created a need for new overnight accommodation, examine relationships between hoteliers, architects and interior designers, seek to explain developments in planning, construction and service technologies. The timeframe spans periods of profound change in the practices and beliefs of those forming mainstream opinion within the architectural profession in Britain and beyond. Furthermore, considerable economic, technological, social and cultural developments took place in the western world as a whole. In architectural theory, modernist belief systems quickly ascended to dominance in the 1930s, then rapidly fell into disrepute as alternative post-modern approaches came to the fore from the latter 1960s onwards.

Buildings providing overnight accommodation to travellers had existed since ancient times. In Britain, the oldest hotels were coaching inns, built to serve horse-drawn traffic using the turnpikes. The modern hotel, however, emerged in the nineteenth century against a background of rapid industrialisation and emergent mass culture, requiring new types of overnight accommodation for business, leisure and social display. The varying levels of comfort and style provided by hotels of the era closely reflected its class hierarchies. Perhaps inevitably, the largest and most lavish examples provoked wonder and envy in the public consciousness. Through their layout and decoration, such hotels' hallway and lounge spaces sought to connote a sense of exclusivity, yet they were in reality very public environments that were also rather anonymous. In such settings, strangers from diverse backgrounds and of both genders could mix and interact while, for a fee, hotel bedrooms offered romantic luxury combined with total privacy.

The Badischer Hof Spa Hotel in Baden-Baden, designed by Friedrich Weinbrenner and built between 1807 and 1809, is widely regarded as having provided an early prototype for the modern European luxury hotel. Set amid ornamental gardens, it offered grand dining and leisure facilities to an affluent and relatively leisured clientele,

consisting of established social elites and those whose wealth had been earned more recently through business and industry. A contrasting American precedent can be found in Boston's Tremont House of 1829, designed by Isiah Rodgers, primarily to accommodate commercial travellers. With 170 rooms, it was much bigger than the Badischer Hof Spa Hotel and had a greater emphasis on practicality and standardisation, each room being provided with a water bowl and pitcher, plus free soap.[2] Thus, from the outset, the particular characteristics that would be developed in European and American hotels were established; in Europe, a romantic aspiration towards royal or aristocratic status was perpetuated – unsurprisingly in a cultural context in which the *nouveau riche* wished to achieve something of the lifestyle of the feudal elites – whereas, in America, a more meritocratic emphasis on comfort and hygiene was advanced.

In the ensuing decades, steam power put people, commodities and finance in motion as never before. Soon, the great modal shift from horse-drawn carriage to the railways brought about a need for large city hotels proximal to stations. Moreover, the steam age and parallel industrial revolution entirely restructured British society. The newly-affluent professional classes – consisting of merchants, financiers, industrialists and administrators – joined the existing upper echelons in demanding a high quality of accommodation, conveniently situated near the major rail termini. In the major European capitals, hoteliers such as César Ritz and the railway companies themselves, codified the palatial city centre 'grand hotel' as a genre that spread across the continent with the express passenger rail network. Perhaps the most celebrated British examples were the neo-gothic Midland Grand of 1873 by George Gilbert Scott at London's St Pancras Station and the Ritz in Piccadilly, dating from 1906 and designed in Louis XV style by Charles Mèwes and Arthur J. Davis. While such hotels catered to the wealthy and provided service levels not dissimilar to those of stately homes, commercial travellers found more modest accommodation in mid-market hotels with comparatively basic facilities. From the latter nineteenth century onward, leisure travel by rail became a further important market and so at seaside resorts and in picturesque town and country locations large numbers of new hotels were built or converted from existing housing to serve its various segments. The era's fashionable 'hydro' hotels, offering hydrotherapy and spa treatments, linked leisure with health – concerns that were subsequently to be important to the rhetoric of architectural modernism. Since then, the rise of mass tourism has gradually changed the status of the hotel into a highly standardised and rationalised 'machine', offering efficient accommodation for often large numbers of travellers.[3] Thus, hotels may be considered as reflective of the dynamic development, mobility and transience of modern life in general.

In wider culture, literary, artistic and filming representations of hotels have tended to represent them either as places of exclusive sociability or bohemian misery, as sites of crime and murder or as hiding place for illicit liaisons.[4] In reality, however, the activities taking place within them on a daily basis tended to be mundane and repetitive. Notwithstanding the fact that several famous hotels have produced lavish coffee table books which emphasise the celebrity guests who have visited, these were a tiny minority of their clientele and most of those checking in would have arrived and departed as barely known strangers. This notwithstanding, hotels, their interiors, and the services they provided were – and still remain – sensitive barometers of changing social, cultural and design tastes. Reviewing the recently-completed Dorchester Hotel on London's Park Lane for the *Architect's Journal* in 1931, the architect and architecture critic Julian Leathart observed how such hotels were replacing private town houses as venues for stylish social gatherings:

> 'Communal eating to the accompaniment of jazz bands supersedes the dignity of the private house dinner party; three- or four-room suites with a bathroom to each bedroom now take the place of a sixteen- or twenty-bedroom mansion with one bathroom for host and guests, respectfully attended upon by a large staff of well-trained servants. Inevitably, the spaciousness and quietude of the old order is being replaced by the fretfulness and hurry of the new'[5]

At hotels such as the Dorchester, architecture and interior design provided backgrounds for social display. Combined with catering, servicing and music, the aim of the hotelier was to engender an atmosphere of collective *bon vivant*.

A jazz band performs in the ballroom of the Royal Hotel in Folkestone; hotels were venues where recent trends in music, fashion, cuisine and lifestyle were introduced to wider audiences.

Hotel architecture and interior design may be interpreted in various ways. As a building typology one might think they would have certain common characteristics in terms of structure, planning and servicing and therefore deserve analysis within these terms. Structurally, a hotel required wide spans on the storeys nearest to ground level to accommodate spacious foyers, hallways, public rooms and kitchens, while the storeys above, containing bedrooms, had short spans. The bedroom storeys needed a building depth no greater than two rooms with a corridor between to be maintained (as opposed to open-plan office buildings that could fill entire blocks). Steel or reinforced concrete framing with concrete floors offered the best solution with a high degree of fire safety.

Yet, from the perspective of users' experiences, hotels – in common with other commercial premises – were primarily understood in terms of style and atmosphere. The commercial question was whether building anew or modernising existing premises to take account of the latest design trends would give a hotelier a slight – or even a large – advantage in what was a highly competitive market. The British and international hotel industry was split between business and leisure sectors which, while occasionally overlapping, more often had their own particular requirements, geographies and clienteles. Hotels in industrial towns and cities addressed the former market almost exclusively, whereas seaside hotels served mainly the latter. Only in London and in picturesque provincial towns with tourist potential did the two genres mix together in the same buildings. Commercial travellers on accounts required a dependable level of comfort and value for money whereas, for leisure travellers, enjoyment and romance were additional important factors. Particularly in the era before the Clean Air Act, seaside visitors from industrial conurbations must have valued the sense of brightness and levity which stylish, up-to-date architecture and design could provide.

In addition to these complexities of choice, the development of British hotel architecture in the mid twentieth century was further complicated by waves of trans-Atlantic influence from the United States of America. While Europe had fought the First World War, in America, which did not enter the war until 1917, developments in hospitality provision continued a-pace and, by the war's end, American hoteliers had taken a decisive lead so far as hotel services were concerned. The ruthlessly efficient 'American System of Manufacture', involving 'Fordist' assembly methods coupled with 'Taylorist' eradication of time-wasting practices could be applied to hotels just as much as to factory-based industrial processes. In each instance, their effect was the same; by focusing on scale and standardisation, the unit cost was driven down while a more uniform quality level could be ensured. The Statler hotel chain was in the vanguard of these developments. E.M. Statler had first built a temporary wooden hotel in Buffalo, New York, accommodating each night up to 5,000 guests visiting the 1901 Pan-American Exhibition. In 1907, a permanent Statler Hotel replaced it, every one of its 300 rooms being fitted with a private bathroom, something never previously attempted on such a scale and achieved through rigorously standardised planning. Bathrooms for adjoining rooms were situated back-to-back adjacent to the corridor, thereby enabling each pair on every storey to share the same plumbing shafts, which were accessed from service hatches in the corridors. Statler's intent was not to compete with the luxury hotels, but rather to offer clean, comfortable and moderately priced rooms for the average traveller and his means of achieving this goal were eventually emulated world-wide in the planning of hotels and, later on, also mass-market cruise ships.

During the inter-war years, the Statler chain expanded, building large hotels in many of America's biggest cities and charging as little as $1.50 per room per night. Its properties invariably were strictly rectilinear in plan, filling whole blocks of the urban grid. On smaller sites, bedroom accommodation and associated corridor circulation was arranged around the perimeter with a rectangular central courtyard, enabling daylight to reach the inward-facing rooms. Hotels occupying bigger plots, by contrast, typically had bedroom storeys laid out with sequences of identical wings coming off a spinal central corridor. In each approach, the idea was to maximise the length of external wall so that every room would have a window, while maintaining a regular modular pattern to enable the inclusion of standard *en suite* units. Viewed from the street, Statler hotels appeared as giant monoliths of facing brick, rising from rusticated stone bases and usually with deep cornices at roof height – the typical beaux arts-inflected 'look' of American commercial architecture of their era. Yet, far more effectively than any hotels in Europe, they addressed modern social concerns for hygiene and egalitarianism in an un-ideological way. They also demonstrated that – contrary to what many modernists believed – social ends and aesthetics were not synonymous, nor were they even necessarily linked. A traditionally-styled hotel could be as up-to-date in terms of technical servicing, if not more so, than one designed with a modernist aesthetic. In competitive commercial contexts, the latter could, however, be relied upon to 'sell' the idea of 'newness' and 'progress' to particular demographics of the population for whom flat roofs, light colours, extensive glazing, tubular steel furniture and modern artworks were aspirational signifiers of better days ahead. As we shall see, during the 1930s, Statler-style *en suite* facilities for every room gradually became a requirement for British city hotels serving the upper middle market.

The British hotel industry's progress during the inter-war era took place against a background of significant social and economic shifts, plus linked modal shifts in transport and mobility, all of which impacted on hotel development. Hotels were a particularly capital-intensive building type to realise due to their many rooms, complex servicing and large amounts of specialised fittings. The period from the end of the First World War until the commencement of the Second- was, however, economically turbulent and politically unstable. The negative effects on Europe's economy of the 1918 Treaty of Versailles, the Wall Street Crash of 1929 and the rise of totalitarian regimes all damaged British economic confidence. Yet, while the poorest often suffered most, the middle classes – who formed the bulk of hotel guests – experienced some of the largest relative income gains. In addition, during the 1920s, middle income earners benefitted from a substantial fall in the cost of living. More

The Statler Hotel in Buffalo, designed by Esenwein & Johnson and completed in 1907, and the Statler-operated (though Pennsylvania Railroad-owned) Hotel Pennsylvania in New York, opened in 1919 to a design by McKim, Mead & White, exemplified typical American planning for very large city hotels.

Early examples of seaside hotels designed according to modernist precepts could be found in Soviet Russia and in Fascist Italy and its colonies. The Institute of Resorts at Sochi on the Black Sea was designed by the Russian architect Alesey Shchusev in 1927-31 and is credited with having inspired the Finnish Alvar Aalto's Paimio Sanatorium design. The Albergo Agli Scavi Leptis Magna, completed in 1928 to a design by Carlo Enrico Rava and Sebastiano Larco, was located near Khums in Libya and was intended to attract Italian tourists holidaying there. While there is ample evidence that British hoteliers and their architects were inspired by American hotel designs, none can be found suggesting that they were even aware of examples such as these. In any case, their manifestation in contexts of revolutionary politics would have made them intrinsically unattractive from a British perspective. In the UK, progressive hotel architecture initially would tend to verge more towards Art Deco.

significantly, the overall numbers of 'white collar' workers grew exponentially between the wars, meaning that a larger proportion of the population had more disposable income for spending on leisure pursuits.[6] This was reflected in growing expenditure on hotel and restaurant services.[7] The Holidays with Pay Act of 1938 further increased demand for hotel accommodation, particularly at coastal locations.

To attract such potential guests, hoteliers and their architects became increasingly enthusiastic about the potential of the Modern Movement to advance hotel design and operation. Indeed, a hotel was arguably an ideal context in which to introduce visitors from diverse backgrounds to new design ideas. In a hotel, every fixture and fitting could be precisely specified, or specially made, enabling a high degree of aesthetic unity to be achieved. Furthermore, guests' experiences of new design would take place while relaxing and enjoying hospitality, meaning that they would be likely to form positive overall impressions. Yet, there remained the option of leaving at any time if 'the shock of the new' proved too great.

Modernism, the commercial 'modernistic' and modern decorative styles

The Modern Movement (or modernism) was characterised by the ready acceptance of modern conditions of industry, technology and urbanism. Its emergence in the early twentieth century reflected a desire to be 'fit for purpose' in the modern world.

In architecture and design, modernism can be understood at three distinct levels. Firstly, it required 'rational' and 'functionally appropriate' planning to address a

building's programme in the most efficient way, making imaginative use of the possibilities of steel and reinforced concrete framing. Façades were to become mere 'skins' enclosing volumes, rather than load-bearing structures as had mostly been the case in the past. This reflected naval architectural practice as a ship's shell plating was similarly a thin cladding over its structural framework. Secondly, modernists sought to apply a variety of futuristic-looking aesthetics, consisting of flat roofs and unornamented façades with horizontal fenestration; again, these were reflective of ship design. In the context of European urbanity, where most existing streets had been developed in the eighteenth and nineteenth centuries with ornate frontages and a distinctly vertical emphasis, modernist buildings represented a break with the past. Thirdly, to declare oneself a modernist was to demonstrate one's adoption of a variety of high-minded ideals about culture and society, allied to concepts of egalitarianism and social reform to enable 'good design' for all – precepts originating in the Arts & Crafts Movement of the nineteenth century. In practice, the Modern Movement aimed to spread widely concepts originating in the European avant garde and in high culture so as to engage with – and to reform – 'the masses.'

Paradoxically, for the 'progressive' leftist intelligentsia, who were most attracted to all three of modernism's prerequisites outlined above, this brought the problem of potentially being copied by 'ordinary' people and therefore losing a privileged position of cultural authority. Indeed, the Oxford-based English literature professor, John Carey, has argued that, although modernism in the arts was promoted as inclusive, it was actually an attempt on the part of cosmopolitan and exceptionally well-educated cultural elites to retain their special status in the face of mass culture and universal literacy.[8]

Notwithstanding the fact that modernist approaches were officially adopted in post-revolutionary Russia during the 1920s and although various prominent modernist polemicists in Britain loudly espoused leftist politics, for most users, at the point of experience, modernist architecture was essentially value-free. To gaze upon a convincingly-realised modernist edifice was merely to see a fragment of a possible 'future' world, manifested in the present one. Furthermore, although modernist principles were promoted by the Movement's polemicists as suitable for 'universal' application across cultures and building genres, in reality, it was possible to vary the level of quality depending on the available budget. Indeed, British commercial developers soon came to realise that selecting a modernist aesthetic was a good way of building cheaply for maximum profit as there was no longer an expectation that money would need to be 'wasted' on carved ornamental stonework.

Highly idealistic though modernist rhetoric may have been, commercial constraints and the need to appeal to existing mainstream taste formulations often led to compromises and even corruption. While property developers were usually more interested in maximising profitability than in formal and aesthetic purity, hospitality providers thought it more important to provide a welcoming aura of comfort with a 'sense of occasion.' This usually meant that expanses of wall, floor and ceiling that modernists would have preferred if left unadorned were 'softened' with upholstery, drapes, chandeliers, wall sconces and figurative artworks that a majority of guests could easily interpret as 'luxurious.' Writing in the early 1960s, a period when the Modern Movement was arguably at its zenith, the British-born, but California-based hotel interior designer Henry End observed:

> 'Perhaps the biggest problem in hotel design is to do things in good taste without the elements of either catering to any popular level or attempting to "elevate" the public taste. A conscious effort at either one will put the designer on dangerous ground with the risk of creating vulgarity on the one hand and uneasiness on the other. Too earnest an attempt to elevate the guest will merely make him uncomfortable. For example, using abstract paintings such as might be found in the Guggenheim Museum would in most hotels be dangerous. There are too many people who would not understand this approach and would get the feeling that someone was making fun of them.
>
> The designer must find that hard-to-find happy medium. He must do things which are high style and different enough to be interesting, without being clichés, gaudy or mundane. A certain amount of exuberance is acceptable, but it must be carefully controlled. Once over the bounds of good taste, there is no return.'[9]

As we shall see, hotel architecture and interior design acted as a prism for such pressures and slippages between design ideals and popular taste.

The *Exposition Internationale des Arts Décoratifs et Industriels Modernes* proved a seminal event in the development of twentieth century visual culture. Initially conceived as an international exhibition, it ended up being primarily a showcase for France to re-assert its authority as the pre-eminent international style leader for fashion and luxury

The cocktail bar of the Forest Hill Hotel at Aberfoyle in Scotland in the late-1930s; the bar counter is formed of glass blocks, augmented with chrome trim and matching tubular steel bar stools. Such forms and materials distinguished fashionable environments of this kind, even if, as in this instance, they were installed within older buildings. Focusing expenditure where it would have the most impact on guests was important and so fixtures that were most easily seen or touched were favoured.

goods design and production. Perhaps inevitably, given the political and economic troubles in the wake of the First World War, the *Exposition* was heavily politicised and Germany – France's main rival in the manufacture of all that was modern and desirable – was not even invited to attend. As Britain had staged its own Empire Exhibition at Wembley in London the previous year, its exhibit was only small. America, on the other hand, claimed that, as it copied all of its 'high end' design output from European precedents, it would have nothing original to contribute – an ironic situation indeed, given that increasing numbers of European architects were, at that very moment, trooping to America in droves to marvel at Manhattan skyscrapers and the chaser lights and billboard advertisements of Times Square.[10]

For the most part, the *Exposition* showcased lavish and exquisitely crafted French couture design, with an emphasis upon interiors and fashion, all of which utilised very expensive materials and aesthetics rooted in the Rococo, mixed with elements of Art Nouveau and an eclectic mix of French colonial styles from North and West Africa, French Indo-China and Central America. Squeezed onto a site on the fringe was a small pavilion demonstrating alternative sets of principles. The *Pavillon De L'Esprit Nouveau*, designed by the French-Swiss architect Le Corbusier, contained a model of a 'future Paris' consisting of identical high-rise buildings set amid parkland and connected by elevated motorways, intended to supersede Haussmann's nineteenth century city centre. Le Corbusier's exhibit was a *coup de théâtre*, representing revolutionary social and architectural ideas which unsurprisingly attracted the positive attention of visiting critics. Thus, at the *Exposition*, a binary opposition emerged between the consumable luxury of the most prominent exhibits and the radical agenda of Corbusier's pavilion. In the era since, such an antagonism has persisted between the decorative arts on the one hand and the quasi-rationalism espoused by followers of the Modern Movement on the other. A closer look at the *Exposition's* many varied exhibits – and, more generally, at the wide diversity of inter-war building and interior styles – shows that a great many actually combined certain elements of each approach. The aim was that users would simultaneously experience the visual luxury of what subsequently became known as 'Art Deco' alongside the 'futuristic' clean lines of modernism. As we shall see, this was a combination frequently found in mid-twentieth century hotel architecture and interior design, as well as in the era's commercial buildings in general.

Within the broad spectrum of commercial modern architecture in the mid-twentieth century, a number of distinct design styles can be identified. To the convinced modernist, however, the very idea of 'style' was to be negated or completely ignored. Instead, architecture was to be seen as a strictly rational, quasi-scientific discipline in which the appearance of buildings would inevitably be 'arrived at' through planning their layout in the most effective way. The nebulous term 'functionalism' has become attached to this belief, which became orthodoxy for many would-be modernists, riddled as it was with inevitable compromises and contradictions.

In the latter 1920s, new and renovated luxury hotels in London's West End were among the first public buildings in Britain in which aesthetics inspired by the Paris *Exposition* could be experienced by members of the public. Indeed, they were among the earliest hotels anywhere to exhibit the new approaches to architecture and interior design.[11] In these and in some subsequent hotels of the 1930s, an angular 'jazz moderne' aesthetic is evident. This was influenced in part by the discovery of King Tutankhamun's tomb in Egypt and the brightly coloured treasures it contained, as well as by the stepped forms of ancient Mayan pyramids, aspects of German expressionism of the preceding decade and, above all, the syncopated rhythms and riffs of American jazz music. Typically, jazz moderne composition was symmetrical with a strong vertical emphasis, thereby seeking to lend even relatively small buildings some of the character of the latest New York skyscrapers, an effect enhanced by applied vertical fluting in faience or stucco and a deep parapet with a stepped in pediment.

Slightly later on, in the early 1930s, 'streamline moderne' emerged with a distinctly curvilinear, horizontal emphasis. This coincided with a widespread fascination with racing cars, high-speed trains, aircraft and Blue Riband-winning trans-Atlantic liners. Fittingly, the origins of streamlining spanned the Atlantic. In 1920s Germany and the Netherlands, architecture by Erich Mendelsohn, Rudolf Fränkel, J.J.P. Oud and others had rounded corners, repetitive horizontal coursing, metal-framed fenestration and extruded balconies. By the mid-1930s in the United States, the French émigré industrial designer Raymond Loewy had begun to 'streamline the sales curve', helping American manufacturers to recover from the Great Depression by encasing their products in fashionable 'streamform' cladding. Both 'jazz moderne' and 'streamline moderne', which to an extent superseded it, were criticised by design reformers of the inter-war era and since for being superficial as they could be applied to buildings and objects little different in terms of structure, planning and technology from those already existing.

This led to the emergence of further binary oppositions between modernism, as practiced by 'European masters' such as Walter Gropius and Le Corbusier, which claimed to have embraced the latest technical innovations and planning techniques, and a commercial 'modernistic', which used 'jazz' and 'streamform' details. For many would-be modernists, 'modernistic' (or 'moderne') styles were positive dangers to their agenda for cultural transformation.

During the periods for study, the *Architectural Review* arguably represented the theoretical and aesthetic 'high ground' in debates about modernism. In these narratives, pro-modernist commentators sought to maintain a clear distinction between themselves and producers of the modernistic. Thus, the journal's editorial policy sought to concentrate on promoting exemplars of 'best practice' while excluding buildings that were deemed too 'compromised' by commercial stipulations or 'hybridised' in terms of

16

style to be worthy of 'serious' coverage. As new hotels typically fell into the latter category, they were more likely to be reported upon in less prestigious building and construction journals and so, notwithstanding their prominence in the urban scene, they were usually excluded from the canon of what was (and is) considered as 'good' British architecture. Yet, so far as popular aspirational taste was concerned, in the 1930s, grand hotels were near the top of a descending order of preference – hence the reason why cinemas, cafés and dance halls – all building genres which served the mass market – often took on the 'Ritz' and 'Savoy' nomenclature that was associated with the most expensive hotels in London's West End.

The hotel industry's own professional organ, the *Caterer and Hotel Keeper*, founded in 1878, had a strong interest in architecture and design matters, but from a much less ideological viewpoint. If design was up-to-date, popular and commercially viable, then it was worthy of positive appraisal. In the early 1930s, almost concurrently with the *Architectural Review*, its content and visual identity changed greatly to reflect emergent modernist visual culture. Whereas the architecture and construction journals were inevitably most interested in the production of buildings in terms of structural resolution and the interpretation and critical appraisal of their appearance, the *Caterer and Hotel Keeper* was more concerned by the ways in which hospitality was consumed and experienced by users in terms of staffing, servicing, catering, table ware, the design of menus and the economics of day-to-day hotel operation for different clienteles. Thus, it encompassed richer, more diverse and – arguably – more relevant discourses than typical architectural writing was usually willing to acknowledge.

For the *Caterer and Hotel Keeper*, the problem of providing hospitality of a sufficiently high standard appears to have been a running theme. Although the journal understandably failed to say so directly, it appears that working in the hotel and catering industries was not an attractive career option for most Britons and so hotel operators constantly had difficulties in recruiting and retaining staff. A consequence of this was that British hotels employed a great many émigrés, mainly from southern Europe, whose presence gave these venues a cosmopolitan – and therefore also modern – atmosphere. Indeed, some émigré entrepreneurs, such as Auguste Oddenino, Charles Forte and Reo Stakis, became hotel-owning tycoons.

Modernism in hotel design

Just as the aesthetic boundaries of modern hotel architecture during the period for study cannot be precisely defined, neither can the boundaries of what constituted a 'hotel.' Within the overarching hotel genre, there were various sub-genres – such as private hotels, spa hotels, chalet hotels, roadhouses and, after the Second World War, motels and motor hotels. These various types had commonalities as well as distinguishing characteristics.

A desire for rationalist planning approaches inevitably led modernist architects and designers to generate archetypes – ideal solutions that could be universally applied. While the results of standardisation are perhaps most clearly seen in the system-building of post-war social housing, similar tendencies can also be discerned emerging in the more eclectic world of inter-war modern commercial architecture. The sudden widespread availability in the 1930s of factory-produced building

Oppsoite: A diverse selection of 'moderne'-style seaside hotels built in the second half of the 1930s; they are (1) the Royale, Penzance, (2) the Queen's, Torquay, (3) the Weydale, Scarborough, (4) the Expanse, Bridlington and (5) Oulton Hall, Clacton-on-Sea. The Weydale's concave frontage appears to have been inspired by that of the Dorchester in London while the Expanse's name not only suggests viewing broad vistas of beach and sea but also sounds a bit like 'Expense.'

components, such as Crittall metal-framed windows, encouraged an increasing aesthetic homogeneity. Viewed externally, many hotels of the 1930s closely resembled buildings of other genres – such as cinemas, light industrial premises, schools and office blocks. Subsequently, several of those constructed during the 1960s had considerable similarities of composition and detailing to the era's hospitals, university buildings and corporate headquarters. The fact that the same architects often designed these different types only reinforced this situation. Yet, in none of the various professional books and articles about hotel architecture produced in the 1960s is style, aesthetics or the appearance of buildings discussed in anything other than the most cursory way.[12]

Paradoxically – given modernism's desire to achieve complete harmonisation and interplay between exterior and interior – many hotels from the period of study demonstrate an unexpected dissociation of these elements. Hotels that did achieve a 'total form' – such as the Midland at Morecambe – were exceptional. By the 1960s, 'styling' a hotel had become work for interior decorators and graphic designers while the job of the hotel architect was often only to create a practical underlying 'framework' in which the sizes of spaces and their inter-relationships would hopefully outlast passing stylistic fads. Façade and interior treatments could always be modernised as need arose, but it was more important that kitchens, for example, were correctly dimensioned, laid out and located, relative to the restaurants, cafés, banqueting facilities and waste disposal points. (By contrast, grand hotels dating from the era before the First World War were more likely to have been designed as complete entities in which the architectural language of the exterior was carried throughout the interior). Dissociating façade and interior mirrored practices in passenger ship design, in which naval architects produced shells to be decorated internally by specialist designers. As we shall see, the latter were sometimes the same individuals as produced interiors for hotels. In each context, only a limited amount of negotiation was possible as to a large degree the structure dictated the arrangement of the content.

Between the two World Wars, there began major modal shifts in transport from rail and sea to road and air. By law, the railways in Britain were a 'common carrier' – meaning that they were required to transport any person or item of freight wherever was required – but although rail offered long-distance travellers the benefit of speed, a private car or van provided flexibility and privacy that public transport was incapable of matching. While manual workers continued to rely on public transport, car ownership gradually expanded to 'middle income' earners, consisting of the lower professions, managers and supervisory manual workers. Motoring by the middle classes not only brought new trade to historic coaching inns, but also gave rise to a need for a new generation of 'roadhouse' hotels, designed and located specifically to serve car owners. As a leisure activity, motoring combined the emerging technology of automotive design with heritage tourism, the latter demonstrated by the publication of the 'Shell Guides.' This Janus-like (simultaneously backward- and forward-looking) experience of the historic past using modern engineering was reflected in the design of roadside hospitality infrastructure. Some new roadhouses exhibited mixes of Art Deco and modernist elements, while others used romantic neo-vernacular styles, depending on whether a particular developer believed that the accommodation they would provide should reflect the modernity of a car, or should instead be subsumed within motorists' experiences of touring through rural 'Olde England.'

Hotels of the post-war era

The Second World War brought a construction hiatus that lasted until 1955. Classified as luxury buildings, hotels were subject to particularly restrictive materials rationing and so it was only possible to gain permits to carry out works that were strictly necessary. Meanwhile, in the USA and neutral Sweden, building work continued without such a lengthy break and so, once Britain belatedly recommended hotel development, Scandinavian and American influences could readily be identified in what was built. These tendencies also reflected the great influence of the Festival of Britain of 1951 on British post-war architecture and design as a whole. At the Festival, the era's 'scientific revolution' was represented through the work of the Festival Pattern Group, which developed abstract, though repetitive, designs based on the chemical structures of atoms and molecules. The event also popularised a new range of slanted fonts with heavy serifs for architectural graphics which soon were adapted by numerous businesses seeking to update their visual identities.

The Loch Lomond Hotel at Balloch in Scotland and Punch's Hotel at Bessacar, near Doncaster, were examples of the many 'moderne'-style roadhouses built near to trunk roads and tourists spots during the latter-1930s. In each instance, there is a distinctly horizontal emphasis with streamlined detailing.

By the mid-1950s, architectural modernism had achieved such widespread acceptance that it had become the prevailing mode of design for many building types, from housing and schools to offices. In the reconstruction of bomb damaged British towns and cities, it was necessary to be pragmatic about cost and reasonably consensual in terms of aesthetics. Ideally, as at the Festival of Britain, a sense of uplift was introduced through the judicious use of colour and pattern and through the avoidance of overly grandiose gestures. The type of cosy, Scandinavian-influenced modern architecture arrived at was often described as 'contemporary' and has since come to be known to some as 'herbivorous modernism.' Britain's initial post-war hotels of the mid-1950s were often good examples of this approach. As Elain Harwood observes:

> 'Hotels had a cachet, hinting in the 1950s at a growing service economy, more leisure time and sophistication. Yet, few were built, because of high capital and staffing costs, while loan restrictions limited local authority investment… Most new hotels were for breweries, notably Watney, Ind Coope and Whitbread…'[13]

For Britain's expanded municipal authorities, many at that time engaged in planning ambitious comprehensive urban rebuilding schemes, attracting a hotel developer was a sign of prestige. Not only would a new hotel encourage renewed business and possibly tourist travel but it would also impress visiting bureaucrats from government and other municipalities, who would enjoy the latest in local hospitality and luxury, hopefully leaving with a very favourable impression of post-war progress.

Meanwhile, American hotel design continued to make further leaps ahead – as best seen in the Hilton chain's large and glamorous premises. With the De Havilland Comet's first flight in 1952, the jet age was under way and one of Hilton's aims was to develop hotels to accommodate air travellers. Jet travel also helped to inspire an accompanying futuristic corporate visual language and so, very quickly, inter-war Art Deco felt passé, associated as it was with transport by ocean liners and steam-hauled express trains.

The Royal Hotel at Ryde as it appeared after the Second World War, looking somewhat weary and neglected following years with little maintenance. Few of the 1930s seaside hotels fully re-gained their pre-war élan.

In America new Hilton hotels in the 'International Style' reflected jet age aspirations and soon Hilton expanded overseas too, its hotels projecting American cultural power in major foreign cities that were now within easier reach for the wealthy by jetliner. The term 'International Style' had first been coined by Henry Russell Hitchcock and Philip Johnston, who curated an exhibition about European modernist architecture at the Museum of Modern Art in New York in 1932. Unlike many European architects and theorists, who emphasised modernism's social aims, Hitchcock and Johnston focused on its rationalist aesthetic and eschewed reformist political agendas. Thus, in the post-war era, the 'International Style' moniker came to be associated with Americanised corporate modernism. Indeed, the term has come to be applied most often to post-war buildings exhibiting similar detailing and finishes to Ludwig Mies van der Rohe's glass-clad office towers in New York, Chicago, Toronto and elsewhere. Furthermore, it is arguable that there was a considerable similarity between the design, layout and detailing of a typical American-style executive office suite of the 1960s and a hotel bedroom of the same era, intended for use by executives. While ceiling, wall and floor finishes, architectural servicing and a majority of furnishings would have been comparable or even identical, the prime difference was that in a hotel room, the desk was pushed into a corner with the bed taking the central position instead.

Sociologically, the American hotel reflected a meritocratic ethos, tempered with strong cultural aspirations towards a life of leisure – surely the perfect fulfilment of 'the American Dream.' As the interior designer, Henry End, observed:

> 'In America, the hotel became the focal point of social activities for a growing middle class. It is today the place to salute achievement, whether this be the installation of a realty board president, or the $1,000-a-plate dinners for charity and politics… And typically American is the fact that the grandeur of hotel life is available to all who have the price, whether it be the bootblack who strikes it rich in the stock market or the red-necked cattleman come to town to sell his thousand head of white-faced Herefords.'[14]

In terms of planning, architects designing the new generation of post-war urban hotel tended to solve the problem of making efficient use of valuable city centre sites while maintaining a regularly-shaped bedroom block through a 'podium and tower' solution. Public rooms on the two lowest floors thereby filled the hotel's plot – whatever its shape – often to the margins with a rectangular, cylindrical or cruciform tower rising above. On more spacious suburban or provincial sites, either an approach similar to Le Corbusier's Unités d'Habitation – with an accommodation block raised on piloti and the public rooms tucked beneath – was used or, alternately, accommodation was planned as a series of wings radiating from a central core, following the mid-1920s precedent of Walter Gropius's Bauhaus school at Dessau.

Britain's first post-war hotels, the Westbury in London's Bond Street and the Hotel

Leofric in Coventry, were both completed in 1955. Both occupied bomb sites and they heralded a new phase of hotel construction that lasted throughout the 1960s. An aggressively profit-orientated property development boom was among the period's defining characteristics as entrepreneurs sought to cash in on cheap land acquisitions that they had made during the previous years of rationing. In 1964, the Labour Secretary of State for Economic Affairs, George Brown, intervened to limit the number of speculative office blocks being built in London. An outright ban on new schemes was followed by the introduction of a permit system to limit their number. This measure caused property developers to focus their efforts instead on alternatives, and, as tourism was increasing, building hotels was an obvious choice. Subsequently, the government actively encouraged hotel development nationwide through the Development of Tourism Act of 1969, which – among other measures – eased planning restrictions and provided subsidies for hotel developments amounting to £1000 per room.

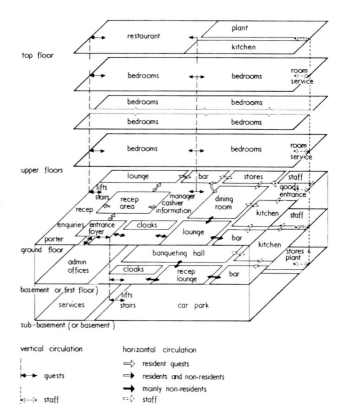

A diagram showing 'flows' and 'adjacencies' within a typical British 'podium and tower' urban hotel of the 1960s.

In commercial architecture, meanwhile, debased versions of the 'New Brutalism' – a term borrowed by the architecture critic Reyner Banham from Le Corbusier's use of the French 'béton brut' to describe raw concrete – became briefly fashionable. This was largely on account of being potentially the most cost-efficient way of building and therefore appealing to developers keen to maximise their earnings. Similarly, system-building and prefabrication enabled cheaper, faster construction on a bigger scale than ever before. As the architecture historian Barnabas Calder observes, the 1960s construction boom was brought about through a combination of economics and engineering:

> 'Cheap energy made concrete and steel available in quantity, and engineers' understanding of reinforced concrete developed rapidly… Architects could slide the constituent parts of their buildings around at will, massively increasing the number of ways they could arrange rooms and routes… escaping the architectural restrictions of ground level… and opening up completely new shapes of building… The 1960s building boom was an orgiastic celebration of these exceptional conditions.'[15]

Such new possibilities were exploited to the full by British post-war architects such as Alison and Peter Smithson, Ernö Goldfinger, Denys Lasdun and James Stirling, whose designs are nowadays justifiably celebrated by architectural connoisseurs. None of these practitioners is featured in this book, however. Instead, the focus here is upon

A selection of hotels and motels of the latter-1950s and early-1960s, developed in association with an ongoing modal shift from rail to road and air. These buildings all demonstrate an emerging tendency to emphasise structural framing, reflecting the New Empiricism in British post-war architecture. They are (1) the Dover Stage Coachotel, (2) the Oxford Motel, (3) the Dalkeith Motel, (4) the Epping Forest Motel and (5) the Skyway Hotel at London Airport.

the types of modern architect favoured by commercial property developers, who were more likely to have viewed their work in terms of the maximalisation of revenue-earning floor space than on earning critical plaudits for producing buildings of high aesthetic merit. Their outputs, while often massive in scale, usually lacked the sense of sculptural drama so appealing to architectural writers at the time and since. Here, we encounter Fitzroy Robinson, Michael Lyell, James A. Roberts, Philip Russell Diplock, Sidney Kaye, Nelson Foley and others who are equally barely known to most enthusiasts for post-war British architecture. Yet, the buildings they designed were much more likely to have appeared in the centres of British provincial towns and cities than works by the critically acclaimed 'big names.' Very often, they faced severe challenges in interpreting complex briefs and seeing projects through to completion on schedule and within budget. Too often, the results of working under pressure were buildings that were at best missed opportunities to have produced superior designs that would have better withstood the test of time. Thus, along with office blocks and shopping centres, hotels as a genre came to exemplify what increasingly came to be viewed as unfortunate qualitative and aesthetic compromises in 1960s architecture. Sadly, those that were of genuine quality – of which there were actually a surprising number – have tended to be overlooked, subsumed as they were with the many banal commercial developments of their era. Yet, arguably, even the less good examples are deserving of closer study and possible re-appraisal due to the profound impacts they brought upon British culture and society.

So far as interior design was concerned, as the 1960s progressed, new hotels came to have increasingly louche décor, combining modernist design elements with psychedelic patterns, pop art and historicist pastiche, the resultant aesthetic hedonism reflecting new-found and wide-spread affluence, social mobility and the coming of age of a critical mass of youth, some of whom at least were determined to experience fun and romance in stylish surroundings. The 'baby boomers' may not yet have become the hotels' main clientele, but the fresh cultural ideas they generated were so infectious that corporate clients and their designers were quick to cash in.

In 1973 hotel development came to a sudden halt. In part, this was due to the ending of the Development of Tourism Act's subsidy regime. This was followed by the Oil Crisis, when Arab members of OPEC quadrupled the price of Gulf crude as a protest against American and Western support for Israel in the Yom Kippur War. The ensuing pause enabled architecture critics to assess the outcome of the frenzied hotel development programme carried out during the previous years; their verdict was overwhelmingly negative. Hotels exemplified what had gone 'wrong' with modern architecture in Britain, too many of the latest examples being incongruous in scale, brutal in detailing and disregarding of context. Yet, before such superficial glamour as they may initially have possessed wore off, they were also emblematic of what at least some considered positive progress.

Theory pertaining to critical readings of hotels

The present work makes some use of theory, although it is deliberately kept light in touch to avoid overpowering the subject matter. Theory is used more as a framework for selecting and juxtaposing particular sources, for reading them in certain ways and

Hotels from the mid-1960s onward, showing the various faces of 'the international style', involving the use of a variety of designs of curtain walling, piloti and 'podium and tower' layouts. They are (1) the Royal Lancaster in London, (2) the Hotel Piccadilly in Manchester, (3) the Caledonian Hotel in Inverness, (4) the Skyway in Southampton and (5) the Breakspear Motor Hotel, near Hemel Hempstead.

for an analysis of architecture and interior design approaches. In the context of studying commercial modern architecture, Henri Lefebvre's *The Production of Space* (1974) provides an over-arching philosophical stance. Lefebvre argued that man-made spaces are actively produced as consequences of socially-produced meanings and values which affect spatial practices and perceptions. Lefebvre stated that every society – and therefore every mode of production – brings into being distinct spaces and spatial forms, reflecting its intellectual and cultural climate.[16] In the context of a market-led, profit-driven sector such as the hotel industry, his neo-Marxist rationale seems reasonable in comparison with more traditional architectural-historical readings, which tend to celebrate only 'exceptional' buildings, somehow 'conjured' by the outstanding 'creative genius' of the most celebrated artist-architects. By comparison, nearly all British hotels were the work of less known, or largely forgotten, practitioners who mostly viewed their work within strictly commercial terms.

Another significant theoretical construct of considerable relevance for the present work is the concept of 'the gaze' as an ideologically-charged way of looking upon other peoples and cultures with an implicit and unequal power relationship between the observer and the observed. As John Urry argues in *The Tourist Gaze*, when we travel, we bring with us certain amounts of wealth and particular assemblages of educational and cultural capital. We then look upon the environments and lives of others whom we visit through a prism of that with which we are already familiar, judging the objects of our gazes by our own standards of what is considered 'normal' and, conversely, what is 'strange' or 'exotic'. For Urry, tourism is predominately a visual practice, a 'way of seeing' in which business 'stages' visual experiences and tourists consume them visually.[17] Furthermore, Urry highlights the paradoxical situation whereby tourists simultaneously desire to experience difference through the consumption of sanitised versions of other cultures while at the same time retaining ready access to familiar comforts and soothing banalities. Indeed, Urry points out that, often, tourists' desires for special experiences means that they expect destinations to be filled with the types of 'highlight' they have seen in brochures. This means that their expectations are different from those of locals for whom the same environment must constitute their everyday experience of normality. Urry also observes pessimistically how

The Forth Bridges Motel at South Queensferry in Scotland was an unusually pugnacious hotel example of concrete brutalism. The building was located adjacent to a new suspension bridge over the River Forth, which its bedroom block faced.

An advertisement for the London Hilton emphasises its plush, foliated interior – a highly-serviced environment of calm and ordered tranquillity in which to retreat from the bustle of the city.

The London Hilton's grandiose, but rather banal, exterior – a prominent building on the London skyline, yet one with remarkably little visual coherence.

'isolated from the host environment and the local people, the 'environmental bubble' of the familiar American-style hotel insulates the tourist from the strangeness of the host environment'.[18] Yet, in first establishing, then modulating, norms of comfort and hospitality that are increasingly universally understood by tourists and travellers and blending these with hints of the exotic, the escapist and the aspirational, the modern hotel arguably performs a vital, though largely unsung, task in the cosmopolitan metropolis.

Variations in modern hotel architecture also related to context and thus to Britain's changing cultural geography since the early steam age. As London was an imperial capital, its late-Victorian, Edwardian and inter-war public buildings were expected to reflect its seriousness as the location of royalty, government and affairs of state. Moreover, London's feudal landlords initially had traditionalist views about the architectural expression of any new edifice built on their estates, meaning that imperialist neo-Classicism and façade dressings of Portland stone or London brick were preferred. Conversely, London's large and relatively pluralistic population made it usually the first location in Britain where new trends in music, fashion, cuisine and service provision could be experienced. It was through the interior design and decoration of nightclubs, cocktail bars, restaurants, cafes, ballrooms and hotels that these trends were first manifested in the built environment, invariably within building shells of much more traditionalist design and detailing. Consequently, in the streets of inter-war central London, modernism most often was hidden from view. London's hotels served not only business (including – very importantly – government officials) and tourism markets but also were relatively informal meeting places for social and wealth elites – as opposed to royal palaces and private members' clubs, with their strict regulations to control social mixing.

Britain's provincial industrial towns and cities, by contrast, were primarily sites of commerce and manufacturing, where industrial wealth was generated and so hotels in these locations were aimed at business and commercial travellers. They were predominantly male and travelling on expense accounts, therefore requiring a level of service befitting their status in the managerial hierarchy and with commensurate 'value for money.' Historic and picturesque provincial settlements, by contrast, usually had some industry and so needed hotel accommodation to serve the business market but, as with London, tourism was also important. In comparison with the capital's centrality, provincial settlements formed one kind of periphery. The seaside – serving mainly British but also some overseas holidaymakers – was another 'fringe condition', as were the suburban hinterlands where roadhouses, airport hotels and motels were developed. In *Places on the Margin: The Alternative Geographies of Modernity*, the British sociologist Rob Shields observes:

> '…Marginal status may come from out-of-the-way geographical locations, being the site of illicit or disdained social activities, or being the other pole to a great cultural centre. In all cases… geographic marginality… is a mark of being a social periphery… Marginal places… are not necessarily on geographical peripheries but, first and foremost, they have been placed on the periphery of cultural systems of space in which places are ranked relative to each other. They all carry the image and stigma of their marginality which becomes indistinguishable from any basic empirical identity that they might once have had. From the primary ranking of cultural status they may also end up being classified in what geographers have mapped as systems of 'centres and peripheries'.'[19]

Shields relates concepts of 'centre and periphery' with those of 'high' and 'low' culture, observing that 'places on the margins expose the central role of "spatialisation" to cultures and nation-states'.[20]

In offering hospitality to large numbers from diverse backgrounds while in transit, while simultaneously providing financial returns on the investments of remote shareholders, hotels belonging to international corporate chains have been accused of exemplifying what the French anthropologist Marc Augé describes as 'non-place'.[21] Augé argues that true 'places' are 'read' in terms of culturally specific meanings. For example, Trafalgar Square in London is unique as a site for national celebration of 'Britishness' or 'Englishness' and has gathered an accumulation of associations with important historical figures who are commemorated there and events – ranging from wartime victory celebrations to Poll Tax riots. By contrast, non-place is corporately homogenous and devoid of any obvious or profound 'auratic' meaning and signification.[22] Assembled from standard factory-produced elements and with generic notices and other 'formulaic' and 'corporate' fixtures and fittings superimposed, such environments tend to offer an adequate level of comfort – but are designed not to be 'homely' and to subtly control their users' behaviours. Augé's position is arguably conservative in that he is more critical of jet age travel environments than those of the previous railway age. Although he tends to ignore manifestations of 'the local' in the 'corporatised' environments he critiques, his ideas nonetheless have a validity for any study of modern hotels – as anyone who has found themselves experiencing *ennui* in a generic chain hotel bedroom will realise.

One of the most challenging tasks in assembling this volume has been to select case studies from the multitude of hotels completed during the periods being analysed. I have chosen to represent a broad range of hotel types within an overall chronological narrative frame work. They span from 1920s modern eclecticism to the late-modernism of the

The Skyline Park Tower hotel. Fine traditions in a beautiful setting.

An advertisement showing the Skyline-operated Park Tower Hotel, located close to Knightsbridge, as viewed from Hyde Park; the building's bulky form – from a distance resembling a giant roll of kitchen paper nestled among the trees – hardly contributed positively to its setting. The cityscape was best enjoyed from within, gazing outward.

early-1970s. The selections have been based on a variety of criteria, including a building's historical significance, its innovation in terms of planning, servicing and aesthetics – or merely because it is a typical example of an architect or a hotel chain's approach. Unlike the many existing books on aspects of the Modern Movement in British architecture, this is not primarily a conservation manifesto, seeking to find exemplars of 'good' architecture, potentially suitable for listing. On the contrary, it is fully acknowledged from the outset that many British hotels from the periods being studied were fairly mediocre and nearly all of the better examples have been so heavily altered by subsequent 'improvers' as to have retained little or nothing of their original *élan* (one of the key characteristics of modern conditions being constant change). Rather, this is an investigation through hotels of how British modern architecture percolated from elites to the masses, and from cities to peripheries and of how an increasingly mobile populace was accommodated in transit during periods of profound social and cultural change.

Interiors of Albany Hotels in Birmingham (1964) and Glasgow (1973) designed by Dennis Lennon's office; (1) shows a bedroom in the Glasgow Albany with a model posing as a businessman working at the desk/dressing table in the corner. The room's detailing with wiring in a duct at waist height and a Bertoia easy chair demonstrate 1960s design advancement and a tendency to simplify and standardise for ease of maintenance. By comparison, (2) shows a bedroom in the older Birmingham Albany, where the detailing is less refined. Images (3) and (4) show parts of the Glasgow Albany's foyer and restaurant, yet, devoid of occupants or any details specific to the city, they could be almost anywhere. Hotels of this kind were intended to cocoon their transient clienteles amid universal signifiers of comfort and modernity, such as fitted carpets, glass-topped coffee tables and television sets.

CHAPTER 1

London West End sophistication

In the second half of the 1920s, considerable investments were made in new and refurbished hotels in London, particularly in the city's wealthy and fashionable Mayfair district, where, as Sir Francis Towle, the Chairman of the upmarket Gordon Hotels Ltd, explained in the *Caterer and Hotel Keeper* in 1927:

> 'One of the most remarkable features which distinguish the 'after the war' period is the immense increase in travel. There is not a nation in the world today whose citizens are not travelling more than they did before the war. This development, which is probably only in its infancy, has emphasised the importance of the hotel industry.
>
> The older generation can remember a time, not so long distant, when foreigners and business men from the provincial cities stayed when they visited London, either on pleasure or business, in the private houses of their friends, or acquaintances to whom they had been furnished with introductions. This practice, so far as the stranger and the businessman are concerned, has ceased. The hotel keeper of today is the host of his country's guests. The proper development of the hotel industry is therefore a matter of national interest.'[23]

Towle and his younger brother, Arthur, each made a very significant contribution to the modernisation and improvement of British hotel, hospitality and catering services during the inter-war era. Their father, William Towle, had been a pioneering railway hotelier who in 1871 had been appointed as manager of the Midland Hotel in Derby. Over the ensuing two decades, Towle senior was responsible for developing the Midland Railway's hotel operations. He was also instrumental in improving railway catering in stations and on trains. Both his sons were educated at Marlborough College, Francis studying thereafter at Cambridge University while Arthur spent several years working in hotels in Europe and the USA to gain practical first-hand experience of the latest emerging approaches to hospitality provision. The two were subsequently employed by their father as assistant managers at the Midland Grand Hotel at St Pancras Station and, when their father retired, they became joint general managers of all the Midland Railway's hotels. During the First World War, Francis Towle served as Controller of the Army and Navy Canteen Board, leaving Arthur in sole charge at the Midland Railway. After a brief return, Francis resigned from the railway to become the head of Gordon Hotels Ltd. When the Midland Railway was amalgamated with others in the 1923 Grouping to form the London, Midland and Scottish Railway (LMS), Arthur Towle – of whom more later – became its Controller of Hotels, Refreshment Rooms and Restaurant Car Services. Both brothers believed that hotels should be at the forefront of design, incorporating the newest technologies and servicing.

In an era of rapid change and modernisation, the question for hoteliers, their architects and interior decorators was whether a modern British luxury hotel ought to seek to engender a cosmopolitan atmosphere, reflecting emerging American and/or European developments in hospitality design, or one characterised by romantic nationalism and tradition. This dichotomy was indeed reflective of the period's wider architectural debates – and the issues at stake were perhaps most keenly felt in Britain, an imperial nation

A late-1920s view of the exterior of the May Fair Hotel near Berkeley Square, which was intended to represent state-of-the-art British (or English) hotel design, but actually more closely resembled a smaller version of recent American examples.

proximal to the European mainland while sharing a common language and commercial culture with the USA. Francis Towle – who was an instinctive moderniser in terms of incorporating the latest technical advancements into the hotels he controlled – nonetheless initially favoured a traditionalist approach to their public expression:

> 'The English hotel of the future… must develop along lines suitable to English taste; it must carry to perfection the comfort, freedom and personal service, that 'good taste' and rightness in the small details of life which have made English home life famous the world over.'[24]

Towle's position was reflected in the design of Gordon Hotels' eight-storey, 404-room May Fair Hotel in Berkeley Square. Designed by the London architect William H. White and developed by a Doncaster builder and property entrepreneur, A. O. Edwards, who owned the construction firm Edcaster, it was completed in 1927. Towle, who had been heavily involved in specifying its aesthetics and facilities, observed in the *Caterer and Hotel Keeper*:

> 'It is a modern hotel – the first put up in London for the last twenty years – and it draws its inspiration not from Versailles, not from Fifth Avenue, but from English life.'[25]

Yet, although decorated internally in Adam and Queen Anne styles, from the outside, the May Fair more resembled a smaller rendition of the newest American hotels. This was largely due to its flat expanses of brick, punctuated by a rhythmic pattern of window openings. Try as Towle and his architect might to have created a hotel reminiscent of an English stately home, its true commercial purpose was betrayed by its repetitive fenestration.

By the latter 1920s, Mayfair was being swept by the jazz age and so the fashionable debutantes and flappers required new styles of social environment, reflecting the latest 'sophisticated' trends in music and *haute couture*; Lucile (Lady Duff Gordon) *ensembles* did not look their best in the Roman classical settings hitherto favoured for London's grandest hotels and other public buildings. The literature historian Faye Hammill has shown that the concept of 'sophistication' gained a new, positive meaning in the latter 1920s. The term was popularised through the media by the 'Bright Young Things' – the emerging 'cultural entrepreneurs' of the literary and entertainment worlds, whose stylish appearance, elegant dress, deportment, sharp witticisms and cosmopolitan lifestyles were linked to progress and aspiration. Hammill sees the actor and playwright Noël Coward as exemplifying the inter-war era's ideal urban sophisticate, forever associated with cocktail chat, cigarette holders, evening dress and stylish nightclub environments.[26] Modern hotel interiors in London's West End were created concurrently with new clubs, cocktail bars and theatres which not only shared their design language but also were often by the same architects and designers.

In comparison with speedy changes in fashion and music, architecture necessarily develops at a slower pace, while interior design arguably straddles fashion and the social scene on the one hand and the architectural world on the other. New trends in music and fashion are often precursors to similar imagery in interior design and, only subsequently, does commercial architecture follow suit. Thanks to the influence of the Paris *Exposition* and of jazz music, the seriousness of the macho imperial neo-classicism of London's public buildings since the late Victorian era – and, by extension, its tendency in commercial settings to segue into nationalistic kitsch – was challenged by a new visual culture that was fashion-conscious, fun-loving, frivolous – and also often delightfully camp in its theatricality.

The Strand Palace Hotel in London before (1) and after (2-5) interior reconstruction to a design by Oliver Bernard, whose scheme swept the original neo-classical design with baroque detailing away in favour of flat planes, extensive concealed illumination and mirrored surfaces. Although the 45-degree angled corner sections in the architraves served no structural purpose in this instance, the detail reflected the typical column and beam junction of Hennebique concrete framing, commonly used for modern commercial buildings of many kinds. This became a leitmotif of many 'jazz moderne'-style interiors of the late-1920s and early-1930s. The building's neo-classical exterior, shown in (6), remained unaltered by the rebuilding work.

The Strand Palace's dining room shows fragments of its original neo-classical design, overlaid with Art Deco finishes. The winter garden – with rattan furnishings – appears to have been more thoroughly reconfigured. In both instances, indirect lighting plays an important role in lending a sophisticatedly up-to-date ambience.

Very soon after the Paris *Exposition*, the first British Art Deco hotel interiors appeared in Central London, in each instance within a refurbished shell of earlier vintage. During the winter of 1925-26, the very upmarket Claridge's Hotel, – originally completed in 1898 and owned by Savoy Hotels Ltd, was tentatively modernised. The Chairman, Rupert D'Oyly Carte, had business interests straddling the hospitality and theatre worlds; he was heir to the D'Oyly Carte Company, which staged Gilbert and Sullivan operettas in the Savoy Theatre, located adjacent to the Savoy Hotel, and elsewhere. His circle of acquaintances in the world of entertainment meant that he was constantly abreast of the latest trends. Since assuming control of Savoy Hotels Ltd in 1903, he had ensured that its flagship Savoy Hotel had continued to attract a fashionable clientele by a continuous programme of modernisation, including the introduction of jazz music and dancing. At Claridge's, he commissioned the Scottish-trained London architect Basil Ionides to redecorate a few suites and to modernise the restaurant. In the latter space, Ionides – working with the craftsmen Byron Inison and William Rankin – installed engraved glass panels and Chinese-inspired light fittings resembling elephants surmounted by pagodas. Commenced within months of the Paris *Exposition*'s closure, Ionides' work at Claridge's enabled the fashionable Mayfair set to experience a little of its cosmopolitan exoticism for the first time in a public setting in London. Shortly thereafter, Ionides co-designed with Frank A. Tugwell a striking Art Deco renovation of the Savoy Theatre (this was completed in 1929).

Not far from the Savoy complex, a much more substantial hotel rebuilding was shortly underway. The Strand Palace Hotel dated from 1909 and was operated by Strand Hotels Ltd, an offshoot of the commercial catering company J. Lyons & Co, which had been established 1884 as a subsidiary of the Salmon & Gluckstein tobacco company. Apart from hotels, J. Lyons & Co ran popular and prominently-located city cafes and restaurants. The company's 'Maison Lyons' and 'Lyons Corner House' premises were aimed at a mass market. In order to drive down costs while ensuring a uniformly high quality of delivery, the company's business model applied essentially Fordist and Taylorist methods of economy of scale and standardisation. Thanks to Lyons' forward-thinking approach, its cafés and restaurants were renowned for their good value and relatively high quality. Enabling as they did large numbers from diversities of social background to enjoy up-to-date service in elegant, convivial environments, they were important sites of modernity and sensitive barometers of cultural change. Whereas the Savoy and Claridge's were aimed at social and wealth elites, Lyons' large London hotels, the Strand Palace and the Regent Palace, sought to attract a broader, predominantly middle class clientele. To achieve this aim, the company perpetuated its tried and tested strategy of 'quality in quantity.'

J. Lyons & Co's Chairman, Sir Isidore Salmon, evidently believed that there was also a commercial advantage to be gained through 'mainstreaming' the latest trends in interior design. As the middle classes were expanding in number and growing relatively wealthier, this approach was prescient. Moreover, by the mid-1920s, many of J. Lyons & Co's venues dating from the pre-war era needed modernisation to remain fresh and appealing. To prepare designs for this work, the company appointed Oliver P. Bernard as Consultant Artistic Director. The son of a London theatre manager, Bernard had first become a stage set designer. Following distinguished First World War service in the Royal Engineers, he was next employed by the British Government's Board of Overseas Trade with responsibility for exhibition design. In the mid-1920s, he designed exhibits for the British Empire Exhibition and for Britain's small contribution to the Paris *Exposition*. Evidently, Bernard was greatly inspired by the latter event and soon he gained an opportunity to emulate its showy, luxurious forms and materials when J. Lyons & Co appointed him.

The Strand Palace was a 980-room hotel, designed in the Roman classical manner by William J. Ancell and Frederik J. Wills. It was intended to serve mostly an upwardly-mobile tourist market. After nearly two decades' use, the hotel was considered ripe for a thorough renovation and this task was given to Bernard with technical assistance from the architect James Maude Richards. They transformed the interior from ponderous neo-classicism into one of smooth planes, triangulated forms, concealed lighting, polished chrome, mirrors, 'jazzy' patterned carpets and upholstery. In particular, the hotel's L-shaped entrance foyer grabbed attention with its revolving doors surrounded by internally-lit glass panels and a 'grand staircase' with matching illuminated balustrades. In a British context, Bernard's re-design, which was completed in 1928, was a trend-setter and, subsequently, the approach was widely emulated – for example, in theatre and cinema foyers. In all instances, the contrasts between hard and soft materials, concealed lighting and endless reflections engendered an escapist atmosphere – a fashionable, ethereal setting for leisure and relaxation which, in the hotel, enabled holidaymakers to feel like their favourite celebrities.

Back in Mayfair, at the junction at the junction of Park Lane and Park Street, the very large 494-room Grosvenor House hotel and apartment development was under construction on the site of the former London residence of the Dukes of Westminster. This had been acquired in 1924 by the philanthropist and patron of the arts, Lord Leverhulme, whose intention was to build an art gallery. An elderly man, he died the following year with his scheme unrealised and so a re-sale took place, the purchaser being the May Fair Hotel's developer, A. O. Edwards. He no doubt wished to ensure further large-scale construction work in London to keep his builders and surveyors from that project in employment. The Grosvenor House development was intended to appeal to the American market and, before commencing work, Edwards collected information about the layout of large hotels and serviced apartment developments there. All the bedrooms would have private bathrooms with the further refinement of extra taps for running iced water. Furthermore, each room would have a private entrance vestibule to ensure silence and privacy.

To produce a suitably grandiose design, he employed as architects Wimperis, Simpson and Guthrie.[27] The firm's senior partner, Edmund Wimperis, was the Grosvenor Estate's surveyor, but as he was now acting on behalf of the developer, the Estate sought independent architectural advice. In 1926, Sir Edwin Lutyens – arguably

A brochure for the Grosvenor House Hotel from the period immediately after its completion; emphasising proximity to parkland was – and remains – an attractive selling point for city centre hotels of this kind.

Britain's most prominent architect, whose prestigious commissions were spread throughout central London and across the British Empire – was approached to comment on the proposed elevations. Rather than merely advising, however, Lutyens seized the opportunity significantly to re-design the building's exterior, making it truly 'his', much to the initial frustration of Edwards. As the Duke of Westminster approved of Lutyens' enhancements, and as Edwards wished to commence construction as soon as possible, there was little option for the developer but to concede that they were indeed superior.

Lutyens added four stone pavilions to the building's roofline, features that were his 'signature' elements in several recent projects, and he simplified the detailing of the frontages to emphasise their cliff-like masses of brick. None of this façade work changed Wimperis, Simpson and Guthrie's underlying plan, however. On ground level, the hotel and apartment sections were joined by a single-storey reception area, surmounted by a curved colonnade. Despite Lutyens' best effort to produce a distinctly British exterior, celebrating the nation's imperialism, as at the May Fair Hotel, the outcome looked overwhelmingly American. Correspondents to *The Times* criticised the Grosvenor House Hotel's monumental scale and *Country Life*'s architecture critic, Christopher Hussey, expressed dislike for the repetitive

Right: The exterior of the Grosvenor House as it appears today, viewed from along Park Lane and emphasising its arrangement as a series of large blocks, topped by pavilions. As with the May Fair in Berkeley Square, American design influence is very evident.

Below: The neo-Tudor Grill Room of the Grosvenor House which followed the 1920s trend for themed historicist interiors, but soon appeared out of date.

fenestration.[28] The hotel was completed in 1929, except for one wing that remained unbuilt until the late 1950s due to a land acquisition dispute.

The interior decoration was mainly by Chappelow and Son of Charles Street, Mayfair, and included a Tudor grill-room. Other facilities were Turkish baths, a swimming pool, squash courts and a gymnasium. The large 'Imperial Suite' was, however, furnished by

Above: Two views of the interior of the Grosvenor House's Imperial Suite, decorated in Art Deco style by Oliver Hill with murals by Clara Fargo Thomas; extensive use was made of silver leaf and mirrors, finishes seen in several notable residential and public interiors of the era.

The grey, silver and black entrance to Claridge's Hotel, as designed by Oswald Milne in 1929 and little altered since; the sleek finishes contrast with the red brickwork of the surrounding building.

Oliver Hill, an up-and-coming architect and interior designer whose parents were friends of Lutyens. He worked jointly on the project with the New York artist and socialite, Clara Fargo Thomas, who was a member of the wealthy Wells Fargo family and known as a painter of colourful and abstract decorative murals. Consisting of 'Military' and 'Navy' rooms – which initially were intended primarily for use by the aristocratic officer class, their partners and guests – the spaces were (in these circumstances) somewhat incongruously decorated with mirror panelling and silver leaf, presumably chosen for their ability to generate endless reflections, thereby enhancing the sense of animation during private parties. The furniture was bespoke and in the manner of the Paris *Exposition*. Thus, there was a significant disjunction between the British traditionalism of the Grosvenor House Hotel's exterior and main public spaces and the continental modernity of Hill's furniture, fabrics and colour palettes. Indeed, the Imperial Suite's only overtly neo-classical references were its triangular door pediments – but even these were stylised interpretations.

As Hill went on to design one of the most architecturally innovative and critically-acclaimed British hotels of the inter-war era, the Midland in Morecambe (completed in 1933 and described below), his background and early career are worth summarising. Well-off, well-educated and well-connected, his parents owned homes in London and at Sharnbrook in Bedfordshire, the latter of which had a gilded Aesthetic Movement drawing room by William McNeil Whistler. Having worked with the architect William Flockhart while attending evening classes at the Architectural Association, Hill established his own practice in 1910, designing mainly for friends of his family. After the First World War, Hill designed Arts & Crafts-style country houses, inspired by those of Lutyens. For his interior designs of Mayfair apartments, however, Hill was early to embrace emerging French and Scandinavian trends in the decorative arts, even in advance of the Paris *Exposition*, producing beguiling schemes distinguished by their shiny finishes, subtle colouration and bespoke furnishings. The Grosvenor House Imperial Suite was strikingly up-to-date and its fashionable decoration may have made the hotel's management wish that they had invited Hill to design more of the building's interiors, the remainder of which soon appeared hopelessly behind the times.

Meanwhile, back at Claridge's, where Basil Ionides' recent modernisation work had been well-received, a more substantial renovation was being planned. As Ionides was fully occupied redesigning the Savoy Theatre, the project was awarded instead to Oswald Milne, who had recently designed D'Oyly Carte's summer house, Coleton Fishacre in Devon; this had been completed in 1926 and had an Arts & Crafts-style exterior with some vaguely 'moderne' interior elements. For Claridge's, Milne devised a new surround for the entrance doors; this was faced in grey Roman stone with an Art Deco canopy and matching doors, above which were granite urns abundantly filled with fruit. Within, Milne added mirrors to the foyer, which was otherwise redecorated in primrose, silver and glossy black. During the ensuing years, silver and black finishes were used in numerous Art Deco hotel, restaurant, theatre and even domestic interiors. Silver provided a shimmering effect that reflected coloured lighting, yet was distinctly more modern-looking than gilding (which had typically been used in the grand historicist interiors of the preceding period). Indeed – as is still the case today – silver was considered as the colour of the future, similar to the polished metal finishes used for new technologies, such as aircraft fuselages.

Milne also updated Claridge's restaurant, replacing its ceiling arches with flattened, angular forms. Next, in 1930, the billiard room was replaced by a new grill restaurant, also by Milne. There followed a much bigger rebuild in 1930-31, brought about by the owner securing the hotel's freehold plus an additional plot of land adjacent from the Grosvenor Estate. This enabled Milne to design a tall, red brick extension block. While this harmonised with the existing hotel, its detailing was simpler and more cubic in outline. Shop units were located along the street frontage and, inside, on the ground floor, a new suite of reception rooms was added. These were separated from those of the main hotel by a wide passage leading to ballroom facilities at the rear. The new rooms' Art Deco interiors involved contributions from a variety of craftsmen, the decorations including a skylight depicting aeroplanes by the Birmingham Guild, wall lights by Walter Gilbert and bold, geometric carpets by Marion Dorn.[29]

While Claridge's was undergoing modernisation, a third significant Art Deco hotel interior was being created at the Park Lane Hotel, an edifice with a short, though remarkably complex history worthy of briefly recounting. The 302-room hotel had first been conceived as a 'millionaire's home from home' by Sir Richard Vincent Sutton, a wealthy young baronet. Construction had begun in 1913 to a design by Sir Henry Tanner, whose London-based practice worked mainly for H.M. Government's Office of Works, designing numerous imposing city centre post offices which, like the hotel, were in the French Renaissance manner. Almost concurrently with the Park Lane Hotel, Tanner's office was also designing a large hotel for J. Lyons & Co, the Regent Palace on Regent Street. While the latter was completed as intended, work on the Park Lane site was abruptly halted in October 1914 when Sutton was seriously wounded while serving as a lieutenant in the First World War.

The structural framing stood empty for the next fourteen years and became known to Londoners as 'The Bird Cage'. Finally, in 1924, six years' after Sutton had died as a consequence of his war injuries, the site was acquired by a highly ambitious up-and-coming hotelier and property entrepreneur from Yorkshire by name of Bracewell Smith, who since 1919 had run the Shaftesbury Hotel in London. He took a substantial financial risk to complete the Park Lane project, commissioning the original architects to update

Claridge's hallway with concealed lighting from wall sconces and a ceiling cove, jazz moderne mirrors, easy chairs upholstered in jazzy patterns and a spectacular geometric carpet by Marion Dorn.

the design, taking into account the latest service standards. Indeed, Smith spent five months in the USA studying hotel design and seeing advice from E.M. Statler, whom he befriended. Consequently, the hotel was to be Britain's first ever with a private bathroom for each bedroom. Rather than following the spatially efficient Statler approach of locating these adjacent to the corridors, due to British building regulations not yet recognising the possibilities offered by forced ventilation, they were instead located behind the façades with opening windows.[30] The hotel was eventually opened in 1927, some thirteen years after the original intended date.

Within, the *nouveau riche* Smith wanted a showplace and so an eclectic variety of historicist decorative styles were deployed. The smoking room, decorated by Harrod's Contract Furnishing Department, was a half-timbered neo-Tudor ensemble, complete with a baronial fireplace, while the Oak Room bar was a replica of the interior of the 16th century Reindeer Inn at Banbury. The Grill Room, by contrast, was in Louis XIV

style, furnished by Robertsons of Knightsbridge and incorporating panelling from J. Pierpont Morgan's house on Princes Gate. This latter 'gimmick' was probably aimed at attracting American visitors.

In 1930, Smith purchased the adjacent Savile Club, thereby enabling an extension to be added to the Park Lane Hotel. As with the existing structure, the new wing was designed by Sir Henry Tanner's firm and its purpose was to provide more bedrooms plus a ballroom, located in the basement and accessed via a separate entrance with its own commodious hallway and grand staircase. Completed in 1931, their interior design was an opulent-looking *tour de force* of Art Deco mirrors, murals, balustrades and illumination, all 'skilfully carried out with a view to night-time use.'[31] Walter Gilbert – who had previously worked on the recent Claridge's interiors – designed the many and varied light fittings, most which were wall-mounted on backgrounds of silver leaf with gold lacquer. Between these, Gilbert's daughter, Margot, painted murals depicting exotic dancing girls watched by musical cherubs.

Architraves and skirtings were in Swedish green marble while the doors were stained soft green and framed in chrome 'jazzy' mouldings, the patterns of which were repeated in the wrought and cast iron balustrading. The Ballroom featured:

> '…Chandeliers in ice-cream colours of frosted glass, and against the walls, a series of light fittings resembling cascading fountains set against shaped peach-mirror panels. Upstairs the light comes from clusters of vertical strips topped with Chinese pagoda motifs in matt chromed metal. There is also lighting hidden in the cornices. Decorative plasterwork panels of winged horses being restrained by muscular youths in loin cloths. Soft pastel colours with metallic finishes [have been chosen] to provide a brilliant background to the dresses of the guests without providing any predominant colour which might be unsuitable to any individual.'[32]

With their languorous curves, reflective surfaces and indirect lighting, the new Park Lane Hotel interiors had a dreamy, ethereal quality. Most fortunately, they survive today in intact condition, providing a potent reminder of the profound influence the Paris *Exposition* had on London's fashionable night life.

As the Park Lane and Grosvenor House hotels demonstrated, by the latter 1920s, American hotel planning and operational practices had come to be widely admired and emulated by hoteliers in Europe. Meanwhile, thanks to the swish internal design of the 1927 French trans-Atlantic liner *Ile de France*, the interiors of which were mainly the work of Paris *Exposition* designers, Art Deco had travelled in the opposite direction. For Americans as for Europeans, the ideal modern urban luxury hotel came to be one that would combine American technology with European decorative style. Just such a hotel was The Dorchester on Park Lane, completed in 1931.

The project was conceived by Gordon Hotels Ltd whose Chairman, Sir Francis Towle, had abandoned his previous desire for 'traditional English' aesthetics in favour of what was up-to-date, no matter the point of origin. Reviewing the hotel upon completion, the *Architect's Journal*'s critic, Julian Leathart, whose architectural practice specialised in designing cinemas, observed of its trans-Atlantic design influence:

> 'In this country we are beginning to follow the example which the great cities in the United States have set in hotel planning and equipment for the last twenty years or so. This imitative movement is long overdue, and as the hotel promoters consider that 'places are judged by the hotels they possess, and the skill with which they are conducted, more than by any other single set of circumstances…'[33]

The Park Lane Hotel's spectacular silver Art Deco ballroom entrance foyer and ballroom remain superbly well preserved. Their reflective surfaces, subtle palette of colours and complex arrangements of illumination reflect the new decorative possibilities brought by the Paris *Exposition* and by advancing technology.

To design the Dorchester, Towle initially had commissioned the progressive architect-engineer Owen Williams and the building contractor Sir Robert McAlpine – both of whom had extensive knowledge of reinforced concrete construction techniques. Indeed, Williams' career had begun as an engineer with the Trussed Concrete Company and, from there, he had established his own practice specialising in concrete structures. In the mid-1920s, he engineered the Palace of Industry and Wembley Stadium for the British Empire Exhibition.

In plan, the Dorchester's ground and mezzanine floors were an irregular pentagonal shape, fitted into a triangular location between Park Lane and Deanery Street, the main entrance facing south towards their junction. Above, the eight bedroom storeys comprised a main wing running parallel to Park Lane, a shorter adjoining wing above the entrance, plus two short wings projecting from the rear. The Dorchester's seemingly complex geometries were actually developed from a rigorously geometric grid of concrete columns on a 56 foot by 35 foot module. (The fact that, when viewed from Park Lane, the bedroom storeys formed a unit distinct from the ground and first floors prefigured the post-Second World War preference for 'podium and tower' planning solutions for large city centre hotels.) To lessen the building's mass, the main façades were slightly concave; as we shall see, curved frontages would become a leitmotif of 1930s hotel frontages throughout the country. Perhaps these were intended to signal a sense of grandeur tempered with a polite deference to their surrounding milieus.

Williams was very keen that the hotel should have unadorned concrete façades, but its owner apparently considered this 'industrial' solution a step too far for a luxury venue and likely to antagonise local amenity groups and potential guests alike. When no satisfactory compromise could be reached, having designed only the new hotel's structural frames, Williams' practice was superseded by another structural engineering firm, Messers Considère, and by the architect William Curtis Green, who was a graduate of Birmingham School of Art and who had in recent years designed power stations and large commercial premises for banks and insurance companies. On the Dorchester project, Green was assisted by James Maude Richards who had recently worked with Oliver P. Bernard on the Strand Palace Hotel modernisation and so was well acquainted with the specific requirements of the building type.

In his *AJ* review of the Dorchester, Leathart was intrigued by the architects' and engineers' efficient all-concrete construction solution, pragmatically concealed from view by a veneer of facing tiles and thereby avoiding any risk of a stylistic conflict with traditionalists who wished Park Lane's environs to retain something of their existing gracious character (no doubt, Towle too wished the hotel to possess an aura of traditional grandeur and dignity).

> 'In these days of architectural conflict, when the advocates of modernism hold worldly warfare with the forces of traditionalism, it may be of interest to recall the abhorrence expressed by certain people for the use of reinforced concrete in Park Lane... The chief point of criticism levelled against reinforced concrete construction is on aesthetic grounds... Concrete walling untouched from the forms as it must be to express sincerely the construction is not elegant, however much the design may indicate the nature of the construction. At the 'Dorchester', the engineer's ingenious idea of using permanent shuttering to the poured concrete walls has been adopted. [This is] built up of polished concrete slabs containing chips of marble [a finish more widely known as 'reconstructed stone']... The poured reinforced concrete walls between are 7 inches thick for a

height of 100 feet… [and yet] the addition of [a further] 50 feet in height would not have necessitated the thickening of the concrete… The rapidity with which the constructional work was executed is exemplified by the fact that each complete upper storey, external and internal walls and one floor, was built in one week. The total time of eight weeks for the eight upper floors of this building constituted a record for rapid progress in this country.'[34]

The Dorchester is shown during construction; the in-situ concrete method enabled the large structure to be completed very quickly. As the bedroom storeys were mostly similar, the same form-work could be re-used, saving materials and ensuring consistency.

The Dorchester's lofty façades with restrained beaux arts detailing, balconies, patio doors and striped awnings could have looked equally at home on the French Riviera or in an American seaside setting, yet the building initially appeared as an unexpected implant into the London streetscape. Corner bedrooms had protruding semi-circular lantern windows, the vertical repetition of which at the façades' vertices was one of the building's most up-to-date looking design features. The use of reconstructed stone facings gave the building a slightly shiny appearance which looked more modern than the brick or Portland stone of neighbouring edifices. As reconstructed stone was less absorbent of dirt, it also remained pristine for longer.

The Dorchester's cosmopolitan external resonances appealed to moneyed, globe-trotting elites whose lifestyles prefigured those of the 'jet-set' by a quarter of a century and for whom preconceptions of what constituted modern luxury were set by both American and European experiences. Yet, when lecturing in 1934 at the Architectural Association about his career to date, Owen Williams observed disparagingly of the Dorchester project that 'there are two types of racketeer: those who get out their guns

Left: A general view of the Dorchester's frontage to Park Lane, as the building appeared upon completion. The concave frontages of the bedroom storeys reduced the appearance of mass of what was a very large hotel.

Bottom left: A 1930s view showing the Dorchester's main entrance façade with its distinctive verandas and corner windows.

Bottom right: A view through a ground floor hallway in the Dorchester; although the decorative styles of the interiors were mostly historicist, their open planning was notable and this reflected the possibilities of reinforced concrete to open up indoor public space.

and those who get out their elevations.'[35] Williams, evidently, was bitter that his own radical design solution had been rejected in favour of Green's more consensual approach. Indeed, he was wary of working with architects ever after.

Within, the hotel boasted no fewer than eighty public rooms of various sizes and types, including – on the ground floor – hallways, a lounge and bar, restaurant, grill room, sherry bar, ballroom, accommodating up to 1,200 dancers or 700 diners with associated reception lobby and cloakrooms, winter garden, orangery, and Royal retiring room. In addition, there were extensive leisure facilities, comprising a Turkish bath, gymnasium, beauty parlour and hair dressing salon.[36] In planning these, Leathart was impressed by the '…disposition of the great reinforced concrete piers carrying the superstructure…' amongst which had been:

> '…Woven the pattern of the principal rooms. The cruciform shape of the ballroom, the 'Oval' room, the nearly octagonal grill room and winter garden provide a multiformity of room shapes and a sense of variety and a pleasant feeling of surprise impress the visitor as he passes from room to room; not the least skilful part of the plan is the inter-connectedness of all rooms… Unnecessary duplication with consequent confusion to the public is thus avoided. The three large service rooms communicate direct with the kitchens on the floor below.'[37]

Such fluidity of space was a characteristic of modernist architecture, even if the hotel's interior decoration was somewhat eclectic, albeit considerably less so than the recent Park Lane Hotel. Styles ranged from 'Spanish colonial' in the Grill Room to neo-Georgian hallways, all overlaid with a veneer of Art Deco lighting, mirrors, furnishings and fabrics. As with the hotel's external treatment, its interior designs were intended to be attractive both to traditionalists and those of more progressive taste.

Another aspect of the hotel's modernism was its advanced and complex, though largely hidden, architectural servicing:

> 'Ventilation… is by means of the plenum system. Air cleaned, warmed or cooled, according to the season, is pumped in… at ceiling level and extracted at floor level with trunking… communicating telephones, vacuum cleaning tubing, electrical wiring and heating system and the complicated and extensive drainage necessary in a hotel with 300 baths, basins and W.C.s…'[38]

As at the Park Lane hotel, it was necessary for all bathrooms to have natural ventilation, their positions being indicated externally by columns of small windows, the arrangement of which set up a rhythmic pattern between the larger bedroom windows and patio doors.

The Dorchester's blending of elements of modernism and traditionalism meant that it had wide appeal, even within the architectural profession, as a letter from M.H. Baillie Scott to the *Architect's Journal* showed. He felt that it was:

> '…The only modernist building which… contrives to appear gracious and friendly. It has none of the brutal, logical 'take-it-or-leave-it' aspect with which we are familiar in modernist buildings. It represents a definite aesthetic conception… We are all too familiar with the usual modernist solution where the angle windows give the appearance of a structure in which some predatory rat has gnawed away at the corner and yet, with diabolical ingenuity, has enabled the structure to survive the process. But here, at the Dorchester, the angle bays are entirely aesthetically satisfactory in relieving the severity of the façades with a note of gaiety. Moreover, the whole exterior appears as an expression of the

interior. [The] Dorchester Hotel is indeed what we have all been hoping for – a really satisfactory expression of the modern spirit in building.'[39]

In the long run, the Dorchester proved an outstanding commercial, aesthetic and constructional success which greatly influenced subsequent British hotel design practice. Yet, when it first opened in 1931, the negative effects brought about by the 1929 Wall Street Crash were at their most severe.[40]

Although many were left destitute, it was those on lower incomes who were worst affected, while the middle classes were less troubled and the most prosperous elites were able to continue much as before. Notwithstanding the seemingly unpropitious economic climate, J. Lyons & Co elected to press ahead with the construction of a new and very large 966-room hotel – the biggest in Europe, in fact – on an approximately rectangular island site at Marble Arch, opposite the top of Park Lane. Lyons had been planning to build a hotel there for the past fifteen years but had been frustrated by difficulties in obtaining all of the land that was needed. Having finally succeeded, they were evidently in no mood to contemplate postponement, especially as their other prime hotels in London's West End – the Regent Palace and the Strand Palace – remained satisfactorily profitable. As the architect and critic E. Maxwell Fry put it in the *Architectural Review*:

> 'Lyons evolved a system which owed its enormous success to the realisation that, granted sufficient custom, it was possible to supply the richest and most sumptuous comforts at prices which the middle classes could afford... The Regent Palace Hotel was the spiritual home of countless thousands of provincials, whose preference for this of all London hotels was based on the well-calculated financial plan of giving the greatest possible service cheaply to the greatest number of people'[41]

Following these principles, the Cumberland was completed in 1933 and was housed within a monolithic eight-storey, Portland stone-faced neo-classical shell by F.J. Wills, which closely matched the adjacent buildings. On the bedroom storeys, 'inside' rooms were arranged around four light wells and accessed from a cruciform corridor arrangement, while 'outsides' were accessed from a rectangular gyratory corridor following the line of the building's perimeter.

By the time that drawings for the Cumberland were being prepared, British planning guidelines for hotels had been updated to take account of the benefits of artificial ventilation, meaning that, for the first time in the UK, it was possible to fully follow the Statler model with regard to the provision of *en suite* bathrooms. Moreover, every room was sound-proofed, double glazed and air conditioned, placing what was a large upper mid-market hotel well ahead of the majority of more exclusive and expensive rivals – at least so far as technology and facilities were concerned.

As with the refurbished Strand Palace, Oliver P. Bernard designed the Cumberland's interiors – and it was these that attracted positive critical attention both from architecture critics and the hotel and catering trade press.[42] E. Maxwell Fry observed that although there was:

> 'Nothing... to compare with the great and nobly proportioned lobbies of an American hotel, for the proportions generally are low and the public lobbies rather in the nature of wide passages for moving throngs..., in any case, I found my chief interest lay... in the superb craftsmanship in new, rare and strange materials.[43]

The main entrance was on Great Cumberland Place, the foyer taking the form of a broad promenade, flanked by offices, tourist bureaux and a bookshop. This connected with a

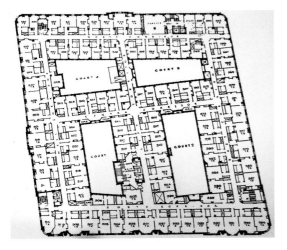

Above: A plan of a typical bedroom floor of the Cumberland Hotel, showing the Statler-derived solution to the layout of rooms with *en suite* facilities; the arrangement is slightly skewed to fit the irregularly-shaped site.

Above right: Day and night exterior views of the Cumberland, as viewed from behind Marble Arch; floodlighting gave a strong hint of the modernity within what was a ponderous neo-classical shell. The external design was very typical of large public buildings of the era in the UK.

subsidiary foyer on Oxford Street. Both were decorated in soothing green and illuminated from large lay-lights in the ceilings, augmented by amber-tinted concealed lighting built into the architraves. In the middle of the ground floor, there was an octagonal central court lounge for the service of teas. Fry noted that:

'The walls are panelled in a West African mahogany, by name of makore, in which a very beautiful figure… is used with extraordinary success, combined with a dark brown marble. In this room, the lighting, where it is not indirect, appears as a series of thin [neon] tubes outlining and accenting the sensuous curves of the dome…'[44]

The main restaurant, behind, was:

'A very large space without pillars, the walls [being] lined with weathered sycamore combined with rosewood and kingwood. Lighting and ventilation provide the end of decoration… for it is in the wall grilles of metal and glass or the suspended trough fittings and coved ceilings that the designer has given his imagination free play… Then again there is the moulded glasswork used to great effect in the entrance hall and lounge…'[45]

The Carlisle Room, a banqueting hall accommodating 300 and of similar internal design, was to the rear of the restaurant, sharing the same kitchen.

A wing of the Cumberland's extensive entrance foyer; the use of marble slabs for the lower walls gave an impression of luxury but were impervious to the wear and tear of heavy daily use. Unlike at the Strand Palace, all corners are curved, rather than angular, reflecting stylistic progress from jazz to streamline moderne. The integrated lighting and furniture exemplify Oliver Bernard's careful attention to detail.

Altogether, the Cumberland's interiors represented a considerable design achievement with a notable sense of continuity and integration. Images (1), (2) and (3) show the foyer and vestibule spaces, (4) shows the central court lounge, which was a lounge space at the centre of the ground floor. (5) and (6) show the smoking room and the restaurant and (7) shows the grill room. With its hardwood panelling the latter is an early example of the approach subsequently used for the interiors of dining saloons on British ocean liners.

The 'streamline moderne' interior design of the Cumberland's public rooms – with their extensive use of 'exotic' hardwood veneers – anticipated similar stylings in British ocean liners built later in the 1930s, not least Cunard's *Queen Mary* of 1936. At the time when the hotel was inaugurated, however, liners with interiors in this manner were yet to materialise and so Bernard's designs may have inspired ship owners and their interior architects to follow J. Lyons & Co's lead.

At the Cumberland Hotel's inauguration in November 1933, Lyons' Chairman, Sir Isidore Salmon, proudly stated that 'this was the first time an hotel of this size, with all the amenities of a super luxury establishment, had been made available to the public at reasonable prices.'[46] Although Lyons built no further hotels pre-war, the company continued to employ Oliver P. Bernard, who applied similar stylings to Lyons Corner House restaurants, which became popular resorts for a broad spectrum of the urban British public who were familiar with such settings from Hollywood movies. Thanks to Lyons and Bernard, they could now enjoy luncheons and dinners in romantic environments which allowed them briefly to fantasise about being their favourite screen idols. In 1935, Bernard additionally designed a new circular cocktail bar at the Regent Palace Hotel with the amusing pun name 'Chez Cup' (pronounced 'shake up').

The advent of the Dorchester and of the Cumberland hotels apparently made the management of the six-year-old Grosvenor House Hotel, which was located between, feel that their premises were already behind the times aesthetically. The drastic solution was to invest in a major refit of the hotel's public areas. In complete contrast with the original design's assertion of British history and imperial might, the new design was more in line with the forward-looking aesthetics of Fascist Italy, where the dictator Benito Mussolini had recently overseen the commissioning of two prestigious trans-Atlantic ocean liners, the *Rex* and the *Conte di Savoia*, which entered service in 1932. The following year, the *Rex* became the only Italian liner ever to win the Blue Riband for the fastest Atlantic crossing.

While the interior of the *Rex* was incongruously an eighteenth century-style 'floating palace', a majority of the *Conte di Savoia* was very progressive, being the work of a youthful Trieste-based architect, Gustavo Pulitzer Finali, who used smooth surfaces, usually finished in costly materials, streamlined details, contemporary artworks and bespoke modern furniture and lighting.[47] In Italy, this approach – which became widely used in the mid-1930s – was known as the 'littorian' style, but it was very similar to what was referred to in Britain and the USA as 'streamline moderne.' In London, Pulitzer designed a travel bureau for the liner's owner, the Italian Line, in a similar manner and also an office for the Italian Tourist Board. It seems highly likely that these projects – and the international publicity given to Italy's new liners – would have brought Pulitzer's work to the attention of the Grosvenor House Hotel's owners.

The circular 'Chez Cup' cocktail bar, constructed within the Regent Palace Hotel, where Oliver Bernard also renovated the dining room.

In late 1933, Pulitzer was commissioned to re-design entirely the hotel's restaurant and ballroom – both of which were two storeys high and therefore akin to equivalent First Class liner interiors – plus their associated lobby spaces. His assistants for the project were two German architects, George Manner and Michael Rachlis, who, like Pulitzer, otherwise specialised in designing ship interiors. In Pulitzer's renovation of the restaurant, the original cornicing

The new Grosvenor House dining room and ballroom interiors, with associated lobby spaces, by Gustavo Pulitzer Finali; their clean lines contrasted with the hotel's previous themed historicist designs for these rooms. Images (1) and (2) show the dining room, (4) shows the dining room entrance, (3) shows the ballroom entrance, (5) shows the ballroom and (6) and (7) show artworks by Georg Ramon and A.R. Thomson, the former adorning a screen in the dining room concealing the kitchen door and the latter decorating the ballroom entrance.

disappeared behind a lowered ceiling with concealed perimeter lighting; this also hid the ionic capitals of the supporting columns and pilasters. On the lower walls, mirror panels and urn-shaped lighting sconces were introduced. In the restaurant foyer, the stage set designer and mural artist George Ramon produced a futurist-style impression of a cityscape and, in the restaurant itself, he painted a rather more soothing decorative panel depicting an undersea scene and concealing the entrance to the kitchen. Pulitzer's ballroom design was particularly stark with flat, unadorned surfaces and indirect lighting (in contrast to the much more ornate Art Deco treatment of a similar space at the Park Lane Hotel seven years before). At the foot of the ballroom lobby's access stair, the artist A.R. Thomson painted a large curved panel of a seascape.[48]

Completed late in 1934, Pulitzer's efforts transformed the hotel's main interior spaces into a land-bound version of the *Conte di Savoia*. Arguably, this approach was rather incongruous within Lutyens' monumental brick neo-classical façades but, as we have already seen with the renovation of Claridge's and the Strand Palace hotels, hoteliers were rarely concerned by any need to maintain aesthetic continuity between exterior and interior treatments. So far as they were concerned, the more important criterion was that guests should respond positively once inside.

The structural and service resolutions for hotels with full *en suite* facilities – such as the Statlers in America or the Cumberland – could potentially also be used for the development of blocks of small serviced flats for short-term rent, bookable in the same manner as hotel rooms. Such was the case with the Cumberland's next door neighbour, the Mount Royal Hotel, which opened in 1935. The seven-storey building was developed by Thomas Crawford Gordon, a London-based hotel and property entrepreneur of Glaswegian origin. He had first entered the hotel trade in his native city in 1901, running the Exhibition Hotel in conjunction with the International Exhibition, which was a major event attracting visitors from around the world. In more recent time, Gordon had developed the Mayfair Court flats in London's Stratton Street, but his Mount Royal Hotel scheme was altogether more ambitious. It would contain 650 furnished so-called 'flatel' units. These were effectively hotel suites, each consisting of a vestibule, kitchenette and bathroom with, in some instances, also a separate sitting room. The idea was to provide 'flats with hotel service at ordinary rents.'[49]

The Mount Royal was designed by Francis Lorne of Burnet, Tait and Lorne, a well-established, highly successful and prominent architectural practice with offices in London and Glasgow. Lorne, the firm's junior partner, was an enthusiastic follower of the Modern Movement and had a reputation for being a vocal polemicist for the benefits of modernist design approaches. Having visited the United States in his early twenties, he affected American manners and dress – though his fascination with all things fashionable and up-to-date initially caused tensions with his more conservative architectural partners. Lorne's competition-winning design in 1930 for a new Royal Masonic Hospital in Hammersmith, however, won widespread praise and an RIBA gold medal on account of its smooth, streamlined modernity, coupled with efficient planning. Lorne brought similar finesse to the Mount Royal scheme.

Externally, the hotel was a brick edifice with curved corners and metal framed windows carried around to the side elevations, the horizontality emphasised by continuous bands of cement at floor and sill height. Its smooth, streamlined appearance represented the opposite extreme of design of public buildings in the 1930s from the Cumberland's ponderous neo-classicism. The 'streamlined' approach, applied to the

Mount Royal

MARBLE ARCH, LONDON, W.1.
Hotel, 800 Rooms, and Restaurant,
Telephone Mayfair 8040 (60 Lines). Telegraphic Address "Mounroy Wesdo, London."

Mount Royal, had first been seen a decade before in the German commercial architecture of Erich Mendelsohn – such as the upward extension he designed for the Mossehaus publishing company's headquarters in Berlin (1923) and the Petersdorf department store in Breslau (1927). In London, an early example was the exterior of the New Victoria cinema by E. Wamsley-Lewis (1930). Nonetheless, the Mount Royal's repetitive curving horizontals were still enough of a rarity in 1935 to be noteworthy. The *Caterer and Hotel Keeper* reported that each of the hotel's flats was:

> 'Furnished in the contemporary style, carpeted with single-colour unpatterned carpets, and with its walls painted one colour also… The most expensive accommodation will be on the top floors, with their 16-ft wide promenade deck or balcony that gives a magnificent view…'

On the ground floor was a restaurant, snack bar, lounge and hairdressing salon while, the flat roof had a garden.[50]

During the construction of the Mount Royal, Gordon became involved in another significant, but much less publicised, hotel project in Walsall in the industrial West Midlands. In 1934, Walsall Corporation had demolished the town's eighteenth century George Hotel, a coaching inn it had purchased in 1927 and, on the cleared site, a new hotel of the same name was constructed to a design by a Glasgow-based architect, James Taylor. This was completed in November 1935 and was leased to Gordon to operate.

The design of the new George Hotel appeared indebted to that of the famous Dorchester in London, which was regarded in the mid-1930s as epitomising the ultimate in British hotel luxury and modernity. As with the Dorchester, the George was concrete-framed with a concave, gently curving façade, faced in reconstructed granite blocks with neo-classical and Art Deco detailing. This suggests percolation of hotel design inspiration from the capital's glamorous West End to provincial towns, where the local worthies aspired to similar facilities and status. The hotel's design was also reminiscent of many of the Burton's menswear stores concurrently being opened all over Britain and, indeed, one such store was included in ground floor retail space, adjacent to the entrance foyer. The George was, however, much smaller in size than the Dorchester and, furthermore, its bedrooms mostly lacked private bathrooms. Its regular clientele of commercial and business travellers probably would not have minded and both locals and visitors would have appreciated its fashionably up-to-date restaurant and cocktail bars.

As well as running the Mount Royal and George hotels, Gordon made numerous additional property investments in the second half of the 1930s and, when the property market declined towards the end of the decade, his losses led to bankruptcy in 1939.[51] Subsequently, the George Hotel suffered neglect in the Second World War and, thereafter, its lack of bathrooms, coupled with industrial decline in the vicinity sealed its fate; it was demolished in 1979.

The George Hotel in Walsall as it appeared upon completion; the design clearly embodies elements of the Dorchester in London, albeit on a smaller scale.

CHAPTER 2
Seaside hotels

The Modern Movement's concern for health and wellbeing strongly linked the new architecture to fresh air and exercise – but, in Britain, this aim was arguably merely a continuation of similar Georgian, Victorian and Edwardian ideals of leaving the polluted city for the coast. The coming of railways enabled the urban masses to travel there and so it was thus in the second half of the nineteenth century that a majority of seaside hotels and boarding houses were built, their variable quality of accommodation closely reflecting the era's social structures and aspirations.

By the inter-war era, a generational shift and the onward expansion of the middle class brought about a need for new hotels, replacing or augmenting those already existing and incorporating fresh spatial, technological and stylistic thinking. Whereas in London, as we have seen, establishment forces usually preferred traditionalist façade designs to modernist ones, the seaside was a 'fringe' condition where there was a tradition of unorthodox and exuberant building – for example, John Nash's Royal Pavilion in Brighton, or the Blackpool Tower complex. Moreover, as modern architecture took inspiration from the appearance of passenger ships, it was arguably more appropriate for 'ship-like' buildings to face onto the sea.

The first seaside hotel to display the new architecture was not, however, prominently located in a major resort, but was instead discreetly hidden on Burgh Island off the Devon coast, which was privately-owned and reachable by invitation only at low tide via a causeway across the sand. Hitherto, the island had been home to just a handful of fishermen who lived in cottages on its grassy slopes, above the sea cliffs. In 1925, it was purchased in its entirety by a theatre impresario and filmmaker, Archibald Nettlefold. He was a scion of the owners of a large engineering firm, Guest, Keen and Nettlefold, the origins of which dated back to the mid-eighteenth century. Nettlefold himself chose a very different career, however, founding the Anglia Films studio in 1923 and, three years thereafter, purchasing Cecil Hepworth Studios, a British maker of comedy films. By the latter 1920s, he also owned three London West End theatres and was a well-known figure in society and entertainment circles.

As one engaged in producing the most up-to-date popular entertainments, it seems reasonable to infer that Nettlefold would have been just the kind of wealthy, progressive individual to have also been attracted to the idea of modern architecture. Besides, he would have been very familiar with the newest cinemas, theatres, private apartments and – indeed – hotel interiors in London's West End.

In the late 1920s, Nettlefold commissioned the architect Matthew Dawson, who was an acquaintance of his, to design a hotel on Burgh Island in which to entertain his friends from the worlds of the theatre and the cinema, as well as accommodating paying guests. When one considers the many youthful and forward-looking architects who were gathered in London at that time, Dawson appears to be a strange choice. Aged 57, he was a graduate of the Architectural Association and subsequently of the Atelier Laloux in Paris. Thereafter, he had designed Arts & Crafts-style housing in Hampstead and Beaux Arts-style bank buildings in various London suburbs. He is, however, better remembered for his career as a lecturer at the Bartlett School of Architecture and at

Cambridge University's School of Architecture than for his architecture practice. His obituary in the *RIBA Journal* nonetheless praises his work for its originality of detail and for the aptitude with which he used the materials he selected. Furthermore, 'His remarks on any problem would always give a fresh view as his observation and critical faculties were acute.'[52]

Possibly influenced by reinforced concrete's advantages in terms of speed of construction and fireproofing, Dawson elected to build Burgh Island Hotel from this material, the use of which was relatively unusual in rural England at that time. Fires in remote country hotels of earlier generations were, however, often impossible to contain and, on Burgh Island, where help would take time to arrive, prevention was better than cure. The main accommodation block was a rectilinear four-storey structure of fairly utilitarian appearance with a flat roof terrace for sunbathing. Within, the use of concrete framing enabled spacious open planning with the columns and beams visible throughout the interior. The junctions between these splayed outwards to accommodate the reinforcing bars, their triangular shapes being not only functional but also contributing to the hotel's 'jazz moderne' interior styling. Throughout, windows were of the Crittall metal-framed variety, a type which would subsequently become so ubiquitous in British commercial buildings.

Yet, as well as being attracted by a modernist approach, Dawson – or more likely his client, Nettlefold – seems also to have wished to reflect the romantic possibilities of Burgh Island's secluded location. Thus, at one end, a rounded tower feature was devised with battlements at its summit. At the opposite end, there protruded a room externally resembling the stern of a nineteenth century warship; inside, this contained panelling and furniture Nettlefold had collected that had originally been in the captain's cabin of HMS *Ganges*. With these diverse elements added, what might otherwise have been a very pure and rational building ended up appearing rather eclectic. Indeed, the juxtaposition of modernist and thematic elements had more in common with the designs of film sets or cinema buildings than with what might be termed 'orthodox' modernism. For whatever reason, it appears that towards the end of the project's realisation, Nettlefold and Dawson fell out and so the building contractor completed it as best possible without the architect's further input.

The interior would have been rather austere, were it not for the jazzy furnishings and fabrics. Throughout, the central heating radiators were mounted vertically on the

Opposite: Burgh Island Hotel in its original late-1920s form, showing (1) the south-east façade, incorporating the stern of HMS Ganges, (2-5) a selection of details of the interior, including a fireplace flanked by radiators forming pilasters with lighting sconces, the entrance doors, a niche in the foyer with a mural map of the Channel and a lounge. The exterior, facing the mainland across a causeway, is shown in (6).

Bottom left: A post-war view of Burgh Island Hotel, showing the large extension designed by William Roseveare; the tower, formerly at the right hand side has, following war-time damage, been demolished to a stump.

Below: A view of Burgh Island Hotel during the Second World War, showing the tower that would shortly be damaged and dismantled.

insides of the concrete structural columns, running from the floor nearly to the splays, where they terminated with glass lighting sconces. In the hallway, between two of these features, an alcove contained a banquette seat behind which was a mural depicting the western English Channel with impressions of the sailing ship Mayflower, which had carried the 'Pilgrim Fathers' to America, and of the Cunard trans-Atlantic liner *Mauretania*. Such integration of services with structure and décor was a frequent characteristic of much modernist architecture and interior design of the period

A couple of years after the hotel's completion in 1929, Nettlefold decided to add a large extension, employing a young Plymouth architect, William Roseveare, to design it. He added a new wing to the rear, again using mostly concrete framing, but with more orderly detailing than Dawson's original section. This included a palm court with a glazed cupola decorated with representations of peacocks and a curving expanse of Crittall windows, enabling guests to enjoy panoramic views southward. Other new Art Deco elements included engraved peach glass mirrors, concealed lighting troughs and a staircase to the restaurant lined in black Vitrolite. These works were completed in 1932, the hotel henceforth boasting 25 rooms and being approximately T-shaped in plan.[53]

During the 1930s, Burgh Island Hotel provided hospitality to select invited guests, such as Winston Churchill, Noël Coward, H.R.H. the Prince of Wales, Wallis Simpson and Agatha Christie (who set her 1941 Poirot detective story 'Evil Under the Sun' at a

similar, though fictional, Devon hotel). Although none of these famous names would have been presented with anything quite so vulgar as a bill, the hotel's more regular wealthy clientele, drawn from the upper middle classes, were expected to pay to experience a little of the era's 'exclusive' celebrity lifestyle.

Notwithstanding Burgh Island Hotel's largely contemporary appearance and advanced construction, it was almost completely ignored by the British architectural establishment and never features in any of the design or construction journals. The protrusion of a pastiche warship stern and of battlements cannot have aided its credentials as 'serious' architecture. Perhaps too the fact that neither of its architects was a known modernist theoretician was also a problem. After a turbulent existence, including bomb damage in the Second World War, during which the tower was destroyed, never to be recreated, Burgh Island Hotel is now maintained in immaculate condition, continuing to serve as an upmarket retreat for the well-heeled.

Three years after his work at Burgh Island, William Roseveare designed a further concrete-framed hotel at Praa Sands near Penzance in Cornwall, a secluded and idyllic location for quiet family holidays. Named the Seacroft, it was located on a slope above the beach and comprised a garage for cars adjacent to the main access road at the lower level, above which was a rectilinear, three-storey accommodation block with a roof terrace. Its proprietors were local entrepreneurs by name of Treloan, whose aim appears to have been to attract prosperous middle-class holidaymakers wishing to enjoy the beach. The hotel's pristine white exterior and uncluttered interior expressed both up-to-date modernity and the pleasures of 'the simple life.' After only a few years, the entire structure was encased by a deep reinforced concrete *brise soleil* within which guests could shelter from strong sunlight or rain while continuing to take in the fresh sea air. Its slender framing and curved corners transformed the hotel's appearance, making it considerably more futuristic and continental-looking.[54] The development from the tentative and experimental forms of Burgh Island Hotel's initial phase, to the Seacroft in its final form exemplify how British modern architecture progressed within a very short timeframe during the first half of the 1930s.

The Midland Hotel at Morecambe

Britain's second seaside hotel to exhibit modernist design characteristics was, in contrast to Burgh Island, very prominently located in the popular Lancashire holiday resort of Morecambe and was a project financed by one of the country's largest businesses, the London, Midland and Scottish Railway. The LMS developed the Midland Hotel at Morecambe as part of a wider diversification strategy in response to the Great Depression's negative effects on its core rail business. Expanding seaside leisure provision was also seen as having the potential to offset a sharp drop in revenue at its city centre hotels as their main source of income – business travellers – had declined in number. Indeed, in the wake of the Wall Street Crash, Britain's major railway companies' hotel receipts fell by at least 10%. Whereas city station hotels bore the brunt of this reduction, the railways' country leisure hotels – such as those at the golfing resorts of Gleneagles and Turnberry in Scotland – suffered less as they still continued to attract the wealthy and leisured who had generally better avoided the Depression's worst consequences.[55] The railways at least had the advantage of scale, meaning that the capital

An aerial view of the Midland Hotel, showing its beach-side location and landscaped surroundings; these separated it from the considerably less aesthetically refined buildings on the promenade. Often, significant modernist buildings were physically distanced from the visual compromises of pre-existing built environments. Below are four views of the hotel from various angles.

costs of their sluggish hotel operations were just about sustainable, whereas independent establishments were more greatly troubled by the suddenly poor trading conditions due to their bigger overheads.

For the LMS, the choice of Morecambe was partly opportunistic. The railway already operated an ageing seaside hotel there and, as the resort was conveniently proximal to the big northern industrial cities, there would be a substantial upwardly-mobile clientele who might be persuaded to travel there for holidays or short breaks in an up-to-date – or even a futuristic – hotel environment. For the local municipality, meanwhile, a new hotel might 're-brand' the town from an unfashionable working class resort, perceived as inferior to Blackpool, to a stylish and desirable leisure destination. (Later in the decade,

many other British seaside resorts used modern architecture to rejuvenate their images.)

During the depression years, most of the existing railway hotels were caught between lower income and the rising expectations of guests. In luxury hotels, it is difficult to reduce costs in line with falling guest numbers without compromising quality. Yet, in the latter 1920s, even the railways' grandest hotels lacked many of the facilities nowadays taken for granted. At the end of 1927, of the LMS's establishments, only Gleneagles and the Adelphi in Liverpool had hot and cold running water in every room. *En suite* facilities – an area where North American hotel chains were setting standards – were scarce. Even Gleneagles, which was opened in 1924, albeit to a pre-war design, and promoted as one of the premier hotels of Europe, had just a quarter of *en suite* rooms. These were serious problems, making it difficult for the hotel to meet its American and European guests' expectations.[56]

The LMS' Chairman, Sir Josiah Stamp, who had trained as an economist and had been a civil servant before becoming a businessman, was in any case an enthusiastic moderniser of the railway's operations. In 1931, for instance, he had head-hunted the talented William Stanier from the Great Western Railway to serve as the LMS' Chief Mechanical Engineer, giving him a mandate to design much bigger, more powerful and modern motive power.

The rebuilding of the Midland Hotel at Morecambe was part of a deal involving the sale of the site of the existing hotel of that name to the local authority, which would then improve the adjacent harbour and establish a new promenade. Alan Powers records that the project was brought to fruition thanks to the persuasive powers of Sir Ralph Glyn, who was not only an LMS director but also Parliamentary Private Secretary to Ramsay MacDonald.[57] The architect was the eclectic and imaginative Oliver Hill who, in the years prior to gaining the hotel commission, had designed several lavish interiors inspired by the aesthetics of the Paris *Exposition* for wealthy London clients and the Grosvenor House Hotel's Imperial Suite, described above. Since then, Hill had come to embrace modernist aesthetics (if not modernism's reformist social agenda). This development followed his visit in 1930 to the Stockholm Exhibition.[58] Thereafter, he designed a few large villas which displayed the latest architectural trends for smooth cubic forms and ship-like curves, flat roofs and metal-framed windows. When designing the Midland Hotel, in addition to modernist influences, Hill's previous exposure to aestheticism, the Arts & Crafts movement and Art Deco were also to an extent reflected in his approach. Notwithstanding his obviously great skill and aesthetic sensitivity, this eclecticism negatively affected his reputation as a modern architect. Making matters worse, Hill was also a *bon viveur* who enjoyed juvenile jokes, fast cars, the company of numerous girlfriends, horse-riding, sailing and holidaying in nudist camps (which, in the 1930s, were regarded by the broad-minded as being another manifestation of progressiveness).[59] Thus, although hard to regard as a serious figure, he did at least possess a strong affinity with cultures of leisure and recreation.

It seems plausible that Hill was recommended to the LMS by Lutyens, who in 1930 had designed an unrealised proposal to extend its Midland Hotel in Manchester and who was a friend of the Hill family. Before the LMS approached Hill, however, a design for a new Midland in Morecambe had already been drawn up by the company's Divisional Engineer, Matthew Adam, who was an architect by training. Although the LMS Hotels and Catering Committee had found this proposal acceptable, they were less than enthusiastic about the business case for progressing the scheme.[60]

Interiors of the Midland Hotel, showing (1) the circular foyer and stair well, (2) Dell & Wainwright's famous view looking upward towards a ceiling mosaic by Eric Gill, (3) the lounge with a Gill bas relief and rug by Marion Dorn and (4) the café with its wrap-around mural by Eric Ravillious.

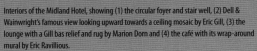

Arthur Towle, the LMS Controller of Hotels, argued that any new Midland Hotel for Morecambe would have to be a new type of establishment for the company, a popular venue that could cater for 'crowds of day-trippers', as opposed to the more exclusive clienteles of the company's existing city centre station and rural golfing hotels. The proposal was, however, opposed by a majority of the LMS Hotels Committee. The prime reason was that its potential for success appeared questionable. Morecambe was primarily a favourite resort of working-class holidaymakers from the industrial towns and cities of Lancashire and West Yorkshire and was not, in the committee's opinion, an appropriate location for a financially lucrative high-quality hotel operation.[61] A winning argument was that Hill's steel-framed, stucco-clad brick design proposal would cost just under £72,000 to build and equip – approximately two-thirds as much as an equivalently sized hotel with dressed stone façades and slated pitched roofs, so the Hotels Committee was overruled.[62] Moreover, the use of a steel structure would enable the building work to be carried out within just 12 months, which was another cost-saving consideration in its favour.

So as far as the hotel's imagined market positioning was concerned, the decision to build it entailed something of a compromise. Although the hotel aimed to be upmarket – albeit catering for a younger, more sophisticated set than was typical of the LMS's usual hotel clientele – prominently located on its ground floor (though operating independently) would be a circular café and bar, able to cater for up to 200 of Morecambe's more traditional visitors and thereby giving them an aspirational taste of stylishly up-to-date design and hospitality. Towle, however, argued to Hill that 'we must not confuse them with the class of people who will be using the hotel… We must walk with kings in the hotel but not lose the common touch in the bar…'[63]

The Midland Hotel was very prominently located on a roughly triangular promontory and surrounded by the newly-formed promenade, gardens and car parking space, suggesting that while users of its café would arrive by train, it was equally likely that hotel guests would drive there. In appearance, the hotel was a gently curving, nearly symmetrical three-storey edifice with a strong horizontal emphasis achieved through continuous external balconies and unbroken window sills and cornices; these features were the typical stylistic tropes of 1920s German Expressionism and had also manifested in Hill's recent villa designs. In the centre was a circular rotunda, containing a dramatic spiral staircase with 'ocean liner' balustrades. Beneath its smooth stucco external finish, the hotel was, however, just a conventional brick structure with load-bearing external walls and reinforced concrete floors. From a distance, the whole ensemble somewhat resembled a beached tropical cruise liner. The *Caterer and Hotel Keeper* commented:

> 'The unusual exterior design is enhanced by the materials employed, the wall facing being composed of white cement and carborundum electrically polished. The dead whiteness is however relieved by a greyish surround to the windows, the architraves having been treated by mixing particles of crushed blue glass with carborundum. Projecting ledges, the undersides of hoods and balconies and the ceilings of the loggias have been glazed to a blue-green tint. By night, flood lighting will render this remarkable building visible for miles out to sea…'[64]

As with Hill's previous projects, the hotel was decorated with considerable skill, the project involving a number of significant contemporary artists. The sculptor Eric Gill contributed four works. On the exterior, a pair of seahorses, said to have been inspired by Morecambe shrimps, were mounted at the summit of the rotunda, high above the entrance doors. Beneath these was a relief panel in Portland stone depicting Odysseus being welcomed from the sea by Nausicaa, who is attended by three female servants bearing fruit, a wine jug and goblet; the scene from Homer's Odyssey obviously alluded to the hotel's role in providing hospitality. Inside, guests were welcomed into a spacious foyer, floored in terrazzo and reaching the full height of the building. Gazing upwards, the risers of the spiral staircase caught slanting light, resembling a nautilus hemi-shell. On the ceiling, three storeys above, Gill designed a medallion depicting Neptune and Triton surrounded by waves; this was executed *in situ* by his son-in-law, Dennis Tegetmeier, who was better known as a book illustrator. As Powers observes, 'nothing like the great spiral main staircase had yet been seen in a [British] public building.'[65] In Berlin, however, Erich Mendelsohn's I.G. Metall trade union headquarters of 1929 had a similar design. Be that as it may, the view from beneath proved irresistible to Dell & Wainwright, who were at the forefront of the 'new wave' of architectural photographers and who dramatically captured the abstract patterns and interplay of light and shadow for the *Architectural Review*.

The café's curved interior walls featured a wrap-around mural by Eric Ravillious depicting fireworks and seaside illuminations against a dark background, the highlights being emphasised through the application of 'glow-in-the-dark' radioactive paint (such as was also used for the hands of alarm clocks). Furniture was light-weight, practical and up-to-date chromed tubular steel. In the bedrooms, there were rugs designed by Marion Dorn, all of the furniture and fittings otherwise being designed or specified by Hill, down to the colours of the towels.

When it opened, the Midland Hotel caused a sensation, it being the first public building beyond London employing modernist design approaches outside and in to which the public had ready access and it set a trend for similar aesthetics at most British seaside resorts. It featured widely in LMS advertising and such was its effectiveness in drawing visitors to Morecambe, if only to sample its café, that the railway subsequently invested in similar-looking buildings for various purposes elsewhere. For instance, it helped finance a new holiday camp at Prestatyn on the North Wales Coast, which was designed in-house by William Hamlyn and also the new Casino building at Blackpool Pleasure Beach, designed by Joseph Emberton; both of these projects were completed in 1939. Unfortunately, as with Oliver Hill's flat-roofed villas, the hotel proved hard to keep water-tight and, within a few years, the Eric Ravillious murals in its café had been so badly damaged by leaks that they were painted over. The harsh climate beside the Irish Sea took its toll on the exterior too and soon the façades were streaked with rust (ironically, thereby resembling a liner in need of dry-docking). To maintain the hotel in the necessary pristine condition to please the intended clientele, an intensive and expensive ongoing programme of maintenance was needed.

Before these shortcomings came to light, the LMS had been so enamoured by the hotel's critical and popular acclaim that it commissioned Hill to restyle the entrance hall, lounge and dining room of its Euston Hotel, where he also designed an American bar, offering over-the-counter service of cocktails, and also to design a similar facility on the concourse of St Pancras Station. These projects were carried out in the 1934-36 period.

With hindsight, however, the Midland Hotel's design and the circumstances leading to its selection raise issues that were reflected and perpetuated in the Modern Movement's subsequent development by commercial interests in Britain. The design approach was chosen to a large degree on account of being the cheaper option and, although the resulting building initially looked splendid, within less than a decade, it had started to become seedy. Image and short-term profit potential were thus more important than substance and staying power.

Back in 1933, the inauguration of both the Midland Hotel and of the conceptually very different Cumberland in London had a profound effect on the British hotel and catering industries. This is most clearly seen in their trade journal, the *Caterer and Hotel Keeper*, which suddenly was re-designed with new *sans serif* fonts while suppliers who advertised in it also changed their graphic identities to align with the latest thinking. Indeed, the *Caterer and Hotel Keeper* quickly became infatuated with modern architecture, interior design and furnishing and with the types of cuisine, staff uniforms, service strategies and entertainment that would complement and extend the new visual culture to form complete experiences for guests and staff. A somewhat fanciful article by the restauranteur Albert L. Louis imagined what the 'Hotel of the Future' might be like, fifty years hence:

> 'The present rate of advancement and progress is such that new hotels now building are nearly out of date before they are opened… For the past two years in my leisure hours I have been designing a hotel that, I am convinced, will be the type of hotel in use fifty years hence. The customer's bill, in my hotel of the future, will be solely for the amount of energy used to fulfil the guest's requirements. I visualise hotels capable of housing 5,000 people, scattered over the country at equal distances apart. Buildings would have a fully-equipped aerodrome on the roof with an 'Attractor Tower.' This tower will draw planes that are tuned into it, in the same way as a magnet attracts a needle, so that a plane cannot miss its destination in fog or darkness. The accommodation will consist entirely of small suites consisting of: Resting Chamber, Cleaning and curative chamber, Meal service chamber, Television and wireless telephone cabinet. The building itself would be composed of several square pylons, fifty floors high, with an electric lift running down the centre of each. There would be four complete suites on each floor. Guests arriving by air would descend straight to their suite from the roof… Meals will be sent to the suite by an electrical conveyance… the containers, when finished with, will be put into a chute for conveyance to an electrical destructive device. The staff of the hotel will consist mostly of engineers.'[66]

While, much later on, some large hotels did indeed count service engineers among their staff, the reality of how British hotel architecture would develop was inevitably far less adventurous.

1935 was the year when the Modern Movement really arrived in Britain's coastal resorts in a major way. The completion of the De La Warr Pavilion at Bexhill on Sea to a competition-winning design by Erich Mendelsohn and Serge Chermayeff was a high-profile and controversial contribution, as to a lesser extent was Wells Coates' Embassy Court apartment block in Brighton. A significant number of hotels were also completed exhibiting modernist characteristics – though these received little or no critical attention from the mainstream architecture journals. Although new seaside hotels were developed all around Britain's coasts in the 1930s, as might be expected, the greatest concentrations of those exhibiting modern architectural characteristics – such as flat roofs, balconies and metal-framed windows – was along the southern coast of England in Essex, Kent, Sussex, Hampshire, Dorset, Devon and Cornwall. There, in summer at least, the weather was more likely to emulate continental dryness and warmth.

Completed in the summer of 1935, the Saunton Sands Hotel, overlooking Barnstaple Bay in Devon, was built to accommodate visitors to the well-known Saunton Golf Links. A large, rectilinear three-storey building, containing 92 bedrooms, it was clad in off-white painted stucco and, from a distance, perhaps more resembled a hospital or sanatorium than a place of hospitality.[67] 'Moderne' styling was most likely selected to reflect golf's fashionability as a healthy outdoor pursuit to be enjoyed equally by men and women. In the 1930s, the heir to the British throne, H.R.H. The Prince of Wales, was a highly-prominent celebrity golfing 'swell', whose sporting garb – consisting of knickerbockers with brightly-coloured stockings, pullover and cap – was widely admired and emulated. Yet the building's architect, Alwyn Underdown, had hitherto worked almost exclusively in the Arts & Crafts style. Born in 1897, most of his work was around Eastbourne in East Sussex, where he produced a series of finely-detailed villas, often built of recycled brick and timber to give a more rustic finish, suggestive of structures that were centuries old, rather than dating from the 1930s. In 1934, three of his housing designs were exhibited at the Royal Academy.

The Saunton Sands Hotel was Underdown's only executed work in the 'moderne' manner – and was a project far greater in scale than his typical output of private housing. In the hotel, the only slight evidence of his love for Arts & Crafts detailing was found in the interior, where extensive use was made of Oregon pine panelling in the lounge and dining room (the overall design of which vaguely resembled ocean liner interiors of the era). In 1936, Underdown produced plans for another hotel which was intended for a site in Seaford, near Eastbourne. It would have had 100 *en suite* rooms and garages for 36 cars. Intended for completion in 1938, the project was never executed, however. After the Second World War, Underdown designed some public housing around Newhaven before retirement in 1959.

Another fashionable golfing hotel, serving visitors to a links course, was the Seabank

Three views of the Saunton Sands Hotel in the latter-1930s; to the rear of the main accommodation block is a garage and staff accommodation.

at Porthcawl on the South Wales coast, facing the Bristol Channel. It resulted from the extensive rebuilding in 1937 of an earlier hotel, which had been converted in the mid-1920s from an Italianate-style mansion of mid-Victorian vintage. In 1932, its neighbouring Royal Porthcawl Golf Club was visited by the Prince of Wales, an event which greatly elevated its reputation among the fashionable set. Capitalising upon this visit and a general upturn in trade, in 1937, the Seabank was encased in a wrap-around extension, transforming it into a substantial four-storey, 89-bedroom hotel in 'streamline moderne' style. The design was by a local architect, E.J. Moore, who had previously designed the Porthcawl Pavilion theatre, and had also produced housing and other smaller projects in the vicinity. Although flat-roofed, the top storey was faced with green glazed pan-tiles facings to give an impression of there being traditional sloping roofs. Only in the section above the entrance was a flat roof hinted at by a small tower feature. In the 1930s, similar hybridised design approaches were actually quite commonplace across a range of domestic and commercial building genres, the aim being to please as many potential users as possible, whether their taste be progressive, conservative, or a mixture of both.

The Oulton Hall Hotel at Clacton-on-Sea – a predominantly working class resort on the Essex coast – was opened in July 1935. It was owned by Travco (Travel Company Ltd), a recently-created joint venture between the Workers' Travel Company and the Co-operative Wholesale Society, the purpose of which was to provide value-for-money holidays for trade union and Co-op members in clean, rejuvenating surroundings. Those taking part had a small proportion of their salary removed each week as holiday savings which paid for their annual break. The Travco system was such a success that by the Second World War it had grown into Britain's second biggest holiday company after Thomas Cook. Travco's hotels and holiday camps were developed in the second half of the 1930s, Oulton Hall being the prototype in terms of its scale and modern architectural style. Designed by a recent London-based graduate of the Architectural Association, Alan Henry Devereux, who was aged only 29 at the time, the main building had four storeys and was approximately H-shaped in plan with additional two-storey blocks to the rear. Altogether, it provided accommodation for 300 guests and, on the ground floor, there was a dining room, lounge and ballroom.[68] Their decoration, though up-to-date, was robust and intended for more punishing usage than equivalent spaces at the more exclusive

Above: The Seacroft Hotel at Porthcawl in the late-1930s; the aerial view shows how a very substantial extension was wrapped around an existing villa, the lantern of which protruded from the middle of the roof, some way behind the new entrance. Although the top storey was clad in glazed pan tiles, the hotel was, in fact, flat-roofed.

Below: Oulton Hall Hotel at Clacton-on-Sea in the late-1930s.

An aerial view of Oulton Hall Hotel, showing its beach context and the adjacent tennis courts.

Saunton Sands and Seabank golfing hotels. Instead of carpeting and rugs, there were terrazzo and linoleum for flooring with tubular steel-framed, leather-upholstered chairs rather than fabric. These tougher finishes reflected the approaches generally applied concurrently in café, holiday camp and cinema foyer décor – all of which were, like Oulton Hall, aimed at mass audiences. Furthermore, despite the hotel's seafront location, few of the bedrooms had private balconies, presumably on account of cost and, moreover, because it was assumed that the typical clientele would in any case have preferred taking part in organised communal activities in the public rooms or on the adjacent beach.

In the genteel South Coast resorts, some very elegant and well-equipped new hotels were constructed in the second half of the 1930s, the intention being to attract a prosperous and relatively style-conscious clientele who were unable to take foreign holidays on an annual basis, or who preferred weekends by the sea, taking the train or car from London.

The ten-storey Palace Court Hotel in the centre of Bournemouth was completed in September 1935 to a design by local architects Arthur J. Seal and Godfrey N. Ellis of A.J. Seal & Partners. Opening a seaside holiday hotel when the summer season was ending may have appeared perverse from an economic viewpoint, but the strategy was actually quite commonplace as it allowed staff gradually to familiarise themselves over the winter so that, by the following summer, the entire operation could handle summer peak visitors paying maximum tariffs in a professional manner. The Palace Court faced towards the sea from Westover Road – one of the resort's major entertainment arteries. Within, it contained 60 bedrooms plus 30 service flats. The *Caterer and Hotel Keeper's* correspondent reported that it was 'an outstanding landmark' and 'the loftiest building on the South Coast.'[69] Its frontage had strong horizontal and vertical emphases, there being continuous bands of cantilevered balcony fronts with protective windscreens between each opening. The top two storeys were recessed, much like the upper decks of a liner's superstructure. Indeed, the entire composition appeared remarkably similar to the more famous Embassy Court apartment block in Brighton, designed by Wells Coates and completed in the same year. At night, the hotel's white frontage was floodlit and its name on the roof was outlined in neon.

The flats at the Palace Court occupied the upper five floors while the hotel bedrooms – each of which had a private bathroom – were on the floors below; every one of these faced onto the sea. Consequently, the hotel was shallow relative to the length of its frontage. The *Caterer and Hotel Keeper* reported that the foyer was:

> '...Light and airy' with 'five first class shops after the style of some of the more modern American hotels... On the first floor is a beautiful lounge with large, high windows opening outwards to a sun balcony. The hotel dining room has

been designed with an eye to… extreme comfort… No part of this mammoth building, however, is more impressive and interesting than the kitchens, which represent the last word in modernity… It is understood that Mr A.J. Seal, the architect, who is one of the co-directors of the hotel, will occupy one of the service suites.'[70]

From the outset, the hotel was a great success and, within a year of opening, its initial local owners had sold out for a profit to London and Southern Properties, a major property company based in the capital.

Subsequently, A.J. Seal & Partners designed the Queen's Hotel in Torquay, completed in 1937, it being in layout and external appearance a smaller version of the Palace Court. The Queen's was, however, aimed at the mid-market and its interior decoration and more limited facilities reflected this situation. Although, once again, all rooms facing the sea had balconies, on this occasion none were *en suite*. Within, 'moderne' treatments were eschewed in favour of themed interiors, consisting of a 'Queen Anne'-style dining room and a Spanish Gothic lounge-bar. Presumably these were demanded by the owner, who was a local publican by name of Gibbons. After all, a traditionally palatial dining room would infer luxury and high status while a Gothic bar would provide a suitably escapist environment in which to become thoroughly intoxicated. The juxtaposition of moderne façades and themed interiors was, of course, commonplace in mass-market pleasure attractions of many kinds during the 1930s – and since.

Back in Bournemouth, meanwhile, the upmarket four-storey Green Park Hotel was finished in October 1937 to a design by another local architecture firm, comprising Henry Collins and his partner, Antoine Englebert Geens.[71] Collins had begun his architectural career in 1912 in his native Barnsley in Yorkshire, subsequently joining the County Borough of Chester where he was involved in designing new 'homes for heroes' who had returned from the First World War.[72] Thereafter, he formed a partnership in Bournemouth with Geens, who was a Belgian émigré. While much of the practice's output was local and small in scale – consisting of café interiors, housing and the like – they achieved greater prominence through winning an architectural competition to design a new Romford Town Hall, completed in 1935, and, three years thereafter, a competition for Newcastle City Hall (which remained unbuilt). Their Romford scheme was a brick edifice in the 'streamlined Georgian' idiom so typical of English public buildings of its era and was selected on account of its offering the best value for money of all the

The Palace Court Hotel in Bournemouth (top), the Queen's Hotel in Torquay (above) and a poster promoting the Green Park Hotel in Bournemouth (below).

projects submitted. The Newcastle design won on account of its similarly rational planning and compactness, tempered by a veneer of grandeur. Similar qualities were, of course, desirable in hotel buildings.[73]

According to the *Caterer and Hotel Keeper*, the Green Park Hotel's 26-year-old proprietor, J.M. Saunders, had specified the building 'with an eye on the future, every bedroom having its own private bathroom.'[74] Built in just six months on a site previously occupied by a large private villa, the L-shaped four-storey edifice contained a large number of two- and three-room private suites, the latter having two bathrooms each; all suites had private entrance lobbies off the main corridors. On the ground floor were a dining room, two lounges, a writing room and a ballroom. Clearly, Green Park was a hotel for wealthier, more discerning guests whom Saunders must have presumed would be a growing demographic. The *Caterer and Hotel Keeper* records that from the outset, the hotel was planned so that, at a subsequent date, a 40-room extension could be added.[75]

The hotel stood in extensive and mature landscaped gardens with lily ponds, ornamental fountains, flowerbeds and topiary. Amongst these were tables and chairs for guests to relax out of doors when the weather was sufficiently clement. The atmosphere was calm and secluded, which presumably would have appealed to a clientele drawn from London's professional class. The interiors were simply decorated with extensive glazing and patio doors to let fresh sea air and sunlight flood in – but the furnishings were mostly traditional, rather than modern in style, having been apparently chosen for their comfort rather than to give a fashionable appearance. The Green Park Hotel soon developed a loyal clientele and subsequently became particularly popular with the Jewish community, whom it served almost exclusively until closure in 1986.

In February 1938, a third large, new Bournemouth hotel opened on a site facing the sea at East Cliff. The Cumberland was designed by local architects, Messers Rowley & Partners, for a London owner, Mrs E.A. Philips, who presumably had chosen the name to emulate J. Lyons' acclaimed hotel at Marble Arch. A five-storey, steel-framed structure,

The exterior of the Cumberland Hotel in Bournemouth and a view of its entrance foyer, which featured concealed lighting, hardwood veneer panelling and comfortable-looking settees.

faced with stucco-clad brick, the ground floor – containing the public rooms – was rectangular in plan. Above this rose a symmetrical bedroom block in the centre of which was a light well. This not only illuminated the bedroom corridors around its perimeter but also allowed natural light to reach the palm court in the centre of the ground floor, which had a glazed roof. All of the hotel's internal partitions were of breezeblock, a recently-developed construction material advantageous for its relatively light weight and cheapness, allied with fire-retardant and sound-proof qualities. Of the 104 bedrooms, only those with a sea view had private balconies and *en suite* bathrooms, while the cheaper rooms on the north elevation shared communal facilities. The *Caterer and Hotel Keeper* reported on the design of the hotel's public spaces:

> 'Four pairs of double glazed doors lead into the card-room, smoke-room, palm court and club-room. The Palm Court is… truly magnificent… It is decorated in cyclamen and green and is entirely lighted by the large dome which is glazed with Flemish glass, tinted a pale pink. Four large rectangular alcoves add to the attractive effect and the angular pilasters and fibrous plaster panels, shaded in green, afford unobtrusive decoration… The floor… is of maple and is sprung for dancing. The lighting is very pleasing with six vertical tubular lamps being provided to each alcove…'[76]

Nomenclature apart, the description of the colour scheme and lighting seems reminiscent of Oliver P. Bernard's treatment of the rotunda at Lyons' Cumberland in London. The idea of a glass-domed hotel 'palm court', however, also suggests an updated version of genteel Edwardian seaside hotel interiors.

Bournemouth's three new hotels represented the very best that a British seaside holiday could provide. Their modern appearance, coupled with relatively sophisticated servicing and comfortable appointments set them apart from earlier generations of hotel in the town and enabled their operators to charge a premium to those who wished to experience the latest in comfort and style.

On the North Kent coast, meanwhile, the Northumberland Hotel, located in the Margate suburb of Cliftonville, was opened in the late summer of 1938. It was a notably clean-lined and confident design in brick by a local architect, Willie Richard Halstone

The clean lines of the Northumberland Hotel at Cliftonville, near Margate, are emphasised by the low-angle of this view, dating from when the building was completed in 1938.

Gardner, who was senior partner in Gardner and Dale, the main specialism of which was designing school buildings for Kent County Council.[77] Gardner's design approach may have been influenced by the new Dreamland cinema and amusement park complex, designed by Julian Leathart, which had opened on Margate's waterfront three years previously. In appearance, both cinema and hotel apparently owed much to the late 1920s German work of Eric Mendelsohn, which in turn, had been heavily influenced by the appearance of ocean liners' superstructures. The Northumberland Hotel was a long, four-storey structure with horizontally elongated balconies. At one end was a curved entrance canopy, indicating the location of the entrance foyer and, at the other, this feature was balanced by an additional storey, giving access to a roof garden.[78]

Impressive designs for seaside hotels by architects from Plymouth, Eastbourne, Bournemouth, Margate and elsewhere provide a counterpoint to the more usual view of architectural modernism in Britain being a phenomenon mainly of concern to London-based theorists, practitioners and critics in the first half of the 1930s. These substantial and costly buildings demonstrate the rapid spread of recent architectural ideas from the continent to Britain's southerly coastal peripheries.

Hotels for Holidays with Pay

The passing of the Holidays with Pay Act in 1938 guaranteed every worker a week's paid holiday each year. Its advent had been widely anticipated as, across the political spectrum, it was viewed as popular and necessary reformist legislation. The consequent need to house much larger numbers of holidaymakers brought a fresh wave of expansion to British seaside resorts in the years immediately preceding the Second World War – and of the development of new out-of-town holiday camps, in which holiday leisure was provided on an industrial scale. The history of the holiday camp as an informal alternative to the seaside boarding house long pre-dates the 1930s, however, and falls outwith the scope of this book. Nonetheless, the first large-scale commercial holiday camp was opened in 1936 at Skegness – a 'bracing' fishing town on the Lincolnshire coast – by the showman and entrepreneur Billy Butlin. He had been born in Cape Town in South Africa to a fairground family originating in the West Country and, as a young man, he returned to Britain where he worked hard to build up an amusements business. He opened an arcade in Skegness in

Butlin's Ingoldmells Hotel was located adjacent to the Skegness Holiday Camp and, like many of the camp's communal buildings, its exterior was reminiscent of light industrial premises of the era.

1927 and subsequently built the camp using his own employees, a decision taken in anticipation of the Holidays with Pay Act becoming law. The camp consisted of rows of identical wooden chalets, built off-site as flat-pack kits and transported to Skegness by rail. By contrast, the communal buildings – containing a reception, dining rooms, ballrooms and changing facilities for the outdoor swimming pool – were designed in a 'moderne' manner, echoing the style of other types of recent leisure and entertainment buildings elsewhere in the country. Initially, Butlin's Skegness camp accommodated 500 but, by the end of the 1930s, this number had increased to nearly 10,000.[79]

In 1938, Butlin's built the Ingoldmells Hotel on a site adjacent to the camp to 'accommodate parents and friends of camp guests who prefer hotel amenities.'[80] Externally, however, the structure appeared to have more in common with the aesthetics of modern factory buildings than anything intended as conventional hotel accommodation. Both holiday camp and hotel were designed jointly by Butlin, who, as an operator of fairgrounds, had considerable building expertise, and the Ipswich-based architect Harold Bradley Hooper, who had previously designed cinemas and other commercial buildings in East Anglia. On such a spacious site, specifying a low-rise pre-fabricated steel structure with wide spans, as would have been used for industrial premises, was a pragmatic solution as it enabled extensive circulation, leisure and entertainment space to be contained indoors at relatively low cost. This meant that, to an extent, a Butlin's holiday was 'weatherproofed' – which was advantageous, given the unpredictable weather conditions beside the North Sea.

On the outside, the Ingoldmells Hotel's rectilinear 'modern factory' aesthetic of facing brick with repetitive horizontal concrete courses was alleviated by 'an impressive fountain, which was constructed at a cost of £10,000. There are seven jet changes, each having its own colour-cycle, and giving a 45-minute display without repetition…'[81] By complete contrast, inside the hotel's entrance block, there was:

> 'A reproduction of a Tyrolean courtyard, gay with flower-decked gabled 'houses' round the walls, a stone-paved courtyard and a central lily pond takes the place of the reception hall… To the right of the reception hall is a licensed restaurant – simple in its decoration – where parties of 800 can be accommodated at a single sitting… The principal ballroom, occupying the left wing, returns to the lavish Tyrolean style. In alcoves along one side are installed bars and refreshment buffets. From a stage, guest artists can entertain an audience of one thousand… A lounge is amply provided with easy chairs, writing desks and tables. The dining room is spacious. Tables are fitted with a full silver service…'[82]

This 'themed' interior was similar in conception to the so-called 'atmospheric' cinema

The entrance foyer of Butlin's Ingoldmells Hotel, incorporating three-dimensional representations of buildings in English vernacular styles; the lounge, however, was decorated in the 'moderne' idiom with horizontal stripes on the walls and globe-shaped light fittings.

interiors which spread from America to Europe in the latter 1920s and had ceilings designed to resemble night skies with three-dimensional 'exotic' buildings arranged around their interior walls, seeking to engender the atmosphere of an outdoor courtyard. Much later on, the idea of a 'leisure shed' became a standard, commercially expedient way of housing wide diversities of hospitality and entertainment functions – but Butlin was an early entrepreneur to realise the benefits of this approach. The hotel's two-storey bedroom accommodation was located to the rear of the entrance block's communal facilities:

> 'Entrance to the residential portion of the building is made through an archway of rustic brickwork. There are 68 bedrooms, both single and double, the beds and fittings being after the style of those on the *Queen Mary*, with sheets and blankets in shades of green. Each room is fitted with hot and cold water, a cream telephone and an electric heater… The curtains are in shades of green and pastel, and the rooms are completely carpeted…'[83]

The high capacities of the restaurant and ballroom suggest that the hotel's public facilities were designed so that either they could accommodate visitors from the adjacent holiday camp, or so that, in future, additional bedroom blocks could be added. The ocean liner reference and the emphasis on soft furnishings are indicative of Butlin's desire that the hotel should be perceived as upmarket.

The Broadmark Hotel at Rustington on the Sussex coast was completed in 1936 and, conceptually, it followed a similar overall approach to Butlin's Ingoldmells Hotel, albeit with greater design finesse. The design was by a Worthing architect, A.T.W. Goldsmith, who was responsible for several prominent 'moderne' buildings in the vicinity, including the town's Connaught Theatre. The hotel's centrepiece was its outdoor swimming pool complex, which included a children's paddling pool and was located adjacent to the beach. The communal buildings, located towards the site's landward end, contained a 60-seat restaurant and a guests' lounge, among other facilities. The bedrooms were in separate two-storey accommodation blocks, each of which had 16 rooms. In terms of overall layout,

The Rustington Lido Hotel's entrance block, one of its chalet blocks, an aerial view of the entire complex and the swimming pool.

the hotel anticipated the typical planning of American and European motels in the post-Second World War era and, indeed, it was intended to attract motorists, for whom ample car parking space was provided. There were also tennis courts, a putting green and, in the evening, the lounge could be converted into a ballroom with a small stage for a dance band and cabaret acts.[84] For the era's motorists, packing the family car and driving to a specially-designed hotel-resort such as this was a new kind of holiday experience. Post-war, the genre became increasingly commonplace – but, in the mid-1930s, the Broadmark Hotel was pioneering.

A late-1930s view of the Silver Waves Chalet Hotel at Dymchurch showing its horizontal layout on a relatively commodious coastal site.

Another notable early example was the Silver Waves Chalet Hotel at Dymchurch on the Kent Coast which also was opened in 1936 but was more compact than either Ingoldmells or Rustington Lido. Its chalets were just single-storey, more like those of a holiday camp. As at Rustington, light-coloured stucco cladding, Crittall fenestration and flat roofs gave an appropriate aura of seaside modernity.

By contrast, the very commodious 400-bedroom Ocean Hotel, located in the rapidly expanding coastal suburb of Saltdean to the east of Brighton, could be considered as a forerunner to the types of 'all inclusive' coastal resort hotel built a generation later in Mediterranean resorts to accommodate package tourists arriving by air. Saltdean itself had been developed from 1931 onward on what had hitherto been arable land.[85] By 1938, when the hotel was completed, the suburb possessed around 800 houses in a variety of modern and neo-historicist aesthetics, an 18-hole putting course and a public swimming pool, Saltdean Lido. Both this structure and the Ocean Hotel were the work of a 38-year-old local architect, Richard William Herbert (R.W.H.) Jones. The two had in common gently curving, symmetrical layouts clearly inspired by Oliver Hill's Midland Hotel in Morecambe – which was at least an excellent source of design inspiration. Indeed, viewed from the main access road, the hotel's main frontage was almost the Midland's spitting image, except in its use of facing brick instead of stucco cladding between the

An aerial view of the Ocean Hotel at Saltdean; the complex made excellent use of a gentle slope to provide accommodation blocks with extensive terraced sunbathing spaces on the roofs.

A panoramic view of Saltdean, showing the suburb's public lido in the foreground and the Ocean Hotel at the top of the slope in the middle distance. The hotel's concave frontage to the street, however, closely resembled that of the Midland in Morecambe (top right). The dining room (above right) was commodious and was decorated with murals reflecting the 'ocean' theme.

window openings. Viewed from the sea, however, the situation was different as the Ocean was a far bigger complex, designed as a series of inter-connected bedroom blocks on the hillside, between which the hotel's swimming pool and children's paddling pool were located. Facing the pool, the rear elevation of the main building had sun terraces and the flat roofs of the bedroom blocks provided yet more sunbathing space. Outwith the main summer holiday season, these blocks – in which the rooms had washbasins rather than *en suite* bathrooms – were closed, leaving only the main hotel building in use, presumably with a more exclusive Midland Hotel-like atmosphere.[86]

The Ocean Hotel boasted a very large dining room in which all guests could be served at two sittings, much as on a passenger liner; this had a mural of the Atlantic Ocean on its end wall, emulating the one in the First Class dining saloon on the *Queen Mary*. In addition, there was a ballroom, an American Bar, a hairdressing salon, a nursery and a gymnasium. Throughout, the décor was ocean-themed with murals depicting undersea scenes and there even were a number of aquaria containing tropical fish built into the internal walls. Adjacent to the hotel complex were outdoor tennis courts, also for the exclusive use of guests.[87] The emphasis on sunbathing, sport and fitness was very much in line with the era's concerns for the 'body beautiful'. Moreover, the fact that the hotel had effectively two classes of bedroom accommodation and a dining regime of fixed sittings for all guests meant that, beyond a visual resemblance to passenger ship naval architecture, its entire operation was remarkably liner-like, perhaps more so than any other shore-based structure of the era in Britain.

Modernism and the modernisation of existing hotels

The ideal modernist buildings – such as Le Corbusier's Villa Savoye at Poissy in France (1927) or Ludwig Mies van der Rohe's Barcelona Pavilion (1929) – were arguably more like rationalist sculptures than places to be occupied by 'real' people. Such free-standing structures were uncontaminated by evidence of the past – indeed, modernism had great difficulty in achieving an accommodation with historic settings, which were often imagined being removed entirely by comprehensive redevelopment (as seen in Le

Corbusier's 1925 Plan Voisin for Paris). By contrast, for operators of commercial buildings – particularly in an era of economic difficulty – the issue was how to achieve the maximum transformation for the minimum investment. This situation affected hotels as much as it did shops, cinemas and numerous other 'high street' building types.

During the 1930s, modernisations were carried out at many British hotels dating from the nineteenth and early twentieth centuries. These invariably resulted in interesting – and sometimes stylistically uncomfortable – hybridisations of Victorian, Edwardian and 'moderne' elements. A typical approach was exemplified by The Savoy Hotel across the Irish Sea in the resort of Bangor in Northern Ireland. The hotel's first phase had been completed in 1931, its owner being an operator of touring coaches by name of J. Gaston who wished to accommodate the holidaymakers he brought from Belfast and elsewhere in Northern Ireland. In appearance, it was a somewhat dour industrial-looking edifice with large brick pilasters. The venture was such a success that, after just two years, it was decided to double capacity. This was carried out to plans by a Belfast architect, John McBride Neill, who otherwise specialised in designing cinemas. He had been greatly influenced by the publication in 1930 of a book entitled 'Modern Theatres and Cinemas' by the British architecture, food and wine critic, P. Morton Shand, which extolled the virtues of German cinema and theatre architecture. Of recent British cinemas, practically the only example of which Shand approved was the New Victoria in London by E. Wamsley-Lewis. Not only did McBride Neill seek to emulate elements of its exterior in his numerous cinema projects but he also applied the same detailing to the Savoy Hotel. Yet, just as the original wing appeared industrial, so too in its own way did the new one, which was externally indistinguishable from many of the latest factory buildings.

Following extension, the Savoy boasted 130 bedrooms, all with hot and cold running water, a lounge, a dining room and a ballroom with a sprung floor. Unfortunately, the designs of the two wings clashed horribly. The solution of re-cladding the original so that both would match took a long time to happen. Indeed, the work was not carried out until the mid-1950s, by which time – ironically – the streamlined style had fallen from fashion.

In late 1935, the terrace of seven houses which formed the Yelton Private Hotel, located close to the pier at Hastings, was rebuilt with a new 'moderne' frontage and upgraded interiors. The conversion was designed by Harold Burleigh of local architects Oxley and Burleigh, based in St. Leonards. The *Caterer and Hotel Keeper* wrote approvingly:

> 'The houses have now been united into one complete building with through corridors on all floors, a spacious lounge, dining room, central lift and an attractive entrance hall… The hotel has been entirely re-furnished throughout,

Two images of the Savoy Hotel in Bangor, showing its gradual transformation into a streamline moderne design through the addition of a new wing and the subsequent re-cladding of the original.

Two views of the Yelton Hotel in Hastings; prominently located at the head of the pier, it was ingeniously fashioned from a terrace of houses.

hot and cold water have been installed in all bedrooms and all corridors are centrally heated…Though the improvements involved virtual rebuilding, the whole of the work was carried through in 9½ weeks.[88]

Further along the Sussex coast in Worthing, the Beach Hotel had similarly begun life as a row of mid-nineteenth century private houses, facing the sea across Marine Parade. In the same year as the Yelton was remodelled, it too was given a new, flat 'moderne' façade with a continuous balcony projecting from the first floor, a deep parapet to hide the pitched roofs and flagpoles on either side of an Art Deco pediment. (By the early 2000s, unfortunately, this frontispiece was beginning to detach from the somewhat ramshackle pre-existing structure, leading to the hotel's closure for demolition.)

In Blackpool, Britain's biggest seaside resort, only a few relatively small private hotels were built during the 1930s, but many of the larger existing properties were extended and modernised. Perhaps the town's predominantly working class clientele could not have afforded higher tariffs similar to those levied by the big new hotels on the South Coast – or maybe the Midland in nearby Morecambe had already cornered that market. A typical example of modernisation in Blackpool was the Carlton Hotel, which was thoroughly rebuilt in 1937 with the addition of a streamlined single-storey extension, clad in cream and black faience and containing a new reception hall, sun lounge and public bar. The contrast between this and the existing structure, which was faced in

The Beach Hotel in Worthing was another re-faced terrace, the appearance of which convincingly concealed its origins. In the long run, the reconstruction proved sadly lacking in structural integrity.

Lancastrian brick with ornate terracotta dressings, was extreme.[89] Within, the existing public rooms were re-configured with lowered ceilings, new flooring in jazzy patterns, fresh paintwork, furniture and lighting. The *Caterer and Hotel Keeper* recorded the outcome of these changes:

> 'Inside, all the woodwork... is in polished light oak, the door fittings in black with chromiumised steel and the decorative schemes have gold as the basic colour. The sun lounge, overlooking the Irish Sea, has a maximum of Vita glass in its frontage and roof... Adjoining is the lounge foyer, planned on novel lines. Seascapes have been neatly worked in frosted design on the windows and the green rubber flooring is patterned with white to give the impression of billowing waves, on which the occasional fish and sailing yachts are shown. The walls are shaded in attractive style to match the green and gold upholstery of the armchairs and tables... Occupying the south-east corner of the extension, the bar and its companion lounge combine colour and artistry with utility and comfort... The curved bar counter is of solid oak relieved with horizontal chromium bands and is backed by a series of mirrors...'[90]

These bright, up-to-date finishes suggest a fashionable, yet warm and welcoming holiday environment to be enjoyed in all weathers – a remarkable partial transformation from the hotel's previous rather dark and heavily ornate internal atmosphere.

By the mid-1930s, a fairly standard hotel modernisation formula had developed. In order to update an existing property's exterior appearance, sometimes all that was felt necessary was to cover architectural mouldings with smooth stucco, adding an Art Deco pediment, flagpoles and new signage in neon-lit *sans serif* lettering. Internally, ornamental cast iron stair balustrades could be encased in plywood, while new carpets, rattan chairs, potted palms, 'moderne' light fittings and tiled fireplaces would complete the new image. In some instances, as we shall see, what was intended to connote 'modern architecture' in hotels could be very superficial indeed.

In 1938, a terrace of houses forming an annexe of the neo-Tudor-style Paignton Hydro Hotel was 'modernised' by the simple expediency of sheering off the cornices, pilasters and other architectural details, which were superseded by a new flat stucco layer and a 'jazz moderne' pediment with sunburst. The hotel had been built a decade before with the aim of attracting coach parties, for which a garage with space for eight of the largest types of motor coach existing at that time was provided. In addition, there were fuel pumps and special bedrooms for drivers and conductors which, unlike those for their passengers, were equipped with private bathrooms.[91] Such was its success that,

Operators of private hotels in British seaside resorts had to decide whether to update their premises or build a-new to keep up with advancing expectations. Consequently, numerous new hotels were built, such as the Seafield and Fally's hotels in Blackpool, exhibiting a variety of hybrid 'moderne' details. Meanwhile, existing hotels, like the Carlton, also in Blackpool, were extended and modernised. The latter's ground floor addition contrasts markedly with the existing structure.

Two views of the Hydro Hotel in Paignton before and after its annexe, formed of a terrace of houses, was modernised in the 'jazz moderne' idiom.

as the 1930s progressed, adjacent houses were acquired to provide more rooms. The neo-Tudor main building, which remained unaltered, and the 'modernised' annexe formed a most remarkable juxtaposition of highly diverse inter-war design styles.

The Babbacombe Bay Hotel at Babbacombe, near Torquay and the White House Hotel in Bournemouth Bay were both rebuilds of hotels converted from seaside villas of nineteenth century vintage. In each instance, an extra storey with a flat roof was added (the latter even had a rooftop sun terrace) and as much three-dimensional architectural detailing was removed from the façades. The Babbacombe Bay Hotel's sun lounge with metal-framed windows provided a final 'authentic' touch of modernity. A further example of this genre was the Grantham Hotel in Newquay, where a new top storey's smooth stucco was alas not continued in the pebble-dashed frontages of the two villas from which the hotel had been fashioned.

Conversions such as these raise intriguing questions about the ways in which the 'idea' of modern architecture percolated from centre to periphery. It would appear that for local hotel proprietors, architects and building contractors alike, 'modernism' meant applying to buildings certain stylistic characteristics, which had been illustrated in each of these professions' journals. Of course, to the Modern Movement's emerging 'establishment figures', who formed and regulated opinion in the 'mainstream' design debates and who were mainly based in London or in the other major European capitals, such superficial approaches were anathema. For many holidaymakers, however, moderne styling, however inconsequential, signalled that money had recently been invested, hopefully increasing the potential for pleasurable experiences and, in the wake of the Great Depression, suggesting that better days perhaps lay ahead.

'Moderne' at its most ephemeral: the White House Hotel in Bournemouth, the Babbacombe Bay Hotel and the Grantham Hotel in Newquay, all converted from existing villas.

CHAPTER 3
From rail to road and air

During the inter-war era, there began major modal shifts in transport from the railways to road and air travel. Each of these new modes had its own emergent geography and, whereas in the nineteenth century major hotels had been built to serve rail termini, now it became necessary to build suitable overnight accommodation in the suburbs or on largely green field sites close to trunk roads or new airport developments.

Apart from the Midland Hotel at Morecambe, the hotels operated by the 'big four' railway companies of the inter-war era mostly dated from the Victorian era and now faced stiff competition from more modern and better serviced upstarts. In December 1934, the *Caterer and Hotel Keeper* reported that the LMS railway was planning to close its 1868-vintage Midland Grand Hotel at St Pancras, which the Chairman, Sir Josiah Stamp, declared was 'hopeless as an hotel.'[92] One reason was that its fire-proof reinforced concrete floor construction – which in 1873 had been state-of-the-art – now prevented the retro-fitting of the vertical pipework necessary for the installation of either central heating or *en suite* facilities. The LMS's solution was to modernise as best possible its remaining hotels to a standard similar to the recent Morecambe Midland. Arthur Towle, who ran the LMS hotel chain, had a strong desire to have a new hotel built at London Euston Station, but this was put on hold pending the completion of a wider plan to redevelop the entire station complex, expected to come to fruition by the end of the decade. Due to fresh economic instability ahead of the outbreak of the Second World War, in the end, the project never was realised.

An early recipient of attention from the LMS was the prestigious but already old-fashioned Gleneagles Hotel, the bedrooms of which were retro-fitted with *en suite* facilities in 1935 while the cocktail lounge and restaurant were transformed with new 'moderne' style interiors. These were designed by George James Miller, who was the son of James Miller, one of Glasgow's best-known and most prolific architects of the early twentieth century. His interventions mostly involved installing suspended ceilings, formed of expanded metal and sprayed with plaster, to give a fashionably smooth, streamlined effect. Much as with Gustavo Pulitzer Finali's recent work at the Grosvenor House Hotel in London, the existing now unwanted neo-Classical decorative enrichments were thereby hidden from view. The 'new' restaurant was named the

Gleneagles Hotel was first proposed in the Edwardian era, but remained unrealised until the mid-1920s. Within a decade, its design was considered out-of-date and so, among other works, the dining room was modernised with a suspended ceiling to conceal its original neo-classicism. The room's semi-circular shape and large windows adapted fairly well to the new style.

The dining room of the Royal Hotel at Paddington Station following mid-1930s modernisation; the appearance of height has been lessened by three concealed lighting coves.

'Restaurant du Soleil' and was considered among Scotland's best. Subsequently, at the request of the British Government, its design was precisely replicated for a restaurant at the Empire Exhibition in Johannesburg in 1936.[93]

At London Paddington Station, meanwhile, the Great Western Railway's Royal Hotel was causing railway management similar concerns to the hotels at the LMS's London termini. The *Caterer and Hotel Keeper* reported that the edifice had been 'built over eighty years ago and [had been] left behind both in interior appearance and equipment by modern public taste.'[94] The solution was modernise the hotel in three stages, this work being carried out to designs by the GWR's in-house architect, Percy E. Culverhouse. The first was 'an extension of accommodation by the construction of a new wing giving 52 more bedrooms, each with a bathroom, and new public rooms, including a big lounge, smoke room and cocktail bar.'[95] In the second and third stages, all existing bedrooms were renovated with bathrooms, the dining room was redecorated using a similar approach to that used by the LMS at Gleneagles, a new grill room was added and the kitchen modernised. After all that, the exterior would be cleaned and painted. Visiting between stages two and three, the *Caterer and Hotel Keeper*'s correspondent observed:

> 'The hotel presents most interesting contrasts between the old and new. First there is the new section of the building, modern in every particular; second comes the modernised section in which high, spacious rooms have been cleverly conformed to present-day practice and the third section awaiting treatment with its Victorian solidity of decoration and furnishing, somewhat depressing atmosphere and indifferent illumination. Revelation of the changes achieved is impressive when, standing in an upstairs corridor one looks up, on the one hand, to a brightly-decorated, well-lit passage and, on the other, to a dim, gloomy corridor as a fitting entrance to its old-fashioned bedrooms.[96]

The GWR also invested in modernising its hotels at St Ives (the Tregenna) and Morehampstead (the Manor House) and had plans for a large new hotel in Looe but, due to economic uncertainty, it decided not to proceed with the scheme.[97]

The only new city centre railway hotel constructed during the inter-war era was the LMS' Queen's Hotel in Leeds which opened in 1937 to a scheme worked out jointly by William Curtis Green, the main designer of the Dorchester in London, and the railway company's in-house architects' office, under William Hamlyn. Within a stone-faced shell in the stripped-back neo-classical idiom then commonly used for major public buildings, it boasted a 'moderne' reception foyer, cocktail bar and restaurant.

A much smaller example of a hotel built in the 1930s to accommodate mainly rail travellers was the privately-owned Hotel Windsor in Exeter, located opposite St Davids Station. Completed in 1939, this three-storey structure replaced the St Davids Family and Commercial Temperance Hotel which had been converted from a terrace of houses. Its operator, a local hotelier by name of Albert Appleby, must have realised that the existing premises were no longer of an appropriate standard to impress guests arriving by the latest Great Western express trains. As a new station hotel run independently of the railway, the Hotel Windsor was a unique example of its kind. Even then, the future appeared to lie with road and air transport, rather than with rail.

During the 1930s, a new generation of so-called 'roadhouses' was built to serving a growing clientele of motorists, who were mostly of the upper middle class and with consequently high expectations with regard to comfort. Roadhouses were, in many respects, a revival of the English inn-keeping tradition of providing food, drink and overnight accommodation to passing travellers. Yet, as the car-owning clientele was insufficiently large to be enough of a business proposition, they also aimed to attract local visitors to enjoy a 'glamorous' evening out, sometimes by offering dinner-dances and live entertainment. Indeed, some roadhouses were in essence large pub-restaurants and had no hotel rooms whatsoever.

Roadhouses varied widely in their looks. Some examples were in neo-Tudor and Arts & Crafts styles, aiming to create a romantic feeling of tradition, while others were neo-Georgian, usually faced in brick with parapets. It was often only a short step away from the latter to varying degrees of 'streamline moderne', which tended to use the same palette of materials, albeit with a more flamboyant emphasis on horizontals and curving corner details. Usually, the choice of style depended on a roadhouse's location and on the taste of its proprietor. In many instances, their sites were suburban, often at road junctions or visible from busy arterial roads, meaning that visitors by car to towns and cities could stay overnight and complete their journeys to the centre the next morning.

Top: The Hotel Windsor, located close to Exeter St David's railway station, was a rare example of a new hotel of the 1930s built primarily to accommodate those arriving by train.

Above: The roundabout at Scotch Corner near Richmond in Yorkshire was a new type of transport environment for the UK. There, a 'roadhouse' hotel in the neo-Georgian manner was completed in 1939 to accommodate motorists in transit. Roadhouses in a variety of historicist and modern design styles were built in the 1930s. Indeed, the difference between this example and numerous others in the 'streamline moderne' idiom was mostly a matter of detailing.

Below: The Comet Hotel at Hatfield looked rather like an airport terminal of the same era and was fitted with a lantern and flagpole, resembling a control tower with a radio transmitter.

The Abbey Hotel at West Twyford was a fine example of a roadhouse containing bars, a restaurant, function rooms and overnight accommodation.

Some of the most impressive roadhouses with hotel accommodation were located on the fringes of London and in the Home Counties. A good example was the Comet Hotel in Hatfield, completed in 1937 to a design by Ernest Brander Musman for Benskins Brewery. Musman's firm specialised in planning roadhouses and pubs in a variety of traditional and modern styles and the Comet, with its wide, drum-shaped projecting frontage was perhaps his most determined effort at streamline moderne. As the roadhouse was located practically opposite the gates of the de Havilland aircraft factory, it seems likely that there would have been a desire to reflect aviation styling in its design. (Subsequently, de Havilland applied the 'Comet' name to its pioneering civil jet airliner, first tested in 1949.)

The Abbey Hotel on London's North Circular Road at West Twyford near Ealing was completed the following year. Owned by the Barclay, Perkins brewery, it was designed by Major Henry Oliver, a London-based architect who, like Musman, dealt mainly with pub design and renovation projects. Oliver's original estimate of £17,000 was described as 'ludicrous' by his client but, in the end, the final cost for the building was nearly four times that sum (including the unexpected demand for a footbridge to be constructed over the road). The architect took ill with stress and the project was completed six months later than anticipated in the early summer of 1938.[98] A symmetrical building with prominent vertical elements, its ground floor contained bars, a lounge and restaurant with function rooms above and bedrooms on second floor.[99]

Another was the Park Royal Hotel in West London; in both instances, the similarity to contemporary cinema architecture is striking.

Perhaps the finest of all was the Park Royal Hotel on London's Western Approaches

by Welch, Cachemaille-Day and Lander, all of whom had previously been involved in designing buildings for the garden suburbs and garden cities around London. H. A. Welsh had worked in Hampstead and Felix Lander in Letchworth and then Welwyn, where he had first encountered his subsequent colleague, N. F. C. Cachemaille-Day, who was an employee of Louis de Soissons before becoming a specialist designer of churches, in partnership and latterly independently.

Welch, Cachemaille-Day and Lander's design for the Park Royal Hotel was asymmetrical, faced in brick and with a distinctly horizontal emphasis. Their approach was in line with that typically favoured by de Soissons, which was itself derived from that of recent buildings in the Netherlands by Willem Dudok. At one end was a short tower feature, from which a cinema-like fin-shaped name sign protruded. Within, the building contained a saloon bar, public bar and cocktail bar on the ground floor and a double-height restaurant at first floor level with bedrooms adjacent on both levels.

While the vast majority of roadhouses were intended to serve private car owners, in Blackpool, the

Manchester Hotel, which opened in 1936, was conveniently located adjacent to the bus station to offer immediate refreshment and possibly lodgings to visitors by bus and touring coach. These forms of transport grew greatly in popularity alongside the car in the 1930s, opening up the road network to the lower-middle and working classes. As with the Abbey and Park Royal hotels in London, the Manchester Hotel's exterior used the attention-grabbing design tactics of cinema architecture, having repeat vertical fins protruding beyond its roofline. The design was by a Blackpool architect, J. C. Derham, who, earlier in his career, had

The Manchester Hotel in Blackpool, sited beside the bus station, was a pub and restaurant complex with bedrooms on the upper floors. The external design was very similar to that of Victoria Coach Station in London, a much larger edifice completed four years previously.

been employed by the London-based theatre designer, Bertie Crewe. Subsequently, in the latter 1920s, Derham was appointed as in-house architect of Blackpool Tower and Winter Gardens, where he oversaw the design of various new attractions. From the mid-1930s onward, he entered private practice, specialising in designing and renovating hotels in the Blackpool area.[100] Evidently, he brought to these projects a sense of theatricality from his earlier career. In seeking to please visitors, who were seeking entertainment and escapism, this approach was highly appropriate. Sadly, Derham died only shortly after the Manchester Hotel project was finished.

New hotels for international travellers

In addition to the need to accommodate growing numbers of motorists, whose journeys were mostly within Britain, there was also an increasing requirement to provide

The Polygon and Royal hotels in Southampton were built to accommodate liner passengers, their design echoing the standard of accommodation found in tourist class on vessels such as Cunard's Queen Mary of 1936. The Polygon, designed by a London architect, James E. Adamson, had an aesthetic affinity with recent public and private housing in the capital, while the Royal's exterior was cleaner-lined and used faience dressings to highlight its 'moderne' curved corners and balconies. The Polygon's foyer (below) featured potted palms and a bright carpet – but none of the polished woodwork found on liners, or in the public spaces of more upmarket hotels.

overnight hospitality to those travelling overseas by passenger liner or civil aviation.

The completion in 1936 of the giant Cunard-White Star trans-Atlantic flagship *Queen Mary*, the construction of which had been suspended for several years due to the Great Depression, gave a significant boost to national confidence. The Clyde-built liner's magnificent Art Deco interiors captured the public's imagination and, as with other new passenger ships of the same generation, these were aimed more at the tourist market than earlier Cunard vessels, which had instead carried large numbers of migrants. Consequently, additional 'tourist class' hotel accommodation was also henceforth needed ashore in the liner's home port of Southampton to accommodate passengers prior to embarkation. In anticipation of this demand, the Royal Hotel was completed in 1935 to a design by A. Haynes-Johnson of Winchester. Externally, its flat brick frontages were enlivened with full-length balconies, clad in faience and with curved corners while, within, it provided an appropriately up-to-date milieu commensurate with typical shipboard tourist cabins in recent liners; of course, most of the bedrooms shared communal bathroom facilities. Subsequently, in late 1937, a further new tourist-orientated hotel was completed. Named the Polygon, it was designed by a London-based architect, James E. Adamson. The five-storey structure occupied a corner site and, externally, was brick-faced with horizontal banding and an Art Deco pediment above its corner entrance. The canopy and signage appear to have been of the same design as used for new cinema buildings of the era and the foyer – with its bright paint, jazzy carpets, potted palms and comfortable settees – also owned more to cinema front-of-house spaces than it did to the *Queen Mary*, which instead contained lavish expanses of polished exotic hardwoods.

Airport Hotels

While liners impressed on account of their great size and complexity, air travel was regarded as being the inter-war era's great transport miracle, offering those who could afford it a sense of freedom, levity and a frisson of daring; little wonder airmen were the heroes of H.G. Wells' popular 1933 novel 'The Shape of Things to Come.' Everything about flying lent itself to futuristic aesthetic interpretation and this included the architecture of airport buildings and the new hotels built to serve them.

The High Post Aerodrome Hotel, near Salisbury, was in essence a roadhouse built to attract fliers and spectators. Dining and dancing were attractions for day visitors.

An early example was the High Post Aerodrome Hotel, constructed adjacent to a private aerodrome opposite Salisbury Golf Course and easily accessible from Salisbury, Andover, Southampton and Bournemouth.[101] Designed for the Wiltshire School of Flying by the Salisbury architects, Botham and Brown, the two-storey structure was effectively a 'roadhouse' with the added attraction for guests of being able to spectate as planes took off and landed. Indeed, the runway could be viewed from a lantern projecting from the hotel's flat roof and somewhat resembling the control tower of an airport building. Within, the hotel contained a dozen bedrooms, the Silver Grill restaurant and a ballroom, these latter facilities being intended largely to cater to local visitors arriving by car and merely wishing to view aircraft in action, rather than to fly themselves.

The Birmingham Airport Hotel, built adjacent to the entrance to Birmingham Airport at Elmdon, featured an outdoor viewing gallery, a restaurant, lounge, cocktail bar and ballroom amongst its attractions. Constructed in the late-1930s, it only opened for business post-war, having been occupied in the interim by the RAF.

The hotel's relatively small number of rooms for overnight guests, several of whom would probably have arrived by plane, indicates the newness of this travel mode and the consequently speculative nature of the project.

Unfortunately, the hotel proved much more expensive to build than the Wiltshire School of Flying had anticipated and this led to a legal case being brought against the architects. Whereas they had estimated that the entire project could be delivered for £3,500, its actual cost was £2,000 greater. Although the judge conceded that the hotel was of an 'unusual character', he nonetheless took a stern view of the fact that the quantity surveyor's advice had been ignored and therefore ruled that the architects should forfeit their fees.[102] During the Second World War, the High Post Hotel was requisitioned as housing for additional workers at the nearby Wessex Aircraft Engineering Company's factory.

In 1933, Birmingham Corporation prepared initial plans for a new airport at Elmdon, eight miles to the south-east of the city. Due to the difficulty in raising enough capital in the depression years, the project was not completed, however, until July 1939, when flights began to Glasgow, Liverpool, Manchester, Southampton and elsewhere.[103] To accommodate airport users, the local brewers and inn-keepers, Mitchells & Butlers, who owned large numbers of pubs around Birmingham, in Warwickshire and beyond, built a large, new roadhouse on Coventry Road, within walking distance of the terminal building. This was designed by the Birmingham architect Archibald Hurley Robinson, who was otherwise best known as a designer of cinemas as well as of other commercial work. A handsome brick edifice, it was L-shaped in plan and with a lantern on the roof above its curving entrance block. Unlike the High Post Hotel's lantern, this feature, containing a light, was inaccessible to the public. Similar examples could be found on Robinson's cinema buildings, though the point of origination was the campanile on the City Hall in Stockholm, completed in 1923, various aspects of which were subsequently emulated in public buildings of diverse types throughout Britain. One of

Fantasy drawings from 1938, showing how a future Grosvenor House Hotel on Park Lane might look, featuring a multi-storey 'aircraft park' above which airships could be tethered.

the hotel's two wings contained 25 bedrooms with a restaurant below while the other had a cocktail bar, ballroom and viewing terrace, from which the airport's activity could be observed. As at the High Post, the inclusion of dancing and plane-watching as additional activities indicates the commercial potential arising from the public's curiosity about flying.

Shortly before the hotel was due to be opened, however, the Second World War broke out and so the entire airport and its immediate surroundings were taken over by the Royal Air Force Flying Training Command. For the war's duration, the hotel proved very useful, serving as its operational headquarters. It was only handed back to Mitchells & Butlers for civilian use some time after the cessation of hostilities.

In the latter 1930s, a growing belief that, in the years ahead, air travel would develop rapidly and that, as with the increase in car ownership, the upwardly-mobile would soon have their own private planes. This expectation led to remarkable fantasy hotels of the future being imagined. In the *Caterer and Hotel Keeper*'s Diamond Jubilee edition in July 1938, A.H. Jones, General Manager of the decade-old Grosvenor House Hotel in London, was invited to imagine how an eventual successor to the existing property might be designed to serve the needs of guests in the year 2000:

> 'The controlling factor will be the demand for sunlight and natural air... The great tapering turrets have been designed to admit and maximum of sun and air. From the inside, the rooms suggest light and spaciousness. There will be no sense of being overlooked. No one will feel "cribbed, cabined and confined." There will be air of lightness and freedom everywhere... With noiseless and odourless cars, guests will drive down an incline right into the reception office, where the staff will take over the cars and run them away by means of silent escalators to the underground garage. On the roofs of the turrets, there will be restaurants, with sliding roofs, the landing stage for private gyro-planes and gyro-taxis, the tennis courts and swimming pool... A series of aerodromes for long-distance and local traffic [would be built] at Hyde Park Corner...' [104]

Needless to say, as aviation developed, the existing Grosvenor House building proved more than adequate to serve air travellers and such further modernisation as eventually took place was far less radical than Jones predicted.

CHAPTER 4

The influence of the 1938 Empire Exhibition on hotels in Scotland

Since the early nineteenth century and the era of Sir Walter Scott, Scotland had become increasingly popular as a destination for tourists. In the Victorian and Edwardian eras, this led to the construction of large numbers of hotels, often in Scots baronial and other romantic styles to fulfil visitors' Highland dreams. Subsequently, in the inter-war years, tastes changed rapidly, and by the late 1930s, Scotland had accumulated a remarkably high number of flat roofed buildings with balconies, including several new hotels. These features were specified notwithstanding an often harsh, cold and wet climate for which 'moderne' – being essentially derived from 'tropical' architectural approaches – was quite unsuitable.

In *The Scottish Thirties: An Architectural Introduction*, Charles McKean partly attributes Scottish architects and their clients' fascination with the Modern Movement to a belief during the economically stagnant Depression years that modern architecture and interior design represented a promise of better days ahead.

Notable early examples of Scottish hotels in the 'moderne' manner included a substantial four-storey extension to the Marine Hotel in Oban, completed in 1936 to a design by the Glasgow architect James Taylor, who had previously designed the George Hotel in Walsall, and whom McKean states was 'unscrupulous' as he 'refused to register [with the RIAS], and… went to prison for tax evasion after the war.'[105]

The Northern Hotel in the Kittybrewster district of Aberdeen, designed by A.G.R. MacKenzie, then recently returned from London to take over the Aberdeen office of his father's practice, and opened in 1937 also had four floors. Wedge-shaped in plan with a curved corner facing towards the city, its frontage was finished in horizontal strips of light and dark grey granite, giving a somewhat austere effect. This was perhaps more reminiscent of some of Erich Mendelsohn's commercial frontages in Berlin or certain government buildings in Fascist Italy than typical British treatments of the era, which tended to be much lighter in appearance. Within, not only were there a restaurant and a cocktail bar with a circular counter but also a ballroom.

Above: Two views of a large extension added in 1936 to the Marine Hotel in Oban, containing additional bedrooms, a sun lounge, restaurant and roof terrace, overlooking Oban Bay. In plan, the structure was very shallow with corridors to the rear.
Below: The granite-clad Northern Hotel in Aberdeen – a particularly severe example of the 1930s 'streamline' idiom.

Much less salubrious was the Bellgrove Hotel in Glasgow's heavily industrialised East End. Opened in 1935 to a design by the Glasgow cinema architects Charles J. McNair and Elder, it was a working men's hostel with small rooms and communal showers and toilets. This notwithstanding it shared aesthetic

similarities to the more genteel tourism-orientated hotels of its era, as well as to those of many light industrial buildings.

The belief that modern architecture could help stimulate economic recovery was reflected in the discourses that gave rise to the 1938 Empire Exhibition in Glasgow.[106] The event was conceived on an ambitiously grand scale to boost West Central Scotland's flagging industrial base. Glasgow and its environs were largely dependent on heavy industry exporting to overseas markets and, when exports ceased, there was a devastating industrial collapse from 1929 onward. The Government was concerned that, while the South gradually recovered, Scottish manufacturing remained sluggish with 60,000 still out of work by the mid-1930s.

The Empire Exhibition site was at Bellahouston Park in south-west Glasgow, where the architect Thomas Tait was commissioned to coordinate the design. The pavilions were built of lightweight steel frames clad in asbestos cement panelling and painted in pastel hues with floodlighting. The overall effect was a *tour de force* of streamline moderne. Between, wide boulevards with illuminated fountains added to the sense of spaciousness, colour and levity.[107] All of this was in marked contrast with the ornate but crowded Victorian host city. As it was expected that very large numbers of visitors would come to marvel at the exhibits, there was also an opportunity for hoteliers to develop new accommodation in complementary aesthetics.

Glasgow's key new hotel venue for Empire Exhibition visitors was the 198-bedroom Beresford which was opened in April 1938 on a site facing Sauchiehall Street – one of the city's major shopping and entertainment thoroughfares.[108] The hotel was both designed and owned by William Beresford Inglis, an architect-entrepreneur whose practice of Weddell & Inglis was best known in Glasgow for producing restaurants, bars and cinemas, some of the latter of which Inglis also operated. Spotting what he believed was a lucrative opportunity to accommodate Exhibition guests, Inglis sold his cinema interests and founded a hotel company to develop the Beresford. At £200,000, this proved a costly venture, involving considerable excavation of the steeply sloping site to give an unbroken flat expanse aligned with the street. The land above was held in place by the construction of a retaining wall at a cost of £10,000 and only then could the building of the hotel itself commence.

When inaugurated, the *Caterer and Hotel Keeper* described it as 'Glasgow's first skyscraper hotel' – though this was a considerable exaggeration as the building had only eight storeys and was no taller than many another in the city at that time. Nonetheless, it occupied:

> 'A commanding position… and its striking yellow, green and scarlet front has been attracting attention for months. Mr W. Beresford Inglis, the managing director told a *Caterer and Hotel Keeper* representative, "Having specialised in cinema design, I decided to introduce the lines and colour of the cinema in the Beresford. The result is certainly surprising, but has gained universal approval."'[109]

The hotel's exterior was entirely clad in faience tiles – a typical facing of 1930s cinema buildings that was easily kept clean, in sharp contrast with the grimy, smoke-blackened sandstone of typical Glasgow buildings. What would otherwise have been a pure cuboid, fitting the city's grid-plan, was enlivened by two drum-shaped projections rising from the first floor to above roof height. These broke the frontage into three sections. In between, a series of fin-shaped verticals was outlined at night in neon.

The *Caterer and Hotel Keeper* also gave a detailed description of the hotel's interior

Opposite: Glasgow's Beresford Hotel of 1938, showing (1) the exterior, (2) and (3) parts of the building's hallway, (4) the sitting room, (5) the dining room and (6) the cocktail bar, which was added later. The dining room's walls are adorned with murals showing Glencoe, Ben Lomond and other Scottish beauty spots.

design, from which it may be concluded that its cinema-like characteristics extended to its public rooms. The spacious entrance foyer had a terrazzo floor, patterned with waves and the main feature was an illuminated archway, through which the stairwell as accessed:

> 'Straight through from the entrance is the restaurant which seats 250. The architectural treatment here is bold and massive. The dado is in straight-grained mahogany, and the walls are treated with honey-coloured Opaltex [a multi-coloured spray paint finish popular for cinema auditorium walls]. Woven into the texture is a faint suggestion of well-known Scottish landmarks, such as Edinburgh Castle and Ben Lomond... Almost the entire front of the hotel is given over to a writing room and lounge for residents only. The furniture is bleached oak and the walls are fawn coloured with motifs indicating the purpose of the room. The first floor is entirely devoted to public rooms. The hotel lounge, although very large, has been so broken up architecturally that it has a distinctly intimate atmosphere. The woodwork is of walnut and the furnishings are crushed strawberry with blue spots. The walls are in soft shades of orange, and the columns are copper spattered with red. Parts of the ceiling are done in apple green.'[110]

Contrasting with all this colour and comfort was 'the smoke room, for men only' which was 'severely plain in dark, reddish oak panelling with hide-covered chairs. The walls are in tones of sepia with motifs of a sporting character...'[111] Its inclusion perhaps suggested a perceived need to cater to the Scottish male psyche by providing a strongly masculine haven in which to bond over cigarettes and whisky.

The bedrooms filled the hotel's upper six floors. The *Caterer and Hotel Keeper* reported that:

> 'In each of these, the carpet is blue with a wavy black line... the walls are papered horizontally with a rough speckled shade of orange. The ceiling is a sunshine yellow... Curtains are a rich cream with a design in blue, black and orange. The bedspread matches the curtains and the quilt is of powdered blue... There is a wash-hand basin and a telephone in every room. The bathrooms, of which there is one to every four bedrooms, are placed at each of the four inside corners of the [stair]well so that no one has to walk more than a few steps from their bedroom...'[112]

The hotel reportedly had 'many novel features' including an all-night restaurant with kitchens located along its full length to enable fast service to hungry guests arriving back late from the Exhibition and a 'telewriter' to duplicate food orders in the kitchen and for the cashier, loudspeakers in all the public rooms for announcements and music, a telephone exchange with 275 lines and two fast passenger lifts.[113] Yet, bathrooms were only provided for every four bedrooms which by 1938 was a poor show and would ultimately become the hotel's Achilles heel. Another strange omission was of a cocktail bar as by 1938 these had become very popular, not least elsewhere in Glasgow – but perhaps Inglis' novice status as a hotelier was to blame. This lack was, however, rectified in October, by which time the hotel had successfully accommodated around 50,000 guests. Also designed by Inglis and located near the entrance in what had previously been part of the (presumably under-utilised) sitting lounge, it was 'very colourful' and featured 'a tangerine carpet with black and faun lines [and] a dado of gambodge with a green horizontal motif.' The upper parts of its walls were 'sprayed in yellow, black, red and gold.'[114] The retrospective insertion of this bar, of course, meant that Inglis could legitimately transfer additional fees to his own architectural practice.

The Newhouse Hotel, opened in May 1938, was a two-storey roadhouse located in industrial Lanarkshire on the main Edinburgh-Glasgow road and completed in time to accommodate those visiting the Exhibition by car. It had a flat roof on which there was a terrace, from which the passing traffic could be watched while refreshments were supplied by means of an electric service hoist. Unlike at the Beresford Hotel, each of the ten bedrooms had its own private bathroom, lined in slabs of shiny Vitrolite glass; this suggests that car owners were a pickier clientele, prepared to pay a premium for these additional comforts.[115] Adjacent was a smaller, separate building for the use of lorry drivers which contained four bedrooms, each with four bunks, and a kitchen where they could cook. The hotel's proprietor was Angus McNab Chassels, who was the son of a Lanarkshire hotelier and also a highly regarded breeder of spaniels. Consequently, he ensured that spacious kennels were provided so that dog lovers would be attracted to stay. The hotel's lounge featured a bandstand and dance floor and the *Caterer and Hotel Keeper* reported that the dining room was 'large and well-lit with windows on two sides… The chef, Mr John Girdwood, was previously at the Imperial Hotel, Edinburgh and at the Waldorf-Astoria, New York… The kitchen can cater for 300 people.'[116] The appointment of a more experienced and well-travelled chef than might have been expected at a small hotel on the fringes of an industrial conurbation suggests that it was intended to serve motorists coming from a wide catchment area to enjoy a stylish evening with dining and dancing before driving home in hopefully not too inebriated a state.

On the Clyde Coast at Gourock, where there was a busy steamer pier and railway station from which regular trains ran to Glasgow – many stopping *en route* at Cardonald, close to the Empire Exhibition's site – a third hotel was developed. Opened in May 1938, the Bay Hotel was a four-storey edifice with a curved frontage, featuring in the centre a glazed stair tower. It was designed by James Austin Laird of Laird and Napier – a Glasgow practice which had also designed cinemas as well as housing. As with the Newhouse Hotel, it had a roof terrace; both this and the rear-facing bedrooms enjoyed spectacular panoramic views across the Firth of Clyde. Apart from the reception areas, the hotel's ground floor was given over to shop units, its public rooms being located on the level above and distinguished externally from the two bedroom storeys by a band of brickwork. As Gourock was a transfer point for large numbers of Scottish holiday-makers bound for the islands of Cowal and Bute, it was hoped that, after the Exhibition's closure, the hotel (and the unconnected development of an outdoor swimming pool on a site adjacent) would encourage more visitors to stay in the town, using the steamer routes for day trips to other places.

The Newhouse Hotel, a roadhouse on the A8 Edinburgh-Glasgow road, and the Bay Hotel at Gourock on the Clyde Coast were both developed in anticipation of a need to accommodate Empire Exhibition visitors.

Subsequently, Laird also designed the incongruously large, but remotely-located five-storey Keil Hotel at the south end of the rugged but picturesque Argyll Peninsula, which was only accessible by car and coach. Its proprietor was a former sea captain, James Taylor, who apparently thought that there would be a market for such a coastal retreat. Almost immediately after opening in 1939, however, it was requisitioned by the Admiralty for wartime use as a hospital. Having completed the project, Laird retired and his practice was dissolved.[117]

In the Scottish Highlands, new hotels aiming to appeal to motorists were developed on sites well away from the railway stations, which for the past century had been considered vital sources of guests. The Drumossie Hotel near Inverness was intended as a large and upmarket 'roadhouse', accommodating motorists using the A9 trunk road. Its owner, Loch Ness Hotels, purchased land for the hotel towards the end of 1937 – but it took three years to complete the project, delays being attributable to a lack of capital and then to the outbreak of the Second World War. The architects, Ballantyne & Cox, were Inverness-based, where they had previously designed a number of 'moderne' villas. The senior partner, Roy Carruthers Ballantyne, was reputedly highly equivocal about the virtues of modern architecture in the Highlands' harsh climate, though nonetheless he seemed to appreciate its visual potential. The hotel was curved in plan with a centrally-located entrance above which was a short tower, a layout somewhat akin to the Midland in Morecambe. In elevation, its three storeys spanned a downward slope and – partly to engender a romantic image rather than an institutional one and also to withstand heavy loadings of snow – the bedroom wings flanking the tower had pitched roofs with lanterns in Arts & Crafts style, rather than flat ones. (Ballantyne & Cox used similar treatments for their housing designs for the same reasons). Upon completion, rather than welcoming the first paying guests, the hotel was immediately taken over by the British Government's Air Ministry (which had responsibility for the Royal Air Force) to accommodate officials and senior military personnel involved in the war effort.[118]

The Grampian Hotel in Dalwhinnie, another A9 roadhouse, some way to the south, was likewise completed in 1940 but, unlike at Drumossie, there was no military requisition, meaning that tourists could be welcomed as planned. The hotel's designer was Colonel Alexander Cattanach, whose practice was based in a nearby village, Kingussie, and whose main specialism was designing cinema buildings all over the Scottish highlands. Occasionally, Cattanach had collaborated in some larger cinema projects with an Edinburgh-based architect, T. Bowhill-Gibson, who additionally had designed a number of 'roadhouse' pubs in the city's outer suburbs. It seems plausible therefore that Cattanach may have consulted him about the Kingussie project, which was a two-storey structure with a stair tower at one end. The lounge and dining room were to the rear, facing the Cairngorm mountain range. While much of the design displayed a clunky angularity more typical of mid-1930s commercial buildings than those completed at the end of the decade, the fire exit stair, serving the bedrooms on the first floor, was a boldly curved concrete structure, more reminiscent of Lubetkin or Corbusier.[119]

The outbreak of the Second World War brought a halt to any further hotel development. There followed a sixteen-year hiatus during which all building works were licensed to control the use of materials that were in short supply, primarily steel and timber, as well as to limit inflation. By the time construction began again, the Art Deco age was just a memory.

The Drumossie Hotel, near Inverness, and the Grampian Hotel at Dalwhinnie were built towards the northern end of the A9 trunk road; the design of the former mixes 'moderne' and Arts & Crafts elements, while the latter is rectilinear and with a flat roof unlikely to cope well with heavy loadings of snow. While Drumossie still exists in good condition, the Grampian has long-since been demolished.

The Westbury in London, Britain's first post-war hotel, was completed in 1955. Images (1) and (2) show the building's symmetrical massing with a recessed centre block. This reflected a well-established design approach, the main difference from pre-war examples being the complete elimination of any form of ornamentation. Nonetheless, the quality of construction and of finish was high, reflecting the availability of skilled labour at a time when few such projects were as yet underway. The interiors were, by contrast, in neo-Regency style, as (3), showing an annexe to the restaurant for private dinner parties, decorated by White Allom Ltd, demonstrates. Following American practice, some of the bedrooms had beds which could be flipped over, Pullman-style, converting them into sofas for daytime use, as shown in (4).

CHAPTER 5

The first hotels of the post–war era

In the post-war era, such building materials as could be found were aimed at what were considered crucial building categories – namely, housing, schools and industry – while those for leisure purposes, including hotels, were at the bottom of the order of preference. Austerity thinking affected nearly all aspects of British culture – a 'make do and mend' philosophy being widely applied, including in the worlds of architecture, interior design and hospitality provision. Restrictions were actually tightened in 1947-48 following the withdrawal of American land-lease arrangements and only began to ease in 1950 with rationing finally coming to an end in November 1954.[120] In that year, approximately 900,000 foreign tourists visited the UK – and the figure was expected to rise in the years ahead.[121]

The foreseeable ending of rationing enabled the first post-war hotels in Britain to be planned with completion scheduled for the spring of 1955 in anticipation of what was expected to be a bumper tourism season. The major problem was raising finance to construct such complex and therefore capital-intensive edifices. One obvious solution was to make use of American finance as the USA was unprecedentedly prosperous at a time when Britain was heavily indebted and focused mainly on attending to basic needs, rather than 'luxury' building.

Britain's first post-war hotel was the eight-storey, 240-room Westbury, constructed largely with American money on a bomb site at the junction of New Bond Street and Conduit Street in London's West End. The Westbury was intended as an upmarket hotel to accommodate visitors from the USA in which they would enjoy the up-to-date technologies to which they were accustomed back home. Its promoter was the New York-headquartered Knott Hotel Corporation which entered a joint agreement with Pearl Assurance to raise the half-million pound development cost. Knott was owned by an American businessman and former champion polo player, Michael Phipps, whose family wealth had been created two generations previously. His grandfather, Henry Phipps, had been a British émigré to the United States, where he was a life-long friend and business partner of Andrew Carnegie and, like him, became extremely rich. At the end of the nineteenth century, his eldest son, John, built a mansion, Westbury House, in a secluded and rural part of New York State favoured by plutocrats and it was from this that the hotel chain took its name. The first Westbury Hotel was developed in New York and opened in 1927.

The London Westbury was designed by the Viennese émigré architect Michael Rosenauer, who was best known in Austria for having designed a 'modern baroque' villa in the gardens of Vienna's Belvedere Palace for his friend, the composer Richard Strauss. Otherwise, Rosenauer specialised in designing mass housing in a quietly modernist idiom that was respectful of context. His designs won such international acclaim that the British Ministry of Health invited him to London in 1928 as one of its housing advisors. There, he settled, becoming a British subject. Cultivated and cosmopolitan, in addition to practicing as an architect, he was an accomplished pianist and a sculptor and, in London, he made several influential friendships in artistic and aristocratic circles. In 1940, Rosenauer moved to America, where he advised in Washington D.C. on the re-housing of war refugees and, there, he made further useful business and social contacts. Post-war, he taught interior design at the University of Pennsylvania, returning to London in 1951 to design the Time-Life Building in New Bond Street, which was built in 1952-53 also with American money on a site almost directly opposite the one to be occupied by the Westbury Hotel.

In terms of structure and external design, the two buildings were very similar, both using reinforced concrete framing and having comparable façade treatments. The Westbury's overall massing with seven-storey wings and a taller, recessed central block reflected 1930s practice, albeit with none of the applied horizontal detailing so typical of that period. The consequently neutral façades with evenly spaced window apertures were clad in Portland stone; their understatement was indicative of a context of ongoing materials rationing, yet also reflected Rosenauer's desire to produce edifices that would transcend temporary architectural fashions, a position very much in line with modernist thinking. A bas relief by Henry Moore was the hotel's only external adornment and its inclusion was typical of Rosenauer's great interest in promoting modern art.

Reflecting the hotel's relatively exclusive status and the greater costs of operation in London's West End, as well as the availability of many dining opportunities nearby, the hotel's internal volume was almost entirely given over to bedrooms, there being only a small lounge with cocktail bar, a tea room and a 150-seat restaurant, all for the exclusive use of guests. This model was commonplace in American city centre hotels as maximising the number of bedrooms was felt to be the most cost-effective solution. The ground floor mostly consisted of leasable shop units.

In complete contrast with the Westbury Hotel's neutral external appearance, its interiors were entirely decorated in whimsical neo-regency style, the designs and furnishings being supplied by well-established, mostly London-based interior decorating firms. Hampton & Sons devised the cocktail lounge and bar plus some bedrooms while White Allom Ltd was responsible for the tea room, restaurant, ladies' powder room and sitting rooms in seventh floor suites. Other decorators involved in designing bedrooms were Waring & Gillow, Gregory & Co, Maple & Co and H.H. Martyn & Co of Cheltenham.[122] Neo-Regency was a significant strand in British post-war design, particularly when intended for consumption by American audiences, as was the case with the Westbury. Whereas the Council for Industrial Design and almost all prominent design critics and commentators promoted modernism as 'good design', since the war, a shortage of dollars and the imbalance of the Bretton Woods Agreement brought about an 'export drive' with the USA. There, the idea of Britain and of 'British design' apparently centred on history and royalty – two phenomena that the mainstream of the Modern Movement had great difficulty in accommodating.

At the Dorchester, a lusher example of this approach was provided by the up-and-coming theatre set designer, Oliver Messel, who was invited to redecorate suites on the hotel's topmost two storeys. In one of these, he had the entire space panelled with mirrors, upon which gilded ornate fretwork in the rococo manner was applied. The combination of shiny surfaces, naturalistic patterns and endless reflections created a lush and magical backdrop for romance and social occasion. It was gorgeously camp and the ideal setting for ladies to pose in long silk dresses, inspired by Dior's 'New Look' and by the style set by H.M. The Queen and her sister, H.R.H. Princess Margaret. Its extreme glamour was, however, a very long way from either international modernism or the more cosy and informal Scandinavian-inflected aesthetic popularised by the Festival of Britain.

Within two months of the Westbury's early March inauguration, a second, very

The Hotel Leofric in Coventry, opened in 1955, was, in terms of design and decoration, a remarkable essay in the 'Festival of Britain' manner. Here we see (1) the exterior, (2) the grillroom, (3) the snack bar and (4) the ballroom. The chairs in the grillroom are Swedish imports and also notable are the many diversely patterned wall, floor and ceiling finishes, creating a distinctly informal, yet also rather fiddly impression.

different hotel opened for business in Coventry. For the heavily-bombed industrial city, resuscitation presented a unique opportunity to create a spacious, well-integrated and humane public environment that could act as a model for other municipalities to emulate. The inclusion of a hotel was apparently considered a desirable element in achieving that aim – yet, even more so than in London, it was difficult to raise the necessary capital. The best solution was for the city to work in partnership with Ravenscroft Properties Ltd, a developer specialising in the retail sector. To entice Ravenscroft, the hotel would form part of a wider project for the city's new shopping Precinct and so, even if it was not a great economic success, rent income from the shops surrounding it would produce profit. This partnership was, however, against Council policy, which favoured carrying out its own development work, rather than involving external interests. As the government would not support it building a hotel, a deal with Ravenscroft was the only option.

The hotel was to be leased to a commercial operator – in this instance, the brewer and innkeeper Ind Coope of Burton-on-Trent. As we shall see, the strategy of a municipality identifying a need for a hotel as part of a redevelopment masterplan, then soliciting a commercial developer to build it for lease to a third-party operator would become a familiar one.

The seven-storey shell of the Hotel Leofric was the work of prominent local architects, W. Stanley Hattrell and Partners, whose design in terms of building height and external finish was required to fit a master plan already prepared for the city centre.[123] The hotel occupied one of two similar brick-faced blocks, facing Broadgate and flanking the main approach to the city's new pedestrianised Precinct. Their external detailing was somewhat in the Swedish contemporary manner, an approach found in a great deal of British public architecture of the period and often referred to as the 'New Empiricism' on account of its aesthetic clarity and its frequent association with commissions from public authorities and the development of the welfare state.

Much like Kungsgåtan in Stockholm, Coventry's Precinct had bridges crossing between each block with pedestrian access at first floor level. The Hotel Leofric consequently had entrances on both the ground and first storeys. 'Double deck' pedestrianised public space of this kind was untried in Britain and was itself a symbol of starting afresh, offering more public space with room to relax and new viewpoints from which to spectate. Two thirds of the hotel's ground floor area consisted of rentable shop units with a small foyer and lift lobby sandwiched between. Facing the car park behind, there was a suite of public rooms, consisting of a snack bar, cocktail lounge and grillroom. Separately from the hotel, Ind Coope operated the White Lion Pub, a public bar on the corner of Broadgate and the Precinct.[124]

At first floor level, there was a somewhat larger foyer with reception counter, a dining room called the French Restaurant, a lounge and a two-storey ballroom with a balcony at one end and a lay-light above the dance floor. To the rear, these facilities, and the public rooms on the lower ground floor, were serviced by a large complex of kitchens, sculleries and cold stores. Bedrooms occupied the entirety of the three floors above and were arranged around an approximately H-shaped corridor plan. In terms of planning, the Hotel Leofric was relatively complex with a high proportion of public rooms to bedrooms, placing the hotel at the superior end of the spectrum so far as communal facilities were concerned. This was also indicative of its status as a symbol of prestige for the municipality and probably also of commercial pragmatism by its developer in that – at least initially – there might not be very large numbers of visitors wishing to stay overnight in Coventry, whereas restaurant, bar and banquet facilities could be used by non-residents as well. Coventry was surrounded by a major industrial conurbation, producing mainly valuable engineered goods and so, among the managerial class, there was considerable wealth to spend on drinking, dining and entertaining. Of the 100 guest rooms, only 70 had private bathrooms, quite a high proportion by the standards of provincial cities in pre-war Britain, but falling far short of typical post-war international practice, which tended to follow the American Statler approach.

Internally, the Hotel Leofric was the first of a number of British city hotels, showcasing the work of designers previously best known for their involvement in the Festival of Britain, in this instance Ward & Austin, who designed penthouse suites on the sixth floor. Otherwise, the hotel's main architects, Hattrell and Partners, thoroughly applied the aesthetics of the Festival's more frivolous elements – such as its Lion and Unicorn Pavilion, the tongue-in-cheek neo-Regency and Victoriana of Battersea Pleasure Gardens and indeed of the subsequent Coronation pageantry in 1953 – throughout the remainder of the hotel's interior. The approach aimed to appear simultaneously bright, comfortable, informal, whimsical and luxurious. In common with much British commercial design of its era, it was much more fussy and fiddly than the clean-lined hotel interiors of the pre-war era.

The foyer spaces were largely panelled in African walnut with dark terracotta-coloured ceilings to conceal nicotine staining. In the bars, attempts were made to combine modern elements with nostalgic evocations of the past, the aim being to 'recreate the cosiness and intimacy of Victorian pubs.' In the White Lion Pub, for example, 'beer handles, brass spiral and woodwork… mahogany, red leather upholstery and copper table tops' were juxtaposed with a 'dynamic ceiling, the flat surfaces (being painted) mushroom and the inclined ones primrose and purple with off-white stripes.'[125] The Cocktail Lounge featured a wrap-around mural by Guy Egan depicting a fantasy late Victorian Broadgate Square with Emmett-style veteran cars, penny farthings and ornamental street lights, all set against a black background. By contrast, the opposite walls were wallpapered with Roger Nicholson's contemporary 'Attica' design in terracotta, sky-blue and lime-green, while the carpet was similarly in line with 'Festival Pattern Group' principles. The Grillroom, adjacent, had a floating teak-clad ribbed ceiling, beneath which furnishings, lighting and wall finishes were again in the 'Festival' manner. The French Restaurant, meanwhile, featured an 'atomic' wall pattern of white plaster discs with gilded edges.

The largest and loftiest space was the two-storey-high ballroom, panelled in a matrix of triangular strips of Gaboon mahogany and Australian black bean, with Brunswick green-coloured intersections. The extensive use of timber panelling was mainly for acoustic reasons, but it also was easier to maintain in such a potentially smoky environment. Furthermore, it lent the space an 'ocean liner' elegance and sense of exclusivity. The space was lit by six chandeliers with coloured cornice lighting and wall sconces further reinforcing the impression of being located on a luxury ship.

Bedrooms were decorated in four colour palettes – green, red, blue and gold – and these were applied not only to the carpets, furniture, curtains and bed linen but also to such small details as door key tabs. Each room had a telephone and wireless (radio) and details such as bedside and dressing tables were cantilevered to make vacuuming easier. Ward & Austin's penthouse suites featured bespoke built-in cabinets and furniture. Careful consideration was paid to the graphic design of registration forms, menu cards and baggage labels so that the hotel's entire visual identity was homogenous and reflective of Festival of Britain typography.

Altogether, the Hotel Leofric was an impressive achievement, considering the restricted economic circumstances under which it was realised. The hotel lasted for over fifty years, closing in 2008 when its latter day owner, the Menzies Hotel Group, sold most of its properties *en bloc* to Travelodge. The Hotel Leofric was then gutted and a new Travelodge was constructed within the building's shell, nearly all of the spaces originally housing public rooms being converted by the budget operator into additional bedrooms. While the hotel had been superficially modernised at various times throughout its career, it had until then retained most of its decorative woodwork and its lounges, restaurants and ballroom all remained largely intact until the sale. In the end, it was a victim of commercial expediency and changing market trends in the hospitality industry.[126]

Back in London, meanwhile, following the settlement of a land acquisition dispute that had dragged on for over thirty years, the final wing of the Grosvenor House Hotel, containing 92 additional rooms, was finished in 1957 to a design by Gordon Jeeves, whose solution discretely blended with Lutyens' treatment of the original façades. As explained above, however, almost from the hotel's inception in the latter 1920s, its operator had had strong urges to modernise its interiors in line with the latest architectural trends. The new wing provided a fresh opportunity to assert an up-to-date image, if only through the interior design. Fortuitously, at this point, the Grosvenor House General Manager, A.H. Jones, was introduced to the highly regarded furniture designer Gordon Russell and his brother, Richard Drew Russell (known as Dick), who was an architect. The introduction was arranged by their sibling, Don, who was Chairman of the British Tourist Authority and an acquaintance of Jones's. The Russells already had connections with the hotel trade as, during their teenage years before the First World War, their father had owned and operated the Lygon Arms Hotel, a sixteenth century inn in the picturesque village of Broadway in Worcestershire, where there was an artistic community. There, the young Gordon Russell had first become interested in furniture making through helping to restore and replicate antique pieces for the hotel.[127] From these beginnings, he joined Joseph Ashbee's Crafts Guild at Chipping Camden, where he learned Arts & Crafts approaches. By the 1930s, Russell had augmented these with a new-found interest in modernism and, having subsequently designed wartime utility furniture and played a leading role in the post-war 'Britain Can Make It' exhibition, by the 1950s, he had become a leading member of the British design 'establishment.'

Russell's bedroom interiors for the new Grosvenor House wing synthesised these influences, combining the practicality of built-in furniture units with fine cabinet making from his own workshop in Broadway. As the new bedrooms were well received by guests and critics alike, Russell was retained by Grosvenor House to re-design the hotel's American Bar, Restaurant and Ballroom, where he replaced Gustavo Pulitzer Finali's glamorous but worn mid-1930s 'moderne' interiors with considerably more sober new designs. Their understated appearance was more in line with contemporary ideas of what represented 'good' design, as influenced by recent Scandinavian practices and the Festival of Britain.

A bedroom designed by Gordon Russell in the 1957 wing of the Grosvenor House Hotel; high quality but rather understated fixtures and fittings typified Russell's hotel output. In line with the era's modernist rhetoric regarding 'good design' and emerging from a phase of austerity, practicality was favoured over glamourous stylistic flourishes.

Russell's work for Grosvenor House set a very high standard for British post-war hotel interior design, though one that was only seldom matched in terms of quality and integrity. Subsequently, as we shall see, Russell, Hodgson & Leigh, the architectural practice founded in 1957 by his brother Dick, produced several fine modernist hotel interior schemes, and these too invariably had bespoke furnishings made at the Broadway workshop.[128]

Concurrently with the completion of the Grosvenor House extension, in Edinburgh, a large new hotel was under construction on a prominent site on Princes Street, the city's main shopping thoroughfare, overlooking the famous city centre gardens and towards the castle. This replaced an existing hotel of late Victorian vintage, the large ballroom of which had been reconfigured as a cinema before the First World War. In 1952, Marks & Spencer began looking for a site for an Edinburgh store and so bought the hotel and cinema for redevelopment. As the adjacent Jenners department store was also keen to expand its floor space, it was agreed that it would share the site and development costs with Marks & Spencer. Above the shops, which were to occupy most of the basement and ground floor, the hotel would fill eight storeys of 'air space', thereby generating extra revenue. The top of the façade would thus align with the roofs of the surrounding buildings. To design the entire project, Marks & Spencer employed the Glasgow-based architects, Monro & Partners, who had designed their existing Scottish stores in the 1930s. The large and complex Edinburgh development was drawn up by one of the senior employees, John Forbes, who produced no fewer than 24 variations before a final scheme was agreed.[129]

A large part of the problem was achieving agreement with Jenners, which eventually pulled out of the project altogether. Another was that the prominent location on Princes Street was subject to unusually close planning scrutiny and lobbying from local amenity groups. Whereas Forbes' initial design proposals – which included retail space for Jenners – were symmetrical with the hotel's entrance located between the two store frontages, the version executed only occupied two-thirds of the site, leaving the remainder empty for subsequent development by Jenners whenever they felt ready to proceed.[130]

Completed in 1957, the Mount Royal Hotel was in appearance an intriguing example of modern traditionalism, for although the materials used for its facing – stone panels and teak window framing – were typical of contemporary practice in Scandinavia, the overall façade composition with numerous bay windows echoed the neighbouring Victorian and Edwardian commercial frontages. At a glance from a distance, the building could indeed have been mistaken for a progressive work of the early twentieth century, rather than one dating from its middle years. The reception and public rooms were on the first floor, accessed from Princes Street by a wide spiral stairway clad in travertine. Emulating the approach to service provision at the Westbury in London, these consisted only of a guest lounge, bar and dining room.

Nearly a decade after the Mount Royal opened, Jenners finally got round to

The Mount Royal Hotel in Edinburgh's Princes Street, showing the original structure at left with the subsequent addition to the right. The roof terrace adds a degree of visual continuity.

extending its premises, albeit using different architects, Tarbolton & Ochterlony of Edinburgh. When this happened, the remaining awkward gap disappeared, though the façade detailing of the new insertion was almost entirely different from that of the existing structure. For a succession of lessees, however, the enlarged Mount Royal Hotel was a well-patronised and lucrative part of Edinburgh's growing tourist infrastructure, which it remains today.

Britain's initial post-war hotels show the varied influences affecting the country's hospitality design as hotel operators and their architects tentatively entered a new era. Traditionalism, Festival of Britain aesthetics, American and Scandinavian modernism were all represented. The next generation of British hotels would, however, more closely reflect emerging international trends as the next stage of hotel development was greatly affected by the rise of jet air travel.

Continental Exemplars

In 1955, the same year as the Hotel Leofric was opened, in Istanbul, the fourth of a series of international Hilton-branded hotels was inaugurated. It was designed by Gordon Bunshaft of the New York branch of the architects Skidmore, Owings and Merrill, but the finance enabling its realisation was largely provided by local investors. The building was a sleek and stylish essay in Americanised 'international modernism', offset with carefully selected picturesque elements of the 'Ottoman vernacular'.[131] In design terms, it was at least a decade in advance of the Hotel Leofric, whose 'Festival of Britain' detailing and homages to Victoriana were, by comparison, inward-looking and lacking any sense of sweeping 'jet age' chic. While the *Architectural Review* merely described the Leofric's interior design in factual terms, the Hilton seemed to provoke a certain degree of awe – the *AR*'s correspondent observing that every room had not only a private bathroom but also a balcony, accessed through aluminium-framed plate glass doors. Furthermore, there were special taps in each room to supply iced water and, to the rear of the hotel, 'the garbage is also refrigerated'.[132] In August 1957, the *Caterer and Hotel Keeper* carried an article, written anonymously by one of the Hilton architects, in which he explained to curious British readers the ten most important 'rules' for American hotel design:

- Construction cost per room should be $1,000 per dollar of average room rate (this included the cost of public and service areas).
- Bedroom floor area should be equal or greater than total public and service space.
- The hotel should operate with fewer employees than the number of rooms – the Dallas Statler Hilton having 1,001 rooms but only 600 employees.
- Land acquisition costs should be less than 10% of the total project cost.
- Profit should come 70% from rooms, 20% from sale of beverages, 10% from shop rentals and 0% from food.
- The occupancy break-even point should be between 60% and 65%.[133]

While these statistics only directly related to recent hotels in the USA, it may be assumed that, to an extent, they were also used in only slightly modified form to formulate the business cases and architectural solutions for numerous American-financed examples developed all over the western world in the ensuing decade, not least in Britain.

Soon after the inauguration of the Istanbul Hilton, in Copenhagen, where Scandinavia's 'hub' international airport had been built at Kastrup, Scandinavian

Airlines System (SAS) commissioned the Danish modernist architect Arne Jacobsen to design a 'flagship' luxury hotel and airline terminal. The SAS Royal Hotel was not finished until 1961 but, upon completion, it came to be widely regarded as the example *par excellence* of a city centre prestige hotel for the international jet set. As with all of Jacobsen's work, the building was immaculately detailed and, seemingly, no aspect of its interior design was too trivial to avoid a bespoke solution, meaning that even door handles, ashtrays and candle-holders were purpose-designed. Critics regarded it as being a modernist masterpiece and, for some, merely spending a night there became a reason for visiting Copenhagen.

The Istanbul Hilton and the SAS Royal Hotel were thereafter held up by British architecture and design critics as setting the benchmarks for design quality to which British hoteliers, their architects and interior designers should aspire. Unfortunately, due to a complexity of circumstances, British hotels of the ensuing period rarely if ever came even close to these supposed exemplars of 'best practice.'[134] The reasons for this failure related in part to the ongoing political and economic after-effects of the Second World War. In the post-war period, British architectural modernism firstly became associated with a public sector keen to make money stretch as far as possible and often resulting in rather austere solutions, rather than luxurious ones. Following the re-election of a Conservative government in 1951, modernism next interfaced with equally miserly commercial developers, who almost invariably prioritised profits per square foot over high aesthetic sophistication.

The clean-lined and precisely-proportioned Istanbul Hilton was widely admired and became an international exemplar of modernist hotel design at its best. Later on, the SAS Royal Hotel in Copenhagen won even greater plaudits on account of the remarkable level of attention to detail applied to every element of the design, including furnishings and tableware.

As Harold Macmillan, the Conservative Minister of Housing and, later, Prime Minister, explained in 1952 when justifying his plan to abolish development taxes, 'the people whom the Government must help are those who do things – the developers, the people who create wealth, whether they are humble or exalted.'[135] The removal of wartime building controls followed in 1954 and, by then, a new consumerism, allied to growing 'white collar' work in offices and generally increasing affluence combined to give rise to a strong market for commercial building. Developers, who had since the early war years bought up as much land as they could while prices remained low, now began speculatively building high-rise office blocks, shopping precincts and hotels and, as we shall see, sometimes these were combined into single monoliths. Legislation was also passed obliging local authorities in certain instances to compensate developers for losses resulting from schemes being delayed or rejected in the planning process. As Fitzwalter and Taylor explain:

> 'By the end of the fifties, the property boom was in full swing. Shares soared eight-fold in as many years. Inflated land values multiplied fortunes and the dismantling of dividend restraint pushed share prices still higher. The tax system discriminated in favour of the developer. Whereas any other manufacturer was taxed on the difference between the cost and the selling price of finished goods, the developer who bought land as a raw material, and improved it by building

on it, was allowed to make his capital gain tax free. Truly, developers never had it so good as under the Macmillan government'.[136]

Initially, the development boom was centred on London and its environs, where vast numbers of new office blocks were speculatively built. So many appeared in central London that, in 1964, the Labour Secretary of State for Economic Development, George Brown, insisted on a temporary moratorium. This merely had the effect of making property tycoons concentrate their efforts instead on building in provincial towns and cities and on developing types of building other than offices, hotels being an obvious choice. Sadly, many of Britain's historic town centres were marred by their piecemeal redevelopment schemes, while at the same time greatly increasing car ownership caused traffic bottlenecks.

Earlier on, the Town and Country Planning Acts of 1943 and 1944 had viewed comprehensive redevelopment of the kind first mooted in the 1920s by up-and-coming modernist architects such as Le Corbusier and Ludwig Hilbersheimer, as a sensible means of addressing bomb damage. For Britain's provincial municipalities, this approach became the great panacea for housing, commercial development and traffic pressures. By the mid-1950s, however, it had come to be accepted that financing such schemes would require partnerships between public authorities and private interests. In theory at least, these would be mutually beneficial. Yet, in practice, as Fitzwalter and Taylor observe:

> 'Throughout the country, butchers, bakers and candlestick makers sat on council committees negotiating multi-million pound deals with some of the sharpest business brains in Britain. Not surprisingly, the councillors tended to come off second best. By advocating comprehensive town centre renewal without controlling the way it was to be achieved, Whitehall played into the developer's hand…'[137]

Macmillan's desire to return to the liberal, de-regulated business culture of the nineteenth century had profound implications for architecture and planning. Technology, meanwhile, moved on considerably, enabling vast and highly intrusive schemes to be built at unprecedented speed in urban environments otherwise created long before. As the architect and architecture critic J.M. Richards reflected in 1955 when Britain's new development boom was beginning: 'Coventry is almost unique in having made a plan after the bombing and (subject to minor changes) carried it though with determination, while other British cities were allowing laissez-faire to take charge'.[138]

The commercial property developer – so important in the realisation of the next generation of British hotels – represented, according to the architect and town planner Sir William Holford:

> '…A new social phenomenon, a middle-man, often starting with nothing and continually putting out antennae to any scent of putting together a site and a client… There is a way of life with a technique of promises and threats. For example, Charles Clore [of whom more below] promising Liverpool a new civic centre and bus station in return for a slice of development land, on the one hand, and Shell threatening the London County Council on another. "One million square feet or we move to the continent."'[139]

As we shall see, it was in this context of rapid change and unprecedented possibility that a majority of Britain's post-war hotels would be realised.

Chapter 6

Motels and airport hotels

From the mid-1950s onward, new hotel development in Britain played a vital role in economic expansion and in the creation of a modern mobile nation. The pattern of development of new hotels was linked to investments in new transport infrastructure – the 1955 British Railways Modernisation Plan, motorway developments and simultaneous projects for new and expanded airports. During the 1960s, the tourist industry grew greatly as a result of increasing wealth and mobility – and, indeed, governmental and regional policies were aimed at attracting visitors from overseas.

Notwithstanding the expense of the railway Modernisation Plan, towards the latter 1950s, the British Transport Commission's deficit had only increased, while the railway trade unions became more forceful in their demands for greater pay and improved working conditions. This seemingly hopeless situation appears to have caused the government to become disillusioned with rail and increasingly infatuated with road and air travel. Private car ownership was seen as a signifier of increasing wealth and social mobility. In December 1958, Harold Macmillan opened Britain's first motorway, the M6 Preston Bypass, and his controversial Secretary of State for Transport, Ernest Marples, was strongly supportive of the development of a nationwide network. Marples had a vested interest in the road lobby as he had recently been a director of Marples-Ridgeway, a road-building contractor which had constructed the Chiswick Flyover. In November 1959, the M1 motorway was opened between Birmingham and St Albans and, as car ownership soared, a succession of similar developments was announced.[140] By the early 1960s, such was the power of the road lobby within government and regional authorities that most of the major airports, some ferry ports and the Scottish new towns were developed with no rail links whatsoever, meaning that users were obliged to travel by car, taxi or bus.

Since the latter nineteenth century, grand hotels aimed at business travellers and tourists had tended to be located in the vicinity of railway stations, or within a moderate distance of the passenger terminals of major ports – but the rapid modal shift from rail and sea to road and air brought about a new geography. As has been shown above, this trend began in the inter-war era with the construction of large roadhouses close to significant road junctions on the urban periphery – but, from the latter 1950s onwards, the development of motels and airport hotels increased exponentially. Since mass car ownership happened first in North America, the United States had a design lead in planning buildings of these types. Typically, these were located on relatively spacious rural or outer suburban sites, which allowed for sprawling low-rise development, in contrast with the denser planning of city centre hotels to maximise revenues from their expensive sites.

Reviewing post-war British motel design for the *Architect's Journal* in March 1973, the critic John Carter observed:

> 'Motels…seem to have come, like takeover bids, supermarkets, planned obsolescence and diversification, from the U.S. Their promoters are not necessarily people with any previous interest in the hotel tradition, but entrepreneurs who 'buy in' the requisite expertise and deploy it as an investment.

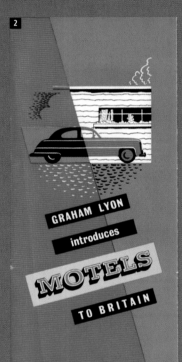

GRAHAM LYON

introduces

MOTELS

TO BRITAIN

GRAHAM LYON *MOTELS* FOR FINE FOOD & ACCOMMODATION

Each Motel Unit includes Private Bath or Shower, Private Garage, Telephone, Radio, Tea-making Machine, Valet Service, Single and Double Rooms, Twin Beds.

32/6 PER PERSON (including Continental Breakfast) - FIRST CLASS RESTAURANTS · FULLY LICENSED · ALWAYS OPEN

THE ROYAL OAK MOTEL built around the famous old Mackeson Inn on the A20 Road to Dover is specially sited to serve cross-Channel tourists using Dover and Folkestone or the airports at Lympne and Lydd. It is also an excellent stop for visiting the Cinque Ports area and Canterbury.

Telephone: HYTHE 66580

NO. 1 · ROYAL OAK MOTEL · NEWINGREEN · NR. HYTHE

Thus, they are in theory free to re-interpret the age-old 'travellers rest' problem in modern terms, but are outside the Swiss-trained hotelier or French-trained restaurant traditions… The 'motelier' caters, in any case, for a different type of guest who does not expect and might be embarrassed by the attentive finesse and meticulous craftsmanship of the old tradition.'[141]

Carter also observed how the development of motel infrastructure reflected profound and rapid cultural and sociological changes:

'Architectural historians and theorists, immersed in traditional concepts of geography and 'influences' have neglected this source of style and form. The motel appears to have been developed to meet two changes. First, mobility, the destruction of distance and locality, the feverish restlessness of modern man. This gives the motel (and to some extent the tourist hotel) its purpose; overnight accommodation and conference facilities. But such a change could as well be serviced by far simpler, plainer buildings… This brings us to a second change, the emergence of a new social class in the last 20 years; the middle management executives, which gives the motel its luxury image… A fantasy world must be created corresponding to the aspirations of this newly possessed class… The creation of a motel, from the promoter's point of view, is not a functional/architectural purpose at all; it is a marketing exercise… Air conditioning keeps the air sweet for several score of well-dined and cigar-smoking conferences, under a comparatively low ceiling with clear acoustics. But it is also a selling point; it symbolises for the grandsons of dole queue grandfathers the "good life."'[142]

Britain's initial post-war motels were, however, considerably less sophisticated than the generations to follow. The earliest example was probably the Kenilworth Auto Villas, built in 1952 on a site adjacent to Roucil Towers, a country house near Kenilworth in Warwickshire. The motel was developed by the 'millionaire showman' and entrepreneur, John Collins, whose father ran the Crystal Palace Amusement park in Sutton Coldfield. At Kenilworh, Collins erected 17 air-conditioned chalets with parquet floors, twin built-in beds, electric cookers and private bathrooms with iced water on tap. These refinements suggest that he directly copied in almost every detail the established American design formula for such premises. Stylistically, the chalets looked somewhat Scandinavian in manner, rather than from the USA.

In subsequent years, a major figure behind British motel development was Graham Lyon, a travel trade entrepreneur who in the 1930s began offering tours of Europe by coach. Later on, he established the Autocheque company to offer independent British travellers to the continent an ability to pay easily beforehand for motoring services and to make hotel reservations. After the Second World War, Lyon bought two hotels in Dover – the White Cliffs and the Hotel de France – to accommodate coach parties arriving and departing by ferry from France and Belgium. He also ran the Merry Dolphin Restaurant within the car ferry terminal in Dover's Eastern Docks and a restaurant in the Ferryfield Airport terminal at Lydd (also in Kent).

Next, Lyon entered into a partnership with the brewery Watney, Combe, Reid & Company, which also ran a chain of pubs and inns, to develop a new motel at a roundabout at Newingreen near Lympne in Kent on the A20 road from London. Its neighbour was the Mackeson Inn, a historic pub operated by Whitbread. Lyon and Watney & Co chose as their architect Louis Erdi, an émigré modernist who had been born Lajos Érdi in Slavonia in what was then Hungary (now Croatia) in 1909. Erdi had

Opposite: Kenilworth Auto Villas, shown in (1), constructed in the grounds of Rouncil Towers, a mansion house in Warwickshire, was a very early example of the British motel seeking to emulate North American planning and service standards. Each chalet had its own garage while communal facilities were located in the mansion, visible to the right. Images (2) and (3) show a brochure promoting Graham Lyon's Royal Oak Motor Hotel at Lympne in Kent, while (4), shows garaging interspersing the bedrooms. Images (5) and (6) show the lounge and a bedroom at Lyon's subsequent New Forest Motel, near Southampton.

studied architecture at the Swiss Federal Institute of Technology in Zürich, from which he graduated in 1930. Although the Institute was traditionalist in its teaching approach, the young Erdi and several of his fellow students were greatly influenced by the example being set by Switzerland's architectural *enfant terrible*, Le Corbusier.[143] In the 1930s, Erdi practised architecture in Yugoslavia, leaving for Britain in 1939. There, he first found work as a porter at the Royal Court Hotel in Sloane Square in London, where he befriended its owner, Auguste Wild.[144] Post-war, Erdi established an architectural practice in London but his wartime experience of hotel work led to a great architectural interest in the possibilities hotel design appeared to offer. So, he submitted a series of articles to the *Caterer and Hotel Keeper* and the publication of these led to him being contacted by Watney & Co, thus beginning a lucrative collaboration in motel design.

The Royal Oak Motor Hotel was opened in 1953. Intended for summer use only, it was a single-storey, timber-framed structure of light construction with mono-pitch roofs, the external walls being clad in elm rustic weather boarding. The *Caterer and Hotel Keeper* recorded:

> 'The modern traveller's rest has ten double and six single suites designed… in 'the human style.' Each double bedroom has a garage into which the visitor may drive at any time. Each room has its own telephone, radio and automatic tea-making machine… By the window is a divan which can be converted into another bed, very useful for the small family… In all rooms the furnishings and décor are in bright contemporary squares and checks. In the restaurant, which can accommodate 60 to 80 people, furnishings are again contemporary, in a Swedish style… There is a parquet floor for dancing and a feature of the service is a drinks bar on wheels…'[145]

Soon Lyon and Watney & Co announced their intention to develop further new motels at points of entry, or close to major roads in southern England. In 1955, Erdi designed the New Forest Motel, located seven miles to the north of Southampton on a site adjacent to the Vine Inn; it followed a similar approach to his previous Royal Oak project. Later the same year, the Devon Motel was constructed beside the Exeter by-pass. A project for a motel at Ferryfield Airport, from which Silver City Airways ran an 'air car ferry' shuttle service to France, did not come to fruition, however.[146]

In an era when air travel was expensive and therefore the mode of choice only for a prosperous elite, going to the continent involved taking a packet steamer across the Dover Strait or North Sea. Then as now, Dover was the busiest Channel port and one of the key 'gateways' to Europe. In the early 1950s, passenger shipping services were rail-connected and operated from the Western Docks, where the former South Eastern & Chatham Railway station stood on the quay with a hotel adjacent. During the decade, the Eastern Docks grew as Dover's car ferry port (by 1958, four ferries were using this facility with the promise of more to come). For many Britons visiting the continent, the prospect of driving on the 'wrong' side of the road was daunting, as was making one's own hotel and dining arrangements. It was perceived by many as safer – and cheaper – to tour overseas by coach as part of an organised group. According to *The Times*, in 1956, 2,716 coaches, carrying approximately

An impression of the New Forest Motel, completed in 1955 and, like the Royal Oak, added to an existing inn.

The Dover Stage Coachotel in Dover was structurally adventurous and, being designed specifically to house coach tour parties, conceptually unusual. Here, we see (1) the exterior, (2) the Dover Sole Bar, (3) the restaurant, (4) the building's relationship to other post-war development along the promenade and (5) a 1950s advertising postcard featuring a touring coach in the centre. The coach's design speaks more of 1930s approaches and seems rather dated in comparison with the hotel.

1

GROUND FLOOR PLAN
SCALE : 1 IN = 32 FT

SECTION AND
FIRST FLOOR PLAN OF
BEDROOM BLOCK

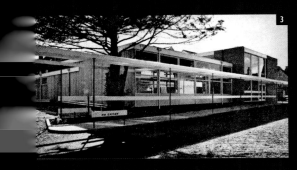

3

4

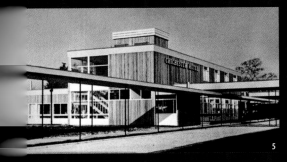

5

6

75,000 passengers, passed through Dover, creating a major accommodation problem.[147] Not only did a proportion of these brief visitors need sleep and feeding, but the coaches in which they had travelled required overnight parking space.

To serve this market, Graham Lyon and Watney & Co commissioned Erdi to design a dedicated 'coachotel' on Dover's waterfront, located between the Eastern and Western dock systems. Inaugurated in 1957, it boasted 30 double and 12 single rooms, which was enough space for two coach parties. In addition, a commodious and lofty-ceilinged dining room enabled many more coachloads to be fed while passing through the town.

Erdi's design for The Dover Stage was striking, making expressive use of reinforced concrete delta frames to cantilever the five-storey accommodation tower perpendicularly across a two-floor block, containing the foyer, bars and restaurant. The bedrooms on the eastern elevation had windows angled at 45 degrees towards the sea, while balconies enabled holidaymakers to experience a foretaste of continental chic before even leaving the country.[148] (These features were otherwise relatively rare in British seaside hotels, particularly ones aimed at a mid-market clientele, as opposed to a wealthy elite.) Inside, the hotel's semi-open plan public spaces were finished with varnished timber ceiling soffits, multi-coloured ceramic tiles, mosaic, Formica bar and table tops and terrazzo flooring – all up-to-date and showy yet conveniently wipe-clean finishes, akin to the easily-maintained interiors of the touring coaches and car ferries transporting the hotel's guests overseas.[149]

As Lyon and Watney had difficulty in obtaining credit for further construction, it was not until the early 1960s that further motels were commissioned by them. In the meantime, their business was re-structured with the brewer becoming the majority shareholder in what was henceforth known as Watney Lyon Motels Ltd. The plan was now to develop motels nationwide, all offering similar facilities and charging standard fixed rates, while following American practice in terms of the facilities on offer. Restaurants and bars were intended as useful amenities for local residents, as well as for motorists passing through. By this point, Erdi had gone into partnership with his young assistant, Ronald J. Rabson, to form Erdi & Rabson. Rabson recalls Erdi as 'a highly imaginative and dedicated architect from whom streams of ideas just seemed to flow.'[150] Certainly, although his output shared a common modernist design language, each project responded differently to its site and context.

Erdi & Rabson's first projects for Watney Lyon were the Mendip Hotel at Frome in Somerset and the Epping Forest Motel at Epping in Essex, both of which were opened in 1962. Planned as 'resort motels,' the intention was that tourists would stay for several nights, using them as bases from which to tour the surrounding countryside.

The Epping project was unusual as, rather than occupying a spacious rural site as had been the case with the majority of Erdi's previous motel designs, it had a constricted location in the town centre, next to the High Street. This was adjacent to Watney's Cock Inn, the structure of which dated from the fifteenth century, albeit with a Georgian street frontage. The solution was to build the motel two linked sections, comprising a reception block, which filled a narrow strip adjacent to the inn, and, to the rear, a wider, three-storey structure containing bedrooms on its two upper levels. This was held aloft by reinforced concrete delta frames between which was a drive-in car park. (These elements were similar to the frames supporting The Dover Stage's accommodation block.)[151]

Although Graham Lyon died suddenly in 1963, Watney Lyon Motels continued developing the motel chain, inaugurating the 34-bedroom Chichester Motel, located

Opposite: The Epping Forest Motel, shown in images (1)-(4), featured a communal block with extensive glazing, adjacent to which the bedroom accommodation was raised on delta frames with car parking beneath. Image (5) shows the timber-clad Chichester Motel, (6) shows the motel's bar, and (7) shows the concrete-framed Oxford Motel. Picturesque when new, these buildings weathered badly and were further compromised by numerous infelicitous changes made by subsequent owners.

near the town's by-pass, in 1964. This was built using a factory-made, pre-fabricated steel frame and panel system, devised by the Swiftplan division of the Taylor Woodrow construction company and faced in vertical strips of varnished oak. For the 60-room Oxford Motel, opened the following year next to the Oxford by-pass, Erdi & Rabson reverted to exposed concrete framing with an over-hanging mono-pitch roof for the reception, bar and restaurant block, beneath which an access road passed through to the car park and bedroom blocks.[152]

In 1966, Watney Lyon Motels opened the 60-bedroom Forth Bridges Motel on a nine-acre site adjacent to the South Queensferry approach road to the recently-completed Forth Road Bridge near Edinburgh. While the bridge was under construction, in February 1965, the *Caterer and Hotel Keeper* had predicted that the traffic flows it would generate would greatly boost hotel trade in the vicinity.[153] The motel included a 120-seat restaurant and a 150-seat cafeteria, indicating that it was intended to cater to large numbers of passing motorists who wished to pause and admire the vista across the river, framed by the historic cantilevered railway bridge and the new suspension road bridge. Once again, Erdi & Rabson's design made extensive use of exposed reinforced concrete, the large car park being ramped upward to meet the entrance block at first floor level, where the reception and a sun terrace were located, with a bar and cafeteria tucked underneath. Meanwhile, the waiter service restaurant enjoyed a commanding position, it being cantilevered outward from the second floor, giving diners had a grandstand view of the two bridges. In appearance, this structure somewhat resembled a contemporary British Rail signal box, such as were found beside recently-electrified lines. To the rear, a separate three-storey accommodation block offered similarly dramatic views across the river and, as with the Dover Stage, all the bedrooms had private verandas. The motel's interior design was rather Scandinavian in manner with timber slatted ceilings and matching furniture.

In 1968, Erdi & Rabson designed an extension for Watney Lyon's sixteenth century Falcon Inn in Stratford-on-Avon, comprising an exposed concrete-framed annex containing additional bedrooms, beneath which there were two storeys of car parking.[154]

The Forth Bridges Motel, viewed from the corner of the site closest to the Forth Road Bridge. The bedrooms, in the block to the left, and the lounge-bar on the first floor had balconies facing the river. The restaurant on the top floor had extensive glazing, reminiscent of a railway signal box of the era. The public bar and cafeteria for motorists, however, were buried beneath a parking deck to the rear.

A selection of views of the Forth Bridges Motel, showing (1) the terrace of the lounge bar at night, (2) the view from the approach road with parking for motel guests at first floor level, adjacent to the motel entrance and for visitors on the level below, (3) the cafeteria with tip-up seating much like a motorway service station, (4) the motel dining room and (5) a corner of the lounge bar.

This quite successfully complemented the old inn's exposed timber structure. Subsequently, the firm produced a design for a motel near Manchester, but before it could be executed, in 1971, the Watney brewery was taken over by Grand Metropolitan, which ceased further development. Louis Erdi died in 1975 and, subsequently, most of the motels designed by his practice were either greatly altered, or demolished. Highly imaginative though these buildings were in terms of planning and in their use of structure, they did not weather well and received insufficient maintenance. The Dover Stage and the Forth Bridges Motel in particular were latterly regarded as eyesores; the former was demolished in 1988 and the latter in 2004.

Esso Motor Hotels

In 1963 Standard Oil Corporation of New Jersey – better known as 'Esso' – began a programme of hotel development in Western Europe, its aim being to create a continent-wide chain of conveniently-located roadside hotels. The description 'motor hotel' sought to engender an image upmarket of typical British motels of that era. The eventual idea was that motorists should be able to drive across Europe, 'from Trondheim in northern Norway all the way through western Europe as far south as Sicily' staying each night in an Esso-owned hotel. The Corporation hoped that, eventually, these would become as ubiquitous as its existing chain of filling stations.[155] In order to give a sense of variety and 'locale' to travellers staying in one such hotel after another, Esso decided to commission a different local architect to design each. The aim was:

> '…To reflect the national character and blend in structure and landscaping to that of the community. Similarly in the decoration of the interior, furniture, fabrics and other appointments produced in the area are used as far as possible and from this it follows naturally that the food in these Esso hotels and drink also features what is traditional to the locality along with internationally called-for specialities…'[156]

In Britain, this ambitious project would initially require hotels and to the north and west of London, followed by ones in central Scotland. In 1966 the first Esso Motor Hotel to open was at South Mimms near Hendon at the southern end of the A1 London-Edinburgh trunk road. Thirty years previously, South Mimms had been a sleepy village on London's northern fringe but in the post-war era, the growth in car ownership transformed its environs with new roadside service spaces where motorists, coach parties and truck drivers could all pause for re-fuelling.

An advertisement for the Esso Motor Hotel at South Mimms.

Views showing the Esso Motor Hotel's coffee shop, with a mural by Michael Caddy adorning the left-hand wall, and one of the bedrooms.

The hotel was designed by Derek Lovejoy and Associates. Born in 1925, Lovejoy had studied at Harvard University in the 1950s, where he became greatly interested in landscape design. Thereafter, he established a practice in Croydon, subsequently setting up branch offices elsewhere. His American connections probably made him an attractive choice for Esso's management. The hotel's interiors were by the New York-based Walter M. Ballard Corporation, which specialised in hotel and other commercial interiors – though selecting an American interior design firm would seem to have run counter to Esso's aim of engendering a sense of locale within.

Occupying a spacious green field site, set back from the roadside, the hotel consisted of a single-storey restaurant, bar and reception building with a two-storey accommodation block adjacent, arranged around a courtyard with car parking nearby. The structure was clad in brown facing brick with oxidised copper facias. Although the 'motor hotel' concept was American, the understated detailing was similar to that of many contemporary English schools, healthcare facilities and university buildings. Within, the public rooms consisted of a lounge and bar, separated by a brick feature fireplace, a grill restaurant, which was lined in cedar, and a coffee shop with a yellow-tiled servery counter and, on the adjoining wall, a bright abstract polyester montage by the artist, Michael Caddy.

Adjacent to the hotel was an Esso filling station; this was to be a feature of all the corporation's subsequent motor hotels and was not only convenient for motorists, but also enabled Esso to retail its core product. (Just as brewery owners of hotels tended to incorporate numerous drink outlets, it was unsurprising that an oil giant would seize opportunities to sell petrol at its hotel sites.)

The second Esso Motor Hotel was at Maidenhead; completed in 1968, it too was designed by Lovejoy's firm. A significantly larger development than the one at South Mimms, it was again planned as a series of wings. The one containing the reception and public rooms had a vaulted cast concrete roof, while the bedroom block had three-storeys. These were linked to the filling station by a roof structure with deep facias and over-hangs. For the interiors, rather than using Ballard's firm again, a London-based consultant, Cope Notter Associates, was employed. From the latter 1960s onward, they became leading designers of British hotel and motel rooms and, at Maidenhead, their approach was Scandinavian-inspired with floating ribbed timber ceilings and timber-framed modern furniture.

By 1966, there were a total of 83 motels operating across Britain, up from 75 the previous year, and, altogether, these provided approximately 3,500 rooms. Operators ranged from chains such as Watney Lyon, Esso, Rank and Forte to numerous private entrepreneurs with single properties. Architecturally, the most visually interesting were

The Esso Motor Hotel at
Maidenhead, showing the block
containing the reception and
communal facilities with the
bedroom block to the left.

those designed by Louis Erdi for the Watney Lyon chain and the Lovejoy projects for Esso. Many others simply consisted of rows of pre-fabricated chalets with mono-pitched roofs, or two-storey accommodation blocks with deck access, both approaches being reminiscent of contemporary holiday camp accommodation.

Airport Hotels

In 1952, the first jet airliner, the DeHavilland *Comet 1*, was introduced, heralding the rapid development of a new transport geography to serve the jet age. Shortly thereafter, the British government announced that London Airport would be significantly expanded. The airport's first terminal, the Europa Building, was completed in 1955 (subsequently this became Heathrow Terminal 2) and its infrastructure was subsequently further enlarged to cope with a steep rise in demand. While car ownership had expanded by the latter 1950s to include sections of the skilled working class, jet air travel initially was expensive and therefore was perceived as an elite activity, requiring a high standard of ancillary services to satisfy those who could afford to fly, or for whom a plane trip represented a very special event. Moreover, as Americans were on average wealthier than Britons in the 1950s, they formed a large proportion of the jetliners' trans-Atlantic clientele. Consequently, British airport hotels required to reflect their expectations with regard to facilities and service provision. As the British-born, but California-based, hotel interior designer, Henry End, observed:

> 'The twentieth century jet traveller can circle the globe and stay each night in hotels that strike the same note of style and comfort… He will certainly look for local colour but this is something he prefers to see from the balcony of his air-conditioned bedroom or through an expanse of glass as he sips a very cold Martini and tests the rareness of his sirloin or prime rib. He will enjoy walking through a lobby that provides a look of the native arts of a strange land, but the craftsmanship will go for nought if the beds are uncomfortable and the hot water pipes are not constantly filled.'[157]

By the mid-1950s, the legacy of the 'wartime mentality' had made much of the British hotel industry parochial and conservative and the fact that it was largely led by former military men cannot have helped matters. Although a 400 per cent increase trans-Atlantic travel was forecast from the mid-1950s onward, the industry initially did little to prepare. As Henry End commented, 'the visitor from America would expect to find a bathroom in his room but few British hotels could provide it.' [158] End cited a debate he had witnessed at a 1956 Hotel and Restaurant Association conference in London at which one prominent British hotelier after another had expressed doubt as to whether new buildings could be afforded. Group Captain B.G. Carfoot of the brewer and inn-keeper Ind Coope stated that his company was 'not too concerned with tourist business' in any case and did 'not think that new hotels can ever be built to give a reasonable return just for the tourist trade alone.'[159] With regard to projected American-financed hotel developments in London, Captain K.C. McCallum, the Managing Director of Trust Houses, Britain's largest hotel operator, said 'wait until they burn their fingers.'[160] Despite this, McCallum admitted, however, that his 'observations of the American tourist led him to believe they expected more luxurious accommodations and a higher standard of service than the British hotels were providing.'[161] As Henry End concluded, with the benefit of hindsight, 'the subsequent American successes must have been unnerving.'[162]

In January 1959, the Canadian-owned Seaway Hotels Corporation, headquartered in Toronto, announced plans to develop Britain's first post-war airport hotel, to be located on Bath Road, adjacent to London Airport. The Skyway was opened a year later to a design by Fitzroy Robinson & Partners. Born in Bangalore in 1914, Robinson was

Views of the Skyway Hotel at London Airport, showing the exterior, which was enlivened by a wing-shaped concrete entrance canopy and by a series of flagpoles along the frontage. The reception area was spacious and high-ceilinged. An American-style long bar was located adjacent.

a graduate of the Bartlett School of Architecture. Following the end of materials rationing, he established his own practice in 1956 and thereafter successfully rode the post-war construction boom. Within a decade, his firm had become one of Europe's biggest and its subsequent commissions included projects for The Stock Exchange and The Home Office, as well as numerous London bank headquarters.

Occupying a relatively spacious site, the Skyway consisted of a T-shaped, four-storey accommodation block, containing 160 bedrooms. From this, a single-storey block – containing the reception foyer, restaurant, bar and banqueting suite with services to the rear – protruded at a 45-degree angle. In the hotel's immediate environs were a car park and an open-air swimming pool for use by guests, interspersed with copses of trees, lawns and flower beds. From the outset, the hotel was planned with the possibility of subsequently adding an additional 100-room accommodation wing.

The exterior treatment was somewhat frugal for a building that, had it been in North America rather than austerity Britain, would surely have been designed to signal jet age glamour. Looking just like a new office block at a provincial factory or an up-to-date secondary school, it was clad in brick with metal-framed windows and coloured glass infill panels. Only a cast concrete canopy over the entrance, which was shaped like an aircraft wing, a row of flagpoles along the main frontage and a free-standing, American-style vertical name sign by the main road hinted at anything more international or exotic.

Ever since, such rows or groupings of flagpoles have become common features of hotels attracting international clienteles of jet air travellers. (By contrast, pre-war British seaside hotels typically had no more than a couple of flagpoles attached to their frontages which were used to re-inforce patriotism by flying the Union Flag). The use of flags to animate and make modern architecture 'festive' perhaps began at the 1930 Stockholm Exhibition – and was an approach frequently used at subsequent expos and as frontispieces for venues of international diplomacy, such as the United Nations, the European Economic Community or the Commonwealth. Flagpoles were inexpensive to install, yet looked impressive and satisfactorily orderly. For visiting guests arriving from afar, the presence of their national flag would make them feel welcome and secure. Furthermore, the hotel chain could always insert its own corporate flag among the others, reinforcing the importance of its brand in the minds of visitors and passers-by.

The Skyway's interior was distinctly American, it being the work of Mary Ornstein, the wife of Seaway Hotels' managing director, Charles 'Chuck' Ornstein. She chose a variety of up-to-date furniture and fabrics supplied by Hille, offset by ostentatious brass lamps, to give a sense of trans-Atlantic luxury and modernity. Consequently, the Skyway's internal atmosphere was much more swish than its façade treatment inferred; as we shall see, this would be a common trait of many British hotels developed in the ensuing decades. The *Caterer and Hotel Keeper* records that translucency and spaciousness, coupled with modern synthetic finishes and American furnishings, were among the distinguishing characteristics of the interiors:

> 'Two whole walls of the lounge are made entirely of glass… the reception desk… features contrasting veneer, timber, ebony and white Formica panelling. The floor is part-carpeted in soft shades of green, beige, black and pink and part terrazzo-covered. Many modernistic 'coconut' armchairs are scattered about the lounge and there are several choice pieces of statuary. The chairs, in green with white enamelled steel shells, are American-designed… Divided off from the lounge, behind a mahogany and glass screen, is the American cocktail lounge and bar,

with an attractive leather-upholstered crescent-shaped bar. Beyond the bar is the dining room – a well-illuminated area because two of its walls are made of glass… with fitted carpet of deep red and square black motifs. There is accommodation for 140 people on Albany dining chairs and at tables with heavy cast pedestals and tops in Formica light mahogany. There is 24-hour service… To the rear is the heated floodlit open air swimming pool, pear-shaped and claimed to be the only hotel swimming pool in London.'[163]

The bedrooms were decorated in turquoise, mauve, grey and gold stripes and all had American-sized baths and built-in furniture with mirrored fronts on the wardrobes. The large windows had full black-out, enabling jet-lagged guests to simulate night-time conditions whenever they chose.[164]

As a result of his work on the Skyway, Fitzroy Robinson became involved in several other hotel development projects. One was to replace the existing Cavendish Hotel in London's Jermyn Street with a new building boasting up-to-date facilities.[165] Another was to supersede the small family-run Yelton Hotel in Hastings with a 22-storey skyscraper hotel and apartment block.[166] Between May and September 1960, 30 million visitors were expected to stay at British seaside resorts, meaning that developers wished to cash in with projects such as this, but as room prices were relatively low, financiers were unwilling to underwrite large-scale hotel construction away from London or the more prosperous provincial cities.[167] The Skyway's building contractor, Bernard Sunley, was also an entrepreneurial property developer and perhaps as a result of his experience with the project, as we shall see, he too became enthusiastic about investing in hotel schemes.

Shortly, a second hotel for London Airport was built on a site close to the Skyway. The land on which it was built belonged to the Watney brewery and its intention had been to develop jointly with Graham Lyon another addition to its roadside motel chain. A shortage of credit coupled with an attractive offer from the J. Lyons hotel and catering company to lease the location caused a change of plan. By the latter 1950s, J. Lyons & Co had grown into Britain's largest and most prominent food manufacturing, restaurant and hotel company. Observing the possibilities resulting from rising car ownership and the growing popularity of jet air travel, in 1957, J. Lyons set up a new hotel-operating subsidiary called Palace Hotels (this used the 'surname' of the Strand Palace and Regent Palace in central London). It was this company that leased the Watney's London Airport plot for a new hotel, timing the project's completion to coincide with the opening of the airport's new Oceanic Terminal. This was developed specifically to handle long-haul international flights and was commissioned in 1961 (nowadays, this is Heathrow Terminal 3). The name Ariel Hotel was chosen following a competition among J. Lyons' staff.[168]

The Ariel was designed by Philip Russell Diplock and Associates with F.J. Wills & Sons as consultant architects; both firms were London-based and the latter had recently carried out minor renovation work on the Strand Palace and Regent Palace hotels. Born in 1927, Diplock had studied at Liverpool University's School of Architecture, beginning practice in 1950. The hotel was his firm's first large-scale project and remained arguably its best work. Subsequently, he became heavily involved in designing for property developers and much of his latter output – which included a high-rise block of flats in Margate and several major redevelopment schemes for Brighton, including the Churchill Square shopping precinct and Brighton Conference Centre – was widely disparaged on account of its incongruous scale and crude detailing. Subsequently, in the 1970s, Diplock briefly collaborated with an Oxford-based church architect, Peter Bosanquet, on a few fairly small and discreet Roman Catholic churches (he also supported church-related charities). In later years, he ceased architectural practice in favour of property development, moving to Sark in the Channel Islands, a well-known tax haven. It was indeed ironic that an architect whose typical designs were so disregarding of context in terms of scale and style should retreat somewhere as unspoiled, pastoral and bucolic as Sark.

The Ariel Hotel was a novel, circular building, four storeys high with a void in the middle, constructed around concrete framework. The *Architect and Building News* explained the rationale behind this arrangement in purely rational terms; according to its correspondent, this layout meant that there were relatively few rooms directly exposed to runway noise, yet the design was no doubt also preferred for aesthetic reasons as shape appeared sleekly futuristic and was thus easily distinguishable in customers' minds from the comparatively dreary-looking Skyway next door.[169] Public rooms were arranged around the ground floor, where there was a central 'courtyard garden', isolated acoustically from the noise of the airport runway.

The entrance foyer had two sets of automatic sliding plate glass doors, activated by pressure pads. Facing these was a curving feature staircase with a small 'water feature' beneath. The lifts and reception desk were on either side with a plate glass wall overlooking the courtyard garden. Such transparency, engendering a heightened sense of spaciousness, echoed the latest international hotel design practice. The restaurant was by a Chicago-based designer, Sam Horowitz, presumably employed in an attempt to out-do the Skyway's interiors. In both instances, the aim was to make American guests feel more at ease while delighting Britons with an added sense of trans-Atlantic glamour. Horowitz's contribution looked as Scandinavian as it did American, having modern wooden-framed furniture and Danish-style pendant lights. The Circle Inn bar, by contrast, combined 'the décor of the Victorian era with that of the present day' to give guests from overseas a taste of what a traditional English pub might be like (and thereby demonstrating international

The Ariel Hotel's sleek exterior, photographed when the building was nearing completion for publicity purposes (hence there are still barriers evident around the ground floor). To show its proximity to London, a typical red double-decker bus has been included.

modernism's apparent difficulty in reflecting local character).[170]

The three storeys above contained a total of 185 bedrooms, all with private bathrooms. These were ingeniously arranged with twin and double rooms around the perimeter of the hotel's 'doughnut' plan, a circular corridor and single rooms around the more constricted 'inner core', facing the courtyard. The rooms were relatively compact, some having sofa-beds but, as most guests would be staying for one night only while waiting to catch flights, or for onward travel, spaciousness was perhaps less important than in hotels elsewhere.

The Architect and Building News emphasised that the Ariel Hotel's external walls were particularly thick and well insulated for noise abatement purposes. Its entrance was flanked by expanses of white marble slabs and, on the floors above, the exterior was faced in white mosaic while the window frames were of teak; all of these materials commonly featured in recent works by the acclaimed Finnish modernist architect, Alvar Aalto, whose approaches to materials and detailing were certainly well worth emulating. The hotel's most important visual features were broad dark blue bands at first floor and roof height, unifying the drum-shape horizontally and making it appear to float above the recessed ground floor.

Functionally, aesthetically and commercially, the Ariel Hotel was an immediate and enduring success. Indeed, it was the first British post-war hotel to equal the better examples of recent international practice. At some point during the 1980s, the exterior was re-clad with an extra external layer of curtain walling; this somewhat impaired the original visual effect, but doubtless made the bedrooms even quieter than before.

Shortly after the Ariel was inaugurated, the construction of a third substantial London Airport hotel began in 1963. The proprietor was Charles Forte (born Carmine Monforte), an Italian émigré to Scotland, who had become a catering tycoon and who already was operating all of the food concessions in the airport's terminal buildings. Forte had learned the catering trade as a teenager in the early 1930s in seaside cafes operated by other members of his family at Weston-Super-Mare and Brighton. In 1935, aged 27, Forte had opened the Meadow Milk Bar on London's Regent Street. Soon, the energetic and entrepreneur was expanding his business with further outlets. Although Forte was interned on the Isle of Man as an 'enemy alien' for the duration of the Second World War, thereafter, as his wealth and influence grew, he became an 'establishment' figure. In 1949 he purchased the Criterion Brasserie at Piccadilly Circus and, two years later, he won a catering contract for the Festival of Britain. In 1954 he added the Café Royal, also in London, to his restaurant portfolio and four years thereafter he

Images showing the Ariel Hotel's entrance with plate glass sliding doors, part of the foyer with an ornamental pond plus a spiral staircase, and the restaurant. The latter featured both table service and an American diner-style over-the-counter service.

An advertisement for the Ariel Hotel, dating from around the time of its opening and emphasising the 'jet age comfort' to be experienced there.

entered the hotel trade, purchasing the Waldorf on Aldwych. Believing that people on the move were good sources of catering income, in 1960, Forte opened his first motorway service station at Newport Pagnell, by the M1 in Buckinghamshire and more of these soon followed.

So far as new hotel developments were concerned, Forte initially entered into an agreement with the Cardiff-based Rhymney Breweries Ltd to finance jointly the 40-room Dolphin Hotel in Swansea; this was completed in 1963. Occupying a long, narrow high street site, the three-storey structure was architecturally nondescript but, within, it was furnished with materials imported from Denmark, indicating Forte's belief in the importance of modern and attractive interior design to engender a welcoming atmosphere.[171] Having begun his career serving in Italian cafés, which were well-known for their glamorous and up-to-date interiors, Forte appears subsequently to have preferred focusing investment in internal decoration for the motorway service stations, hotels and other catering outlets, which his company went on to operate. For the most part, he seems to have viewed his buildings' architectural envelopes as mere 'boxes' in which attractive and profitable enterprises could be housed.

Forte's Hotel at London Airport was designed by a recently-established London-based architectural practice, Michael Lyell and Associates.[172] Born in 1924, Lyell had trained at the Architectural Association, being employed upon graduation by Wells Coates, the eminent Canadian émigré modernist whose 1930s architecture and industrial design output had done so much to promote the Modern Movement in Britain. In 1954, Wells Coates made the ambitious and hard-working Lyell a partner,

and, thereafter, the two were jointly credited with a number of villas in the Home Counties. Reflecting the picturesque design influences of the Festival of Britain – for which Wells Coates had designed the Telekinema – their architectural expression was softer and more respectful of context that had been typical of his pre-war output. By then, Wells Coates' health was failing and, following his death in 1958, Lyell set up his own practice, the office of which was in Knightsbridge.

Lyell was yet another youngish architect to have established

Forte's London Airport Hotel was the third to be completed there. The reception was designed in the Scandinavian manner with dining facilities located in a separate block in front of the main building. The latter utilised a variation on a standard design for Forte motorway service stations.

himself at a propitious moment at the beginning of a major property boom. Although Wells Coates was an influence, Lyell's own approach to architecture was far less idealistic as he embraced with enthusiasm the lucrative possibilities offered by large-scale commercial development. In restaurants and on the golf course, he proved highly adept at 'schmoozing' with potential clients.[173] Much of the design work, however, was carried out by a variety of partners and assistants, though frequently based on outline ideas supplied by Lyell himself. An early major scheme by Michael Lyell Associates was the Forum in Chester, which was a theatre, retail and office development submitted in 1961 but not constructed until the latter 1960s; alas, it was widely regarded as a disastrous intrusion into the town's centre.

Forte's London Airport Hotel was designed by Lyell's assistants Michael Philips, Arthur Wilter and Issy Spektor with interior design by Glen Reece. The architects were faced with a green field site where, unlike in Chester, the selection of textured pre-fabricated concrete panels and strictly regular fenestration could not be compared unfavourably with charming-looking historic edifices. Charles Forte demanded an efficient building, expressing particular disdain for the neighbouring Ariel Hotel because he felt that the wedge-shapes of its bedrooms wasted space unnecessarily and, in addition, would have been more expensive to outfit than rectilinear rooms. Consequently, Forte's London Airport Hotel was given a T-shaped layout, conceptually much like that of the Skyway, though Forte's was slightly the larger of the two hotels, having five storeys containing 128 single plus 152 twin rooms. In front of the hotel, adjacent to the main entrance, was single-storey block containing the restaurant, coffee shop and 'Autogrill' (a steakhouse concept already popular at Forte's motorway service stations). This structure had a roof consisting of shallow-pitched red-tiled pyramids – a feature also seen at Forte's roadside premises which was becoming a company trademark.[174]

The hotel's reception foyer and the adjoining lounge and cocktail bar were one-and-a-half storeys high and arranged in open plan, giving a welcome sensation of spaciousness, in contrast to the claustrophobia of an airliner cabin. On entering, visitors faced a white marble wall featuring a 12-foot-long plate glass panel, etched by the artist Michael Caddy with signs of the Zodiac and incorporating eleven clocks, showing the time in major cities around the world. The carpet was gold and this extended into the lounge and bar, where the counter was 40 feet long and illuminated so as to give an impression of floating in space. One wall was faced in panels of quartzite in which the mica glittered slightly. Adjacent to the reception counter was a car hire office. To the rear were large banquet and conference rooms, panelled in rosewood with folding partitions faced in moulded fiberglass panels. The bedrooms were panelled in Canadian black walnut and, like those of the neighbouring hotels, were heavily sound-proofed.[175] As with the Skyway, to the rear were landscaped gardens and a heated swimming pool. Forte soon announced plans for further similar hotels at Manchester and Glasgow airports. In the meantime, the company completed a Forte Motor Lodge in Oxford June 1964 with single-storey accommodation and another red pyramid roof on the grill and restaurant block.[176]

Forte's London Airport Hotel and all of his subsequent new hotels in Britain were built by Sir Robert McAlpine, whose firm took responsibility for managing the entire projects, including technical and interior outfitting. This approach saved effort for Forte and his own company's staff. Forte, however, quickly developed design guidelines for

The Forte-owned Excelsior Hotel at Manchester Airport; here too flags create a welcoming and festive initial impression.

what he considered to be the optimum bedroom and bathroom sizes and other details which the architects were expected to follow unquestioningly. These techniques – which became increasingly commonplace across the hotel sector as the 1960s progressed – enabled large and complex buildings to be built to a reliable schedule and with little budgetary risk for their operators.[177]

As soon as Forte's London Airport Hotel had been designed, Michael Lyell Associates was commissioned by Forte to design a further airport hotel at Manchester Airport. Named the Excelsior Hotel, a title subsequently used by Forte for other new hotels, it was completed in May 1965 and boasted 150 rooms in a four-storey accommodation block, faced with brick. The reception, public rooms and conference facilities were in a separate block, clad in vertically-ribbed cast concrete panels, facing the airport's access road.

In the second half of the 1960s, a convergence of service standards between motels and airport hotels took place. By then, the two types were serving similar clienteles due to jet air travel having been democratised by the introduction of larger planes with more capacity, thereby enabling cheaper ticket prices.

Notwithstanding the obviously air travel-associated nomenclature of the Canadian Skyway hotel brand, in 1966 the company opened its second British hotel in Southampton, close to one of the port's main entrances. This was to accommodate increasing numbers of cruise passengers and also those taking liner voyages who arrived days before their scheduled embarkation time. Between 1959 and 1961, many new passenger liners had entered service from the port – the *Canberra*, *Oriana*, *Transvaal Castle*, *Windsor Castle*, *Northern Star*, *France* and *Rotterdam* – all offering higher standards of shipboard accommodation than their predecessors. In future years, the numbers of Britons taking cruises was expected to grow exponentially.[178]

The design of the 10-storey Southampton Skyway was by the local architects, W.H. Saunders & Son, a firm established in 1922. They appear to have been inspired, at least to an extent, by the design of the

The Beachcomber Grill at the May Fair Hotel in London – an early example of a Polynesian-themed hotel interior in the UK.

Istanbul Hilton, which had been widely publicised in the British architectural press. Certainly the external detailing of the Skyway's 125-bedroom accommodation block – from which panoramic views across the city, the docks and over the River Solent could be enjoyed – was remarkably similar. In particular, the vertically-slatted grilles enclosing fire exit stairs at each end and the deep parapet at roof height were very Hilton-like. Within, the hotel's interiors were themed and this approach was also reminiscent of aspects of Hilton design, as well as some of the era's cruise ship interiors (themed approaches were also found in post-war Butlin's holiday camps). Inside the roof structure, there was a 'Polynesian'-themed bar and 'nightspot', the décor of which featured bamboo structures, 'tropical' foliage and canvas parasols. There, guests could 'drink and dance in exotic surroundings.'[179]

In the first half of the 1960s, there was an international trend for Polynesian-themed hotel, nightclub and restaurant interiors, a prominent, early British example being the Beachcomber Grill and Aloha Bar, inserted into London's May Fair Hotel in 1960. This had been devised by a film set and interior designer, Erik Blakemore, of Garnett, Cloughley, Blakemore and Associates, a London-based multi-disciplinary architecture and design practice, the other partners of which were the architects Patrick Garnett and Anthony Cloughley, Shortly after, Blakemore designed six similar South Seas-themed bars for various Butlin's holiday camps.

In part, the fashion for Polynesian styling may be attributable to American soldiers having experienced elements of Pacific island culture during the Second World War with those who subsequently entered the hospitality trade in the USA seeking to create similar 'tropical beach bar' aesthetics within premises there. The great popularity of Roger & Hammerstein's 1949 musical and 1958 film 'South Pacific' may also have been a factor. Another was that a 'Polynesian'-style setting could be relatively cheaply and quickly made with rough and fairly basic materials, and this had obvious commercial benefits (even if such facsimiles only passingly resembled 'the real thing'). In a sense, pastiches of the Polynesian style were arguably merely another manifestation of western design taking inspiration from the 'exoticism' of the East, a phenomenon that stretched back as far as the eighteenth century.

Adjacent to the Skyway's nightclub was the Nautical Bar, which had old lifeboats suspended over the counter and drinks barrels with brass hoops for tables. In the Solent Room Restaurant, located in the ground floor, there was polished wood panelling with strap-work in neo-Georgian style and framed illustrations of sail-powered British warships of yesteryear to evoke something of the atmosphere of a naval officers' wardroom.[180] Needless to say, the architectural press was deeply unamused by such 'lapses' of taste. The hotel also featured an outdoor heated swimming pool. The combination of themed décor and attractive leisure facilities, however, meant that guests checking in prior to embarking a liner or cruise ship could effectively extend their holiday by enjoying the hotel's own cruise ship-like facilities.

During the 1960s, as the British economy grew, foreign holiday travel became available to larger sections of the population. The growth of cruising was one manifestation of this, but so too was the development of charter-flights carrying 'package tourists' to Mediterranean resorts. The advent of charter flights led to a growth in the provision of hotel accommodation at British provincial airports. One such burgeoning airport was Birmingham where, in 1969, Forte added a second Excelsior Hotel to his chain by leasing the 30-year-old Birmingham Airport Hotel

124

The Skyway in Southampton was located close to the docks, the cranes of which can be seen to the left of the accommodation block, shown in (1). The interiors illustrated are (2) the Solent Room restaurant, (3) the Polynesian nightclub, (4) part of the foyer and (5) the Nautical Bar.

(described above) from the brewers Mitchells & Butlers. As the premises were considered ripe for expansion and modernisation, Forte commissioned Garnett, Cloughley, Blakemore and Associates to refurbish the interiors and to add a new wing with 66 additional rooms.[181]

They had recently attracted widespread attention for having designed flashy interiors for the 'Top of the Tower' revolving restaurant in London's Post Office Tower and for the Chelsea Drugstore bar and café. With shiny mirrored finishes, moulded fibreglass and pop art references, these projects were the epitome of 'Swinging London' stylishness. Thereafter, they designed Forte's Newport Pagnell, Scratchwood and Corley motorway service areas. The diversity of these projects, clients and expected customer demographics, as well as the memorable solutions achieved, shows a remarkably imaginative and un-snobbish approach to practice. Although retro-styling became increasingly commonplace in the latter 1960s, Garnett, Cloughley, Blakemore and Associates carried it off with more wit and finesse than most other designers of their era.

The Draitone Manor restaurant in the Excelsior Hotel at London Airport.

At the Birmingham Excelsior, the 1930s façade was partially obscured with a parabolic canopy, clad in shiny aluminium and studded with twinkling lights. The Art Deco interiors were stripped out entirely and replaced with new designs which mainly exemplified late 1960s design fashion while new bedroom wings were built to the rear. Soon after, Forte decided to expand the London Airport Hotel with additional accommodation wings and an enlarged restaurant complex and it too became an Excelsior. Although the hotel's original architects designed the shells for the new wings, again it was Garnett, Cloughley, Blakemore and Associates who devised their interiors. For the restaurant, Erik Blakemore elected to pay homage to a local neo-Georgian mansion, Draitone Manor, his design mixing elements of its ornate plasterwork with dark red walls, carpets, upholstery and a mirrored ceiling.[182] The scheme was carried through with such brio that it appeared surprisingly convincing, particularly once a significant quantity of alcohol had been consumed on a corporate expense account.

Hotels with multi-storey parking

By the mid-1960s, when Dr Beeching's rationalisation of British Rail was reducing the national network by a third, urban planners' infatuation with car culture reached its peak. Apart from motels at major road junctions, it was also felt necessary to build city centre hotels integrated with multi-storey car parking so that motorists arriving via the new urban dual-carriageways could find ample space for their cars next to overnight accommodation.

In 1963, Parcar Utilities Ltd, a Bristol-based developer of multi-storey car parks,

announced plans to build in the city a 228-bedroom hotel integrated with an adjacent multi-storey car park, from which drivers could access the bedroom accommodation directly. Its site was close to the docks, which were by then experiencing decline, meaning that land there was comparatively cheap and plentiful.[183] Completed as the Unicorn Hotel in the autumn of 1966 to a design by Kenneth Wakeford, Jarram and Harris, the hotel wing was faced in repetitive rows of moulded concrete facing panels while the parking element was contained within a criss-cross pattern of diagonal concrete lattice-work. The hotel's operator was The Rank Organisation, a sprawling leisure conglomerate hitherto best known for film-making and for running cinema chains. It had recently begun to diversify as an operator of motorway service stations and it was this division that ran the hotel. In 1964 Parcar announced plans for a further project with Rank to develop a similar hotel to the Unicorn in Gibraltar, but this did not come to fruition.[184]

Top and above: The Unicorn Hotel in Bristol, showing the accommodation block in the foreground with multi-storey car parking beyond; motorists could check into the hotel at the car park entrance, gaining direct access to the appropriate bedroom storey from the corresponding parking level.

In Leicester, the most radical example of a combined hotel and car park appeared in 1967. The Abbey Motor Hotel was operated by Scottish & Newcastle Breweries and occupied the top two storeys of the city's new Abbey Road multi-storey car park.[185] Initially, the hotel's 'rooftop' location and impressive views outward had novelty value but, soon, its sense of isolation above

Below left and right: The Abbey Road car park in Leicester with the Abbey Motor Hotel occupying its uppermost storeys; the structure has an awkward relationship with its immediate surroundings and the external design of the motel element appears not to have been resolved with any significant aesthetic consideration.

The Strathallan Hotel in the Birmingham suburb of Edgbaston and the Round House Hotel in Bournemouth were slight variations on a standard concept, featuring hotel accommodation above multi-storey parking.

numerous bleak concrete layers of parking spaces led to its decline. In 2012, it suffered a serious fire, as a result of which it was closed with the intention of demolition but, at the time of going to press, it remains derelict and is an unfortunate eyesore.

In March 1966, the *Caterer and Hotel Keeper* published a proposal by a company named Panorama Hotel Properties, for a circular, seven-storey, 100-room hotel for Bournemouth with two levels of car parking sandwiched between the ground floor public rooms and the bedroom storeys and restaurant.[186] Its site, which was at a road junction to the north of the town centre, had previously been occupied by the 1888-vintage Imperial Hotel, which was demolished in its entirety. The new property was designed by the architects Duke & Simpson and named the Round House, its lessee being the Hall Woodhouse brewery. Upon completion in April 1969, it was Bournemouth's first new hotel for over thirty years.[187]

The rotunda shape and the detailing of the façades on the bedroom levels showed obvious similarities to the Ariel Hotel at London Airport. The parking levels were accessed via internal ramps and clad in honeycomb concrete panels. The design's advantage was that all the outside rooms enjoyed elevated views of the townscape but unfortunately those facing inward to the central light well had only a dreary outlook to other bedroom windows and exposed vertical services. Nonetheless, the Round House concept undoubtedly aspired towards a kind of science fiction urban future, in comparison with which the reality experienced by guests unfortunately fell somewhat short.

Subsequently, Duke & Simpson designed for Scottish & Newcastle Breweries the very similar Strathallan Hotel in the Birmingham suburb of Edgbaston and this opened in 1971 (see below). Yet, central Bournemouth and a Birmingham suburb were very different types of urban context to which neither hotel specifically responded. These were buildings which related primarily to the universality of car culture, rather than to any particular locale.

A series of views of the Carlton Tower Hotel in London; (1) shows the foyer when new, with Feliks Topolski's glass mural filling the right-hand wall around the reception desk, (3) shows the cocktail bar and (4), a penthouse suite. The advertisement for the hotel in (2) links its fine appointments with proximity to Buckingham Palace. Image (5) is a recent view of the exterior, facing Cadogan Square and showing Michael Rosenauer's precise attention to materials, proportion and the arrangement of the fenestration.

CHAPTER 7

The first 'skyscraper' hotels in London's West End

Hotels were the first commercial edifices to pierce the low-rise horizontality of post-war central London. The importation of design models that were very obviously American in origin aroused strong passions and hotels – as much as office towers – became notorious focal points for impassioned debates about the capital's redevelopment, future appearance and character. Since the opening of the Westbury in Bond Street, little new hotel accommodation had been built in the West End, even although numbers of visiting tourists continued to increase year on year.

One relatively small project to come to fruition in 1958 was an extension for the 1911-vintage Washington Hotel in Curzon Street in Mayfair; this was designed by Bronek Katz and his architectural partner, Reginald Vaughan. Katz, who was an émigré from Poland, had previously worked in the UK for Walter Gropius and Maxwell Fry, in whose office Vaughan was also employed. Post-war, Katz and Vaughan designed the 'Homes and Gardens' exhibit at the Festival of Britain, as well as shops and overseas factory housing for the Bata shoe company. The Washington Hotel annexe, though no taller than the existing building, had a distinctly vertical emphasis, its exterior being faced in pale grey granite panels with black spandrels, teak and aluminium window frames and blue glass infill panels. The crisp detailing and use of black framing and shadow-gaps continued throughout the interior. Top floor rooms were set back with private balconies. Katz – who had tended to specialise in particular areas of practice (exhibition design, shoe shops and so on) might also have made hotels a further speciality but, alas, he died in 1960 in a skiing accident, just when a post-war hotel construction boom was starting to gain momentum.

Opened in 1961, the 318-bedroom Carlton Tower Hotel, adjacent to Cadogan Gardens in Chelsea, was a building of an altogether more impressive magnitude; indeed, it was the first high-rise structure in central London.[188] The hotel was the one realised fragment of a mid-1950s grand project by the landowner, William Gerald Charles Cadogan, the 7th Earl of Cadogan, to replace most of Sloane Street and Sloane Square with a neo-Corbusian development of high-rise commercial and residential blocks, connected by elevated walkways. The masterplan for this scheme was prepared jointly by the architects J. Douglas Matthews and Partners and the architect and planner Lionel Brett (later Lord Esher). Unsurprisingly, the scheme proved highly controversial and an influential local amenity group, The Chelsea Society, campaigned vigorously for it to be scrapped. Although it succeeded in achieving this aim in 1959, the project for the Carlton Tower had already gained assent and so proceeded as intended.

The 1958 extension to the Washington Hotel in Curzon Street with the original building to the rear; note the roof terrace around the top floor suites.

In 1953, the Chelsea Property Company had identified the hotel's rectangular site, which was at that time occupied by a neglected Georgian terrace, and they contacted the Cadogan Estate with a view to acquiring the lease. Negotiations were protracted and eventually an American partner was found in the Hotel Corporation of America – a grandly-titled upstart established only in 1956 by a Bostonian property development entrepreneur, Sonny Sonnabend, who was the son of a jeweller from Austria. In the short time since its formation, Sonnabend's hotel business had expanded quickly and by 1960 it was operating several prestigious hotels, including the Plaza in New York. A further project partner and investor in the Carlton Tower project was the construction company, Sir Robert McAlpine, which commissioned the architect of the Westbury Hotel, Michael Rosenauer, to produce a suitable design. Perhaps inspired by his own American experiences and by a belief that the future of commercial development lay with tall buildings, Rosenauer's solution was quite revolutionary, at least for a London context.

The hotel consisted of three main elements, the centrepiece of which was an eighteen-storey accommodation tower, on either side of which were blocks of ten- and three storeys. The entire ground and first floors were given over to a complex of hallways and public rooms. As with Rosenauer's Time-Life and Westbury buildings, the Carlton Tower's exterior treatment was rather understated, its soaring flat stone-clad façades being punctuated by a rhythmic pattern, alternating windows and balconies with patio doors, from which guests could enjoy unprecedented views across central London. At the base of the tower, adjacent to the entrance, were bas relief sculptures by Elizabeth Frink, one of Britain's most sought-after modern sculptors.

The hotel's interiors were designed by Henry End, an Englishman who had moved to California after the Second World War, where he had founded a successful interior design consultancy in Los Angeles. An acknowledged hotel design expert, he would subsequently publish the *Interiors Book of Hotels and Motor Hotels*, which illustrated the latest world-wide (though American dominated) trends in design and decoration. As Henry End observed, producing spaces reconciling American-inflected international practices with a sense of locale while avoiding cliché was a challenge:

> 'In designing the Carlton Tower, caution was needed against the trap of trying to copy British period design, something the British themselves are best at. A real effort was made to avoid the use of synthetics, relying instead on natural materials turned out by British craftsmen. In some cases, materials were imported and crafted according to designs from our office. There were rosewoods from Bombay, silks from Italy and Thailand… The art work with its genuine flavour of British life helps greatly in keeping the Carlton Tower from presenting such an international picture that the guest might forget he is in England. All the furnishings in the hotel were designed to give a contemporary feeling which would not fall completely in the international idiom. They were also designed to be sumptuous without violating the British desire for understatement.'[189]

In contrast to the Westbury's opulent but somewhat kitsch neo-Regency interiors, for the Carlton Tower, End used a distinctly 'California modern' approach. The lobby, fronted by expanses of plate glass, was spacious with veined white Italian marble flooring and indirect lighting playing off a flat, textured ceiling. Colours were muted; large leather-upholstered lounge chairs in the manner of Mies van der Rohe were located around glass-topped coffee tables. The inner wall, with a long horizontal slot for the reception counter, was tiled with a decorative panel in glass depicting London scenes by Feliks Topolski, a Polish émigré artist who had been commissioned by Buckingham Palace to paint murals commemorating the coronation. This royal connection may have made him an attractive choice for the hotel's American owner. The columns in front of Topolski's panel were rectangular and faced in rosewood.[190]

Adjoining the lobby was a steak restaurant, the Rib Room with a wall of windows facing Cadogan Place. Its dark red colour scheme was intended to conjure 'an atmosphere of masculine hearty good cheer.' It too had Topolski artworks on the walls, this time 'caricatures' of typical Londoners.[191] The *Caterer and Hotel Keeper* records:

> 'Here, prime beef is actually carved in the room beneath a copper canopy. English oak panelling and regimental red felt cover the walls… The whole atmosphere is one of deep sophistication with the ruby red glass candle lamps… Chairs are of teak and black leather from Denmark…'[192]

The Chelsea Room, on the first floor, offered French cuisine in surroundings of 'subdued opulence', while the ballroom, adjacent, recalled 'the grandeur of a historic past amid today's functional beauty.'[193] What this amounted to was a Miesian combination of flat ceilings and dark veneered wall panelling with slim shadow gaps, juxtaposed with chandeliers and Austrian 'festoon' blinds. This was, of course, the typical American international luxury hotel aesthetic of the period – but it was new to London. On the Carlton Tower's topmost floor, there were a number of large, open-plan suites with floor-to-ceiling, edge-to-edge glazing, enabling spectacular panoramic views of London, while the adjacent lower block's uppermost level had conference-function rooms overlooking The Mall and Buckingham Palace.

Despite initial scepticism, as completed, the Carlton Tower was a splendid hotel – suave, sophisticated, immaculately-detailed and expensive-looking. Although the exterior survives today much as Rosenauer first designed it and has withstood the test of time superbly well, sadly, little of Henry End's beautiful interiors remain; even the Topolski reception panelling has been ripped out and replaced with generic neo-Georgian woodwork, stylistically quite inappropriate in such an advanced building.

While the Carlton Tower was under construction, even bolder redevelopment schemes were announced for other substantial tracts of central London. Next to Royal Festival Hall on the South Bank, for example, plans were announced for a very large, rectilinear hotel and office development. A skyscraper hotel was also proposed for Hammersmith, to be designed by Gollins, Melvin, Ward & Partners.[194] Shortly after, a yet more ambitious redevelopment scheme was announced for Piccadilly Circus, at the centre of which was a vast slab-block hotel with 1,000 rooms. This had been drawn up by the influential architect and urban planner, Sir William Holford, who was a vocal supporter of rebuilding British cities along Corbusian lines to aid the flow of road traffic. A rival scheme for Piccadilly included a 12-sided hotel tower, designed by Kuok Choo Soo, Courage Tobogo and Rory Westmaas – but, perhaps fortunately, none of these projects came to fruition.[195]

In London, bringing about any major redevelopment required large amounts of capital, great determination, considerable political and diplomatic skills, a lack of shame in bullying opponents into submission whenever necessary and vast reserves of patience. The individuals behind London's next high-rise hotel, the Hilton, would demonstrate all of these traits. The project was to prove every bit as controversial and, as we shall see, took far longer to materialise than its promoters ever anticipated.

As the American academic Annabel Jane Wharton has argued, Hilton's expansion

Views of the London Hilton when newly completed in 1963, showing (1) the exterior, (2) the entrance with twinkling lighting built into the soffit and plate glass doors and (3) The London Tavern.

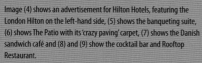

Image (4) shows an advertisement for Hilton Hotels, featuring the London Hilton on the left-hand side, (5) shows the banqueting suite, (6) shows The Patio with its 'crazy paving' carpet, (7) shows the Danish sandwich café and (8) and (9) show the cocktail bar and Rooftop Restaurant.

outwith the USA was not only related to the jet age's bringing about a requirement for up-to-date luxury hotel accommodation in destination cities but also to a desire shared by Conrad Hilton and the US Government to demonstrate overseas the superiority of American technology, hospitality and style over that of the Soviet Union.[196] Thus, the European cities selected as early recipients of 'International Hiltons' – Istanbul, Cairo, Athens and Berlin – were all relatively near to the Cold War's front line, or in countries where there was an American perception of an imminent Communist threat. The buildings were all financed locally, either by the host state or private investors rather than by the Hilton Corporation itself (though American foreign aid and loans guaranteed by the USA also were sometimes used). Hilton, however, retained complete oversight of each hotel's design and operational management, receiving a third of the profits. Subsequently, this approach to contracting became widespread throughout the international hotel industry.[197]

In London –another relatively early recipient of a Hilton in 1963 – the situation was different, it being a city already popular with American business travellers and tourists and the capital of a vital military and diplomatic ally. The London Hilton was one of a number of International Hiltons subsequently developed in western European capital cities, others being in Paris, Amsterdam and Rome. Wharton records that, as early as 1950, Conrad Hilton had sought to build a hotel in London. Notwithstanding ongoing strict rationing of materials for 'luxury' buildings, the Board of Trade had decided to prioritise the construction of one new hotel. Fortuitously, Hilton representatives attending a congress in Nice encountered Sir Francis Towle, whose company, Gordon Hotels Ltd, had developed the Dorchester Hotel in the early 1930s and had a great enthusiasm for up-to-date American hotel design. They hatched a plan to collaborate in developing an 80,000 square foot site owned by Prudential Assurance at an unidentified location in central London with Gordon Hotels investing 60% of the required capital.[198] Although this proposal failed to come to fruition, in October 1953, Hilton announced in the *New York Times* the development of a 550-room London hotel – but probably due to the complexities of obtaining land, planning permission and building permits plus the fact that – unlike in the cases of Istanbul, Cairo or Athens – the British Government would not become involved as a major sponsor, this project likewise failed to materialise.[199] (By contrast, the fact that the Westbury's was financed solely with American capital overcame building licensing difficulties.)

In 1955, Conrad Hilton was contacted by Charles Clore, a London-based impresario, business tycoon and property entrepreneur, who wished Hilton to become a partner in a take-over bid he was planning for London's Grosvenor House Hotel; the plan was that, should the outcome be successful, the two would share the hotel's profits between them.

Small in stature, irascible in temperament, cynical in nature and fiercely ambitious in his desire for wealth, Clore was the son of a successful tailor from London's East End. During the 1930s he had invested in cinemas in Walthamstow and Cricklewood and in 1937 had taken a cheap lease on the struggling Prince of Wales Theatre in Coventry Street, near Leicester Square, which he had turned around by staging 'non-stop revues' with fashionable, high-kicking chorus lines. These had proved so popular that soon Clore was in a position to replace it with a new theatre of almost twice the original's capacity. During the Second World War, he had earned a fortune from his investment in a South African gold mine, and used the proceeds to buy bomb sites in London for subsequent redevelopment. After the war, Clore had continued to make diverse property and business acquisitions; asset-stripping to release short-term value became a familiar hallmark of his approach. In 1953, Clore had joined forces with a rival property developer, Harold Samuel, to mount a hostile take-over of the Savoy Hotel Group – which owned the Savoy, Berkeley and Claridge's hotels – but they were thwarted when Savoy's directors controversially handed control to their own staff pension fund, thereby freezing out the two corporate raiders.[200] Evidently, Clore's appetite for hotels had been whetted, however.

Clore's attempt with Hilton to win the Grosvenor House Hotel also failed as not enough shareholders were convinced to sell out and so Hilton withdrew his support, forcing Clore to concede defeat.[201] Shortly thereafter, however, Clore and Hilton must have decided instead to develop jointly a new London hotel of their own.

During the latter 1950s, Clore continued to attempt corporate raids; he won control of the shoemaker Sears, but failed to acquire the prestigious Selfridge's department store on Oxford Street. Clore's mercenary boardroom interventions to extract the highest possible dividends made him very popular among investors and so he had little difficulty in raising capital, no matter what the effect of his parsimony was on the long-term health of the businesses he controlled. So far as property development was concerned, Clore masterminded a number of controversial schemes, benefitting from the removal of post-war licensing and Harold Macmillan's Conservative government's entrepreneurship-friendly policies.

Hilton's discussions with Clore regarding their London hotel project proved to be lengthy and convoluted; Clore was a tough negotiator who insisted that Hilton should fund half the cost of the project, rather than claiming a third of the profit through his preferred 'franchise' model for hotels outwith the USA. Clutterbuck and Devine's biography of Clore records that:

> 'For some time, it looked as though negotiations with Hilton would come to nothing… Unless [Clore] could show a clear income from the building, he would not be able to persuade the [investment] institutions to provide the cash to construct it… The Hilton negotiators improved their offer a number of times, but always based on the same formula. In desperation, [Clore] persuaded Conrad Hilton himself to come over… Eventually [Clore] snapped 'This is London, England, not Addis Ababa. And here you'll pay the rent.' Hilton stared at him for a moment, then nodded and said 'it's a deal.' The rent would be based on the cost of the building.'[202]

In 1957, initial design drawings for the London Hilton were produced but whereas its continental namesakes benefitted from expansive sites with long street frontages and, often, open space across which their façades could be viewed, the London hotel was required to fit within a relatively cramped location near the foot of Park Lane, the environs of which already boasted a number of large hotels. The development plot was created by Clore through combining damaged properties and bomb sites he had previously purchased. For overseas tourists, favourite shopping and museum attractions – Oxford Street, Harrods and The Royal Academy – were conveniently close at hand and the hotel would overlook the leafy expanses of Hyde Park. To gain enough capacity, the obvious solution was to build upward and so a 34-storey skyscraper was proposed. This consisted of a two-floor podium, from which rose a tower containing 700 rooms that was crescent-shaped in plan, the form being chosen so that the maximum possible number of rooms could have views over Hyde Park. Thus, although the site's length on

Park Lane was only 180 feet, the convex façade gave 216 feet on the bedroom storeys.[203] As this would be London's tallest building, dwarfing the height of distant St Paul's Cathedral, and the city's first proper skyscraper, the Hilton/Clore proposal enraged many influential Londoners – some of whom worried that the hotel would enable guests with binoculars to spy through the windows of Buckingham Palace. A public enquiry was therefore commenced in November 1957 and in May 1958, the London County Council voted against granting planning permission.[204] The LCC did, however, concede that a hotel of some sort should indeed be built on the site selected for the Hilton. Yet, for influential naysayers, the idea of an American-owned and -branded hotel dominating the West London skyline may have felt too much like US cultural imperialism. In the wake of the recent Suez Crisis – when the USA had supported Egypt's nationalisation of the Suez Canal in the face of British and French objections – popular sentiment in Britain had recently hardened against America. (Elsewhere in London, other very tall buildings were being given permission, most notably the 32-storey Millbank Tower, finished in 1963, and the 37-storey Post Office Tower, completed in 1965.)

Consequently, Hilton and Clore were forced to produce a revised design, this time with a smaller tower that was Y-shaped in plan and thus with concave façades, which not only appeared much less imposing than the original proposal but also had 100 fewer rooms. In scale, the hotel remained grandiose, even though its architectural expression was now rather apologetic. This scheme was produced by one of Clore's regular associates, an architect by name of Sidney Kaye. Born in 1915, he had trained at the Brixton School of Building and at the London Polytechnic. As a young man, Kaye had first encountered Clore when working for Lewis Solomon, Son & Joseph, which had carried out a number of early Clore property conversion projects. When the senior partner, Joseph Morris, died, Kaye, who was then a junior partner, inherited the business. Evidently, Clore was impressed by Kaye's eagerness to please and, more especially, to work strictly within an agreed budget. Within a short time, thanks to Clore's patronage, Kaye's architectural practice grew from ten assistants to over 100 with Clore's development companies as its major client. Little archival material exists on Kaye, who died in 1992, though Clutterbuck and Devine's biography of Clore does contain an insightful interview in which Kaye recalls Clore as having been:

> 'A man who put up a very brusque front and was difficult to get close to. His time was limited and in spite of the enormous amount of business our practice had with him, I don't recall being with him in his office at any time for more than five minutes…'[205]

Furthermore Clutterbuck and Devine record that:

> 'Clore approached construction with the eye of a financier. He rarely felt any aesthetic interest in the buildings he constructed; so long as a building yielded a comfortable profit, was put up by the promised date and fulfilled its purpose, his task was done. Many of the office buildings he developed are strikingly plain and functional… Clore…didn't believe in any great architectural triumphs which result in bankruptcy.'[206]

Several of Kaye's designs for speculative office blocks showed the influence of commercial work by Ludwig Mies van der Rohe – albeit without the great German-American architect's concern for proportion, luxurious materials and precision of detailing. Shorn of these qualities, a superficial veneer of Miesian minimalism could be achieved relatively cheaply, giving a profiteering developer buildings that appeared satisfactorily 'up-to-date' and 'international' in style. In a rare 1970 interview by *Architect and Building News*, Kaye emphasised the prime importance of profitability which he considered the most objectively measurable sign of a building's success.[207] An obituary written in 1992 by Kaye's former architectural partner, Eric Firmin, recalled his pride in gaining the Hilton commission and in the hotel's subsequent economic performance, but says nothing about his thoughts on the building itself.[208] Kaye's evident belief that buildings were primarily 'beautiful' on the balance sheet was actually a perfect functionalist argument – but it ran contrary to architecture's historic and modern aspiration to represent and perpetuate 'high culture' and to be considered as 'the Mother of the Arts.'

Although the Royal Fine Arts Commission objected to the latest design proposal for the London Hilton and sought to persuade the LCC to limit any development to a height of no more than 100 feet, in 1960 the pro-business Conservative government of Harold Macmillan intervened to over-rule both it and the local authority, giving the Hilton project permission to proceed at last.[209]

Clutterbuck and Devine's interview with Sidney Kaye records that:

'The agreement with Hilton was not without stringent conditions. Hilton wanted the hotel built within a tight time schedule of two years, in order to catch the summer tourist trade, and to his specifications. The annual rental would depend on the cost of the building, then estimated at £4 million. Hilton was taking no chances and put pressure on Clore to start construction almost immediately. After all, the longer the delay, the higher the costs; and the higher the costs, the greater the rent. Even though Kaye's plans were far from finalised, the bulldozers moved in.

"Can you imagine the quandary I was in, in case the building was over the budget?", Kaye asks. In his view, the building was under-priced by £1 million. The Hilton management breathed heavily down everyone's neck and asked Kaye how many hotels he had built. "None", was the reply. From start to finish, the building of London's most prestigious hotel was a stressful affair. It was a nightmare keeping to the budget with everything half decided upon. Workmen, architects and surveyors were all working under severe pressure. While the foundations were being laid, adjustments were still being made to the design drawings.

Kaye chose a cement render as the cheapest finish to the upper walls enclosing the hotel's ballroom. "Then the contractor said to me "why don't you use reconstructed stone? I've got a special deal with a company." I re-did the drawings and got blasted for causing an increase in price… The final bill for the hotel came in at £4.5 million, only marginally above the budget."'[210]

Whereas the other International Hiltons were all impressive works by significant American and European Modernist architects, aesthetically and experientially, the London hotel was a disappointment in comparison. Although its podium was crisply detailed in the 'International Style', the tower rising above not only appeared deflated due to its concave façades but also it was incoherently detailed, having rather clumsy Portland stone-faced balconies protruding from its vertices that bore little relation to the design of the curtain walling adjacent. This was framed in gold and black anodised aluminium, the whole ensemble appearing fiddly and failing to make a clear architectural statement. The building's roof-scape appeared particularly ill-resolved, it consisting of a series of relatively small and uncoordinated concrete lumps, whereas either a clean silhouette or a dramatically sculptural solution *à la* Le Corbusier would surely have been preferable. While the floors containing bedrooms were ingeniously laid out, the public circulation spaces within the podium were rather cramped in comparison with those of other Hiltons.

Most of the interior design was by Hilton's in-house specialist, David T. Williams. Guests entered the hotel through frameless plate glass automatic sliding doors. Following the tower's structural grid, the lobby was Y-shaped with an elevator bank towards the rear and check-in and concierge desks to either side. While the internal finishes were of high quality – both floor and walls were panelled with slabs of Botticino marble with rosewood detailing – the space was too small in both its horizontal and vertical dimensions and so lacked the sense of grandeur that guests who had stayed elsewhere in the Hilton chain would have come to expect. The hotel's vertical circulation was also under-dimensioned; to save money it had only four elevators, rather than the six recommended by Sidney Kaye. In the two unused lift spaces on each bedroom floor, Kaye was asked by Clore to squeeze in two additional rooms, rather than making them into lounges for adjacent rooms as had been his wish. As Clutterbuck and Devine record:

> 'Some years later, Hilton, realising they would need to spend money putting sound insulation in the bedrooms nearer the lifts, tried to make Clore pay for his own earlier penny-pinching. He arranged for Clore to stay in one of these bedrooms… Clore… saw through Hilton's ploy to make him, as the freeholder, pay for the noise insulation. Guests in the rooms around the lifts continue to pass uncomfortable nights.'[211]

(Nowadays, the two outer lifts, closest to these rooms, are switched off during the night, thereby resolving this problem.[212])

Back on the ground floor, the space to the north of the lobby contained 'The London Tavern', which was an informal (though expensive) steakhouse restaurant, attempting to recreate some of the atmosphere of an old coaching inn, albeit within a modernist design framework. Its walls were lined with rustic facing brick, the bar canopy was of beaten copper, the ceiling was finished in dark slatted timber and the furniture combined some of the characteristics of up-to-date Scandinavian design with a nod to the English vernacular. Janus-like, it simultaneously endeavoured to look forward and back, giving foreign guests a very sanitised and air conditioned 'hint' of what was supposed to be traditional London-style hospitality. On the other side of the entrance was St George's Bar and it too attempted a modern re-working of 'Olde England' with etched glass panels of St George and the Dragon by the Edinburgh artist Don Pottinger to the rear of the bar counter. Beyond the elevators was 'The Patio', a double-height lounge space which served as a vestibule for the very large banqueting suite further behind; this facility filled the rear half of the hotel's site at first and second floor level, above a car park. 'The Patio' had potted plants, Spanish-style lighting sconces and balustrades and its carpeting had a 'crazy paving' pattern, somewhat resembling the interior design approach of some British colonial passenger liners and cruise ships of the same era. On the first floor, facing Hyde Park, was The International Restaurant, the hotel's main dining room, which was intended to present a variety of global cuisines, changing daily on a rolling basis. Its walls incorporated four sets of vertical sliding panels which were painted with murals depicting North American, Mediterranean, Central and South American scenes, any one of which could be selected to modify the room's character according to the theme desired on a particular day. Staff uniforms, menus and coloured 'mood lighting' could likewise be adjusted to enhance the desired effect. On 'Oriental' evenings, for instance, the waiters wore British 'Raj' tunics and so British imperialism was nostalgically represented, albeit within an Americanised globalising framework.[213]

The interior design of the banqueting suite and of the top-storey Rooftop Restaurant was given over to a different architects' firm, Casson-Conder Associates. It was a prominent and respected London-based practice, co-led by Sir Hugh Casson who was at that time among Britain's best known design personalities. As well as being a practicing architect, Casson was also an architectural journalist, cartoonist, educator and 'public figure' who had first come to widespread prominence as Director of Architecture of the South Bank Festival of Britain exhibition. The Hilton's Rooftop Restaurant – offering spectacular views across London – and its banqueting suite were widely marketed as key features. The former space was reminiscent of Casson's interior design work for the P&O liner *Canberra*, having rich woodwork and dark, saturated upholstery colours. The banqueting suite, meanwhile, was promoted as a 'wonder' of up-to-date servicing, design and technology and the fact that a 'known name' such as Casson had been commissioned to decorate it only added to its cachet. At the entrance, Casson commissioned a tapestry by a former Royal College of Art student of his, Joyce Conwy Evans, and this was woven by Dovecot Studios in Edinburgh.[214] A further notable space on the ground floor was a Danish sandwich café, the interior of which was finished with ceramic wall decorations by the Danish artist and craftsman Bjørn Wiinblad.[215] When the London Hilton was new, Danish cuisine was being widely promoted by the country's Ministry of Agriculture and open sandwiches ('smørrebrod') were considered the height of good taste in every sense. This situation echoed the international acclaim for Scandinavian architecture, design and lifestyle in general, all of which the café's interior sought to reflect. In the basement beneath – and in complete contrast stylistically – was a Polynesian themed restaurant called 'Trader Vic's', the 'exotic' décor of which featured bamboo framing, fabric panels, straw parasols and other 'tropical' decorations. Its inclusion was probably a riposte to the highly popular Beachcomber Grill and Aloha Bar at the May Fair Hotel in Berkeley Square which, since opening in 1960, had become a popular haunt of celebrities and London's fashionable set. Trader Vic's at the Hilton was, however, politely ignored by such architectural critics as deigned to write about the hotel at all when it opened, yet it actually proved to be among its most successful facilities and is indeed the only original interior to survive today. Staff uniforms for the hotel's approximately 700 employees were designed by Hardy Amies, H.M. The Queen's favourite couturier.[216]

Upon completion, the London Hilton was reputedly the biggest hotel in Europe in terms of its overnight capacity (though within months, it was usurped by the Westbury in Brussels).[217] Yet, despite its size and the difficulties overcome in bringing it to fruition, it did not even seem to find favour with Clore's closest business associates, who far preferred entertaining at the considerably more spacious and grand Dorchester further along Park Lane. Clore's colleague, Charles Gordon, records in his biography of the property developer:

> 'We strolled down Curzon Street to the Mirabelle [an exclusive Mayfair restaurant]…The Hilton's arrogant tower smirked as if it was signalling to us from Clore. Peter [Folliss, another of Clore's business acquaintances] and I looked up and smirked back. 'I would never stay there if you paid me,' said Peter with unusual fervour. We sat down at the Mirabelle, the *maitre d'* put Peter's drink on the table without asking.'[218]

Arriviste and rather venal though the Hilton's British owners were, evidently they had quickly developed an aristocratic sense of entitlement and a strong desire for separation from 'ordinary people' – even those of the sort who were Hilton guests.

While the London Hilton was nearing completion, Charles Clore was already involved in the development of a further large hotel at the opposite end of Hyde Park, on Kensington High Street, adjacent to Kensington Palace Gardens. This occupied the cleared site of the bomb-damaged Royal Palace Hotel, which was in the ownership of City Centre Properties, a company established in 1955 by one of Clore's rival property development entrepreneurs, Jack Cotton. His initial wealth had been made in Birmingham, where, in the early 1930s, he had bought land on the urban fringes from farmers to sell on at a profit to builders of suburban housing estates. Post-war, he moved to London, establishing City Centre Properties in 1955 and becoming, like Charles Clore, a multi-millionaire. Cotton ran his business from a suite in the Dorchester Hotel and, in 1960, he and Clore merged their London property interests, retaining the City Centre Properties name.

The hotel project had been initiated by Cotton in 1961 and was to have formed part of a much larger mixed development, in addition containing offices and retail space. As architect, Cotton and Clore chose the suave but famously iron-willed Colonel Richard Seifert. He too was very wealthy thanks to his recent collaborations with various London property developers, whom he sought to oblige with the most lucrative design solutions, sometimes at the expense of considerations such as continuity of streetscape and relationship to context. Elain Harwood states that 'Seifert credited his war service with honing his confidence and management skills.'[219] Certainly, he gained a formidable reputation for holding seemingly every detail of a project at his fingertips and, with the haughty authority of a military officer, politely instructing planners to accept whatever his practice and clients wished to see constructed. Seifert stated that 'commerce… offers the architect a completely new role as a financial wizard capable of getting the most out of the development, the client and the authorities.'[220] Until the late 1950s, Seifert's practice had been small and his output of housing and small offices was mainly traditional in style. A design for a substantial office block on Marylebone Road, Woolworth House, then greatly impressed the property developer Harry Hyams, who thereafter used Seifert's firm as architects for subsequent, even larger schemes. To handle this work, the number of staff Seifert employed grew exponentially from a dozen in the mid-1950s to around 300 in 1969. Of Seifert's employees, the key designer was George Marsh who was responsible for coordinating most of the practice's output. Interviewed in retirement by Elain Harwood, he recounted how Seifert's own office space was fitted with hidden microphones, connected to a loudspeaker in the main drawing office, so that clients' wishes could be relayed live. That way, Seifert's teams of architects could immediately begin sketching suitable ideas for showing clients immediately after their supposedly 'private' meetings with Seifert.[221]

As *The Architect and Building News* recorded in 1965, in Kensington, Seifert and City Centre Properties:

> '…Were not given an easy time when their plans were submitted more than four years ago. The hotel is all that remains of a great bulk of proposed building. Part of the scheme was opposed by the Kensington Society because the 250 ft tower proposed would have dwarfed St Mary Abbots, and it was eventually rejected by the LCC. Although the hotel was given the go-ahead, the developers were made

to lop 73 ft off the height, so that no-one in it would be able to see into the grounds of Kensington Palace. The architect rescued the lost space by driving the building 40 ft down and thus finding room for three more floors for parking, conference rooms, a banqueting hall, a coffee bar and grill room.'[222]

Seifert's staff managed to include these latter facilities by half-burying below ground the floor immediately beneath the main entrance level so that only the windows protruded. Consequently, the hotel's entrance, on the floor above, was accessed via ramped approaches. Furthermore, the storeys above ground had the lowest possible floor-to-ceiling heights to enable as many to be fitted in as possible. The hotel was to have 527-bedrooms and would be known as the Royal Garden.

While intense efforts were being made to maximise the commercially viable floor area of what would be Britain's largest hotel in terms of capacity, there was trouble within City Centre Properties as Clore and Cotton had a clash of personalities. Where Clore was self-contained and detail-focused, Cotton was flamboyant in his risk-taking. Clore soon became infuriated by what he saw as Cotton's lack of precision. The outcome was that Cotton was out-manoeuvred then ousted by Clore and so by 1963 – when construction of the new hotel in Kensington began – Clore was in sole charge of the company. Cotton withdrew altogether and, within a year, had drunk himself to death.[223]

Outside and within, the Royal Garden Hotel was unapologetically brash; even the *Architect and Building News* – rarely the most trenchant critic of new buildings – commented on its 'startling presence and jolly vulgarity.'[224] It consisted of a pair of rectangular 10-storey, concrete-framed blocks, forming a T-shape with a courtyard filling the space in front, giving the hotel an awkward relationship with Kensington High Street. The *Architect and Building News* interpreted its being set back from the street as reflecting an unappealing pretence to aloof grandeur. The east elevation over-shadowed Kensington Palace Gardens, spoiling the park's sense of separation from the city. The façades were clad in aluminium-framed glass curtain walling with black infill panels and the end walls of the accommodation blocks had vertical ribbed aluminium, giving a slick and shiny effect somewhat reminiscent of recent commercial architecture in Italian cities. Massive, tapering concrete pillars and a deep entrance canopy were the principle elements near to street level. While the individual elements were fairly typical of big, modern hotels around the world, at the Royal Garden there was insufficient space to make properly the monumental architectural gestures apparently desired by Seifert's architects and so they appeared meanly squashed together.

The hotel opened in the summer of 1965 and was operated by the Oddenino company. This had been established by Italian émigrés to London who in the late Victorian era had first became well-known hoteliers and restauranteurs, famous for their eponymous hotel in Regent Street. After the Second World War, their company was more associated with property speculation. To design the hotel's interiors, Oddenino's management employed Design Research Unit, a very prominent and prolific London-based multi-disciplinary design consultancy. Its co-founder, Misha Black, had been the co-ordinating architect for the substantial 'Land of Britain' exhibits on the South Bank. Since that time, Black and his DRU colleagues had become major figures in the British design establishment, their work encompassing motorway signage, the British Rail corporate identity programme and critically-acclaimed First Class interiors for the Orient Line UK-Australia ocean liner, *Oriana*. This vessel shared the Southampton-Sydney route with P&O's *Canberra*, designed internally by Hugh Casson,

142

A series of views of the Royal Garden Hotel when new, showing (1) and (2) the building's façades to Kensington High Street, (3) the Garden Room restaurant and (4) its façades facing Kensington Gardens.

The Royal Garden Hotel's foyer, the Garden Room on the top storey, part of the adjacent night club with a David Partridge metalwork panel on the ceiling and the cover for a brochure promoting the hotel when it opened.

subsequently of London Hilton fame. Indeed, it seems likely that DRU secured the Royal Garden project as a result of the widespread positive publicity their *Oriana* designs had received. Although the hotel's publicity emphasised its 'luxury', its main market was tourists and so DRU's approach was generally more colourful and informal than on the liner. The project was led by one of DRU's senior employees, Kenneth Bayes, who was a close colleague of Black.

The foyer was clad in jacaranda, a tropical hardwood and was furnished with black leather Mies van der Rohe 'Barcelona' chairs and decorated with a large abstract mural by the artist Joe Tilson. The adjoining stair lobbies and first floor lounge space were similarly treated – but there the 'international style' aesthetic ended abruptly.[225] The bedrooms were decorated in pink with floral chintz curtains to resemble rooms in English country houses and thus appeal to overseas guests' sense of British tradition – this notwithstanding the spaces' low ceilings and wall-to-wall fenestration. There were three restaurants – a grill room just below ground level, the Garden Room, which overlooked Kensington Gardens at the hotel's entrance level (featuring a frescoed ceiling by Leonard Rosoman), and the Royal Roof Restaurant on the top floor, offering views across London.

This had red striped wallpaper and was adjacent to a nightclub, decorated with metalwork panels by David Partridge.[226] The *Caterer and Hotel Keeper* records that DRU's brief was to create 'a timeless atmosphere… synonymous with England… in a modern idiom, avoiding pastiche or traditional treatment' while avoiding 'a wholly avant garde treatment which would… become dated in time.'[227] Despite this apparently contradictory set of ambitions, the journal concluded optimistically that the Royal Garden was a hotel 'suitable for the rocket age' and emphasised the 'scientific marvels' of its kitchens and service infrastructure.[228] By contrast, *The Architect and Building News'* critic was less sanguine, noting the Roof Top Restaurant's 'crinkly walls' and the nightclub's 'badly stained black marbelised tables standing on brassy cones' and observing that, at best, the interiors 'only hinted at English elegance.'[229]

In the mid-1990s, part of the Royal Garden Hotel's curtain walling collapsed, leading to its closure for a major rebuild, during which the exterior was entirely re-faced in rain-screen cladding and the interiors were completely redesigned. Thus, although the building still looms over Kensington Gardens, in appearance it is unrecognisable from how it was first conceived.

Hotel design books and manuals

The London Hilton architect Sidney Kaye's recollections of designing large and complex buildings for Charles Clore indicate that those involved in the property development business were subject to a great deal of pressure and stress to keep within tight budgets and time schedules. Evidence of Richard Seifert's approach to architecture and property development reveals a similar situation.[230] To assist architects involved in the high-octane world of hotel design, by the early 1960s, the first examples of a growing number of specialist books had been published.

So far as can be ascertained, the earliest of these for an audience of European architects, designers, planners and hotel owners was *Hotelbauten* by the German Alexander Koch, which was self-published in 1958 with parallel texts in German, English and French. Koch's lavish illustrations gave primacy to the latest American-owned large hotels and hotel-resorts and his text achieved an effective balance between analysis of the buildings' 'functional' aspects of planning and servicing and their external and interior atmospheres, as he imagined that guests would experience them. In the introduction, he observed:

> 'The present-day guest's desires are for a private, intimate atmosphere, together with every modern comfort during the time of relaxation and rest. Not less important is the commercial traveller who needs a haven in which he can relax in comfort and quietly concentrate after a strenuous day. In many new hotels the elevations, lobbies and dining halls have been adapted to conform with modern architectural styles and one finds among them many outstandingly good solutions. If many hotel proprietors are, on the contrary, of the opinion that the guest's demand for representation is better met by a traditional style of furnishing, then the examples shown here will convince the reader that modern living certainly includes comfort and ease.'[231]

Commencing his book with the Istanbul Hilton, Koch not only addressed its overall planning, but also commented favourably on the colours and finishes of its Sadrivan

Restaurant, the gold foil ceiling of the Karagöz Bar and the flower beds surrounding the rooftop Maramara Bar.[232] Of the Hotel Statler in Dallas, Texas by William B. Tabler of New York, he observed with approval that 'the social rooms open towards a charmingly arranged patio with a fountain beautified by abstract sculpture.'[233]

By contrast, the first British publication on hotel design, *Hotels Restaurants Bars* – which was written by the Coventry architects of the Hotel Leofric, W. Stanley Hattrell and Partners, and published four years after *Hotelbauten* – reflected only a clinically utilitarian analysis, even in the very first sentences of its introduction:

> 'All hotels, restaurants and bars have a common denominator – Man. They are designed to cater for his three basic needs: eating, drinking and sleeping. In each of these types of building, the design problem is basically the same since restaurants and bars are only specialised units performing part of the function of a hotel. Wherever they are located, whatever their size or standard of service, they are all built with one object – to enable food, drink and lodging to be provided for paying customers… The broad principles of hotel design have been established by experience and to some extent by tradition…'[234]

Yet, it was acknowledged that 'it is not possible to design a standard hotel, restaurant or bar, but it is possible to determine the principles which govern their design.'[235] Chapter 1 on 'Hotels: Basic planning and design' focused on choice of site, the orientation of a hotel building, its structure, public and service circulation routes, while Chapter 2 concentrated on servicing. Only in Chapter 3 were hotel guests' expectations discussed – but in a manner which largely sought to concentrate more on issues of technology than on popular taste, 'climatic conditions' being the first sub-heading. Towards its end, however, the chapter included just two short paragraphs on the issue of 'Fashion', acknowledging that:

> 'Fashion has its effect on the planning and more particularly on the decorations, for fashions in buildings change almost as rapidly as fashions in clothes. But to alter a hotel every few years to keep up with fashion is obviously uneconomic. In the long run the attraction of the building will depend not so much on whether it conforms to what is in vogue for the time being but whether the materials used will withstand the hard wear they will get…'[236]

The section concluded with the observation that:

> 'A man can travel the world today in such a short time that he has no opportunity of adapting himself to a changing environment… Hotels designed to cater for such a man, complex though they may be, are conforming to one of the fundamental principles of hotel design – to make him feel at home. Already there is a universality in architecture unknown twenty years ago. There is a sameness about hotels built in England or America or Turkey which reflects the fact that although they are subject to different climatic conditions, although they may be built of local materials and by local craftsmen, there is a uniformity of use which imposes a recognisable pattern.'[237]

Needless to say, the obvious paradoxes inherent in this statement went uncommented upon. In line with modernist rhetoric as it had evolved in Britain at that time, the tone was absolutist and unconcerned by the obvious differences between 'homeliness' and 'universality' and by the effects of different accumulations of educational and cultural capital upon peoples' formulations of taste. So far as the authors of 'Hotels Restaurants Bars' were concerned, just as Le Corbusier had imagined in the 1920s, the 'Man' of the future would respond to a hotel environment – or any environment for that matter – in purely a rationalist manner.

In captioning the illustrations, the authors continued their policy of emphasising underlying 'functionality' at the expense of style and glamour; their 'take' on the Istanbul Hilton was that 'the need to provide in a hotel large-scale public rooms and domestic-scale bedrooms nearly always leads to a design having a podium of large areas with a block of small units above.' No mention whatsoever was made of the hotel's décor. Later on, in a section on interiors, images of the expansive, luxurious foyer spaces in the Americana Hotel at Bal Harbor, Florida and of the Istanbul Hilton were arranged alongside a photograph of the rather banal, constricted, low-ceilinged reception of the recently-completed Keirby Hotel in Burnley. The accompanying caption made the trite comment that 'from the reception area of an hotel there must be direct access to all other parts of the building… The staircase to the bedroom block is immediately adjacent to the reception counter…'[238] In attempting to argue for a universalist approach to hotel design, the authors could not bring themselves to acknowledge the very significant spatial and stylistic differences between the two large and flamboyant American-owned hotels and the smaller, drearier, provincial British one.

The approach of *Hotels Restaurants Bars* was similar to other design guides published during the same period about hospitals, schools, offices and housing, all of which sought to adopt an emotion-free and 'institutional' approach. Unfortunately, those using these other building types usually had far less choice in the matter than hotel, restaurant or bar customers.

While it is difficult to assess how influential *Hotels Restaurants Bars* might have been, one may assume that most British architects subsequently involved in hotel design would have purchased it. Moreover, its tone is highly indicative of a wider culture in British architecture and architectural publishing that was afflicted by peculiarly narrow readings of the rhetorical statements of continental and American modernist pioneers, such as Louis Sullivan ('form follows function'), Adolf Loos ('Ornament and Crime') and Ludwig Mies van der Rohe ('less is more'). The formative experiences of British modern architects in the Great Depression, followed by wartime and post-war austerity must also have affected this line of thought, or at least influenced what architectural writers felt that they dared to say or write about how buildings should be designed.

Furthermore, in attempting to occupy the ethical high ground in debates about 'Good Design', accusations of having found pleasure in what might have been viewed by fellow practitioners or critics as 'kitsch' or 'pastiche' apparently had to be avoided at all cost. (By comparison, Alexander Koch's analysis was much more inclusive, pragmatic and with a strong hint of post-war levity.) One may conclude that, for many British architects who subsequently involved themselves in designing the shells of hotel buildings – or who specialised entirely in this field – and who decided to follow the austere principles emphasised in *Hotels Restaurants Bars*, the design process itself cannot have been particularly satisfying either. Indeed, the book's utilitarian tone would seem to imply that service engineers, rather than architects, should be the most important contributors to hotel design processes. This may partially explain the often dreary and derivative characteristics of the exteriors of large numbers of the hotel buildings subsequently developed. By contrast, the interior designers who outfitted them appear to have had more pleasurable tasks, very often demonstrating the application of considerable imagination.

CHAPTER 8

The big hotel chains

Hotel development was a capital-intensive business and so, just as a majority of operators came to favour bigger hotels on account of their welcome economies of scale, for the same reasons, it became advantageous to grow large chains of properties, across which administrative costs could be spread. With these advantages in mind, Charles Forte – arguably Britain's most successful hotelier of the post-war era – explained in his autobiography that in the early 1960s he was:

> '…Interested in expanding the company but found, however, that there was a limit to how fast and how large a private company could grow. A public company can raise capital much more easily and, without that, capital expansion is difficult. I had only to look abroad to see American hotel companies, such as Conrad Hilton's, building hotels all over the world. I could see clearly that my determination to pursue a policy of vigorous acquisition and expansion could only be achieved if the company went public.'[239]

So far as hotel guests and their travel agents were concerned, reputable hotel chains engendered confidence that a known and dependable level of facilities and service would be provided. In America, Hilton, Holiday Inn, Marriott and others set the benchmarks in these regards with each company's corporate brand and 'signature features' to an extent usurping the more traditional perceived need for distinctive or unique forms of architectural expression. During the 1960s, as we shall see, British hoteliers generally expanded on a far smaller scale than the American chains, which became world-wide organisations. Furthermore, in Britain, hotel designs and layouts were rarely standardised as they so often were in the USA. Partly this was due to the involvement of property developers in financing and overseeing the construction of new hotels, which were usually past the stage of modification by the time operators negotiated to lease them. It may also have been attributable to Britain's tradition of inn-keeping in which individualistic properties were favoured for their 'charm' and 'character.' A third factor was that certain British hotel entrepreneurs entered the business very quickly, leasing whatever new properties they could, irrespective of their size or style.

In the 1960s, the economic benefits of standardisation for hotels and restaurants were reflected in the commercial catering industry's dominant narrative of applying quasi-scientific methods to the mass-manufacture of foodstuffs in modern industrial premises. During the period, the *Caterer and Hotel Keeper* carried increasing numbers of advertisements, often featuring men in scientists' white coats, pouring liquids from test tubes to discover how best flavours and textures could be synthetically created. Thanks to innovations in food science, it was claimed that a single carton of powdered tomato soup, when re-hydrated, could feed an entire conference delegation. While convenience was emphasised, nutritional value and the possible negative side-effects of food additives were not discussed. In January 1967, Edward Reynold, Senior Lecturer at the Scottish Hotel School in the University of Strathclyde in Glasgow wrote a controversial letter which the *Caterer and Hotel Keeper* published, expressing the view that the traditional restaurant kitchen was 'dead as a doornail' and that the future of catering lay instead with factory-prepared convenience foods. Commenting on the ensuing impassioned correspondence this suggestion generated, the journal acknowledged that there would remain a niche for *haute cuisine*, yet it observed that 'for the less exalted and more numerous establishments, the modern range of convenience foods is a boon and a blessing, enabling economies to be made in labour and equipment and, wisely used, providing a more consistent menu standard than would otherwise be possible at the prices charged.' Furthermore, it was pointed out to sceptical readers that even the great chef Escoffier had produced and marketed bottled versions of his own sauces, enabling others to emulate his signature tastes.[240] Perhaps unsurprisingly, hotel chains serving the mid-market found these approaches particularly attractive. The idealisation of scientific methods of production also related to modernist beliefs, though, with hindsight, the way these were often applied within the catering industry demonstrates how such ideals could be compromised by the profit motive.

As we have seen already, the earliest British hotel chains were railway-owned and associated with major stations. Subsequently, between the two world wars, London-based chains such as Gordon Hotels Ltd and J. Lyons & Co's Strand Hotels expanded to attract particular elite and mainstream market segments with up-to-date, well-serviced properties.

A further significant established London hotelier serving mainly the capital's tourist market was Imperial London Hotels, founded in 1837 by Thomas Henry Walduck whose descendants subsequently developed a number of large hotels around Russell Square in Bloomsbury. The company's properties were thus well located to attract visitors arriving by rail at Euston, King's Cross and St Pancras stations, as well as enabling ready access to the nearby British Museum, West End theatres and other attractions.[241] In the post-war era, Imperial London Hotels' properties were suffering neglect and, moreover, they had too few rooms with private bathrooms to please the more discerning guests. A programme of new construction was therefore instigated, commencing with a large extension to the Tavistock Hotel in Tavistock Square to a design by C. Lovett Gill & Partners; this was carried out in a neo-Georgian style to match the original and completed in 1957.

Gill was a London-based architect of Scottish origin who, pre-war, had worked in partnership with Sir Albert Edward Richardson, a famous architectural practitioner, historian and educator. Both Richardson and Gill favoured the revival of eighteenth century classicism and, by the time of Gill's initial projects for Imperial London Hotels, he too was a senior and respected figure in the architectural profession.

C. Lovett Gill & Partners was retained to design Imperial London Hotels' subsequent new properties, commencing with the Hotel President on corner of Guild Street and Russell Square. Completed in 1960, the year Gill died, the hotel was fully air-conditioned, its 450 *en suite* rooms each having a television (this was an unusual refinement for a mid-market venue of the era). The brick and granite-faced frontage had curved corners and many of the bedroom windows formed V-shaped, fin-like vertical projections, enabling guests to enjoy oblique views along the street. While such features were more typical of the 1930s 'moderne' aesthetic, the use of glass mosaic around the entrance was reflective of more recent practices in the styling of commercial frontages.

Watercolour renderings of the hotel's rather unadventurous exterior treatment were displayed in the architecture section of the Royal Academy's 1960 Summer Exhibition.[242] *The Architectural Review* was, however, scathing of the timidity of its design when compared with other schemes for large new hotels in and around London. Noting the

The Hotel President's exterior and an advertising brochure produced at the time of its opening; externally and within, the design was rather unadventurous.

hotel's unusually large number of single rooms – totalling 390 – for the accommodation of transient guests arriving at nearby rail termini, the *AR* regretted:

> 'That this radical assessment of hotel function has not been matched by an equally radical architectural treatment; the marked difference in style between the President and the other hotels… serves as negative proof of the revolution that has taken place.[243]

Evidently, the *AR*'s critic would greatly have preferred a design in the international style with a podium and tower. Ironically, while the Hotel President's slightly conservative design blended well with the locality and withstood the test of time, in only a decade, as we shall see, the *AR* began to re-assess its own enthusiasm for universally modernist design solutions.

Imperial London Hotels marketed the Hotel President as offering 'new world comfort in an old world setting', its air-conditioned accommodation and American-sounding name providing a hint of trans-Atlantic glamour for British guests still used to recent post-war austerity while also providing visiting Americans with the type of amenities with which they were already familiar. Decoratively, the interiors were, however, every bit as fusty as the façade treatments, their design more reflecting British 'middlebrow' domestic taste of the period than anything of which Hilton would have approved.

Subsequently, C. Lovett Gill & Partners designed for Imperial London Hotels the Bedford Hotel in Southampton Row (1963), the Imperial Hotel in Russell Square (1970), and the vast Royal National Hotel in Bedford Way (1974) which, boasting 1,630

bedrooms, today remains London's biggest hotel building in terms of capacity. (It and the Imperial superseded older hotels of the same names.) In appearance, these projects fluctuated from the Imperial's exuberant zig-zag treatment of glazing and cast concrete panels – which at the time of its completion, was derided by critics – to the Royal National's dull expanses of flat brickwork, intended to harmonise with nearby Georgian terraces. Indeed, it seems possible that the Imperial's brashness was a response to criticism of the President's conservatism with the Royal National's design, in turn, responding to disapproval of the Imperial.

Gordon Hotels, Strand Hotels and Imperial London Hotels each owned no more than a handful of properties, located in and around central London. Apart from the railways, the one really big nationwide hotel operation in mid-twentieth century Britain was Trust Houses, whose hotels and inns – though large in number – were mostly quite small and old.

Trust Houses had its origins in the latter nineteenth century when the fourth Earl Grey – an aristocrat, liberal politician and colonial administrator whose seat was in Northumberland – decided to intervene to stem the decline of England's historic roadside inns, a result of the stagecoach having been usurped by the Railway Age with its new transport geography. He wrote to his fellow Lords Lieutenant (the Queen's representatives in each county), suggesting that Public House Trust Companies should be established to rescue and upgrade the inns. The scheme was first put into effect in 1904 when the Waggon and Horses at Ridge Hill in Hertfordshire was sympathetically renovated as a prototype for a nationwide resuscitation scheme. Fortuitously, the inn's revival coincided with a growing fashion for cycling and so, particularly at weekends, it became very popular with middle-class riders exploring the countryside on their machines. Soon, more Trust House

A mid-1960s brochure promoting the Trust Houses chain, most of which at that time consisted for former-coaching inns.

Hotels in the Trust Houses Group 1965/66

With the compliments of Trust Houses Limited

Companies were formed to acquire further inns. To all of these a similar formula was applied, moving upmarket and offering good quality accommodation, food and service in historic – and therefore romantic – environments. Soon, the Trust Houses were amalgamated into a single company which, by 1913 possessed 43 inns and, by the First World War's end, had over 100. Once car ownership began to grown in the inter-war era, the Trust Houses chain expanded further, acquiring rural properties near beauty spots to which motorists would wish to drive. In 1938, the company had accumulated 222 inns and small hotels. In the post-war era, another phase of expansion occurred, Trust Houses initially purchasing a number of hotels of Victorian and Edwardian vintage in London's West End.[244] By this point, the company was purely a commercial business, its aristocratic and philanthropic origins having been consigned to history.

In anticipation of the 1960s tourism boom, a major programme of new construction was instigated under the chairmanship of Sir Geoffrey Crowther, who had first joined Trust Houses' management in 1946. A former editor of *The Economist* magazine and a director of several companies, he was a reputed workaholic whose drive transformed the company in the space of only a decade into Britain's most extensive and up-to-date hotel operator. In recognition of this and other business achievements, he was made a life peer in 1968.

The first Trust Houses new build project to come to fruition was the eight-storey Dragon Hotel in Swansea, opened in May 1961, which was

the first new hotel in Wales since the war and the town's tallest building.[244] Trust Houses' appointment of Burnet, Tait, Wilson & Partners as architects indicated their high design ambition. Formerly known as Burnet, Tait & Lorne, the firm was one of the most highly regarded in Britain and, apart from the mid-1930s Mount Royal Hotel (described above) and co-ordinating work for the 1938 Glasgow Empire Exhibition, its output included numerous prestigious public and commercial buildings in the UK and overseas. The Dragon Hotel had an exposed concrete-frame and consisted of a two-storey podium, which, in plan, was trapezium-shaped to fit a road junction.[246] This contained the reception, bar, restaurant and banqueting suite with retail space around the perimeter. From this rose a six-storey, T-shaped bedroom block with 117 rooms.[247] In external appearance, the building was crisply detailed, yet somewhat austere, being reminiscent of several recent hotels in West Germany. Doubtless, its architects would have justified the design approach as being merely a latter day version of Trust Houses' Tudor inns, with their exposed oak framing. Within, the hotel offered all modern conveniences, being air conditioned and with *en suite* rooms throughout. The ceilings of its public rooms were lofty and the spaces were decorated in a modern Scandinavian idiom, using light colours and timber-framed furniture. The hotel's up-to-date design and fine facilities were welcomed in Swansea and the building remains a popular and externally well-preserved landmark in the city today.

Meanwhile, in London, construction of a second new Trust House was underway. The nine-storey, 77-bedroom Hertford Hotel on Bayswater Road overlooked Kensington Gardens and was intended to provide comfortable but inexpensive accommodation with

Trust Houses' Dragon Hotel in Swansea (top left), a baggage label for the hotel (top right), the restaurant of the Hertford Hotel in London and the building's exterior.

a fairly basic level of service. The hotel was a ten-storey tower, designed by Lam, Biel & Partners, a London practice otherwise specialising in offices and multi-storey car parks.[248] This filled the air space above a garage and petrol station, which was the work of different architects, Royce, Stephenson and Tasker, for whom such premises were a speciality. As the garage was recessed between columns supporting the hotel block, it made little impact on the overall composition. The framing of the tower was clad in Empire stone with blue mosaic infill beneath the window openings, making for a crisp composition. The hotel's entrance was narrow and those entering immediately ascended stairs or took the lift to a small reception on the first floor, adjacent to which a bar and restaurant were located. The latter featured a mural depicting the history of Trust Houses and both the hotel's name and its interior design commemorated the company's Hertfordshire origin.[249] Initially, Trust Houses considered the Hertford as a 'flagship' property, but such was the company's subsequent pace of expansion that it soon gained control of several much more impressive and splendidly appointed hotels in central London.

For their next London project, Trust Houses entered into a deal with the Laing Construction Company whereby the hotelier leased the upper six floors of Henry Wood House, a new 14-storey combined hotel and office development, designed by Burnet, Tait, Wilson & Partners and occupying the site of the blitzed Queen's Hall in Langham Place.[250] This was close to the BBC and to the new Post Office Tower, which had a revolving restaurant near its summit. The idea of a 'hotel in the sky' perhaps reflected similar urges to move occupants into the air, thereby reflecting advanced technologies and jet travel.

The St George's Hotel's interiors were the work of Dennis Lennon's practice. A London-based architect and interior designer, Lennon was a graduate of the Bartlett School of Architecture (part of University College London). Following distinguished army service in the Second World War, he joined Maxwell Fry's practice where he dealt mostly with exhibition work as it proved difficult to gain building permits for anything

The St George's Hotel in London, located above office space in Henry Wood House and featuring a restaurant on the top storey.

more substantial. From there, he was headhunted by the Rayon Industry Design Centre, where he made influential contacts in the fashion and textiles industries. Having established his own firm in 1950, he worked initially on Festival of Britain exhibits, designing furniture for the Transport and the Homes and Gardens pavilions on the South Bank. Lennon's first hotel interior project was in the mid-1950s when he was commissioned to renovate the bomb-damaged Mandeville, located near to his office in Fitzhardinge Street. This had been purchased cheaply by the property entrepreneur Maxwell Joseph (who subsequently founded the Grand Metropolitan hotel, pub and brewing conglomerate). The St George's Hotel interiors were designed jointly by Lennon and one of his assistants who later was made a partner, Bernard Wiehahn, an architect of South African origin who was married to Lennon's sister.[251]

No sooner were the projects for the Hertford and St George's hotels underway than Trust Houses announced further schemes for new hotels in Winchester and Sheffield.[252] In addition, the company planned to extend and sensitively upgrade some of its historic inns, transforming them into motor hotels by adding new bedroom wings with up-to-date comforts adjacent to the existing buildings. (In combining old and new, this approach was much like that applied in recent years to some of the Lyon Watney motel projects, described above.)

In Winchester's historic town centre, meanwhile, Trust Houses appointed Fielden & Mawson to design the Wessex Hotel, completed in 1964. The practice's senior partner was Bernard Feilden, a Bartlett graduate who had since worked in Norwich designing housing, churches and on the conservation of the cathedral. As a result of the latter, Feilden had become well known for his concern for the preservation and enhancement of historic urban environments. The hotel was a three-storey concrete-framed structure, constructed on a falling site and thereby allowing two floors of accommodation to be built over a car park located below street level. Its frontages were clad in local red brick to harmonise with neighbouring buildings. Inside, the hotel's bar, adjacent to the reception, had a decorative panel in coloured glass by John Piper and Patrick Reyntiens depicting the 'Green Man' of local legend.

Uniquely in the British hotel trade, Trust Houses at this point established its own in-house architecture department to handle subsequent hotel schemes. Nelson Foley was appointed chief architect in February 1961 with D.G. Millett as his deputy. Born in 1915, Foley had studied architecture at the Regent Street Polytechnic, from which he graduated in 1937. Remembered by his son as a quiet and unassuming man, he had wanted to become an artist and to do stage design, rather than architecture, but his parents thought these careers were too risky.[253] In 1953, Foley was employed by Norman & Dawbarn, who were specialists in designing airport and college buildings. They sent him and his family to Jamaica where he assisted in designing and overseeing the construction of the Palisadoes Airport terminal and also parts of the Jamaica Institute of Technology,

The bar of the Wessex Hotel in Winchester, showing John Piper's stained glass panel on the end wall. The interior typified the high standard of design achieved by Trust Houses in the earliest of its new properties of the 1960s.

both of which were completed in 1958.[254] Thereafter, he returned to Britain where he was appointed as senior architect responsible for the design of residential areas in Crawley New Town.[255] Foley's early career trajectory suggests that he was a hard-working and dedicated technician with a suppressed artistic streak. In nearly all existing accounts of the history of British modern architecture, however, architects employed in-house by commercial clients are frequently ignored due to their perceived lack of creative independence; despite his substantial output, Foley's rather 'invisible' career with Trust Houses reflects this bias.

Foley's initial projects for Trust Houses were to modernise sensitively some of the company's historic coaching inns, providing rooms with added *en suite* bathrooms and making adjustments to take account of current-day fire escape requirements. Foley – who had a liking for the picturesque – apparently enjoyed working on these buildings. His subsequent modernist approach to the design of Trust Houses' new hotels seems to have been dictated more by economic and time constraints that by any strong convictions regarding modernism.[256] Foley's first such project was to extend the 400-year-old Ship Inn at Alveston, 11 miles north of Bristol, with the addition of two modern wings, transforming it into an up-to-date motor hotel, albeit one in which guests could drink and dine in a charming and historic setting.[257]

In 1965, the first batch of new Foley-designed hotels for Trust Houses was completed, with varying degrees of success in terms of quality and composition. The Eastgate Hotel in Lincoln – a three-storey concrete-framed structure with brick infill – was accused by the *Architect's Journal* of 'fail[ing] to meet its responsibilities to the past on an important site near Lincoln Cathedral.'[258] In particular, the presence of an expanse of car park in front of the hotel was felt to be 'an eyesore.' Yet, Foley – whose earlier work at Crawley had demonstrated thoughtful planning – initially intended to arrange the hotel around a pedestrianised courtyard with parking to the rear. As this would have partially blocked a view to the cathedral, planning permission was refused, forcing a most unfortunate redesign. Another point of contention for the *Architect's Journal* was the building's 'gimmicky roof line', the canopy over the top floor balconies having a suggestion of crenellation.[259] This, the *AJ* noted with regret, had incited 'no objections from the town's planners.' Yet, the detail was rather jaunty and in line with similar features on buildings of many kinds in the wake of the Festival of Britain, albeit a rather late example.[260] In Lincoln, it appeared that Foley was arguably more sinned against than sinning – but the situation does demonstrate very clearly the compromises inherent in designing and developing hotels, many of which were beyond their architects' direct control.

In complete contrast, the Hallam Tower Hotel in Sheffield was an imposing 11-storey edifice, somewhat incongruously located amid leafy suburbia on Sheffield's western fringe, close to the main road to Manchester. Inevitably, its clientele comprised almost entirely motorists, who enjoyed superb views from its upper floors towards the Pennines in one direction and across the city in the other. The hotel was designed mainly by Foley's assistants H. Tiktin and J. Hounsell, who devised a cruciform plan. This comprised a reinforced concrete accommodation tower containing 136 bedrooms, standing on broad pilotis, perpendicular to the ground and first floor entrance and public room block.[261] In contrast to the tower, this long, low structure had lightweight steel structure with large windows in slender stainless steel frames (an appropriate finish for a hotel in Sheffield, given the city's reputation for cutlery-making). In front of the main entrance, the pilotis and soffit of the tower formed what was effectively a lofty port cochère, within which

was suspended a 'canopy' of pendant lights. On the tower's end elevation above the entrance, the facings on each floor level were adorned with abstract bas relief sculpture panels by Henry and Joan Haigh.[262] In common with most of Foley's subsequent hotels for Trust Houses, the Hallam Tower's extensive grounds were carefully designed with flower beds, copses of trees and other informal elements to soften the building's sharp lines, Indeed, Foley had a particularly strong interest in landscape architecture, which he had studied subsequent to his initial architectural qualification.[263]

A brochure from the hotel's inauguration records that, as with other hotels of its era in northern industrial cities, the interior design, which was by London-based interior decorators, Sibyl Colefax and John Fowler, combined modernist elements with references to nineteenth century industrial heritage. The foyer had a spiral open-tread stairway to the first floor, where the banqueting suite was located.[264] The Vulcan Room restaurant, on the ground floor adjacent to the foyer, had an 'orange, yellow, pale wrapping paper brown and sour green' colour scheme while the Sheffield Plate Grill was decorated with 'a series of Sheffield trade signs, none of them later than 1910 and most of them mid-19th century', set against a colour scheme of pink, red, black and white. The Downstairs Bar, meanwhile, was a 'dark intimate room with a club-like atmosphere enlivened by turquoise blue upholstery, dark Lincrusta walls and reproductions of eighteenth century Hogarth engravings with silver trimmings.'[265]

While the Hallam Tower was nearing completion in Sheffield, on a site between the new town of Hemel Hempstead and the M1 motorway a much smaller, though equally well conceived, Trust Houses hotel project was being built to a design by Foley and his colleagues. The Breakspear Motor Hotel was Trust Houses' first attempt to break into the upmarket end of the growing British motel trade, following the successes of Watney Lyon, Esso, Forte's and others in this growing sector. Its layout was largely horizontal, there being separate entrance and accommodation blocks, the latter of two storeys and containing 28 'studio rooms.'[266] Perhaps surprisingly, the entrance block appeared as the more substantial element, having four storeys and, with its podium and tower layout,

The Star Inn in Alfriston was one of several historic Trust Houses properties for which Nelson Foley designed extensions upon his appointment as the company's in-house architect. Typically, as in this instance, the new structures were added to the rear of the existing ones and arranged around courtyards with car parking.

At the Eastgate Hotel in Lincoln, Foley's desire to create a court-yard was frustrated by local planners and instead the hotel ended up being built as a single block with the car park in front.

The Hallam Tower Hotel in Sheffield, showing (1) the entrance, (2) the exterior, (3) and (4) the foyer, (5) the Sheffield Plate Grill and (6) a typical bedroom.

An image of the Breakspear Motor Hotel's entrance block, showing its distinctive variegated cladding and concrete bas relief panel, and a view of two of its bedroom blocks.

appearing from a distance like a complete hotel building in miniature. The idea was that it should act as a 'signpost', to 'attract attention from a considerable distance', and thereby enable the hotel to be spotted by motorists passing on the M1.[267] As with the Foley office's concurrent Sheffield scheme, the Breakspear Motor Hotel's entrance block emphasised contrasting horizontals and verticals. At first floor height, a canopy with deep white facias projected outward, supported near one corner by a concrete screen wall featuring a bas relief panel.[268] Above, the service block was faced in closely-packed slim vertical enamelled steel fluting, interspersed with panels in graded colours. Just as Robert Venturi, Denise Scott-Brown and Stephen Izenour would observe of roadside commercial buildings in the USA in 'Learning from Las Vegas' (1972), it was obviously advantageous for a hotel such as the Breakspear to have a frontage disproportionate in scale to what lay behind. The reception and public rooms were located on the ground floor, the storeys above being occupied by the manager's flat, staff service accommodation, offices and heating plant.

At the Breakspear, Trust Houses' introduced a new catering concept, perpetuated in all of their subsequent new hotels. 'The Buttery' was a grill with a semi-circular bar at which guests placed their orders directly with the chefs, who cooked in a semi-open kitchen. This approach not only saved the cost of employing a large waiting staff but also enabled diners to have a more direct involvement in specifying how they wished their food prepared as well as being able to enjoy the experience of watching the chefs in action.[269] In an era with high employment and difficulties in recruiting serving staff to the hospitality industry on account of its long hours and low wages, such ingenuity was necessary.

A combination of new hotels and a growing economy meant that, for the 1964-65 financial year, Trust Houses' turnover and profit increased by around a quarter, the former from £31.7 million to £47.7 million and the latter from £1.6 million to £2.1 million. The relatively small yield demonstrates the tight margins within which even large hotel chains operated.[270]

Trust Houses soon found that the Breakspear was its most profitable hotel, exceeding all expectations with regard to occupancy. Indeed, it was often forced to turn would-be guests away. The solution was quickly to add new wings containing additional rooms. So far as the company's management was concerned, this hotel appeared to be an ideal model for future developments, which would henceforth be aimed at providing a

uniform standard of service and modern amenities to a mobile, car-owning public consisting of leisure and business travellers alike.

Construction of the company's second motor hotel, the Bell at Epping Forest in Essex, was soon under way with opening scheduled for the autumn of 1965. This incorporated an existing eighteenth century inn of that name, which Trust Houses had acquired in 1917. The inn was augmented with a significant new structure adjacent, consisting of separate reception and bedroom blocks faced in matching local brick. Having acquired their room keys, motorists drove beneath a glass-enclosed pedestrian bridge to enter a courtyard, around which the accommodation was arranged. Unlike at the Breakspear, at the Bell, the rooms were off-set at an angle, breaking the monotony of the façades and giving each one a little extra privacy.

As well as Trust Houses' commissioning new hotels from its own architecture department, in 1965 the company also took over two existing hotel companies, each of which had major new hotels under construction. Its greatest coup was the acquisition of Grosvenor House, the owner of the eponymous hotel on Park Lane. In Sheffield, the company had agreed to lease a large, new 118-room city centre hotel being built by Town & City Properties Ltd, a prolific London-based property developer. It had originated as a rubber estate company in British colonies which, from the mid-1950s onward, had re-invested its profits in commercial property all over the UK. With Trust Houses' take-over of Grosvenor House, it would thereby operate two major hotels in Sheffield, giving it a monopoly over the upmarket end of the city's hotel trade. Sheffield's Grosvenor House hotel was, however, more centrally located than the Hallam Tower and with bigger rooms and arguably better facilities.

The building was designed by Ian Fraser & Associates of London; an Architectural Association graduate of 1952, he was yet another of his generation to have grown successful as a designer of large office, commercial and residential projects. The hotel was located on a sloping site with car parking filling half of its podium at first and second floors with public rooms in other half and on the floor above. From this structure rose a seven-storey accommodation block, square in plan with a central core and 16 rooms on each floor. A smaller number of penthouses were located on the top-most storey.[271] Unfortunately, the facings of the Grosvenor House's podium were rather poorly resolved while its upper storeys had significant areas of plain concrete facing panels with only small windows set in vertical channels between. It was thus a rather utilitarian addition to the cityscape, lacking the Hallam Tower's sleekness and artistic adornments.

As the intended tenant, Grosvenor House had been responsible for completing the hotel and specifying its interiors. To lend the upmarket image they desired, a decision

The Grosvenor House Hotel in Sheffield, showing (1) the concrete and glass-faced exterior, (2) and (3) the restaurant, with columns clad in mosaic, (4) to (6) hotel lounge furniture, designed by Dick Russell and, (7) to (9), Russell-designed tableware.

was taken to continue their relationship with Gordon and Dick Russell, employing the latter's architectural practice, Russell, Hodgson & Leigh, to carry out the interior design work. The project architect from this and other hotel schemes was Ray Leigh, who had first been employed by Russell as a 23-year-old student to assist in making exhibits for the Lion and Unicorn Pavilion at the Festival of Britain. (This structure, which was meant to symbolise the British character, was designed by Robert Gooden.) As a child during the Second World War, Leigh had been evacuated from London to Morecambe, where the sight of Oliver Hill's Midland Hotel had greatly enthused him about a career in architecture. Subsequently, at the Architectural Association, he had encountered several modernist luminaries, including Le Corbusier and Alvar Aalto, the latter proving an important influence. Leigh, therefore, had a long-standing appreciation of the possibilities hotel design offered and a particularly Scandinavian-inflected approach which, when coupled with the Russell brothers' Arts & Crafts inclinations, resulted in work of a very high quality.

For the Sheffield Grosvenor House Hotel, complete ranges of fixtures, fittings and tableware were designed, thereby echoing the approach used by Arne Jacobsen when devising interiors for the SAS Royal Hotel in Copenhagen. The fact that Grosvenor House accepted this, rather than choosing the more commercially expedient approach of ordering existing items from catalogues, was impressive and almost unique for a British hotel interior of the era. Unfortunately, the hotel's awkward internal layout, predetermined by its architect and developer, mitigated against spatial clarity; it was a case of making the best of a less than ideal situation. The best public room was the restaurant, a long volume with timber-lined alcoves along its inner wall. All of the furniture was made by Gordon Russell's Broadway workshop and was inspired by recent Scandinavian precedents, it having rectilinear beechwood frames. The lounge chairs had demountable upholstered arms, backs and seat cushions. The tableware was also purpose-designed and each item was shaped for easy stacking. Given Sheffield's reputation for cutlery, the hotel's unique range would have been a point of pride.[272] It was, however, most unfortunate that all these items were concealed within a shell of such comparative banality. For the next forty years, the Grosvenor House and Hallam Tower hotels operated with varying degrees of success, the latter's out-of-town location making it something of a 'white elephant' at quieter times of the year. Both hotels closed in the wake of the 2008 recession and are now derelict; the Hallam Tower has been reduced to a vandalised shell.

In addition to Trust Houses' acquisition of the Grosvenor House company in 1965, it also purchased Queen Anne's Hotel and Properties Ltd, the owners of London's new Cavendish Hotel in Jermyn Street, which at that time was nearing completion. Plans to replace the original Cavendish, a building of Edwardian vintage that had never recovered its pre-war élan, had first been announced in 1961 with Fitzroy Robinson as architect. By the time the project came to fruition, however, he had been superseded by Maurice Hanna of Hanna and Manwaring, who designed an impressive-looking 252-bedroom hotel, albeit with just one smallish restaurant plus two residents' bars and no banqueting facilities. As with other hotels in the vicinity, most guests were expected to dine out (the famous Quaglino's restaurant was immediately adjacent).[273] That way, a smaller staff could be employed with consequent cost savings. A typical 'podium and tower' solution was again used, the exterior of which was faced in cream textured cement panels. The proportions were elegant and the detailing neatly handled, each end of the tower tapering inward with the side elevations slightly concave. Before the Cavendish project, Hanna and Manwaring's most noteworthy design was a warehouse in Victoria Street, which attracted technical interest on account of its unusual tubular steel framing. The warm praise critics gave the hotel, however, apparently led to further more prestigious commissions being received, such as designing new premises for the Yugoslav Embassy near Earl's Court and a scheme to extend the Park Lane Hotel in Piccadilly (though this was never executed).

As with the Hallam Tower in Sheffield, Trust Houses chose Colefax & Fowler to decorate the interiors, their designer, Michael Raymond, selecting pastel shades with patterns and foliage in an attempt to evoke something of the atmosphere of the old Cavendish Hotel, the rococo decoration of which had apparently been very popular with regular guests. Its replacement's foyer had mosaic-covered walls and seating in soft green and pink. Its ceiling was composed of small hanging metal pieces, forming a diffuser over the concealed fluorescent lighting. The *Caterer and Hotel Keeper* commented that 'the effect is stupendous but, oh, the cleaning!'[274] The restaurant and cocktail bar were decorated in bright apricot and yellow tones with vertical slats forming a screen between the two elements. The Sub Rosa Bar, adjacent, was designed to memorialise Rosa Lewis 'that colourful Edwardian character who at one time owned the old Cavendish Hotel' and had black buttoned leather banquettes, red walls and rococo chandeliers to 'recreate the good old days and provide a cosy drinking spot.'[275] The Terrace Room Bar, on the first floor, had a Wardian case containing tropical plants as its centrepiece, lit from above by a skylight through which the accommodation block could be viewed soaring upward.[276]

Following Trust Houses' purchases of Grosvenor House and Queen Anne's Hotel and Properties, a trading loss was recorded for the first half of 1966 and so the Chairman, Sir Geoffrey Crowther, announced a temporary slowing in the pace of expansion.[277] Nonetheless, an unrealised scheme taken over with the Grosvenor House acquisition for a five-storey 104-room hotel in Worcester was given the go-ahead for completion in 1967. Named The Gifford in memory of a well-known local bishop, this formed part of a highly controversial new mixed-use development, comprising a shopping arcade and a 400-space car park, occupying a prominent site in the historic and otherwise picturesque town centre directly opposite the cathedral. From any angle, the scheme was a crass intrusion, neither its 'podium and tower' design nor the concrete aggregate and engineering brick facings making any reference to the surrounding townscape.

Within, the hotel was, like the Grosvenor House in Sheffield, designed by Ray Leigh of Russell, Hodgson & Leigh, who made every effort to provide an environment of high design quality. The restaurant, conference room, cocktail bar and lounge were on the first floor, the latter having floor-to-ceiling windows, looking towards the cathedral. The inner wall was decorated with a 30-foot-long decorative panel by Jennifer Campbell, comprising embroidery and resin, emulating the repeat patterns of the cathedral's vaulting and stained glass. Throughout, there was a preponderance of dark woodwork with contrasting mosaic panels in recesses, designed to resemble panels of illuminated manuscripts. Opened in the summer of 1967 in time for the tourist season, the hotel was popular with visitors, but so far as many locals were concerned, the structure in which it was housed never found favour; the arcade and car park were eventually demolished in 2016, though the hotel itself – which by this point had become a Travelodge – survived.

By the latter 1960s, Trust Houses' policy of sympathetically upgrading its existing

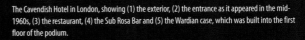

The Cavendish Hotel in London, showing (1) the exterior, (2) the entrance as it appeared in the mid-1960s, (3) the restaurant, (4) the Sub Rosa Bar and (5) the Wardian case, which was built into the first floor of the podium.

old coaching inns and augmenting these with new hotels of high design quality and with distinctive design features had changed significantly. Instead, the company now began selling off its historic town centre properties and replacing them with edge-of-town 'motor hotels' of generic design. A spate of recent fires in its old premises may have hastened this approach, as did the difficulties guests reported in finding enough parking spaces.[278] The first of this new batch of standardised motor hotels, the Post House at Newcastle-under-Lyme in Staffordshire, was opened in the autumn of 1967 and this formed the prototype for those to follow. The hotel's name was chosen to commemorate the fact that some of Trust Houses' historic inns had been places where letters were posted for dispatch by stagecoach. Subsequently, the 'Post House' name was applied to nearly every new Trust Houses hotel, creating a more uniform brand identity, linked to a vague sense of nostalgia for a historic past that no longer had a place in the company's business strategy.

Nelson Foley's design for the Newcastle-under-Lyme Post House was adapted from that of his recent Breakspear Motor Hotel – albeit without repeating its attention-grabbing entrance block and public artwork. Instead, the entire structure was clad in aggregate-faced cement panels. A year later another even more tightly budgeted Post House was opened at Sandiacre by the M1 motorway between Nottingham and Derby.[279] It was an indirect replacement for Trust Houses' Flying Horse Inn in central Nottingham but was similar in layout to the Post House at Newcastle-under-Lyme. Thanks to an increased use of prefabrication – for example, all the bathroom units were made off-site and delivered complete for installation – the construction cost was lowered to £5,000 per room. As the *Caterer and Hotel Keeper* records, the accommodation was comfortable but formulaic, comprising:

'…A standard design bedroom with modular fitted furniture. Rooms are studio

Below left: An aerial view of Worcester, showing the Cathedral Square shopping complex incorporating the Gifford Hotel, which is the tall building near the top left corner.

Below right: The lounge and bar of the Gifford Hotel, from which the cathedral could be viewed.

Bottom left: An aerial view of the Post House at Newcastle-under-Lyme.

Bottom right: A lounge space in the Post House at Sandiacre, which was designed with economy in mind, hence the exposed brick finish on the end wall.

style [i.e. entered directly from the exterior, rather than via an internal corridor] and mostly twins; the second bed forms a couch by day or when the room is let as a single, and fittings include radio, telephone and television. Guests are provided with electric kettles, milk, sachets of instant coffee and sugar and tea bags.'[280]

Half-a-century later, the lure of easy parking, clean beds, a shower, TV and being able to make a warm drink remains generic in the present-day equivalent mid-market hotels and motels.

A third new Post House was planned for Sherbourne in Dorset and this opened in 1968, but whereas those at Newcastle-under-Lyme and Sandiacre benefitted from their placement in the busy and densely-populated Midlands, the one at Sherbourne was expected to be quieter outside the summer tourist season. With these hotels up and running, Trust Houses' future direction as an operator of modern hotels of increasingly standardised design was set.

The Albany Chain

Following the success of the Ariel Hotel at London Airport, J. Lyons' Strand Hotels subsidiary began a policy of expansion with plans for large and up-to-date hotels in the centres of major British provincial cities to serve business and leisure travellers. In Birmingham, an opportunity arose to develop the first of these thanks to the municipality's enthusiasm for commercially-led urban redevelopment and its willingness to be very flexible in accommodating developers' requirements. Birmingham was among the earliest local authorities to include the creation of an inner ring road as a key planning policy, for which it had first begun to purchase land in 1943, although it was not until 1956 that construction actually began. When building sites began to be cleared along the ring road's route, the municipality became enthused about finding a commercial development partner. The road's builder, John Laing & Son, and a local property tycoon, Jo Godfrey, offered to prepare a single, coherent scheme. The outcome was the long, ribbon-like, six-storey office development lining Smallbrook Ringway; this was designed by a local architect, James A. Roberts. As Elain Harwood comments of the project, 'It was among the first examples of a new kind of speculative modernism that was busy, curvaceous and altogether 'pop' in its styling and easy admittance of signage, shop window displays and frequent alteration.'[281] Born in 1922, Roberts was a graduate of the Birmingham School of Architecture who had formed his own very successful and prolific practice in 1952, specialising in large-scale commercial developments, including the design of hotel buildings.

As part of the Smallbrook Ringway project, both Godfrey and the municipal authority wished to include a hotel, the shell of which was to be designed by Roberts and his assistant, Norman Higginbottom. To design its interiors, J. Lyons & Co, however, chose Dennis Lennon, whose firm had recently worked on Trust Houses' St George's Hotel in London (described above). From the later 1950s onward Lennon had also produced interiors for a chain of steak house restaurants that Lyons had developed. Concurrently with these, he had been engaged to update some public spaces in its Cumberland and Regent Palace hotels, gradually replacing Oliver P. Bernard's early 1930s Art Deco designs, which had come to be considered passé.

The new Birmingham hotel was named The Albany. Externally, it was a rather mundane 12-storey podium structure, the accommodation block of which was brick-faced with the edges of the concrete floors exposed as horizontal bands. The vertical structural elements were similarly treated and extended upwards by an extra storey at roof level to frame the plant room. One of Lennon's assistants, Brian Beardsmore, had a significant role in the hotel's interior design and in that of subsequent Albany hotels.

Lennon argued successfully with the developer for a double-height foyer space and this featured plate glass doors, a stone slab floor, teak panelling, smoke-tinted glazed balustrades in brushed aluminium frames, brass ceiling lights and chandeliers to give a warm glow, the overall effect being rather Scandinavian. As Lennon had discovered that the hotel's site had previously been famous for gun-making, its public bar was 'The Gunnery Room' and featured displays of old locally-made weapons. Otherwise, it too was mostly Scandinavian in style with painted brick walls and light oak furniture of Lennon's own design. The cocktail bar had a teak counter and matching ceiling panelling, while the Carvery restaurant was decorated in royal blue and white and featured a bandstand and dance floor for dinner dances. Carvery restaurants, in which large joints of meats were pre-cooked and served by chefs at hot counters, with vegetables, salad and desserts adjacent, became popular in the 1960s. To an extent, this trend was following the lead set in Scandinavia by 'smorgasbord' buffet dining, albeit with hot dishes rather than only cold ones. As with Trust Houses' 'Buttery' restaurants, described above, Carveries saved on the need to employ large numbers of waiting staff, while enabling diners to choose precisely how much of each dish they wished to eat. For anybody aged over 20, for whom memories of wartime rationing would have remained fresh, the sight of large quantities of succulent meat – and having carte blanche to eat as much as one pleased for a fixed sum – must have seemed the height of pleasurable luxury. The Albany's other restaurant was 'The Garden Room', offering an à la carte dinner menu; this had red decorative screens and troughs containing foliage.

Each of the 250 bedrooms had a private bathroom. For the rooms, Lennon's staff designed cantilevered dressing tables and mountings for the radios, telephones and televisions (which were on swivel-stands). Beardsmore recalls Lennon's 'very neat attention to detail and insistence on orderliness, including the placing of electric sockets and ventilation inlets.'[282]

In 1969, a second Albany was developed in Nottingham, using the same team of Godfrey as developer, Roberts as architect and Lennon's firm as interior designers. The 160-room hotel formed part of a larger development, including an office tower located adjacent, both structures rising from a common two-storey podium block. The office element was, however, by different architects, John P. Osborne & Son, also of Birmingham, and its curtain wall cladding bore no relationship to the hotel's continuous brick skin. Concurrently, with the Nottingham Albany project, much of Lennon's office was engaged in coordinating and designing spaces for the Cunard liner *Queen Elizabeth 2* and so Beardsmore – who was at that time uninvolved in the *QE2* project – worked on the hotel largely single-handed. Its darker, richer colours reflected taste changing away from light Scandinavian palettes to the strong, saturated hues associated with 'Swinging London' psychedelia. Deep reds and bright oranges, purples and browns were also less likely to show tobacco staining. The foyer had travertine flooring and wall panelling with orange shag-pile rugs and easy chairs with black buttoned leather upholstery. The reception counter was clad in rosewood.

Lyons' 'Carvery' self-service dining concept was used for the main restaurant. In

The Albany Hotel in Birmingham; (1) shows Smallbrook Ringway with the hotel on the left, (2) shows the reception foyer, (3) shows the main restaurant, (4) and (5) show the cocktail bar and Gunnery Bar, (6) shows a standard bedroom and (7) shows a dining area for private parties.

A series of view of the Albany Hotel in Nottingham, showing (1) the exterior by night, (2) the foyer, (3) a table setting in the Four Seasons Restaurant with lobster served, (4) a general view of the Four Seasons Restaurant, (5) The Carvery and (6) one of the bedrooms.

addition, a smaller à la carte restaurant called 'The Four Seasons' was inspired by the eponymous dining room in the Seagram Building in New York. The Nottingham version had indirect perimeter lighting, casting on off-white textured wall panelling. The carpets were midnight blue and William Plunkett chairs of the same design as those used for First Class rooms on the *QE2* were selected. A 400-capacity banqueting hall occupied one end of the podium and was divisible by sliding retractable walls into three smaller spaces. The Forum cocktail bar likewise had Plunkett furniture, while The Mint bar served the same role as The Gunnery at the Birmingham Albany, its theme being selected to recall that, in the past, Nottingham had minted its own coins. As we shall see, such nostalgic evocations of times past would play an increasingly important role in British hotel interiors of the latter 1960s.

The Rank Hotels Chain

In the early 1960s, the Rank Organisation realised that catering and hospitality would be lucrative areas in which to expand operations. Rank was stuck with a sprawling chain of over 500 cinemas in Britain and the Commonwealth, many of which were experiencing declining patronage in the television age and so there was an urgent need to diversify. The company also owned ballrooms and both these and its larger cinemas had cafés and, in some instances, also restaurants. Rank's diversification was spearheaded by its Chairman, John Davis, who had come to the company through its pre-war absorption of Odeon Cinemas, where he had been employed as an accountant. Unfortunately, he gained a reputation for being a bully who hired and fired senior staff seemingly at will and so, under his leadership, Rank's initiatives often appeared unpredictable, the company being prone to sudden restructurings and changes of direction. New activities for Rank commenced by Davis in the 1960s included recorded music, the Rank Xerox office duplication machine business, television set manufacture,

Following the Nottingham Albany project, Dennis Lennon's firm was engaged to add an extension to the Birmingham Albany Hotel, containing a swimming pool and fitness facilities; this was known as the 'Albany Club'. The interior design apparently shows the influence of Le Corbusier, although the architect responsible, Brian Beardsmore, recalls that he had Carlo Scarpa's work in mind when drawing up the scheme.

the conversion of failing cinemas to bingo clubs – and investment in the development of motorway service stations, motels and, thereafter, a hotel chain. In these latter activities, Rank was following the lead set by its American cinema industry counterparts, Metro-Goldwyn-Mayer and Loew's. The first Rank-operated service station was by the M2 at Farthing Corner in Kent and it opened in May 1963.[283]

Rank's involvement in hotel operation developed from its roadside service operations, both initiatives having been spearheaded by a youthful and ambitious manager called John Hastings, whose background was as a hotelier. In contrast to its major competitors, however, Rank's approach to hotel development appears to have been opportunistic. Having agreed to lease the Unicorn hotel-cum-car park in Bristol, Rank quickly became involved in the operation of a number of more conventionally-designed hotels elsewhere in Britain and overseas. In 1964, plans were announced additionally to operate hotels on the Algarve in Portugal and in Sardinia. At the same time, a project was unveiled for a tourist hotel near Aviemore in the Scottish Highlands, aimed at attracting winter skiers. A further scheme was for a 108-room hotel in Gateshead, to be known as the Five Bridges in recognition of the various River Tyne crossings, with completion scheduled for late in 1965.[284]

For its Aviemore project, which would mean large-scale construction work in an area of outstanding scenic beauty, Rank set about currying local favour by promising a £10,000 loan to assist in the ongoing development of ski facilities on the slopes of nearby Cairn Gorm. Already in the mid-1950s, the mountain had been identified as offering obvious potential for such development. From 1954 onward, the Central Council for Physical Recreation – a government-sponsored organisation – had lobbied for the development of downhill skiing there and so a Strathspey Winter Sports Development Association was created. This was led by the local landowner, Iain Grant, who was Laird of Rothiemurchus and it received funding from central government, the local authority and private enterprise. Access roads and ski facilities were built and the first phase of the Cairn Gorm ski development was inaugurated in 1960.[285] As skiing was expected to attract large numbers of winter visitors, a number of prominent businesses – including The Rank Organisation – appeared interested in providing resort-style hotel accommodation.

Rank's well-publicised gesture of offering to fund the development of additional skiing infrastructure on Cairn Gorm helped to endear the company to locals. Soon, a deal was struck to acquire a site already earmarked for a hotel-resort project at Coylumbridge on Ian Grant's Rothiemurchus Estate. Until Rank concluded its purchase from Grant, it had seemed likely that the department store tycoon Hugh Fraser and the Scottish & Newcastle Breweries company would be the project's joint developers, but Rank's bid was the more generous. (The Fraser/Scottish & Newcastle scheme eventually materialised elsewhere in the vicinity.)

Following planning advice and the wishes of the Rothiemurchus Estate, Rank developed its Coylumbridge Hotel with unusual sensitivity, employing Russell, Hodgson & Leigh, who had previously designed several hotel interiors for Grosvenor House. According to the project architect, Ray Leigh, Rank's selection of the firm happened as a result of its Hotel Division's Managing Director, John Hastings, coincidentally staying overnight at the Lygon Arms Hotel in Broadway, Worcestershire, which Dick Russell's father had once owned and which his brother, Gordon, had helped to restore. Enthused by the hotel's rustic charm, Hastings was directed by its present owner to Russell's nearby furniture workshop. As a result of his encounter with the

1

2

An aerial view of the Coylumbridge Hotel's exterior, showing the two accommodation wings on either side of the reception with the swimming pool to the rear; the hotel's picturesque layout was complemented by interiors featuring stone rubble walls, pine-framed furnishings and checked fabrics, as shown in (3) to (6). The swimming pool, shown in (7), had a laminated timber roof.

3

4

5

6

7

Russell brothers, responsibility for the Coylumbridge project was given over to Russell, Hodgson & Leigh.[286] As Ray Leigh recalls:

> 'John Hastings and his colleagues were so busy dealing with numerous hotel schemes all at once that they had no time to interfere with what we were doing and so we had almost complete freedom. We were even required to deal with issues more commonly addressed by clients than their architects – such as land acquisition and applying for a drinks license.'[287]

A condition of planning permission was that the hotel should also provide inexpensive youth hostel-style accommodation for young people and families wishing to explore the surrounding scenery and to undertake outdoor activities. Thus, as well as 113 hotel rooms, lounges and restaurant facilities, a 'Mountain Lodge' for these guests was included with its own separate cafeteria and sitting areas. A third element was a leisure centre, including a gymnasium and ice rink, housed beneath a laminated timber roof structure (designed on behalf of Russell, Hodgson & Leigh by the structural engineer Tony Hunt).

Shielded from view by mature forest, the hotel was a discreet three-storey structure, approximately T-shaped in plan, with a strong horizontal emphasis and informal massing, the various blocks appearing to overlap slightly. Yet, with its pitched tiled roofs, pine cladding and feature walls of granite rubble, it might equally have been designed for a freeway through the Canadian Rocky Mountains as nestled by the Cairngorms.

Within, a large open-plan foyer, lounge and bar space provided generous public circulation and, from this, the restaurant, cafeteria, pool and conference/banqueting suite were accessed. The centrepiece was an open fireplace, located in a structure formed of smoothly curved granite boulders, around which pine-framed lounge chairs were arranged to engender an atmosphere of warmth and relaxation. As with Russell, Hodgson & Leigh's previous hotels, the interiors were neatly-detailed yet unpretentious in style and there were bespoke furnishings throughout.[288]

The Coylumbridge Hotel and Mountain Lodge opened in November 1965. Reviewing the development, the *Caterer and Hotel Keeper* commented on the hotel's 'warm, welcoming rusticity', noting that the 'beds are fitted with bold chequered covers woven by local craftsmen' and that the furniture 'has been built in Scotland using light Scandinavian-type woods.'[289] Meanwhile, *Interior Design*'s critic was merely relieved that:

The Five Bridges Hotel in Gateshead and the hotel's Bewick's Bar, featuring fibreglass representations of industrial cogs and gear wheels in the ceiling.

> 'There is no suggestion of the domestic or imported *schmalz* which a combination of Scotland and skiing might so easily have inspired, although a high proportion of local products have been used. Only in the restaurant is there an excess of the knotty softwood and random rubble which the architects have allowed themselves…

Visually the most successful area is the cafeteria (the 'Long Room'), where bold
shapes, bright colours and good proportions owe little to Scotland or skiing.'[290]
Rank's next hotel to open, the Five Bridges in Gateshead, was entirely different in
conception, appearance and quality. Designed by the Brighton-based firm of H. Hubbard
Ford & Partners for the Newcastle property developer, Greensatt & Barratt Ltd,
externally, it was a banal structure with exposed concrete floors and brick infill. Indeed,
it more resembled a large secondary school of its era than a place of hospitality.

While the hotel's overnight accommodation was still under construction, its three
bars were opened in August 1965 and these were the hotel's most noteworthy aspect.
The interior design work was by Tributus Design Unit, based in King's Langley in
Hertfordshire, who mixed colourful 'pop' design with nostalgic references to the locale's
industrial history. For example, 'Bewick's Bar' commemorated the eighteenth century
engraver, Thomas Bewick, with reproductions of his work lining the walls, while the
ceiling comprised fibreglass renditions of industrial cogs and gears. The furniture,
however, consisted of wire mesh Bertoia chairs, set against bright orange carpets and
upholstery. 'The Engine Room', located adjacent, was, as its name suggested, themed
around heavy industry, particularly shipbuilding. Within a week, the bars had apparently
sold over 1,000 gallons of beer to a thirsty and curious public. A car park at second floor
level was sandwiched between the hotel's reception and bar facilities and its
accommodation block, the parking being accessed from the rear. Projecting from the
front of the hotel was a lower block containing a conference, banqueting and exhibition
suite.[291] It took until the spring of 1966 for the hotel to be completed, it being
inaugurated in May by H.R.H. Princess Margaret. The involvement of separate
architects, interior designers, developers and operators, coupled with the early opening
of the hotel's bar facilities, demonstrates the commercial pressure under which the
project was carried out.

Rank, meanwhile, had acquired a lease on another substantial new provincial hotel,
located by Trent Bridge in Nottingham. Its curving 10-storey shell had been built in
1961 as a speculative office development but the developer went bankrupt, abandoning
the half-built structure which then lay empty until a new owner was found, who decided
instead to finish it as the 90-bedroom Bridgford Hotel. This re-design was carried out
by Tributus Design Unit. The *Caterer and Hotel Keeper* observed:

> 'The architects and planners were unanimous in saying that their biggest headache
> was the low ceiling beams. They have solved this problem not by going in for light
> ceilings but by making a feature of them. Many are coloured, with sloping or
> cantilevered panels. In the principal bar – the Sheriff's Room – one feels as if one
> is in a marquee, whereas the main function room – the River Room – is rather
> like a bohemian attic. The structural supports along the length of the curved

The Bridgeford Hotel in
Nottingham.

> building made bedroom design difficult. A
> partition wall at each support meant very small
> single rooms and a wall at alternative supports
> gave rooms too large for singles. Therefore,
> there are only three singles… On sloping
> ground, the hotel has on its lower ground floor
> with the reception at the rear. 'The Outlaws Bar'
> – the public bar – is on the upper ground floor,
> as is the Bridgford Restaurant…'[292]

The Pennine Hotel in Derby.

Possibly because the kitchens were too small for conventional cooking, the *Caterer and Hotel Keeper*'s report emphasised the hotel's use of new-fangled microwave ovens. Its manager had been promoted from one of Rank's motorway service stations, where these were used and he enthusiastically believed that they offered the most efficient means of cooking everything from steaks to Dover sole. He expected that the use of microwaves would transform hotel catering during the ensuing years and was evidently very proud of the Bridgford's kitchens being ahead of the curve.[293] In common with most British mass caterers in the 1960s, Rank's management was enthralled by the potential for economies achievable with such increasingly industrialised approaches. An advertisements in the *Caterer and Hotel Keeper* for Smethursts, a supplier of frozen meat and fish, proclaimed that 'To The Rank Organisation, it makes good business sense to use Smethursts' Frozen Foods throughout their Hotel Division.'[294]

Architecturally unimpressive though the Five Bridges and Bridgford hotels were, the Rank hotel chain truly reached its nadir with the 100-bedroom Pennine Hotel in Derby, another design by H. Hubbard Ford, which opened towards the end of 1966 as part of a new central development in which Rank also ran a ten-pin bowling alley. It was a six-storey block on concrete stilts with textured concrete facings and ends clad in dark brown brick. As with the Five Bridges in Gateshead, it most resembled a dreary secondary school. Aiming almost exclusively at the business market, its double rooms were unusually compact in the expectation that they would mostly be let as singles. They were also sparsely decorated, as it was believed that men travelling on accounts would prefer to spend their free time in the hotel's Eagle Bar (which was named after a locally-made Rolls-Royce aero engine). The restaurant was supplied from a kitchen designed for operation by just 11 staff, again making extensive use of pre-packaged frozen foods and microwave ovens. However, the *Caterer and Hotel Keeper* records that 'the chef, Guy Rety, from Rank's Coylumbridge Hotel, Aviemore, felt that it was demoralising to have a dishwasher in the centre. It is therefore to be screened by a rubber curtain.'[295]

During the Pennine Hotel's construction, Rank's Chairman, John Davis fired the Hotel Division Managing Director, John Hastings, after only three years in the post and just when a critical mass of hotels had been opened. Hastings' replacement was an Australian-born marketing manager, John Whittle, who was brought in from the Top Rank ballroom dancing division.[296]

Rank Hotel's flagship property was to be the 416-room Royal Lancaster Hotel in London's Bayswater Road, for the completion of which Whittle was now responsible. The 19-storey podium and tower block, filling a site incorporating Lancaster Gate Underground Station, had been designed by, T.P. Bennett & Son, a company founded in Nottingham in the 1930s which had subsequently established a London office. Pre-war, T.P. Bennett had designed several cinema buildings for Odeon, which had subsequently been bought by Rank. As with the company's Bridgford Hotel in Nottingham, this development had been initiated as a speculative office scheme by the property tycoon Max Rayne and it was only once construction got underway that Rank negotiated to lease it for hotel use. Externally, it was faced in slim pre-cast concrete facing panels which formed a pattern of hexagonal openings for the windows, the spaces beneath which were filled with black mosaic. Around the podium and the topmost

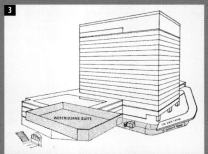

Images of the Royal Lancaster Hotel in London, Rank's flagship hotel property, built within a shell intended for offices. These show (1) the accommodation tower with hexagonal-shaped pre-cast concrete façade detailing, (2) part of the entrance foyer designed by Gordon Bowyer, (3) a diagram of vehicle access to the car park and the conference suite's location in the podium, (4) a Rank Hotels advertisement with models posing as businessmen and (5) part of the top floor bar and restaurant, designed by Leonard Manasseh.

storey, which contained services, the facing panels formed a pattern of closely-spaced verticals. While the detailing was well-resolved, variations of this formula were applied to many office developments of the era.

Initially, John Hastings planned to complete the building as a mid-market 'motor hotel', making a virtue of the fact that the podium's first floor level contained a car park but, upon taking control of Rank's hotel operations, John Whittle decided to move the project upmarket so as to compete directly with the London Hilton and Royal Garden hotels, located elsewhere around the fringes of Hyde Park. Instead of the swimming pool and bowling alley initially suggested by Hastings for spaces within the podium, there would be substantial conference, exhibition and banqueting facilities. Just as at Rank's Bridgford Hotel in Nottingham, converting the shell of an office block meant making compromises because neither the layout of the vertical circulation and servicing, nor the heights and sizes of the windows were ideal for the new usage.[297]

The hotel fit-out was scheduled to happen between January to August 1967 – a very tight time-frame for so large a project. To co-ordinate the work, Whittle appointed one of Rank's regular designers of motorway service stations, Tom Calloway, as consultant architect. As co-ordinating architects, he selected the London-based practice of Cassidy, Farrington and Dennys, with whom he had previously worked successfully in his last managerial position within Rank to convert failing cinemas and bowling alleys into ballrooms and banqueting facilities. Led by Nigel Farrington, who was well-connected within London architecture and design circles, its past projects had included the design of the Shell Centre offices on London's South Bank – a project of similar magnitude to the Royal Lancaster Hotel. Moreover, as the hotel would also contain ballroom, banqueting and exhibition facilities, Cassidy, Farrington and Dennys' known ability in designing such spaces would prove useful.[298]

Realising that there would be far too much design work required for his own firm to handle so quickly, Farrington invited other architects and designers of his acquaintance to devise the principal interior spaces. Thus, Gordon Bowyer & Partners with Keith Townend drew up the foyer and associated hallways, Leonard Manasseh & Partners designed the top-floor Looking Glass Restaurant, Anthony Sharp and Geoffrey Harcourt produced two bars, one for guests called 'Falstaff's Cellar' – decorated with fibreglass panels depicting imagined scenes from the Wars of the Roses – plus a public bar, 'The Glorious House of Lancaster', with an outdoor terrace facing Hyde Park. Margaret Casson (whose husband was Hugh Casson) and Roger Liminton produced a suite of five small private function rooms, Farrington himself designed the very large Westbourne Suite banqueting and exhibition hall while H.T. Cadbury-Brown designed the smaller Nine Kings Banqueting Suite. Bedrooms on the fourth to seventeenth floors were designed by Ray Leigh of Russell, Hodgson & Leigh, who had previously been responsible for Rank's well-regarded Coylumbridge Hotel. Other bedrooms and suites were designed jointly by two Cassidy, Farrington and Dennys employees, Sarah Evelegh and Mary Shand. Evelegh recalls that, although the hotel was marketed as a luxury venue, it was, in her opinion, yet another high-density, tourist-orientated enterprise in which nearly all of the rooms were relatively compact and homogenous.[299]

Nonetheless, with such a range of highly regarded architecture and interior design talents assembled, the Royal Lancaster Hotel might have been expected to be among the finest examples of its kind, reflecting 'Swinging London' at its best. While they all gave of their best, alas, the earlier procurement of the hotel's shell by a property developer for office space undermined its potential to impress. The *AR* reflected with despondency:

'In an age when the client's needs are becoming more specialised…, it makes little sense to design a conventional structure before knowing how it is going to be used. Speculative development might succeed if it were possible to put up a type of structure which allowed infinite degrees of flexibility within it, but the speculative design of the Lancaster Hotel determined the position of staircases and lifts, and such variable dimensions as ceiling and window sill heights, well before the Rank Organisation came to the scene as clients. As many floors as possible were crammed into the overall height of the building and full air-conditioning was only introduced subsequently, reducing the ceiling heights even more. This… has seriously affected the quality of space in the public areas. For example, the site has the finest views over Kensington Gardens, which the fixed sill heights made it almost impossible to exploit.'[300]

Furthermore, the hotel's foyer was 'mean and confusing', making the *AR* 'yearn for beaux-arts axial symmetry.'[301] A shopping arcade with large display cases, presumably to entice tourists to buy souvenirs of their visit to London, was the foyer's most conspicuous feature. The adjacent foyer bar was 'frequently closed, forming a dark and empty space at the end of the reception area' and the white acoustic ceiling was 'marred by the heavy profile of the air conditioning outlets.' These were of a 1930s design in Bakelite, a type still commonly found in British commercial interiors even today. Their advantages were cheapness and easy maintenance, both attractive qualities for service engineers, whereas a more up-to-date design with neat aluminium slits would have harmonised better with interiors. These criticisms aside, the *AR* felt that Gordon Bowyer's treatment of the foyer spaces was 'simple and strong', its various uses being unified by the consistent use of hard finishes and neutral colours, such as honey-coloured terrazzo, travertine and teak. Particularly impressive was 'a remarkable computer which copes with all the billing, registering every charge against a guest's account and producing any bill within thirty seconds'; this was, however, hidden from view behind 'the bland exterior of the reception counter.'[302]

Leonard Manasseh's & Partners' design of the Looking Glass Restaurant also failed to realise its full potential for reasons largely outwith its architect's control. The prior positioning of the stair and lift shaft blocked what – with more considered design of the entire edifice – should have been an unbroken panoramic view over Hyde Park. Manasseh tried his best to disguise this unfortunate blockage with tinted mirror panelling but little could be done to overcome the high sills of the concrete curtain walling, other than to create a raised floor area around the bar – and this only served to emphasise the poor-quality suspended ceiling finishes used throughout the hotel. Around ventilation ducts and light fittings, these darkened quickly, while cigarette smoke caused further colour variations. Yet, beneath this unfortunate finish, Manasseh designed bespoke leather-upholstered bucket chairs on pedestals and did his best otherwise to specify furnishings that were:

'Both rich and restrained… the dark green carpets and leather upholstery introduce a note of intimacy… The overall dark tone is livened up by some orange leather upholstery and by white marble tops in the bar area… the restaurant comes into its own at night when the window glass blends with the black mirror to form a continuous reflecting surface and when the ceiling retreats behind the glitter of hanging glass prisms.'[303]

Alas, budgetary constraints limited the number of these light fittings Manasseh was allowed to specify and so 'the brilliant effect that might have been achieved is only hinted at.'[304]

The Nine Kings Banqueting suite was principally of interest to the *AR* from a technical perspective; it was regarded as a fine example of an emerging type of multi-functional hotel environment which could be used for banquets, exhibitions, sports such as boxing or wrestling and corporate events of various sizes. Horizontal sliding partitions could be brought across to divide the space into three equal (and acoustically separate) parts. The Rank Organisation's expertise in cinema and television was reflected in the 'elaborate facilities for lighting and projection' and there were galleries for 'interpreters with simultaneous translation equipment during international conferences.' The ceiling was on a 4-foot grid so as to be demountable, enabling cabling and lighting to be dropped through wherever necessary and the fixing of temporary partition walls.

Evidently, the architects and interior designers responsible for the Royal Lancaster Hotel's fit-out focused their limited budget where it would have maximum impact on guests and visitors – meaning that furniture, carpets, curtains, counter tops and room fittings were of a high quality, whereas ceiling finishes and other slightly less proximal surfaces were of comparatively inexpensive design. Consequently, the hotel was never going to reflect the very best of contemporary international practice but was, rather, a compromise between that aspiration and the reality of needing to make an existing building shell work as best possible combined within the additional constraints of a slightly too mean budget and too tight a time-frame.

Shortly after completion, the Royal Lancaster Hotel featured on film in the bank heist caper 'The Italian Job', starring Michael Caine and distributed by Rank, the initial sequences of which were set in fashionable locations in 'Swinging London.' In the film, Caine's character, Charlie Crocker, a 'loveable cockney rogue', newly released from jail, is treated to a *ménage a quinze* with bikini-clad 'hip chicks' in one of the hotel's suites.

Competition between the proximal Royal Lancaster, Royal Garden and Hilton hotels was intense. The fact that all three had top-floor restaurants only intensified their rivalry and, having been the first to open with such a facility, the Hilton was also the first in which a drop-off in custom was noted. The management's solution was to strip out Hugh Casson's refined modernist interior, replacing this with a highly ornate scheme by the company's American-based interior designer, David T. Williams. While Casson had sought to avoid distracting from the view outwith, Williams decided instead to make the interior look as obviously 'luxurious' as possible by introducing warmer colours and decorative flooring, wall coverings and ceiling finishes, chandeliers, draped curtains and potted palms – an extravaganza of pseudo Edwardiana, entirely at odds with the hotel's overall design. So far as Hilton was concerned, the approach at least made the restaurant look distinctly different from those of its two competitors.[305]

In the longer run, Rank's hotel chain was out-paced by those of Trust Houses, Forte, Strand, plus the various overseas-headquartered chains that subsequently entered the British market. By the mid-1970s, Rank had begun to dispose of its hotels and, within a decade, all had new owners.

British Transport Hotels

Upon the nationalisation of the railways in 1948, the hotel estates of the 'big four' companies were brought together under the management of the Hotels Executive, which in 1953 was re-configured as British Transport Hotel and Catering Services. It could

The Old Course Hotel in St Andrews, as viewed from the golf links and also from the railway, which was located to the rear.

claim to be the country's largest hotel chain in terms of the number of bedrooms it provided (5,317 in 49 hotels). With few exceptions, however, its properties dated from the Victorian and Edwardian eras. Of the 1930s additions, the Midland Hotel at Morecambe had proved a great disappointment, being difficult to maintain and, due to its location in a working class resort, hard to fill with a clientele willing to pay a premium; it was consequently sold in 1952. When railway management was re-structured in 1963, the hotel division became known as British Transport Hotels.

As with railway management in general, British Transport Hotels' leadership was worried about being perceived as old-fashioned and presiding over a business that increasingly appeared unfit for the future. While the railways struggled to match competition from road and air modes, its hotel division fretted about whether potential guests might prefer the new Trust Houses, Albanys and Rank hotels to the high-ceilinged, rambling and sometimes thread-bare old hotels it mostly operated, grandly designed though they undoubtedly were. As in the 1930s, the best solution to this problem appeared to be to cover up Victoriana with false walls and ceilings and to add up-to-date wallpaper, carpets and furniture in a bid to disguise as best possible this reality.

In the mid-1960s, British Transport Hotels began planning for its first – and only – new premises of the post-war era, the Old Course Hotel, located in St Andrews on the Fife Coast in Scotland. The town is best known for its ancient university and as the 'home of golf', the latter appellation being a big attraction for tourists from around the world. The hotel was completed in 1968 on a site formerly occupied by railway sidings, facing the Old Course's seventeenth hole with the North Sea beyond. The idea was to emulate the success of British Transport Hotels' properties at Gleneagles and Turnberry, albeit with up-to-date design and attractive resort-style facilities. To fund the project, British Transport Hotels entered into a joint agreement with BOAC (the British Overseas Airways Corporation), the forerunner to British Airways. They selected New York-based architects, Nathaniel Curtis and Arthur Davis, whose large practice produced a wide variety of building types, ranging from public housing schemes and university buildings to hotels and Playboy clubs. For the hotel, they collaborated with the London-based practice of Mathews, Ryan and Simpson, who carried out some of the detailed design and also supervised construction. Recently, they had designed university buildings in Aberdeen and so were well acquainted with local building regulations and planning procedures.

Curtis and Davis's design was for a four-storey structure, containing eighty bedrooms, two restaurants and two bars. On a picturesque site, a certain amount of discretion was required and so, to reduce the appearance of mass, the ends were recessed and stepped downward. Given current architecture fashion, however, the

architects were unable to resist the lure of brutalist façade detailing, with the floors forming thick concrete protrusions, matching the top service floor, the sides of which were slightly pitched, perhaps in a nod to country house hotel design tradition. All of the bedrooms had bay windows, again picking up on nineteenth century design approaches while enabling better views towards the golf course for those at the front. For those to the rear, however, a panorama of decaying railway infrastructure had to suffice. The end walls were clad in a thick layer of undressed stone blocks, continuing the brutalist aesthetic, while also vaguely referencing rugged seaside cliffs. Altogether, the composition was a strange and somewhat uncomfortable-looking mix of what the architects really wanted, tempered with what they believed the local planners would allow. More than anything else, the hotel resembled a secure military complex, designed with the intention of being blast-proof. Unsurprisingly, this harsh approach failed to accord with the idea of a refined and romantic Scotland that a majority of its guests came to St Andrews to experience. Worse still, the hotel was one of the town's most prominent buildings, directly facing the Royal and Ancient Golf Club's grand club house across an expanse of fairway. From the outset, many locals secretly wished that they could somehow make it disappear. While the hotel obstinately remained to torment them, after less than a year, the railway to St Andrews was closed, a victim of the notorious 'Beeching cuts.' The newest British Transport Hotel thus became the only one without a nearby rail connection.

British Transport Hotels and BOAC had plans for another new hotel near to London Gatwick Airport. This would have been a very large structure, containing around 900 rooms and again designed in a brutalist aesthetic. The project never came to fruition, however, it being left to private sector operators to build and run hotels there.

Back at St Andrews, after just fifteen years, the exterior of the Old Course Hotel was re-faced in brick with post-modern detailing less likely to be contentious with a traditionally-minded clientele. By that time, British Transport Hotels had become an early target for privatisation by the Conservative Government of Margaret Thatcher. In the long run, the properties it formerly operated have thrived under a variety of owners and most of them are beautifully preserved and maintained. The same cannot be said for many of the hotels run by the other chains described in this chapter.

Chapter 9

Hotels for provincial operators

In the early 1960s, new hotels began to appear in smaller British industrial towns. Just as having a super cinema had been a sign of progress in the 1930s and the development of high-rise apartment blocks had come into fashion in the 1950s, a hotel represented further aspirations to be modern and, even, glamourous. That way, visiting public officials and business travellers could hopefully be accommodated in style, hopefully leaving with a positive impression, rather than one of pollution and decay. Such hotels were also popular venues for conferences and corporate entertainment by the business community, as well as seeking to attract a broad cross-section of the community with for wedding receptions and other special events. Almost invariably, these hotels belonged to brewery chains, who sought to increase their revenues by including several bars to encourage significant drink sales. In a sense, they were following in the traditions of inn-keeping but, over time, the reliance on drinking tended to have negative consequences: though initially considered glamorous, the public rooms risked becoming tainted by stale beer and nicotine. As the *Caterer and Hotel Keeper* observed on several occasions, another challenge was the recruitment of local staff with appropriate *savoir-faire* to provide proper hotelier service.[306]

Perhaps the first of this new generation of smaller hotel was the Keirby in Burnley which was an ambitious project by the local brewer, Massey & Co, to create the only 4-star hotel in Lancashire outside Manchester and Blackpool. For its owner, the hotel represented a very substantial and risky investment outwith its core businesses of making beer and running pubs. The fact that its management decided to press ahead reflected commercial pride and a desire to be associated with a prominent and prestigious facility in the centre of its home town. A soot-blackened industrial town, Burnley was an unlikely setting for the eight-storey, 48-bedroom building, completed in 1960 to a design by H. Hubbard Ford & Partners.

These architects were Brighton-based and otherwise carried out general commercial work, designing supermarkets, banks and shop interiors, a majority of which were in southern England.[307] Many had Festival of Britain-style details and the Keirby Hotel was no exception, the roof of its service storey being arched, much like that of the Royal Festival Hall (though this leitmotif was used in a great many British buildings of the era). The hotel was located adjacent to Burnley's 1930s Odeon cinema, each building being a good example of what was considered fashionable modern architecture in its respective era. Of the hotel's appointments, the *Caterer and Hotel Keeper* reported:

> 'Entering the new hotel through double armour plate glass doors, one comes into the reception and lounge, carpeted in Kingfisher blue and Forest green… There are two settees in turquoise and two low tables of brushed chrome with white plastic tops… Situated on the first floor, the Long Bar is carpeted in two-tone grey and there is a most attractive 31-foot curved bar faced with rosewood and Formica. Built-in seating is upholstered in rust and lemon fabric of a rough weave…The Square Bar has one wall of random stone, while the remainder are panelled. Carpet is French blue with chairs in sherry-coloured hide… Also on this floor is the ladies' powder room, claimed to be one of the most luxurious in

the country with its Honduras mahogany finish and smart mirrored dressing shelf, which is scalloped with blue-grained buttoned leather...'[308]

With two penthouse suites on the top floor, three bars, two dining rooms and a ballroom, the Keirby Hotel was intended to impress locals and visitors alike but, in reality, it mostly attracted commercial travelers. At weekends, visiting football teams patronised it, and it also proved popular as a venue for dinner dances and wedding celebrations. When the economy declined in the second half of the 1960s, it began to struggle and soon its first floor restaurant, which had a sprung dance floor beneath the carpet, came to be used as a venue for Northern Soul dances, attended by hordes of 'mods.' Needless to say,

The Keirby Hotel in Burnley was an early attempt at developing a new hotel as a prestige facility in an industrial town. The building provides a sharp contrast with its immediate environs and, within, appears to have had a fairly high level of design ambition.

these events irrevocably altered the hotel's reputation from a genteel retreat for businessmen to one that was likely to be raucous. Its decline continued until recent time and, after a spell of closure, it was converted into student accommodation. In the space where youths once danced, there is now a gym for students to work out.

The Strathclyde Hotel in Corby, completed in 1963, was of similar dimensions and capacity to the Keirby and was likewise located in an industrial context. Designed by the Canadian émigré architect Enrico de Pierro, its name reflected the fact that large numbers of Scottish steelworkers had come to Corby to find work. It was given 'new town' status and a master plan for new development was devised by the architect and urban planner Sir William Holford. As part of this scheme, a site for a hotel was located adjacent to the shopping precinct, the intention being to accommodate businessmen visiting the steel works.

As a student at McGill University in Montreal in the late 1930s, de Pierro had first been introduced to the architecture of Le Corbusier and Alvar Aalto, which influenced his own subsequent output. Having served in Europe during the Second World War, he returned to North America, became a tutor at McGill, though his wish was to move to London. Through his university colleagues, he was recommended for a post teaching at the Architectural Association and, there, he entered and won a competition to design Poole Technical College, beating over 250 other entrants. Next, he was successful in another competition for a new Civic Centre building for Corby. It was as a result of that project that he was also commissioned to design the Strathclyde Hotel.[309]

De Pierro's scheme was for a 10-storey building with a podium, containing mainly retail space, above which the hotel's restaurant and bar were encased in a glass-faced box. Higher up, the bedroom block stood on piloti, its various floors being slightly offset with recesses and over-hangs, the edges being of exposed concrete. In between, the walls were faced in engineering brick, chosen for being particularly resistant to urban grime. The design was hard-edged, yet remarkably well articulated. Within, the hotel was at first considered as Corby's most stylish hang-out, its Pigalle Bar in particular becoming a local attraction.

Two views of the Strathclyde Hotel in Corby, the exterior of which was boldly shaped. Alas, in the 1970s, it suffered a sharp decline paralleling the fortunes of the town in which it was located.

As with the Keirby in Burnley, such glamour as the Strathclyde may at first have possessed soon wore off. In the 1970s, British Steel ran down its Corby plants and their decline badly affected the town. Against a background of high unemployment and little money for ongoing maintenance, the hotel was closed in 1980 after an outbreak of legionnaire's disease in its water supply. When the nearby Civic Centre began to suffer acute structural problems and was demolished, the vacant building was re-purposed as local government offices.

In Scotland's industrial Central Belt, there were a number of new hotels serving mainly business clients and hosting local events. Motherwell, a steel town in Lanarkshire, had the 40-bedroom Garrion Hotel which opened late in 1962. It was the first new hotel operated by the prolific Glasgow-based restauranteur, Reo Stakis, who was a Cypriot émigré to Britain in 1928 and who thereafter worked hard to establish a successful catering business. The hotel's first floor contained a restaurant, two cocktail bars, a ballroom and a 'canteen' self-service cafeteria, the latter facility outfitted with Rexine-upholstered benches, Formica table tops and a rubber-tiled floor, much like the staff facilities of industrial premises. The other, more upmarket, public rooms, meanwhile, had similar dark wood panelling to factory boardrooms.[310] Clearly, Mr Stakis and his interior designer, Jean Welsh, knew the taste of their clientele. Subsequently, Stakis built or acquired numerous other hotels all over Britain; none of his new builds was architecturally distinguished, however.

In Glasgow, the ten-storey, 115-bedroom Royal Stuart Hotel in Jamaica Street, which opened in 1964, was the city's first new hotel since the Beresford of 1938. Designed by Walter Underwood & Partners, it was a speculative investment by the Great Universal catalogue shopping company for operation by a local chain, Clydesdale & County Hotels Ltd.[311]

Underwood was born in Glasgow's East End in 1906; in the mid-1920s, he studied architecture at Glasgow School of Art, then worked as an assistant in various Glasgow and Lanarkshire practices before switching to local authority work for Dumbarton County Council and Nottingham Corporation. During the Second World War years, he was Chief Architect for the Scottish Co-operative & Wholesale Association and in 1946

The Garrion Hotel in Motherwell, which featured a cafeteria and an a la carte restaurant, thereby attracting two different sections of the local market.

he was made a partner in Wylie, Shanks & Underwood (previously Wylie, Shanks & Lochead). In 1960 he broke away to form Walter Underwood & Partners, the 'partners' being two employees from the previous firm. By the 1960s, Underwood was not only considered a leading Scottish modernist architect but was also highly regarded in professional circles, serving as a Glasgow School of Art governor and as Vice President of the Royal Incorporation of Architects in Scotland. Apart from the Royal Stuart Hotel, Underwood's other major projects of the era included new buildings for the Royal College of Science and Technology (now Strathclyde University) and a major development of high-rise housing and maisonette flats for Glasgow's Cowcaddens area.

The Royal Stuart Hotel in Glasgow, showing the open terrace on the top storey, optimistically intended for an outdoor restaurant.

The *Caterer and Hotel Keeper* felt that the hotel's exposed concrete structure 'brightened a formerly drab area of Glasgow.' Somewhat optimistically, given the city's often wet and windy climate, Underwood left space on the top floor for an outdoor garden restaurant, though unsurprisingly this never came to fruition. The *Caterer and Hotel Keeper* noted the hotel's automatic sliding entrance doors, features that were by then *de rigeur* for any city hotel aspiring to upmarket status. The interiors were described as 'Scandinavian-inspired' but the accompanying illustrations showed floridly patterned carpets and furniture that was more typical of British middle-brow taste than anything from Denmark or Sweden.

The expected clientele were tourists and business executives. For the latter market, there were pairs of single bedrooms with adjoining shared bathrooms, the *Caterer and Hotel Keeper* explaining that 'after extensive surveys it has been discovered that many young businessmen visiting the Glasgow area are willing to share a bathroom but not a bedroom. This system saves both cost and space.'[312] By the mid-1960s, such an approach was unusual, indeed, rather backward. Arguably, the hotel's effective two classes of accommodation reflected Glasgow's uneasy industrial decline and the nascent beginnings of its gradual transformation as a cultural destination instead. By the 1980s, the Royal Stuart Hotel had followed the Beresford in becoming student accommodation as hotels lacking bathrooms for every bedroom were no longer tenable.

Scottish & Newcastle Breweries' 102-bedroom Gosforth Park Hotel, located in Newcastle's northern suburbs, opened October 1966 to a design by the company's in-house architect C.P. Wakefield-Brand and his assistants A. Raine and J. Hetherington. As they otherwise specialised in the design of brewery buildings, their approach to planning and specifying very obviously reflected the era's better industrial architecture. One major problem was that the site had underground mine workings, meaning that subsidence was feared. The solution was to build on concrete rafts with so-called 'frame box' construction to ensure that structural integrity would be maintained in the event of movement underneath.[313]

In terms of clientele, the hotel was expected to rely on the local manufacturing economy to generate much of its business, its proximity to Newcastle Airport and to major roads being advantageous. In plan, it had had three wings, two of these forming an L-shaped, four-storey storey block with a function suite on the first floor and bedrooms above.[314] The remaining single-storey wing contained a very large 6,500

Three views of the Gosforth Park Hotel in Newcastle, showing the main façade, the concrete structure containing the ballroom/event space and the cocktail bar, with its 'moon crater' ceiling.

square foot space for trade shows and dinner dances which, according to the *Caterer and Hotel Keeper*, was the 'showplace of the hotel.'[315] Constructed of exposed pre-cast concrete frames, it was entirely free of internal columns. Its roof was of cast in situ concrete and, in elevation, the ridges and troughs made a zig-zag pattern. These were offset on either side with the result that the area between consisted of a series of inter-locking triangular prisms. The journal *Building* considered it to be the first of its kind in the country, if not Europe, and praised its combination of technical ingenuity and constructional elegance.[316] Although it was undeniably eye-catching, similar repeating wavy forms were also found in better examples of the era's bus garages, warehouses and light industrial premises As the bedroom block to the rear was faced in dark brown engineering brick with continuous horizontal fenestration, the whole *ensemble* somewhat resembled a modern factory complex, rather than a place of hospitality. Nonetheless, it was undeniably well constructed.

Though externally somewhat dour, the hotel's public rooms, designed by Raine, were memorably 'groovy'. The ballroom was decorated with abstract murals on a bright purple background. Its concrete roof structure was exposed and illuminated by coloured lighting. The Stable Bar was open to the public and was robustly outfitted to resemble a stable for race horses, there being a stone floor, bare brick walls and a slatted timber ceiling. The Branding Grill restaurant, adjacent, had sliding abstract fibreglass partitions to adjust its size according to demand while the cocktail bar's ceiling was modelled on 'moon craters.'[317] Just as the interior designs of British seaside hotels had offered holidaymakers colour and escapist glamour, in industrial areas, the latest examples brought an uplifting taste of 'Swinging London' psychedelia. The high proportion of communal space indicates the importance of the hotel's social and corporate functions, supporting the local business community.

In the second half of the 1960s, the use of architectural theming for the interiors of new hotels increased. Partly, this was a design approach that, despite proselytising by would-be modernists in favour of the 'International Style', had never gone away. Partly too, as more new hotels were built, operators now wished to make theirs memorably distinct, rather than homogenous. Indeed, within commercial modernism, the conflict of aims between the universalist approach most often preferred by architecture theorists (who sought to emulate the ideas of modernism's European 'masters') and architects' clients' desires to offer unique experiences, was paradoxical. One way of resolving this problem was to use a futuristic-looking 'space age' theme, within which modernist design 'icons', such as Eero Saarinen 'tulip' chairs, could be accommodated. Another increasingly fashionable solution was to adopt a Danish or a Scandinavian theme, thereby embodying what was considered as

An aerial view of the Gosforth Park Hotel, showing the wavy concrete roof enclosing the ballroom/event space.

'good' design taste while using high-quality 'natural' finishes, such as brick, timber and leather (rather than space-age – and therefore synthetic – materials like fibreglass, formica, nylon and plastic). That way, conservative taste could be reconciled to an extent with modern aesthetics.

In York, the London-based hoteliers and restaurateurs, Spiers & Pond, a company established in the mid-nineteenth century, developed a new nine-storey, 100-room hotel called the Viking, a name conveniently referencing York's medieval past as a Viking capital while justifying interiors filled with up-to-date Danish furniture and lighting; this was completed in 1967 to a design by Fitzroy Robinson and Partners, the London-based architects of the Skyway at London Heathrow Airport. From a distance, the hotel's ten-storey accommodation tower, which was entirely clad in brick, somewhat resembled a grain silo, or similar large industrial structure. Within, however, the interior design approach sought to transport guests across the North Sea to Denmark. While many British hotels and restaurants of the 1960s aspired to emulate Scandinavian design approaches, more than any other hotel, the Viking appeared as though it could actually have existed there instead of in Yorkshire. As the *Caterer and Hotel Keeper* records:

'The Scandinavian décor of the Viking Hotel has already been the subject of

The Viking Hotel in York, the interior of which was designed in the contemporary Danish manner with varnished timber ceilings, bare brick walls and imported furniture.

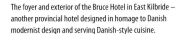
The foyer and exterior of the Bruce Hotel in East Kilbride –
another provincial hotel designed in homage to Danish
modernist design and serving Danish-style cuisine.

boasts by Spiers & Pond, and it is not difficult to see why. As soon as one enters the hotel, one gets the feeling that it is different. The colourful fabrics, the furnishings, all the natural wood and brickwork… The foyer has warm, red brick tiles instead of carpet and the bedrooms as well as public areas include brick and wood in the design. Great attention has also been paid to light fittings and details like candle-holders to maintain the Scandinavian, and frequently Viking, theme… The 'open plan' – there are large glass panels – lounge bar and coffee shop lead off the foyer, and an open tread staircase leads up to the first floor, which houses restaurant, cocktail bar, ballroom, kitchens and functions suite… [which] have been well designed to break up the area – contrasting wood finishes, false ceilings and split level.'[318]

In the expanding Scottish new town of East Kilbride, near Glasgow, meanwhile, the Bruce Hotel went one better, having not only Danish-style décor but also a 'Dansk Coffee Bar', selling Danish pastries and staffed by real Danish waitresses. Recently, a Danish Food Centre restaurant had opened in Glasgow and, as this had proven highly popular, the Bruce Hotel's operator, Lowland Scottish Hotels, had decided to include its own version. Moreover, the latest phases of East Kilbride's development to be completed had been modelled to an extent on the new Copenhagen suburb of Ballerup (and even had a school of that name) – so East Kilbride's perceived cultural affinity with Denmark was strong.

The Bruce Hotel was designed by Walter Underwood & Partners, who had previously been responsible for the Royal Stuart Hotel in Glasgow. It contained 65 *en suite* bedrooms, a 90-seat restaurant and a 120-seat cabaret club. The *Caterer and Hotel Keeper* noted that the 'bedroom furnishings, as much of that in the public areas, has been imported from Denmark and plays an important part in the overall décor… In the night club… the décor becomes more gimmicky with moulded plaster ceilings and coloured lighting.'[319] The Dansk Coffee Bar's trade was expected to come from 'local people, but not teenagers, rather than hotel guests.'[320] It would appear that, in East Kilbride as elsewhere, hotel managements were fearful of young peoples' potential for rowdy behaviour. The fact that Lowland Scottish Hotels' origin was as part of the temperance movement, which sought to cut the consumption of alcoholic drinks to reduce public drunkenness, perhaps also affected its perceptions of some of the local clientele.

Megastructures incorporating hotels

As the 1960s development boom progressed, property entrepreneurs and planners became further emboldened in the scale of projects that were proposed and given assent. Increasingly, very large mixed-use schemes were devised, requiring the total clearance of big tracts of prime city centre land. By incorporating shopping arcades, office blocks, leisure facilities and a hotel in a single complex, it was possible to spread risk as, even if one element failed to generate enough of a return, the others would probably meet or exceed expectations. Among the more ambitious of these initiatives was a project for a large bombsite by Piccadilly Gardens in central Manchester, incorporating the monumental-looking Hotel Piccadilly.

The scheme had first been mooted back in 1959 when the property developer and builder Bernard Sunley became interested in realising the site's potential. Sunley was a Londoner who had undertaken military construction work during the Second World War, building numerous aerodromes for the British government. A workaholic, he rode the post-war construction boom, using his well-placed connections to help win lucrative contracts, including for government buildings and the Gatwick Airport terminal building (completed in 1958). In addition, his company built the Skyway Hotel at London Airport, a project which seems to have wetted his appetite for further hotel developments.

For the Manchester scheme, Sunley initially employed Maxwell Fry and Jane Drew to prepare designs for what was imagined as a megastructure to serve as the northern gateway to the Moseley Street Comprehensive Development Area with linking with pedestrian walkways to Piccadilly Station. In 1961, Fry and Drew were superseded by Covell, Matthews & Partners – a London-based practice first established in 1937 by Ralph G. Covell who in 1948 went into partnership with Albert E. T. Matthews. Initially, Covell had specialised in church design and, during the war, he carried out military work. By the 1960s, the partnership had gained a reputation for handling large office, university and housing projects. Their design for Manchester was expected to be completed in early 1963, but progress was delayed by the need for substantial modifications to satisfy the municipal planners while ensuring that Sunley retained the desired amount of floor space. In the end, construction only began that year.[321] The project was then beset with repeated strike action by construction workers, meaning that it took nearly a further three years to come to fruition.[322] In the final version, the entire site was occupied by a podium, containing mostly shop units and a car park, out of which rose three towers. Two of these were office blocks (named Bernard House and Sunley House in

The Hotel Piccadilly in Manchester, a mighty concrete structure floating above the city on comparatively slender piloti; the hotel's parking deck and main entrance on top of the podium were accessed by motorists by means of a spiral ramp.

A series of interior views of the Hotel Piccadilly, showing (1) the view from the reception to the Coffee Shop, (2) the steak house, (3) a suite with separate sitting room, (4) the King Cotton Bar, (5) the Champagne Bar, (6) the restaurant and (7) part of the King Arthur's Court banqueting suite.

memory of Sunley, who died shortly before their completion) while the third contained the 280-bedroom Hotel Piccadilly. This was to have been leased to an unnamed American hotel chain but, when it withdrew, Ind Coope, the brewer and inn-keeper which ran the Hotel Leofric in Coventry, took over as operator.

The Hotel Piccadilly was a brashly expressionistic 14-storey edifice, the massive overhanging exposed concrete supporting structure of which appeared to 'float' above the city on comparatively slender concrete stilts. These emerged from the shopping arcade, the roof of which was a car park, accessed via a spiral ramp (this was a legacy of the hotel's intended American operator). As guests were expected to arrive by car, the main entrance and reception were adjacent, effectively at second floor level and partially hidden among the stilts. Yet, because the hotel was only a short walk from Piccadilly Station, many visitors actually came on foot and found it very difficult to locate the narrow subsidiary entrance on the ground floor, which was hidden within the shopping arcade underneath the building, rather than adjacent to Piccadilly Gardens (as would logically have been expected). The complex's architects and Manchester's planners must have reasoned that, in future, pedestrians would use deck access bridges but, in the end, these elements were never constructed. So far as the hotel's developer was concerned, however, the lack of a prominent foyer on the ground floor meant that the entire street frontage could be leased out for retail use, thereby increasing the amount of revenue.

The architecture critic Ian Nairn observed the development's '...board-marked concrete, 'sixties plastics, disjointed shapes and constructivist planes' while, within, the hotel contained 'all the ingredients of 'sixties high living.'[323] The restaurant enjoyed panoramic views across Piccadilly Gardens. Adjoining was a splendidly louche champagne bar, the walls of which were lined in padded leather while the ceiling was partially covered in mirrored panelling and partly in shag-pile carpet, from which glass chandeliers reminiscent of champagne bubbles descended. The Coffee Shop had a 'waffle-plate' back-lit suspended ceiling and, next door, the King Cotton Bar's interior walls were decorated with reproductions of nineteenth century etchings, depicting the local cotton industry. Above this was King Arthur's Court, a suite of three inter-connected rooms intended for dinners, banquets and parties, the décor of which was vaguely themed around the idea of Camelot; these had tented ceilings in bright stripes, the copper exterior cladding of which somewhat resembled a series of pagodas.[324]

Alas, due to poor construction, on the hotel's opening night, part of the suspended ceiling in the banqueting suite collapsed on guests, who included numerous prominent and distinguished Mancunians.[325] The delay in completion, coupled with this embarrassing accident, caused the architect Ralph Covell to launch into an impassioned tirade against the British construction industry at the press conference for the hotel's launch.[326] Its high design ambition but somewhat shoddy finishes all too obviously reflected the desires and pressures of commercial development at that time.

Of retail and leisure developments containing hotels elsewhere in England, the Merrion Centre in Leeds, completed in 1964 to a design by local architects Gillinson, Barnett & Partners, was also notable for its ambitious scale. Filling a nine-acre site, it consisted of a bowling alley, cinema, indoor market, shopping arcades, office accommodation, car parking and the eight-storey, 109-room Merrion Hotel. This and the cinema were leased to subsidiaries of the Rank Organisation. In comparison with the dynamic forms of the Hotel Piccadilly in Manchester, the Merrion was a tepid affair, however. What they had in common, sadly, was poorly executed detailing as, within

The Merrion Centre in Leeds with the Merrion Hotel on the right-hand side.

only a short time, the Merrion's cream mosaic cladding began to disintegrate, the eventual solution being to replace it all with red facing brick.

In 1960s Scotland, large multi-use retail and commercial developments were built in Dundee, Falkirk and Edinburgh, but the most remarkable example was in the new town of Cumbernauld. Dundee's Overgate development, completed in 1963 to a design by the locally-based firm of Hugh Martin & Partners, was the first of these schemes to come to fruition. Dundee's municipality was particularly enthusiastic about transforming the city centre through the insertion of a ring-road and the construction of modernist commercial and public buildings on sites surrounding it. As elsewhere, the plan was to give the city a new image through the replacement of as many superficially dilapidated late Georgian and Victorian properties as possible. Above the Overgate Centre's shopping arcades rose offices, a car park and, most prominently of all, the Angus Hotel. This latter element occupied half of a long, seven-storey transverse block, the remainder of which contained office space. The four upper storeys were faced in bands of light grey rough-textured cement slabs with continuous ribbon windows. On the bottom three storeys, the vertical structural elements were exposed and transversely bisected by access roads. Between these, the exterior walls were slightly recessed and faced in dark grey brick, the idea presumably being that, from a distance, the upper part structure would appear to 'float' over the ground.[327] Alas, viewed from closer quarters, this artifice became only too apparent, as did the poor quality of detailing. Moreover, in terms of form, scale and materiality, the Overgate Centre was entirely out of keeping with the still essentially medieval surrounding street plan and with the remaining stone buildings of earlier vintages.

The hotel was leased by Scottish & Newcastle Breweries, who appointed a different Dundee architect, Ian Burke of the Burke Martin Partnership, to fit out its interiors. Burke's firm, which specialised mainly in retail and office design, treated them in a

The Angus Hotel in Dundee, located above the Overgate Centre.

modern Scandinavian manner with extensive woodwork and bright orange and purple fabrics. The hotel's public rooms were the first spaces in Dundee to be decorated in this manner and so it was briefly considered fashionable. After just thirty years, it had declined badly, however, and so was closed for demolition.

In Falkirk, the situation was no better. There, the Callendar Riggs Shopping Centre, completed in 1968, was just as intrusive and destructive. It was a joint project commissioned by a specially-established company, Falkirk Development Ltd, which comprised private and municipal interests with the design work carried out by the Falkirk burgh architect, A.J.M. Currell, and a prolific locally-based practitioner, Baron Bercott.[328] Bercott had recently also designed the town's Municipal Buildings and Town Hall, plus several schools in the vicinity. A graduate of the University of Liverpool School of Architecture, Bercott had moved to Scotland in the 1950s, working initially in Glasgow.

The Metropolitan Hotel in Falkirk, located in the centre of the Callendar Riggs Shopping Centre.

The Callendar Riggs development was externally clad in aggregate-faced cast concrete panels. Rising from the centre of this banal, fortress-like structure was the Metropolitan Hotel, a stubby tower block which, as its name suggested, was operated by Maxwell Joseph's Grand Metropolitan company. The four bedroom storeys were held aloft by three-storey-high concrete stilts, between which the restaurant and bar were slung at second floor height, thereby enabling the mall to continue unobstructed beneath. Within, the bedrooms were relatively large and brightly lit, those at the corners having continuous fenestration, giving wide views towards the surrounding hills and countryside.[329] Like many another of its era, the hotel was best enjoyed from the inside, looking outward. The *Caterer and Hotel Keeper* records how the architect and developer's lack of expertise in hotel operation, however, led to the overall proportions of space allocated to each purpose being inappropriate for the operator's needs:

> '…Grand Metropolitan Hotels have had to surmount problems which all too often face operators of new hotels. Chief among them was the fact that [they] completed negotiations to lease the hotel after it had been designed and construction

The Callendar Riggs Shopping Centre with the hotel's accommodation block protruding above.

started…They cite, for instance, the large amount of corridor…There is probably enough public area for a hotel twice the size…'[330]

The interior design won approval, however, the colour scheme being:

'…Sober – reflecting the industrial character of the area. Carpeting is mostly a figured dark brown and the décor in the public areas is predominantly wood panelling… On ground level and separate from the hotel is the Metro Bar, a large bar designed for passing trade. Décor is brighter than in the rest of the hotel and hot meals and snacks are served at the 50-foot serpentine counter.'[331]

Although the hotel continues to operate in much rebuilt form, Falkirk, alas, never recovered from the damage to its centre perpetrated by Currell and Bercott in the mid-1960s. The subsequent replacement of the Callendar Riggs Centre's original cladding panels with post-modern pilasters, pediments and domes did nothing to reduce its crudity and intrusiveness.

Grand Metropolitan followed up its Falkirk scheme with a more conventionally planned free-standing hotel of similar size in Wakefield, which opened in 1965, and there were also plans for a substantially bigger Scottish hotel in Glasgow's India Street. Forming part of a mixed-use redevelopment scheme, this would have had 230 rooms and a revolving restaurant on the top floor. Perhaps fortunately, the project was never realised.[332]

Cumbernauld's Town Centre was to prove one of the most celebrated and derided architectural projects in post-war Scotland. The new town was built on a windswept escarpment at the foot of the Campsie Hills to house some of those decanted from Glasgow's over-crowded inner city slum districts. The project for a single, very big concrete 'megastructure' to contain all civic and retail requirements, plus residential

The Golden Eagle Hotel in Cumbernauld, attached to the Town Centre megastructure, from which access for pedestrians was gained midway up the block. The hotel's Antonine Bar was one of four in what was a relatively small property with only 29 bedrooms.

and hotel accommodation, was initiated by the Cumbernauld Development Corporation, led by its Chief Architect and Head of Planning, Hugh Wilson. The design selected, however, was by Geoffrey Copcutt, a youthful Yorkshireman who had graduated from Edinburgh College of Art in 1951. Having established a practice in Leicester, he returned to Scotland in 1958 to work for the Cumbernauld Development Corporation on the Town Centre project.

Copcutt's megastructure was built across a dual-carriageway with car parking on the lowest level, a mall above and penthouses in its upper reaches. When the plans were published, the project was hailed internationally by architects and planners for its boldness and innovation. As a result, Copcutt and his boss, Hugh Wilson, became internationally sought-after for advice and inspiration. Both left Cumbernauld in 1963 to work elsewhere. Wilson was knighted for his achievements and Copcutt was soon employed by the United Nations as an advisor on planning. Meanwhile, back in Cumbernauld, it was left to others to oversee the Town Centre's completion.

The Golden Eagle Hotel at Kirkby on Merseyside was another in Tennent Caledonian's provincial chain.

At that time, the greater part of scheme was still to be designed in detail, the idea being that as the surrounding town was expanded over time, the Town Centre would likewise be extended outward from the central core, to which new elements could be 'plugged in' as need arose. One of these additions was to be a hotel, principally for the use of business travellers as well as – presumably – curious visitors, including planners, keen to marvel at the megastructure's design.

The Golden Eagle Hotel, completed in 1967 to plans prepared under the supervision of Dudley Roberts Leaker, who had superseded Hugh Wilson as the Development Corporation's Chief Architect, was a seven-storey building, located at the Town Centre's north-west periphery. Because the centre's lower ranges were occupied by car parking and roadways, the main circulation was at the third and fourth floor levels and so the hotel's reception and main public rooms were half way up, with its 29 bedrooms above. The lessee was the Tennent Caledonian brewery, which recently had taken leases on several hotels located in new retail developments in northern industrial towns. The first was at Kirkby, a new town on Merseyside, and the second was at Thornaby on Tees, where the town centre was redeveloped in the mid-1960s with a sprawling shopping, housing and office complex, designed by Elder, Lester & Partners of Billingham and commensurate in size with Cumbernauld Town Centre.[333] Tennent Caledonian used the name 'Golden Eagle' for all of these hotels. The one in Cumbernauld was a banal, stumpy, building, faced with brick and lacking any of the visual drama of the centre to which it was connected. Within, it had no fewer than four different bars, occupying the greater part of the lower storeys. One of these had a Roman-themed interior, with murals reflecting the proximity of the Antonine Wall, which had marked the northerly fringe of civilisation. Clearly, Tennent Caledonian's intention was that even if there were insufficient overnight visitors to make the bedroom accommodation reliably profitable, local drinkers would be a lucrative and regular market.[334]

What the hotel and centre had in common, unfortunately, was a poor build quality and both soon began to decay. Furthermore, as the centre was planned with expansion in mind, it was surrounded by rough open land, making its environs visually unappealing and difficult to traverse on foot, meaning that, unless hotel guests drove, they were effectively 'trapped' in the sprawling megastructure, in which the shops were closed and shuttered in the evening. Consequently, the hotel only ever attracted disappointing numbers of overnight guests as motorists visiting Cumbernauld on business had the option of staying elsewhere and driving for their appointments in the town. Meanwhile, the hotel's bars gained an unfortunate reputation for being sources of drunken disorder, deterring other potential users. Similar problems apparently affected other recently-opened hotels in provincial Scotland and it soon came to be suspected that investments in such premises was merely a ruse by the breweries to gain seven-day drinks licences (whereas pubs were obliged to remain shut on Sundays, hotel bars could open to serve 'bona fide travellers'). As the *Caterer and Hotel Keeper* recorded in 1971, the Clayson Committee, established to investigate Scottish licensing, concluded that hotels of this kind were merely a 'cynical manipulation of the law.'[335]

In 1980, a truck accidentally collided into one of the Golden Eagle Hotel's frontages, causing a collapse of the brick facing and leading to the its closure after little more than a decade of operation. In 1981, the building was bought back by the Cumbernauld Development Corporation following an engineer's report which highlighted its lack of structural integrity and deemed its ongoing existence a risk to public safety.[336] Shortly after, it was demolished after a pitifully short and undistinguished existence.

The Aviemore Centre and its hotels

Large multi-functional developments, such as those described above, were intrusive enough in the contexts of existing city centres, such as Manchester or Leeds, and also provoked public controversy in new towns – as was the case with Cumbernauld. In a picturesque Highland setting, the effect of such a large-scale development approach was significantly more problematic, as the Aviemore Centre scheme would prove.

About a year before skiing facilities on Cairngorm were inaugurated, in October 1959, the Scottish department store tycoon, Hugh Fraser, visited a nearby village, Newtonmore, accompanied by a high-flying and influential Scottish Office civil servant, George Pottinger, whose brief was to oversee tourism development in the Highlands. In Civil Service circles, Pottinger – who admired and befriended Fraser and subsequently accompanied him on Swiss skiing holidays – was apparently known as 'Gorgeous George' on account of his stylish dress, suave manners and taste for the good life. Their initial plan was to redevelop Newtonmore as a tourist resort – but this idea was unenthusiastically received by locals, who feared that a large influx of external funding would damage the village's character and undermine well-established hotel businesses. Fraser and Pottinger's attention next fell upon Aviemore, a small railway hamlet at a junction, one of the lines from which would soon fall victim to Dr Richard Beeching's restructuring of British Railways. A tourist development would be bound to be more welcome there as an alternative source of income and employment.[337]

By 1962, Fraser had assembled a consortium of investors, including the Scottish brewery magnate Sir William McEwan Younger, chairman of Scottish & Newcastle Breweries and of the Scottish Conservative Party, and Harry Vincent, chairman of the construction firm Bovis. Two-and-a-half million pounds, a quarter provided from the public purse, would be invested in a new resort facility for Aviemore, featuring hotels, restaurants, bars, shops and a range of leisure facilities on a site close to the existing village. This, it was hoped, would transform the village into an upmarket environment similar to Courcheval or St Moritz, where Fraser and Pottinger had enjoyed winter holidays. At first, land on the Rothiemurchus Estate was sought, but its owner, Iain Grant, refused to sell to the development consortium. Hugh Fraser, however, preferred a site to the north where the Victorian-era Aviemore Hotel had once stood; it had burned down in 1950 and was subsequently demolished.[338]

Soon an architect was appointed to design the new resort complex but, rather than holding an open competition, as might have been expected in a project involving a 25% investment of public money, the development consortium made a direct appointment. Harry Vincent of Bovis insisted that John Poulson – an architect-businessman from Pontefract in Yorkshire – was the only man who could fulfil the consortium's vision. An unremarkable – and unqualified – architect, since the mid-1950s, Poulson's firm had grown to be among Europe's largest with 750 employees and several subsidiary offices as far afield as Malta and Lagos. As with many of those serving commercial clients, it employed mainly youthful graduates who could be worked hard for basic pay. Poulson was, however, virtually unknown in Scotland and, notwithstanding his firm's vast output, his projects were rarely sufficiently distinguished to merit publication in the mainstream architectural journals. Indeed, of the many hospitals, shopping centres, office blocks and housing developments produced, most were at best mediocre in terms of their outward appearance and internal ambience. Poulson, however, apparently had a reputation for working within a given budget and delivering plans punctually and quickly. He also was an enthusiast for factory-made pre-cast concrete panel construction systems and, from 1963 onward, his senior assistants, Ron Young and Leslie Pollard, had worked closely with the building contractor, Crudens, to manufacture panels under license using the Swedish Skarne system, which was intended for the construction of housing.

Poulson first visited Scotland in connection with the Aviemore project in March 1963. According to Pottinger, who hosted him and Hugh Fraser: 'There was a sympathetic gleam in Fraser's eye when he looked at someone who promised plans within a week and meant it.'[339] Poulson argued for the expansion of the project to include not only two substantial hotels, each with a choice of bars and restaurants, but also an indoor swimming pool, an ice rink for curling and a cinema-theatre so that there would be alternative attractions during inclement weather. These additions were accepted with a consequent increase in budget to three million pounds.

Construction of The Aviemore Centre by Bovis began in the spring of 1964 and it was opened in the autumn of 1966. Its centrepiece was a terraced piazza called 'Allander Square' (a title reflecting the House of Fraser brand identity), around which were sited the hotels and leisure facilities. While the latter were low-rise structures, built of combinations of reinforced concrete and steel framing with cladding, the two hotels utilised Poulson's favoured pre-cast concrete panels. The more upmarket of the two was the ten-storey, 54-room Strathspey Hotel, by far Aviemore's tallest building. According the architects, it supposedly resembled 'a traditional Scottish keep' but in actuality it appeared more like a grain silo from the American mid-West, unceremoniously plonked into the picturesque Highland landscape. On the lower floors were three bars plus a restaurant with floor-to-ceiling windows. Close by, the six-storey Badenoch Hotel, its more populist counterpart, had 30 rooms, half of which had angled windows to give the best possible views of the Cairngorm massif. It too had a ground floor restaurant, serving a 'continental' menu, plus two bars. The ratio of five separate bars to a total of

The controversial Aviemore Centre initially had two substantial hotels designed by John Poulson's office; these were the Badenoch Hotel, shown in (1) and (2) and the high-rise Strathspey Hotel, shown under construction in (3) and (4). In a harsh climate, the complex's poor build quality soon began to show and decline set in rapidly.

eighty hotel rooms was very high and reflected pressure from Scottish & Newcastle Breweries as joint-owners to sell as much drink as possible to thirsty day visitors and the equally thirsty local populace. Externally, the entire development was painted snowy white to blend with the winter landscape and the Badenoch Hotel's main frontage had varnished timber infill panels. During the first winter, the Aviemore Centre was fully-booked with skiers and Allander Square appeared the lively, elegant Swiss-style space Fraser had envisaged. Thus, the project was officially presented as a considerable positive achievement for all involved and in 1967 it won the British Travel Association's 'Come to Britain' trophy.[340]

The Norseman Hotel in Peterlee was built on a steep slope in a picturesque setting.

From then on, the Aviemore Centre and its hotels experienced a very rapid downward spiral of decline. The site's planning had taken no account of wind direction with the consequence that, during blizzards, snowdrifts filled Allander Square, making it impassable. Meanwhile, the harsh climate quickly exacted a heavy toll on the painted concrete and varnished timber external finishes, meaning that the entire development soon began to look shabby. As a cost-saving measure, Poulson's office had specified an insufficiently dimensioned sewage treatment plant with the effect that untreated effluent spilled into the Aviemore burn and, from there, into the River Spey, which was an important river for the local salmon fishing and malt whisky industries. The smell which permeated the Aviemore Centre was occasionally 'nauseating, challenging its image as a health resort.'[341] Furthermore, the resort developed a reputation for the drunken and rowdy behaviour of day visitors, which caused more genteel staying guests to avoid it.[342]

Yet, notwithstanding the Aviemore Centre's well-publicised problems, Scottish & Newcastle Breweries evidently were so satisfied with the Poulson office's architectural work that he was subsequently commissioned by them to design a hotel in Peterlee, a new town in County Durham. Completed in 1970, the Norseman was a five-storey building perched on the sloping bank of the River Wick. Main access and the reception were at second floor level and, one storey below, facing the river, a semi-circular restaurant space was cantilevered outward, enabling diners to enjoy views of mature trees and across parkland overlooking the town centre. Above was a two-storey bedroom block clad in lighter brick. In comparison with Poulson's earlier work in Aviemore, the building responded fairly well to its context although, as was typical of his firm's output, the detailing was fairly crude. In Stockton-on-Tees, a short way to the south, Poulson's office designed the seven-storey, 140-room Swallow Hotel, one of a number of new hotels in the North-East to be operated by the Swallow chain, which was a recently-established mid-market hotel subsidiary of the Vaux brewery. The hotel was located adjacent to the Castlegate Shopping Precinct, for which Poulson's practice was additionally responsible and both were constructed using 'Urbus System' pre-cast concrete modules.

Quite why so many public and commercial clients remained so loyal to the mediocre Pontefract architect would, however, shortly be publicly revealed to the great embarrassment of all concerned. In January 1972, John Poulson's business went bankrupt, its owner's personal liabilities amounting to £900,000. At the subsequent hearing in Wakefield, a remarkable history of bribery and corruption of public officials by Poulson to win contracts for his practice was uncovered. Evidently, his true skill had been in realising the greed and vanity of the civic, governmental and business figures he had encountered. Poulson's accomplice in this was T. Dan Smith, a prominent and dynamic Newcastle councillor who had been chair of the city's Housing Committee and, from 1959, its civic leader. Subsequently, from 1968 until 1970, he acted as Chairman of the Peterlee and Aycliffe Development Corporation. In addition, he had established a number of 'public relations' consultancies to which Poulson had paid large sums. Smith then passed these on as bribes to councillors in other municipalities – including Durham County Council, covering Peterlee and Stockton-on-Tees – on the understanding that they would ensure that Poulson's firm was awarded upcoming architectural contracts. For over a decade, the strategy had been successful but, as time wore on, it was necessary to give ever larger bribes to win fresh contracts and to buy the silence of those who suspected skulduggery.[343]

In Scotland, Poulson had treated George Pottinger with particular generosity, paying for expensive overseas holidays, Savile Row tailoring, a car and even the greater part of a large villa near Edinburgh's exclusive Muirfield golf course; named 'The Pelicans', it was designed by Poulson's firm. The Civil Service Code, of course, forbade its employees from accepting undeclared gifts of any kind and Pottinger had told colleagues that his fine attire and possessions had resulted from successful speculations on the stock market. Poulson, Smith and Pottinger were jailed for their activities – though, notwithstanding overwhelming evidence of wrongdoing, all three continued to protest their innocence.

Ironically, on his 'home territory' in Newcastle, T. Dan Smith had studiously avoided employing Poulson and had refused to countenance any 'sweeteners' being paid. Indeed, Smith saw himself as a modern 'renaissance man' who believed passionately in the potential of both town planning and the arts to transform citizens' lives.

Shortly after Smith became Council Leader in 1959, he announced a plan to set up an advisory committee of distinguished architects and planners to guide Newcastle's redevelopment, following the best international practice. Names touted included Le Corbusier, no less, as well as Leslie Martin, Robert Matthew and Basil Spence. Subsequently, Smith went on private architectural study tours to Scandinavia where he examined major recent works by top Danish and Swedish architects, including Arne Jacobsen, whose SAS Royal Hotel in Copenhagen had been completed in 1961. While in Sweden on the same tour, he stopped off in Luleå to examine its critically-acclaimed shopping centre, designed by Ralph Erskine. These experiences led Smith to conceive of a plan to redevelop Newcastle's Georgian Eldon Square with a retail development by Erskine, similar to the one in Luleå, and a skyscraper hotel by Jacobsen. The latter was apparently only too pleased to be invited to design another hotel, not least because he would gain additional fee income for large quantities of bespoke furniture and lighting. Indeed, by 1963, Jacobsen was being touted as the designer of both the hotel and the surrounding shopping centre.

The 'new' Eldon Square's Scandinavian modernism was expected to be the lynchpin in Smith's vision for a new Newcastle and, once built, the citizenry would be so impressed that they would give full support to his wider redevelopment vision of transforming the entire city into a British version of Brasilia, the post-war Brazilian capital which was at that time much admired for its modernist architecture and planning. In April 1965, a delegation of Newcastle councillors and officials, plus a Jacobsen representative, visited London to solicit interest from potential hotel operators; these included Trust Houses, J. Lyons' Strand Hotels Ltd, Forte, plus the North American Hilton Hotels and Skyway Hotels. It would appear that Forte soon became the favoured potential tenant as the hotel was subsequently promoted as 'The Excelsior' – a well-known Forte brand, but hitherto only for properties close to airports.

Jacobsen's design would, at thirty storeys, be Newcastle's tallest building. Occupying a site on Eldon Square's South-East corner, its small footprint and great height would enable the square's communal garden to be retained as a public amenity, even though the surrounding Georgian terraces would be demolished for the shopping mall. The hotel derived its structural resilience from four concrete towers, one at each corner, containing service stairs. A further four towers, each containing a lift, defined a central service core. Both the stair and lift shafts projected well beyond the hotel's topmost floor and so one may speculate that, had it been built, the hotel would have possessed similar characteristics of detail to Jacobsen's St Catherine's College, Oxford (1960-66). There, he first realised the expressive potential of over-hanging concrete structural elements, juxtaposed with smooth expanses of metal-framed glazing. Jacobsen, moreover, tended to go through phases in which he would design various building types in a similar manner. During a slightly earlier period when he had sought to emulate American exemplars of the international style (for example, the SAS Royal Hotel and Rødovre City Hall), he illustrated his approach to an architectural colleague by using a matchbox. Resting on end, it represented a hotel, on its narrow side, it became a city hall and, on its flat surface, it was a school.[344]

For the Newcastle hotel, blocks containing bedrooms – clad in bronze anodized aluminium curtain walling with glass infill panels – would have projected beyond the

Architectural models of Arne Jacobsen's unbuilt design for a prestigious hotel for Eldon Square in Newcastle, where the building would have been surrounded by a new shopping centre.

four corner stair towers, creating a bold and clean-lined overall composition. The ground floor would have been recessed between the building's vertices and entirely glazed with the four lift shafts visible from the street, rather like the exhausts of a space rocket. Thus, the bottom storey would have quite precisely replicated the roof scape. Had it been built, the hotel would have been a bold, magnificent addition to Newcastle's rapidly changing skyline.

In 1967, Jacobsen opened a Newcastle office to handle the hotel project and, by 1968, it appeared that it would shortly come to fruition. The *Newcastle Evening Chronicle* enthused:

> 'The famous Danish architect has designed the 30-storey hotel… [which] will cost at least £2½ million. Newcastle Corporation has commissioned the hotel and when it is completed it will be leased to Fortes and Co. Ltd. It is planned to start clearing the site by the middle of next year and to start building the new prestige hotel in January 1970. The tower block will house the hotel bedrooms and there will be a restaurant on the top floor. At the foot of the building, there will be other restaurants, bars and public rooms and a car park in the basement.'[345]

Still, finance was not fully in place and soon Forte became engaged in a merger with Trust Houses, which diverted its senior management's attention away from the project.

In March 1971, Jacobsen died with construction still not begun. The 1973 Oil Crisis and the price inflation it brought finally killed off the scheme, though Newcastle's civil authorities still required to pay Jacobsen's executors' fees of £170,000 for design work, including drawings for new ranges of bespoke furniture and lighting. A shopping mall was eventually built on Eldon Square, to a design by Chapman Taylor & Partners, in conjunction with City Planning Officer, Wilfred Burns – but this was an ugly and unloved structure. It was indeed very sad that, if old Eldon Square really had to be replaced, it was not Jacobsen's design that was chosen. Furthermore, how ironic that Britain's most notorious modern architect – John Poulson – and one almost universally held to be among the world's best – Arne Jacobsen – were tangentially linked through the energetic yet autocratic activities of T. Dan Smith. With hindsight, it appeared that Smith personified a great paradox of the British Modern Movement in architecture as a whole; on the one hand, he was ambitious, visionary, and idealistic, but on the other, he was venal, corruptible and with a tendency towards totalitarianism.

CHAPTER 10
The hotel construction boom

In 1969, Harold Wilson's Labour Government introduced the Development of Tourism Act which sought to provide strategic support for the growth of international tourism to the UK as an important 'national industry'. Among the Act's aims was a more coordinated approach to marketing and the provision of a large quantity of new *en suite* hotel accommodation, attractive to American and European visitors. In the government's typically technocratic and instrumentalist way, it was expected that this measure would finally redress the British lag in hotel development since the introduction of wartime building restrictions in 1939. The Isle of Man had set a precedent in subsidising hotel construction and this measure had apparently been successful in encouraging the expansion and modernisation of the hotel stock there.[346] In July 1966 the House of Lords had forced an amendment to the British Government's Investment Incentives Grant Scheme to include the hotel industry – and it was this change that led to subsidised hotel construction having a central role when the Development of Tourism Act reached statute.[347] The provision was officially known as the Hotel Development Incentives Scheme. In practice, the scheme lessened planning restrictions on hotel developments and provided grants of up to £1,000 for every bedroom in any project begun before 31 March 1971 and finished by 31 March 1973.[348]

Britain's tourism boom was given added impetus by a 14 per cent devaluation of the pound in November 1967, making the country more attractive to foreign visitors due to is relatively cheaper prices. The devaluation was bought about by poor balance of trade figures which, in turn, were largely caused by a lengthy seamen's strike in 1966, subsequently compounded by a dock workers' strike. These events and their negative consequences for the manufacturing economy encouraged the government to focus on developing tourism as an alternative source of wealth and employment. Beyond the government's desire for grandiose 'national plans' to skew market forces in various sectors, the need for new and larger hotels could also be related to the concurrent advent of wide-bodied jet airliners, most notably the Boeing 747, and to the belief that, in the foreseeable future, supersonic air travel would further 'shrink' the globe, thanks to the development of Concorde (which Wilson's government also enthusiastically supported).

In practice, the promise of subsidy led to a rush by developers to get as much hotel accommodation built as possible before the scheme's end date. In October 1970, the *Caterer and Hotel Keeper* reported:

> A record 800 applications for grants for hotel development has been received by the English Tourist Board under the state backed hotel development incentives scheme… and brings the total number of applications received to March 31 (the latest date by which construction must have started) to over 2,000. Planned investment notified now exceeds £320 million, of which approximately half is in the Greater London Council area. The total number of new bedrooms represented by these applications is approximately 66,400 (comprising 46,800 in new hotels and 19,600 in extensions to existing hotels).'[349]

On average, 235 new hotel rooms would be added to Britain's stock every week, transforming the nature of hospitality provision throughout much of the country.[350]

Not only would this boost business and tourism, but it would also generate a great deal of extra employment, it being estimated that 40,000 additional staff would be needed by the time all of the hotels were completed in 1973 – a 12 per cent increase in the industry's total workforce in the UK. This had stood at 380,000 in 1967, but was expected to rise to 414,000. As the *Caterer and Hotel Keeper* admitted, however, 'hoteliers' staffing problems would be much greater but for the foreign labour they employ; in 1969 permits issued admitting foreign catering labour to Britain totalled 19,000 against 15,000 for 1967.'[351] New shorter-term employment would also be created among architectural technicians, structural and service engineers, building contractors and suppliers of construction materials, hotel equipment and furnishings.

While all of this seemed splendid in theory, the reality of building many large and complex structures within a tight timeframe was problematic – at least so far as the quality of the end results was concerned. For Britain's now very wealthy and powerful property entrepreneurs, the inducement of state funding was irresistible and so they set their favoured architects to work, maximising the subsidies claimable for the hotels they planned to build. The outcome was mostly a rash of crude, rushed, frequently banal and too often over-scaled projects. Coming on top of the Ronan Point disaster in May 1968 – in which a recently-completed high-rise block of flats in London's East End had suffered a sequential collapse at one corner due to shoddy construction work – and, quite separately, the trial of the corrupt architect John Poulson, the hotels produced under the Act led to yet another public shaming of British modern architecture. To increasing numbers of observers, some prominent architects – often those involved in hotel development – appeared greedy and amoral. The situation was cruelly but presciently satirised in 'The Architect's Sketch' in a 1970 edition of the surreal television sketch show *Monty Python's Flying Circus* and in a scene in the film *Get Carter*, in which, upon witnessing the murder of a client in a multi-storey car park, the architects only express concern about whether they will still get their fee.

The pattern of expansion under the Hotel Development Incentives Scheme was aimed at attracting prosperous foreign tourists and business travellers. Consequently, hardly any new hotels were built at seaside resorts, particularly not those attracting mainly working and lower middle classes Britons. By contrast, new hotels in tourism 'honeypots' – such as London's West End or Stratford-on-Avon – were given considerable encouragement.

The subsidy regime prompted Trust Houses to embark on a fresh programme of expansion with the company's architect, Nelson Foley, churning out a further fifteen new Post Houses mainly near busy roads on the urban fringes throughout Britain. As the text of an advertisement in the *Caterer and Hotel Keeper* records, by the late 1960s, the company believed that it had arrived at an un-improvable formula for the development of motor hotels:

> 'The experimenting is over. We now know the 'mix' that makes Post Houses successful and the building programme is being stepped up. 8 up to last year. Plymouth, Hampstead and Leicester this year. Tyneside, Swindon, Aviemore, Leeds/Bradford, Teeside, Norwich and York in 1971. And many more on the way. Each one provides guests with centrally heated comfort, a private bathroom, TV, radio and telephone; kettle and sachets for tea and coffee. Many of them have a buttery and a first class restaurant in addition; also lounges and bars; many have rooms planned for function and conference use. By eliminating room service,

porterage and other dispensable functions, room tariffs are kept remarkably low, considering the standard of comfort offered. The staff are similarly well provided for. Naturally, the equipment and layouts are right up to date; everything's planned to make work lighter and easier. And staff accommodation, where provided, is of a very high standard. The experimenting is over, as we said.'[352]
In urban settings, it was necessary to build upward, rather than outward, however. Thus, the Hampstead Post House at Primrose Hill in North London, completed in July 1970, was a six-storey building, faced in brick, though containing precisely the same facilities as the horizontally-planned 'out of town' examples. The 145-room Tyneside Post House close to the A1 trunk road in Newcastle, which opened in February 1971, followed a similar formula. A third example of a vertical layout was the St George's Hotel in Liverpool with 167 rooms. It was located above the city's new St John's Precinct shopping development, a sprawling structure designed by James A. Roberts and, separately from the hotel, incorporating the 138-metre-high Beacon observation tower, which had a revolving restaurant at its summit. Externally, the Tyneside and Liverpool Post Houses were rather mundane affairs with brick and concrete aggregate facings; in seeking to maximise profits, their operator had obviously come a long way from its high design aspirations for new hotels in the first half of the 1960s.

Much more imposing was the very prominent Mayflower Hotel in Plymouth, completed in 1970 and regarded by Trust Houses as a flagship property. For the previous decade, Plymouth Corporation had desired to see a high-rise hotel developed on a prominent site facing Plymouth Hoe and thus with the potential for guests to enjoy grand, sweeping vistas of cliffs and sea from the public rooms and bedrooms. In March 1960 a scheme was published for a 16-storey hotel, designed by Vincent Burr & Partners and, shortly after, three hotels of Victorian vintage were compulsorily purchased to enable its construction, much to the fury of their owners. At an inquiry convened by the Ministry of Housing and Local Government, the owner of the Grand Hotel stated that the proposed new building 'would be unaesthetic. Its concrete and glass structure would not beautify the Hoe.'[353] Permission was rejected and nearly a decade then elapsed before the decision was reversed.

The need for a large new hotel in Plymouth came back on the political agenda in anticipation of festivities planned to mark the 350th anniversary of the Pilgrim Fathers' voyage from there in 1620. In 1970, large numbers of American visitors were expected to attend a series of related events around the Hoe and, of course, the Hotel Development Incentives Scheme was in place to ease planning restrictions and provide a generous subsidy for the construction.

Post House hotels near Newcastle and at Primrose Hill in London.

The St John's Precinct in
Liverpool with the St George's
Hotel protruding above.

Nelson Foley produced a 10-storey, 104-bedroom slab-block, fabricated from weighty-looking, rough-textured concrete blocks and panels. All but eight bedrooms were on the scenic south-east side with corridors, store rooms and vertical circulation, plus one single room on each floor facing landward; this was less commercially expedient than the more typical floor arrangement of rooms on both sides of a central passage. It also meant that the rear façade was a forbidding expanse of aggregate panelling with hardly any windows, more resembling an industrial silo than a hotel. Penthouses on the topmost bedroom floor could access a private patio, running along the building's length. At ground level, the public rooms overlooked a terrace with an outdoor lido area, surrounded by soft and hard landscaping. At the building's south-east corner, a semi-octagonal two-storey projection from the slab block contained the hotel's bars and restaurants.

The architect and critic Michael Blee, who reviewed the hotel for the *Architect's Journal*, explained its brutalist aesthetic in terms of physical context; this was indeed dubious and arguably more reflected Blee's employment by Basil Spence – who was invariably concerned with contextual matters – than the reality of commercial expedience:

> 'The prominence of the site called for a building of broad scale and architectural treatment. Projecting band courses on the south elevation are designed to shade south-facing rooms… External materials have been selected to contribute to the environmental character of both twentieth century and historic Plymouth – a clean, windswept, grey stone city. The exposed aggregate cladding panels were fabricated locally… Both the structure and windows were designed to withstand force-ten gales and upward driving rain…heavily profiled pre-cast cladding panels seem appropriate in both colour and form to the marine context and the bastion aesthetic acknowledged in a relatively blank north façade.'[354]

The hotel was accessed from the north side, 'via a glass box tacked onto the side of the slab.'[355] By contrast, the lobby had glass wall tiles, a dark stained slatted wood ceiling and a pavoir brick floor. A fibreglass bas relief on one end wall depicted the Pilgrim Fathers' departure from Plymouth. The reception and adjoining lounge, beyond, through which the Hoe could be viewed, was decorated with 'gaudy colours of the nautical ship's flag tradition.'[356]

Opposite: Trust Houses'
Mayflower Hotel in Plymouth
was considered a 'flagship'
property and was laid out with
nearly all rooms facing the Hoe.
This resulted in a particularly
severe elevation to the rear,
where the main entrance was
located.

In its conception, layout and massing, the Mayflower was one of the more innovative hotels of its era, yet, as Blee observed, due to the rapidity with which it was conceived, coupled with a tight budget, too many of its details remained 'crude and unsophisticated.'[357] As the hotel aged and became weathered, chunks of cladding began

to fall off and it came to be regarded locally as an unfortunate intrusion into an otherwise attractive setting and so few were sorry to see it demolished in 2016.

Another of the more notable Trust House hotels of the period was the 183-room Leicester Post House, designed by Foley and his assistant John Main and occupying a commodious site near a junction of the A46 and M1 roads. Opened in July 1970, it consisted of a single storey pavilion, containing the public rooms and kitchen, standing in front of a stepped, three-storey accommodation block with 183 bedrooms. The exterior had a strong, horizontal emphasis, the pavilion being faced with large white glazed tiles, set in aluminium frames, rising from white limestone concrete beams and topped with a deep profiled acrylic facia. At the front was an expanse of narrow floor-to-ceiling windows with deep aluminium mullions which were picked out in warm coloured light after dark. This rather bold design contrasted with the quiet detailing of the bedroom block, which was faced in deep red rustic bricks.

Before designing the interiors, Trust Houses' consultants, Alan and Aileen Ballantyne, visited Leicester Museum where, according to the *Caterer and Hotel Keeper*, they were impressed by the unusual Roman mosaic pavements preserved there. These inspired 'a carpet for use throughout the hotel in peacock blue, emerald green and Iona

blue on a background of sienna gold. A variation of the mosaic interlocking pattern was also used on the square ceramic handles of the doors...'[358] Indeed, throughout the hotel's interior decoration, modernist elements were mixed with themed designs:

'The Wolseley Room contains enlargements of drawings by John Leech from 'The Comic History of England... The Bell Bar, named after the old Bell Hotel (demolished in 1969) features artefacts salvaged from the demolition. The bar front features an abstract

design in three-dimensional ceramic tiles by Kenneth Clark.

The Silver Grill enables Post House diners to see their roasts, grills and chicken spatchcock (whole chicken with breast-bone removed and flattened), cooked within their sight… The restaurant's décor is carried into thirteen silver lighting fittings suspended parallel to the long window wall. The Barge Buttery will be of special delight to the increasing numbers of 'longboat' owners who ply Britain's inland waterways for pleasure, and an intriguing place for hotel guests in search of a quick, palatable meal. Its large mural shows a typical longboat scene complete with boat, bargree, family and black Labrador. Rudders, horses tails, painted water cans, a copper kettle or two and table mats with old barge designs help to heighten the effect of this bright, informal room. The two-level hardwood boarded ceiling, with its curved shape, is an abstract version of an upturned boat, and the warmth of its natural colour agreeably softens the vivid red, blue, green and black colours of the interior of this room.'[359]

At locations on the urban fringes, such as this engendering a sense of place evidently required effort, it being necessary for remotely-located designers such as the Ballantynes to begin by finding out what attractive cultural heritage was there to exploit. Objects and images were then carefully selected and brought together to intensify the theme, intriguingly echoing approaches found in the era's museum curation and throughout the growing heritage industry.

Two further broadly similar Post Houses were opened in the late summer of 1971, one on the A660 between Leeds and Bradford and the other on the outskirts of York. The former had 120 rooms and the interior decoration of its public rooms included screens fashioned from the wooden components of dismantled looms from local textile mills. The York Post House was a low-rise structure, inconspicuously occupying a picturesque location surrounded by mature trees with an ancient cedar of Lebanon retained as the centrepiece of the courtyard, around which its 104 bedrooms were arranged. As at the Mayflower in Plymouth, its Buttery restaurant was hexagonal with large windows so that diners could enjoy views over the grounds. Here, Nelson Foley's talent for landscape design was particularly obvious.[360]

Trust Houses' first Scottish Post House was at Aviemore, completed in the autumn of 1971 in time for the winter skiing season and boasting 103 rooms. For this project, Nelson Foley employed an entirely different approach from the brutalism of Plymouth or the low-rise motel aesthetic of his designs in the Midlands and Yorkshire. Instead, he apparently sought to emulate the style of Rank's nearby Coylumbridge Hotel, the pitched roofs and 'rustic' detailing of which had attracted widespread praise. On an undulating site to the rear of the village, adjacent to the Aviemore Centre, the Post House had an informal layout, varying between two- and four storeys, and was faced in rough-surfaced imitation stone blocks, the large roof overhangs lending it something of the aura of a mountain lodge. Inevitably, the interior had a Highland Scottish theme with tartan carpets, feature fireplaces and other supposedly 'local' details. On site, the project was supervised by Burnet, Tait and Wilson, who had earlier on designed hotels for Trust Houses in London and Swansea.[361]

Shortly after the Aviemore Post House's inauguration, Trust Houses was merged with Charles Forte's hotel and catering business to create Trust Houses Forte, one of the Europe's largest hospitality businesses. At that time, Trust Houses owned 181 hotels while Forte ran 43. This was not going to be an easy marriage, however, as Trust Houses

The exterior of the Post House serving Leeds and Bradford, (2) the hotel's restaurant, featuring a screen fabricated from the timbers of dismantled textile looms, (3) the Buttery Restaurant in the York Post House and (4) the Post House in Aviemore.

was run by rather grand 'establishment' gentlemen with a traditionalist 'public school' ethos, whereas Forte was a self-made entrepreneur who apparently had little time for what he saw as their rather patrician approach. When the two managements failed to agree on a future strategy, the former Trust Houses directorate resigned *en masse*, leaving Forte's people in control of the combined business.[362] Shortly after, the former Chairman and mastermind of Trust Houses' great expansion since the mid-1960s, Lord Crowther, died of a heart attack at Heathrow Airport. Forte continued both companies' planned expansion strategies as, with government subsidies agreed, there was little point in changing anything.

Following the merger, the first new hotel to be inaugurated was the Excelsior at Glasgow Airport, which had been developed jointly with British European Airways and was designed by Forte's usual hotel architects, Michael Lyell Associates, whose assistants Michael Pretty and Clive Sturley were responsible for the project.

The ten-storey building had a cruciform plan with four wings emanating from a central service core and was clad in concrete panelling with a surface of white calcite flint.[363] With 320 rooms, it could claim to be Scotland's biggest hotel when it opened in late 1971. The interior design of the two restaurants on the ground floor was by a London-based practitioner, Susan Ferguson; these were the Ranfurly Room, which claimed to offer a 'traditional Gaelic menu, against classic French dishes' and a main restaurant 'epitomising the hotel's vital link in the progress of jet-age travel.'[364] Thus, once again in a 1960s airport hotel, a highly circumscribed version of 'local tradition' was juxtaposed with jet age international modernism.

During the ensuing years, Trust Houses Forte developed further new Post House hotels (at the time of Forte's take-over, the 'in-house' architect, Nelson Foley, had worried that the new management would disband his department). The latest Post

The Excelsior Hotel at Glasgow Airport which, at the time of opening, was the largest in Scotland.

Just because we're Scotland's largest hotel, we don't have to act like it

We have 320 bedrooms — all have a private bathroom, t.v., radio, telephone, air-conditioning and soundproofing. And much more.

But we also offer you the personal attention that you usually only get with small places.

The Hotel also has two restaurants. The smaller more intimate Ranfurly Room offers a traditional Gaelic menu, against classic French dishes. The main restaurant epitomises the Hotel's vital role in the progress of jet age travel.

And it can all cost much less than you think — children under sixteen sharing the parent's room are accommodated free.

For reservations, please telephone (STD 041) 887 1212.

**Excelsior Hotel,
Glasgow Airport,
Abbotsinch,
Paisley, Renfrewshire.**

A BEA Trust Houses Forte Hotel

Above: an advertisement for the Excelsior Hotel in Glasgow.

Below: images of the Penny Farthing Buttery of the Teeside Post House, the Norwich Post House and its Yeoman Buttery and the bar of the Roebuck Post House near Stevenage.

Houses demonstrated an ongoing gradual shift from modernism to themed design approaches. The Roebuck Post House near Stevenage incorporated the seventeenth century Roebuck Inn, which Trust Houses Forte unusually decided to retain, rather than sell. In the new section, designed by Foley with interiors by Dennis Holmes and Pat Palmer, old oak beams, rescued from a derelict barn, were incorporated into the ceilings of the public rooms, which additionally had ladder-back chairs, old trestle tables, rustic brickwork and tapestries to give a 'Tudor appeal.'[365] The 140-room Teeside Post House on the A1044 Middlesbrough-Yarm road in Yorkshire was designed by Foley in what was described by the *Caterer and Hotel Keeper* as a 'Ranch-style' with a strong horizontal emphasis and large roof over-hangs. Within, the Pennyfarthing Buttery was decorated in celebration of the centenary of the invention of the pennyfarthing bicycle, having pendant lights incorporating old bicycle wheels, enamel advertising signs and other Victoriana. Trust Houses Forte's nineteenth Post House was outside Norwich by the junction of the A140 to Ipswich and the A11 to London. Its Yeoman Buttery supposedly reflected Norfolk's agricultural tradition with wooden farm implements displayed on the walls.[366] Another Post House was added just a few weeks later on the outskirts of Ipswich. This time, rather than the flat roofs and modernist fenestration of previous Post Houses, the roofing was double pitched with tiles and the windows were individually set into the brickwork. Inside was the Miller's Bar, featuring 'screens based on East Anglian corn sacks with local millers' trademarks painted on them, an original painting by Mary Adshead of the 'Jolly Miller of Ipswich' and wicker-wood hooded chairs in red willow.'[367] Trust Houses Forte

subsequently even began developing Post Houses in continental Europe, the first of which was located outside Liège in Belgium.

J. Lyons' Strand Hotels subsidiary benefitted from a Hotel Development Incentives Scheme subsidy to build a substantial 14-storey, 250-bedroom Albany Hotel in Glasgow which was inaugurated in 1972. As with the earlier Albanys in Birmingham and Nottingham, the shell was designed by James A. Roberts, whose Birmingham practice was by this point domiciled in that city's distinctive Rotunda office tower, for which Roberts had also been responsible. Sadly, from the outside, the Glasgow Albany – which was located in a heavily redeveloped part of the city centre, close to the M8 motorway and the new Anderston Centre shopping and office complex – was unprepossessing, it being a mass of dark brown brick with relatively small bedroom windows arranged in narrow vertical slots between glass infill panels. This gloomy composition was lent an air of superficial elegance by stylish stainless steel graphics, spelling out the hotel's name, designed by John Diebel, who was responsible for all of the Albany chain's brochures and advertising. The fonts selected evoked the 1930s – and similar 'retro' flourishes could also be found in the interiors, which, as with the previous Albanys, were the work of Dennis Lennon and his assistant, Brian Beardsmore.

Lennon's firm had only recently completed extensive and critically acclaimed interior design work for the Clyde-built Cunard trans-Atlantic liner *Queen Elizabeth 2*, completed in 1969. Their work on the Glasgow Albany was another major achievement and the interior had some similarities to that of the liner. It was also the building's best aspect though Lennon and Beardsmore had tried to persuade Strand Hotels' managing director, Norman Joseph, that their firm should handle the entire project. Joseph refused to countenance this, his slightly perverse argument against being that 'if you got the architecture as well, you'd take your eye off the interiors.'[368]

The lofty L-shaped foyer, featuring cream marble-clad walls and back-lit floating ceiling panels, made a strong initial impression. As Lennon had a liking for contemporary art and was friendly with the London fashion photographer and socialite Elsbeth Juda, who published *Ambassador* magazine and whose circle of friends includes many important contemporary artists and designers, he persuaded Strand Hotels to fund the inclusion of an unusually large number of artworks for the Glasgow Albany's public spaces and penthouse rooms.

The bars and restaurants were located off the foyer. The Carvery and the Four Seasons Restaurant were largely windowless spaces which had slightly vaulted ceilings. The latter had dark brown walls, in front of which apple trees in planters were surrounded by banquette seats. As a gimmick, the trees were dressed by a florist with blossom, leaves or fruit, depending on the season. Across the foyer, the Cocktail Bar had screen prints by Eduardo Paolozzi and Norman Aykroyd. By contrast, The Cabin Bar was, according to a hotel brochure 'all Norwegian rustic and very cosy.'[369] Most impressive of all was a vast banqueting suite for 700 which, this being Glasgow, was put

The exterior of the Ipswich Post House and its Miller's Bar; here, Nelson Foley's modernist approach was fully superseded by post-modern features and detailing.

to regular and effective use as a venue for boxing matches. These were attended by black tie-wearing, predominantly male audiences, mainly from the engineering and construction trades. On the topmost floor, the Ailsa and Iona penthouses had off-white shag-pile carpet, black velour-upholstered 'landscape' furniture with zebra-patterned cushion covers – the height of early 1970s decadence. The louche design approach perhaps not only reflected current fashion but also the imagined taste of a male clientele who aspired to the type of 'lifestyle' popularised by *Playboy* magazine.

The *Architectural Review*'s appraisal of Lennon's work emphasised the interiors' 1930s references – and even found subtle homages to Charles Rennie Mackintosh in elements such as room dividing screens:

> 'It is a cliché now to remark of the current architecture sub-style that it represents a return to the '30s... Then, we were fumbling our way into the unknown... Today, we know what the terminus *ad quem* was. There were and are many good things about this terminus, but among the bad was the total loss of a sense of place. An architecture of planes, when carried to its ultimate conclusion, leaves you with a sense that you are any old where... In strong contrast to this, The Albany... shows that recourse can still be had... if you really try. The entrance is a Savoy-like, marble-dominated space but the bar at the end is dominated by wooden slats in tribute to... Mackintosh. But when we remember what usually happens to bars of new hotels, we have been let off lightly.'[370]

Such Mackintosh references as were distinguishable in the Albany were, however, abstract, Lennon being too much of a sophisticate to indulge in obvious pastiche.

Unsurprisingly, given the Glasgow Albany's many luxurious but delicate finishes and its heavy-smoking, sometimes hard-drinking clientele, it did not remain for long in the pristine form its designers had envisaged and soon modifications were made which 'toughened up' but also gradually fragmented the interiors. After thirty years' use, the hotel had become so degraded that it was fit only for demolition – a remarkably short existence for such a complex and costly building.

In addition to its three city centre Albany Hotels, Strand developed three further much smaller Albany Inns, which were sited in 'out of town' locations to attract motorists, much like Trust Houses Forte's Post Houses. In all instances, they were designed by the Headley Greentree Partnership with interiors by the husband-and-wife team of Peter and Julia Glynn Smith. The first of the Albany Inns was at Hayling Island near Havant in Hampshire, the second was at Crick near Rugby and the third at Ossett near Wakefield. The Hayling Island Albany Inn, completed in 1972, was notable for its seaside leisure-orientated design, the bedroom accommodation being arranged as a series of two-storey chalet blocks with mono-pitch roofs, forming a semi-circular arrangement around a swimming pool and lido area.

The major breweries benefitted from Hotel Development Incentives Scheme subsidies to help pay for their own major hotel construction programmes. Scottish & Newcastle Breweries' recently-formed Thistle Hotels chain negotiated deals with developers to operate five new hotels, all to be opened in the first months of 1973. Thistle was the brainchild of Scottish & Newcastle's Managing Director, Peter Balfour, who was keen to diversify the company into the leisure and tourism sectors. Its approach was – like that of Rank before it – rather opportunistic as none of the properties it leased had much in common with each other in terms of expected market segment, size, appointments or style. This eclectic approach was distinct from that of the large and

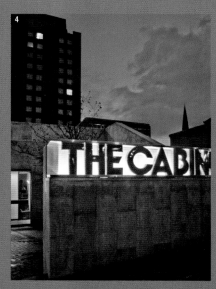

Exterior views of the Glasgow Albany Hotel are shown in (1) to (4); the hotel's brown brick exterior was lent refinement by graphic design and details such as the canopies over the various entrances. Images (5) and (6) show parts of the foyer adjacent to the banqueting suite and (7) shows the entrance to the cocktail bar with a screen referencing Mackintosh and another featuring 'pop'-style graphic design.

Images (1) and (2) show a sign and part of the interior of the Four Seasons Restaurant while (3) shows the Carvery Restaurant, (4) shows the bar, (5) shows the banqueting suite set up for a conference, (6) shows a penthouse suite and (7) shows a standard double room.

The Albany Inn at Hayling Island, arranged around a courtyard with an outdoor pool.

successful American hotel chains, such as Holiday Inn or Marriott, whose thousands of properties, spread across the USA and beyond, all had more-or-less homogeneous characteristics. By contrast, perhaps Scottish & Newcastle saw no problem in perpetuating the British inn-keeping tradition of owning premises that were fairly individual in style.

The first of the new Thistle hotels to be completed was the Strathallan Hotel in the Birmingham suburb of Edgbaston. This was built by the same developer as had been responsible for the Round House Hotel in Bournemouth, described above, and so more-or-less the same design was used with car parking at the first and second floor levels and bedrooms above. The major external difference was that whereas the Round House was faced in aggregate panels, the Strathallan was brick-clad, and, in line with Thistle Hotels' wishes, the interior was Scottish-themed. The Claymore Bar supposedly reflected the atmosphere of a highland shooting lodge, while the Balmoral Lounge was meant to evoke the interiors of the royal castle of that name. The *Caterer and Hotel Keeper*, however, emphasised the hotel's £6,500 Burroughs computer to prepare guests bills – and claimed that it was the first UK hotel to use this type of accounting system.[371]

Thistle's Royal Scot Hotel in London's King's Cross Road had 349 rooms and was aimed primarily at the tourist market. A seven-storey structure faced with brick on a corner site, its front elevation was unremarkable, but, facing Percy Circus to the rear, the frontage precisely replicated that of a demolished Georgian terrace. This was a necessary concession to ensure swift planning approval but also one pointing the way ahead to a coming era when historic cityscape would be increasingly valued, rather than obliterated. In one of the lost houses, the Russian Communist leader Vladimir Lenin had once stayed and so the Soviet Ambassador unveiled a plaque there when the hotel was opened.[372] The bridal rooms, located behind the neo-Georgian rear façade, were decorated in Adam-style and equipped with four-poster beds.

The 151-room Strathmore Hotel in Luton formed part of a large and destructive town centre redevelopment scheme, the centrepiece of which was an Arndale Shopping Centre. It was one of many such centres built in British provincial towns during the 1960s and 70s by the Yorkshire property developer Sam Chippendale and his business partner, a Wakefield bakery magnate called Arnold Hagenbach ('Arndale' combined parts of each of their names). The Luton development was designed by the Tripe & Wakenham Partnership with Leonard V.R. Gorbing & Partners; replacing several grand nineteenth century edifices,

The Royal Scot Hotel, near King's Cross in London.

its crudely-finished elevations and lack of sympathy towards the scale or aesthetics of its surroundings were most unfortunate.

The Strathmore Hotel's lower three stories formed a podium extension to the mall with the bedrooms in an eight-storey brick-clad tower above. Thistle's management believed that there was an opportunity to use the extensive space in the podium for dining and entertainment facilities, thereby making the hotel the centrepiece of Luton's nightlife. The Coffee Shop was open 16 hours a day and a 300-capacity nightclub and cabaret venue called 'Trews' was adjacent. In addition, there was a 350-capacity conference suite.[373] In some respects, the approach of seeking to attract large numbers of locals as well as visitors was similar to the one adopted nearly eighteen years previously by Ind Coope at the Hotel Leofric in Coventry and seems to have continued to be regarded by the big breweries as the most satisfactory model for new hotels in provincial industrial towns.

In central Edinburgh, Thistle's King James Hotel, with 154 rooms, formed a part of the highly controversial St James Centre, which contained a shopping mall, multi-storey car park and New St Andrews House, an office tower leased to the Scottish Office. This development, which necessitated the demolition of eighteenth century buildings by William Playfair, was instigated by Ravenseft Properties and designed by the Burke Martin Partnership. The scheme was of miserably low design ambition for such a prominent urban setting. In a 1974 *Architect's Journal* article by Dan Cruikshank – who was at that time coming to prominence as a conservationist – it was condemned for 'overpowering' everything else in the New Town and making no connection with the surrounding urban fabric.[374] Cruikshank found it to be just one of many recent developments in central Edinburgh that were diluting the city's character through being 'the wrong size, in the wrong material, in the wrong places.'[375] Externally, the hotel, which was the centre's most visible aspect, appeared as a series of three rows of rough-textured concrete boxes stacked above recessed lower storeys. While it served its purpose of accommodating visitors well enough for the ensuing 43 years, its contribution to Edinburgh's otherwise splendid cityscape was not in any sense positive. Both hotel and shopping centre were closed for demolition in 2016.

Thistle's flagship hotel was the Atlantic Tower Hotel in Liverpool, a 13-storey, 226-room edifice designed by Sir William Holford and Partners. Holford – whose prolific urban planning work has already been referenced – was a Liverpool University graduate. In 1970, his firm opened an office in Edinburgh to handle projects in the

An early-1970s view of the 'Trews' nightclub in the Strathmore Hotel in Luton and the exterior of the King James Hotel in Edinburgh, photographed shortly before demolition in 2016.

north of England and Scotland and it was there that the Liverpool hotel scheme was devised. Located on a triangular site at the junction of Chapel Street and New Quay, its external design attempted to evoke the heritage of the nearby River Mersey as a famous departure point for ocean liners. From a two-storey podium rose a triangular bedroom block with slightly convex sides, resembling the bow of a ship. In the centre, the service core was also triangular with lift shafts at its vertices. Externally, the hotel was clad in white-enamelled aluminium curtain walling with continuous ribbon windows around each storey. Although the effect was striking, attempting to evoke passenger ship naval architecture was surely an intriguing early instance of a revival of 1930s design approaches. Moreover, at the very point when the project got under way, the Canadian Pacific steamship company withdrew Liverpool's last trans-Atlantic passenger service and, almost simultaneously, Elder Dempster Lines ceased its passenger route to Ghana and Nigeria, meaning that there were no longer any regular overseas liner routes from the Mersey. Although it may not have been the architects' intention, from the hotel's inception, its shape commemorated a lost industry. Thanks to a high degree of prefabrication, the hotel was built in only six months and opened in the early summer of 1973. The *Caterer and Hotel Keeper* observed:

> 'With four new hotels opened in 13 months, bringing 800 extra bedrooms to the city, Liverpool has become somewhat blasé about new hotel development. But the excitement and mood of great anticipation generated by the Atlantic Tower, the last of the four to open, can be assessed by the fact that 1,000 people went to see for themselves on 9 June, the day the doors opened to the public for the first time.'[376]

A bedroom floor plan of the Atlantic Tower Hotel in Liverpool and a view showing the hotel under construction with the reinforced concrete service core rising upward.

The Atlantic Tower's nautical theme was continued indoors, where specially-commissioned contemporary art works and modernist furniture adorned the foyer and adjacent lounge space:

> 'The romance of Liverpool's association with the sea and the ships has exerted a strong influence on the décor and fitting out of the hotel. Surmounting the foyer, finished in ivory veined marble, is a 5cwt bronze sculpture based on a flight of cormorants by Liverpool sculptor Sean Rice. To the right is a lounge with fixed seating in olive green hide and settees and chairs in fawn coloured leather. Occasional tables are in polished chromium with smoked glass tops. The foyer gives direct access to the National Suite, a five room complex named after former winners of the Grand National and all have access to a landscaped courtyard dominated by the second of Sean Rice's sculptures, which stands approximately 18ft high and is based on the wheeling vortex formation of black-backed gulls.'[377]

The hotel's restaurant was designed both for use by day, when the vistas beyond were an attraction, and at night, when soft illumination, decorative drapes and live music were intended to create an atmosphere evoking imagined shipboard luxury:

> 'The name 'Stateroom' for the restaurant was inspired by the Stateroom on the passenger liners, now part of Liverpool's history as a port. There are ever-changing views of the river scene. There will be a resident trio, the

The Atlantic Tower Hotel in Liverpool viewed at night with floodlighting, the hotel's foyer with sculpture by Sean Rice, the Trade Winds bar and the Stateroom restaurant. To engender an atmosphere of ocean liner authenticity, the latter was equipped with Robert Heritage chairs of the design found in the Britannia and Columbia restaurants of Cunard's recently-introduced trans-Atlantic liner and cruise ship *Queen Elizabeth 2*.

Peter James Trio, for after-dinner dancing six nights weekly. The seating, for 160, is split into intimate dining bays… the full width window overlooking the Mersey is broken up with ceiling-to-floor gold Lurex and white striped curtains, hanging in pairs and illuminated from above to create a shimmering effect…'[378]

In the hotel's two bars, the theming descended into kitsch, however. One of these was named 'Trade Winds' and was:

'Designed to resemble the interior of a galleon and even has its own parrot called Horatio… Some features were inspired by Nelson's flagship, HMS *Victory*. One section resembles the captain's quarters with mock windows fronting an 18ft mural featuring old trading ships and giving customers a realistic impression that they are looking out to sea. In contrast is the 'action' area, with mast, rigging, gun ports and musket holders. Stools shaped like capstans, curtains in heavy brown and faun net resemble fish netting and a carpet incorporating a compass design in shades of blue and plum add character to the bar.'[379]

The other bar, named the 'Highlander' was, by contrast, 'in Scottish baronial style. Carpeted in the rich tartan of the Royal Stuart clan, rough, white plastered walls give a traditional feel. The bar counter in oak is fronted with red leather panels and embellished with Cairngorm brooches.'[380]

On a smaller scale than Scottish & Newcastle, the Greenalls Brewery based in Warrington expanded its De Vere hotel chain. Its project to extend and renovate the war-damaged Cavendish Hotel in Eastbourne was notable on account of the design quality of a new corner wing by Fitzroy Robinson & Partners. Completed in 1973, this had an over-sailing roof, continuous fenestration in recessed bands and projecting balconies. The suites at the corner gave unbroken views along the promenade towards the pier.

A new entrant into the hotel business, attracted by the Hotel Development Incentives Scheme, was the long-established bookmaker, Ladbrokes, which since 1956 had been run by Cyril Stein, an ambitious business entrepreneur who began a programme of diversification. The Betting and Gaming Act of 1961 enabled the opening of high street betting shops and bingo halls. A decade later, Stein moved into the hotel trade too – a 'classier' area of activity than Ladbrokes' existing core businesses.

Ladbrokes' approach to hotel development was more closely aligned with that of the large American hotel chains than those of existing British chains such as Rank or Scottish & Newcastle. Initially, the company commissioned the building of three hotels in Leeds, Bristol and Middlesbrough, all of which were designed by the same architects, Abbey Hanson Rowe, and interior designers, Cope Notter Associates. Furthermore, they all had the same name – Dragonara – and the same facilities. Each had a different plan, however, to respond to its site's characteristics.

The Leeds Dragonara was located close to main railway station and had 240 rooms in an eight-storey accommodation block rising from a podium. The Bristol hotel, between Temple Meads Station and Queen's Square, had only seven storeys to avoid dominating the adjacent St Mary Redcliffe Church, but this was compensated by a larger footprint, giving 210 rooms. The hotel's most noteworthy feature was its Kiln Restaurant, built inside the cone of the city's last remaining glass kiln, which dated from 1780 and was preserved as a condition of planning consent. Within its tapering brick walls, 120 diners were accommodated in what the *Caterer and Hotel Keeper* considered 'extremely attractive and unusual surroundings.'[381] Not only did the kiln's retention reflect an emerging desire for the conservation of industrial archaeology, but also involved its imaginative re-integration with new technical services and furnishings. The hotel's bedrooms were carpeted in brightly coloured shag pile and appointed with 'Yugoslavian open-fronted cupboards and Spanish bedspreads.'[382] The hotel's leisure facilities included squash courts, a swimming pool and a sauna. The 240-room Middlesbrough Dragonara was a 14-storey monolith on a site overlooking the docks, where it was sandwiched between two office blocks of lower height. Due to a land acquisition dispute, however, it proved impossible to demolish a derelict row of brick terraces immediately in front of the hotel, giving an unsightly vista of decay for arriving guests and those looking downward from their rooms. The

The exterior of the extension added to the Cavendish Hotel in Eastbourne and the interior of one of its corner suites, giving an unbroken panorama along the town's promenade.

Images showing the Dragonara Hotel in Bristol, the hotel's Kiln Restaurant and the Dragonara Hotel in Middlesbrough, demonstrating its unfortunate proximity to a derelict terrace of houses.

management resolved this problem by commissioning what was acclaimed as Britain's largest advertising hoarding built around the terrace, thereby hiding the problem. Today, 'wrapping' buildings has become a common solution to situations of this kind.[383]

All three Dragonara Hotel were opened in April 1973, Ladbrokes' advertising slogan being 'Good places to stay when you're working – great places to stay when you're not.' The company proved surprisingly adept at running hotels and soon fresh acquisitions were made. The Beaufort Hotel in Bath, dating from 1972, was purchased from the brewer Myddleton; designed by Snailum, Le Fevre and Quick, a Bath practice otherwise best known for having produced the city's Snow Hill housing scheme. Located near Poultney Bridge, its rear elevation had a terrace facing the river. The hotel was to have formed part of a wider redevelopment plan for the city, which Hugh Casson had been invited to approve – a decision he apparently later regretted. Although its Bath Stone facings attempted to harmonise with the environs, its overall design was most unimaginative.[384]

In terms of standardising hotel design, Crest Hotels, a new company formed in 1970 by the Bass and Mitchells & Butlers breweries went a stage further, employing Tributus Design Unit of London to develop fully modularised structures, comprising bare concrete cubes arranged in groups rather than stacked up to form a single monolith, as was more usual for hotels. At that time, the possibilities of flexible, instant, 'plug-in' architecture were of great interest to those who considered themselves as progressive thinkers – as seen in proposals by Cedric Price or Archigram. While the aspiration may have been to emulate the types of temporary accommodation found on oil rigs or even space stations, in reality, concrete modules were rather heavy and inflexible. Nonetheless, in a few avant garde buildings, such as the Habitat 67 flats in Montreal by Moshe Safdie, an aesthetic of irregularly stacked cubes was used. The initial batch of Crest

The Beaufort Hotel in Bath.

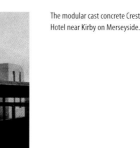

Hotels sought to use a similar strategy, albeit with far less artistry. The first of these occupied a site by the M6 motorway near Kirkby on Merseyside. It was intended to accommodate businessmen visiting the nearby industrial conurbation and consisted of 50 cast concrete modular rooms (described as 'Urbus System low-rise units'), a grill room, coffee shop and two bars. Subsequent examples of the same design formula were planned for sites near Coventry, Derby, Exeter, Immingham and Beaconsfield. The arrangement of the modules could be varied depending on each site's characteristics, but in all cases, the outcome was monotonous; streaky light grey boxes of varying heights were hardly likely to impress either business executives or tourists.

The biggest and arguably also the grandest new entrant into the British hotel market as a result of the Hotel Development Incentives Scheme was the American-headquartered Holiday Inn Corporation, established in 1952 in Memphis, Tennessee by an entrepreneur called Charles Kemmons Wilson. The 'Holiday Inn' name was reputedly derived from an aspirational 1942 musical film, starring Bing Crosby and Fred Astaire. The initial aim was to provide clean, predictable, family-friendly and readily accessible overnight accommodation to road travellers. In 1957, Wilson introduced a franchise model to enable more rapid nationwide expansion; this approach meant that anyone could build and operate a Holiday Inn motel, so long as it was done according to the chain's standardised formula with regard to the facilities offered, the sizes of bedrooms, the furnishings and corporate branding. As the name suggested, there was an emphasis on leisure facilities, such as swimming pools, meaning that a typical one-night-stay while *en route* across the USA would feel more like a mini holiday. This formula proved tremendously successful, the typical roadside signs with their green neon-lit letters, yellow arrow and 'readograph' displaying room rates soon became commonplace near junctions on American freeways. Within a year, there were 50 across the United States, 100 by 1959, 500 by 1964, and the 1000th Holiday Inn opened in in 1968. Next, the company began to expand internationally. Indeed, alongside Hilton and McDonald's it was to become one of America's great post-war hospitality exports.

The Hotel Development Incentives Scheme encouraged Holiday Inn to bring its American formula to Britain as part of a wider incursion into the European hospitality market. The plan was that, by the summer of 1973, there should be no fewer than eleven large new Holiday Inns around Britain, each with between 200 and 300 bedrooms and with indoor swimming pools and other leisure facilities not typically found in many British hotels at that time. The locations selected were Plymouth, Leicester, Liverpool,

A series of views of British Holiday Inns of the early-1970s; (1) shows the American-style sign of the Heathrow hotel, (2) shows Bristol, (3) is a postcard advertising the Liverpool hotel, (4) and (5) show the exterior and a bedroom of Plymouth and (6) shows Swiss Cottage in London.

Marble Arch and Swiss Cottage in London, London Heathrow Airport, Bristol, Birmingham, Dover, Slough and Newcastle.

As if this were not enough to cause British hoteliers to feel threatened, the *Caterer and Hotel Keeper* published an article detailing the workings of Holiday's Inn's mighty corporate machine in the USA:

> 'Design of Holiday Inns comes under the supervision of the vice president of architecture, and co-ordination of all Inn construction is handled through the Projects Development Department. The Holiday Inns' Construction Division is one of [North America's] leading institutional builders. Holiday Inns Inc. has its own legal department for real estate and mortgage loan assistance, and one of the best-equipped accounting departments in the hotel and motel industry.
>
> In the United States, reservations can be made at any Holiday Inn by the Holidex computer system or through a toll-free telephone call to centralised reservation offices in Atlanta, Chicago, Memphis, New York and Salt Lake City… Today, you can even ride via Holiday Inns Inc.… the company… controls Continental Trailways, the second largest U.S. inter-city bus system. Holiday Inns Inc., with Gulf Oil Corporation, pioneered the use of an oil company credit card for charging hotel services…'[385]

The first of the British Holiday Inns to open was in Plymouth, occupying a site directly across Hoe Park from Trust Houses' recent Mayflower Hotel. Completed in the spring of 1971, its operator was Holiday Inn's Canadian franchise holder, Commonwealth Holiday Inns of Canada (known as C.H.I.C.), which would be responsible for four of the British hotels. The architect Alun Wyatt designed a 12-storey structure, making extensive use of pre-cast concrete elements. Because the 225 bedrooms were identical modules with windows on one face only, at the south-west corner, where the best views could have been enjoyed, there was instead an unbroken expanse of concrete. This large blank area, however, enabled the Holiday Inn name to be displayed in large lettering, thereby reinforcing the brand identity. Only on the top storey – where there were suites and a restaurant – did the glazing continue on all sides. The podium contained a large conference suite for up to 300 delegates, an indoor swimming pool and a car park. The *Caterer and Hotel Keeper* records the hotel's appointments and the brand's inspection regime for franchises:

> 'The Plymouth Holiday Inn… is number 1,263 in the global network, which boasts "a new room opened every twenty minutes" and plans to have 3,000 hotels around the world by the end of the 'seventies… Like all Holiday Inns, the rooms are large – minimum size of a double is 21 ft by 12 ft. there are two restaurants - a penthouse restaurant commanding a magnificent view of Plymouth Sound, and a ground floor American-style Coffee Shop. There is an indoor swimming pool and sauna bath and a free underground car park "as big as the playing surface of Wembley Stadium." All of these things can be found in some modern British hotels, but at a Holiday Inn they are just standard items… Efficiency and strict control of standards are also part of the Holiday Inn story. And to ensure that standards are strictly kept, a team of Holiday Inns inspectors will visit the Inn four times a year. If the establishment fails to make a certain percentage of available points the innkeeper is given 30 days to make good the faults and, if he fails to do so, the franchise may be taken away.'[386]

With its top-storey restaurant, spacious rooms and indoor leisure facilities, the Holiday Inn was considered as upmarket of the Mayflower. Following local protests, C.H.I.C.

was not given permission to install a typically American 'Holiday Inn' sign by the hotel's main access road. At Leicester, this type of signage, originally intended to attract attention from passing cars, was installed as planned and soon caused major consternation, as the *Caterer and Hotel Keeper* records:

> 'Even before it opened, the £1 million Holiday Inn had caused quite a stir amongst the good citizens of Leicester who didn't like their sign. "Much too Americanised for us", they declared. Letters appeared in the local papers describing it as a monstrosity, even an abortion. One citizen praised the action of Plymouth Corporation for banning a similar Holiday Inn sign.'[387]

The hotel had a similar capacity to the one in Plymouth, as well as the same range of conference and leisure facilities.

The 245-room Holiday Inn at Marble Arch in London, opened in September 1972, was squeezed into a narrow site off Edgware Road – but its architects, Richard Seifert & Partners, were well used to squeezing the maximum possible accommodation into constricted spaces. Although most of its rooms had balconies, those on the lower floors of the 14-storey accommodation block merely looked towards the gables of surrounding buildings. The hotel's developer was Heron Holdings Ltd, from whom C.H.I.C. leased it.

C.H.I.C. also ran the 300-room Holiday Inn at Swiss Cottage, completed in September 1972 to a design by Dennis Lennon's architectural practice – the first time Lennon's office had designed a hotel's shell rather than its interiors (which were finished according to Holiday Inn's own standard specifications). On a triangular location between Adelaide Road and King Henry's Road, the solution was to build two inter-connected five-storey accommodation blocks, the smaller one with a square footprint being adjacent to the junction while the other was rectangular in shape and located where the site broadened out. Lennon appears to have made his own imaginative interpretation of the Holiday Inn brief, designing a hotel more closely resembling one found next to an Italian beach than at a road intersection in North-West London. The ground floor had arched windows – suggestive of an arcade – while those above had slender projecting balconies, the railings around which had prominent vertical balusters. These details and the white paintwork were slightly incongruous – but a lot more festive and fun than the more typical results of hurried design and construction exemplified by most other hotels of the period.

The Bristol Holiday Inn, designed by the Renton Howard Wood Partnership, formed part of a much larger redevelopment scheme for the city's quaint but neglected Old Market area. The outline plan for this project had been devised in the mid-1960s by Sir Hugh Casson and involved the construction of a new multi-lane road, Temple Way, which formed part of the city's inner ring road and was bulldozed through the site in a cutting. The hotel stood on one side, with deck access bridges linking to its podium level.[388] As at Birmingham, Leicester and Liverpool, the bedrooms were contained in a horizontal rectilinear block, in this instance clad in close-fitting, aggregate-faced panels. These were interspersed with grilles which formed an alternating pattern beneath each set of windows, producing an effect reminiscent of the patterning of the façades of Berthold Lubetkin's pre-war Lenin Estate in Finsbury, albeit within a more obviously brutalist overall design concept. The entire Temple Way redevelopment was, however, disliked by many Bristolians and so, notwithstanding the Holiday Inn's superior quality, it too was widely disparaged by those who regretted the loss of the previous cityscape.

The Holiday Inns in Liverpool and Birmingham, also with around 300 rooms, both opened in December 1972 and were the work of the Birmingham architect, James A.

Roberts, with detailing similar to his Birmingham Albany Hotel of eight years previously. At the same time, another Holiday Inn of the same capacity was opened at London Heathrow Airport.[389] In terms of layout and massing, the latter was, however, closest in style to its North American contemporaries, being a low-rise four-storey structure, faced in brick, with a giant sign by its entrance.

By the end of the 1960s, the growth in jet air travel had caused Heathrow Airport to expand to encompass three terminals, collectively known as 'Sky City' and surrounded by increasing numbers of auxiliary offices, warehouses and, of course, hotels.

In addition to Heathrow's new Holiday Inn, a 350-room hotel was developed by the London-based Capital & Counties Properties who intended to lease it to Hotel Corporation of America (the operator of the Carlton Tower in London's Cadogan Square). When they had second thoughts, it was instead offered to another North American operator, Skyline Hotels of Toronto, Canada. Designed by the Ronald Fielding Partnership, a major London-based commercial practice, the Heathrow Skyline – as it became – was yet another four-storey hotel between the A4 Bath Road and the airport runway. From the outside, its repetitive cast concrete elevations were fairly similar to those of Forte's nearby Excelsior. Its major innovation lay within because the 'piazza' defined by its four accommodation blocks was enclosed by a 'space-frame' roof structure, supporting a Perspex dome. Beneath this, the climate could be kept summery throughout the year, so Skyline Hotels' interior designer, Alan W. Edwards, was inspired to produce 'El Patio Cariba', an indoor pool and lido area with 'tropical plants and birds and West Indian waiters and waitresses. In the evening, a West Indian band plays to guests, who can drink at the bar or in the pool as one side is actually in the water.'[390] The two-storey high reception, with aluminium 'starburst' chandeliers and buttoned leather lounge furniture, overlooked the pool through an expanse of plate glass windows. Other attractions included 'Diamond L'il's' – a wild west cabaret restaurant in which a live country and western show was staged each evening, the Colony Room with conventional a la carte dining, le Café Jardin coffee shop, and a multi-functional banqueting room for 450 diners, or 650 conference guests.[391]

In the bedrooms, Edwards chose a 'rustic French' aesthetic, suggested by the bare brickwork of the incomplete shell (but also in line with emerging taste trends – as demonstrated concurrently by Terence Conran's Habitat chain of homeware stores). Copies were made of 'the traditional furniture of Normandy', the painted finishes of which were partially sanded away. This 'distressed' look was apparently 'highly practical in minimising maintenance costs.'[392] Suddenly encountering such

incongruous décor inside a brutalist building by a busy airport runway must have been strange indeed but, aided by heavy soundproofing and triple-glazed windows, the designs perhaps enabled a degree of temporary escapism for those willing to suspend disbelief.

Esso Motor Hotels, referred to previously and likewise American owned, was also encouraged to begin a fresh programme of expansion. The plan was to augment its two existing, quite small hotels at South Mimms and Maidenhead, both near London, with larger examples near Luton, Bristol, Coventry, Runcorn, Edinburgh, Glasgow and Wembley. The first four of these were similar in height and layout to the original pair, but the two Scottish examples and, in particular, the Wembley hotel, were considerably more ambitious.

The Edinburgh property, which opened in the Spring of 1970, was located on Queensferry Road, a busy artery close to the centre and airport to attract visiting tourists, while also serving Esso's core motorist clientele through proximity to the Forth Road Bridge. The 120-room, eight-storey structure was designed by James Shepherd Morris of Morris & Steadman. In recent years, the practice had designed hospital and university buildings in Edinburgh, Glasgow and Stirling – but never previously a hotel. The outcome was sadly undistinguished, being faced in pre-cast concrete blocks somewhat in the manner of the London architect-developer, Richard Seifert, though without the self-confident swagger of his best work.[393]

Following the Edinburgh project, Morris & Steadman's other senior partner, Robert Steadman, prepared drawings for a second Scottish Esso Motor Hotel, to be located beside the new Erskine Bridge over the River Clyde and also conveniently near to Glasgow Airport. To ensure its timely construction at a time when most suitable builders were fully occupied with hotel projects elsewhere, Esso engaged a European subsidiary of the American Daniel Construction Corporation, which had built some of its other recent hotels on the continent, but none of the previous British ones.

Steadman's design was dominated by a brutalist accommodation block, containing 180 rooms, held aloft on two-storey concrete stilts and clad in a variety of rough, textured concrete finishes. The uppermost three bedroom storeys were corbelled over the four below with the reception and public room blocks being tucked beneath at a right-angle. In a semi-rural location, surrounded by open land, such a top-heavy-looking mass was intrusive and the effect was perhaps more redolent of some sinister government facility than a place offering a warm and hospitable welcome.

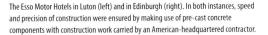

The Esso Motor Hotels in Luton (left) and in Edinburgh (right). In both instances, speed and precision of construction were ensured by making use of pre-cast concrete components with construction work carried by an American-headquartered contractor.

As with Esso's first pair of British hotels, the interior design was by Cope Notter Associates but, unlike in their previous contributions, at Erskine modernism was eschewed in favour of a themed design which sought to reflect Glasgow's trading with the East Indies in the nineteenth century:

> 'The décor of the public areas will echo this era in colourful and sophisticated style. Tones of red and crimson will create a warm and tropical atmosphere and the exotic décor will provide an oriental background. An unusual feature of the Eastern Trader complex will be… cube-faced panels with decorative brass and steel nails, reminiscent of old tea chests. Oriental weapons will be on display.'[394]

The conference and banqueting suite, however, was an early instance of an approach that was subsequently to become very familiar to Glaswegians:

> 'In decorating the Erskine Suite, the designers have produced a striking Art Nouveau look which they attribute to the influence of Charles Rennie Mackintosh… The suite will accommodate up to 400 persons for a conference or banquet…'[395]

The Esso Motor Hotel by the Erskine Bridge crossing of the River Clyde to the west of Glasgow.

The 156-room Bristol Esso Motor Hotel at Hambrook near Bristol was controversially built on what had been a picturesque green belt site near to the M4 and M32 motorways. To qualify for a Hotel Development Incentives Scheme subsidy, the project needed to be under construction by March 1971. To maximise speed and efficiency, Esso Motor Hotels dismissed its initial choice of architect (name unknown) and instead entered into what at that time was a fairly innovative integrated design and construction 'package deal.' This involved handing responsibility for the project to a Bristol-based 'design and build' company, Building Partnership, and its construction subsidiary, JT Building Service Group. According to the *Architect's Journal*, their 'one stop' solution 'provided a quicker answer than more traditional procurement methods' and, indeed, from Esso Motor Hotels' presentation of the initial design brief to the motel's completion, just 15 months elapsed (as opposed to the two years expected when using conventional procurement).[396] The many specialist sub-contractors involved were co-ordinated by Building Partnership and Esso Motor Hotels employed only a consultant architect to monitor progress.

Mature pine trees lined the driveway and the car park – for 250 vehicles – was set among the trees of an apple orchard. The motel's public areas were concentrated in a glass-walled building overlooking the gardens and linked to the three-storey L-shaped bedroom block. As the site was prone to flooding, an artificial lake was built to contain water and run-off; this was 'complete with an island and a red-sailed dinghy.'[397] According to the *AJ*, design and construction work:

> '…Accelerated to a hectic speed… snap decisions saved a good deal of fuss and bother… As an example, the air conditioning consultant insisted on some form of solar protection [to mitigate solar gain]. Tinted glass was decided upon, but the buyer advised that the unit price of tinted glass jumps considerably over a certain pane size. This led to prompt redesign of the glazing pattern to keep to the cheaper rate with no delay on site.'[398]

The fact that quite substantial changes, profoundly affecting the building's appearance, happened on almost an ad-hoc basis inevitably meant that the outcome was fairly banal. The bedroom block's flat frontages with rows of small windows were particularly dreary and monotonous. In an attractive location, this was indeed a pity and a missed opportunity. The motel was, in fact, best experienced from within, looking outward. Here too the interior design was by Cope Notter Associates. Because of the Bristol's history as a trading port, a 'Bristol Trader' theme was adopted for the restaurant and lounge areas. In addition, there were conference and banqueting facilities for 400, divisible into four smaller units.[399]

The Wembley Esso Motor Hotel was sited adjacent to Empire Way, a major arterial road developed in the 1920s for the British Empire Exhibition. Completed in November 1972 to a design by Richard Seifert & Partners, it was the chain's largest addition – a 12-storey concrete monolith containing 335 rooms plus conference facilities for 900 in three large suites. The ends of the accommodation block folded over the fire escape stairs, their angled shapes reflecting those of the roof structure of the conference suite, located in front. These bold forms lent a sense of visual cohesion and were commensurate with the overall scale of the structure. The Seifert office was usually good at detailing of this kind; no matter how over-scaled its schemes were, they tended to appear confidently unified.

The hotel's public rooms were by Garnett, Cloughley, Blakemore & Associates with the bedrooms by Cope Notter Associates. Erik Blakemore designed a standard carpet pattern in a variety of colour combinations for use throughout the building. This had a medallion motif, which was repeated in other prominent interior elements such as door handles. The walls of the reception were panelled in walnut and the public rooms were furnished with modernist items imported from Finland which at that time was emerging as a major exporter of 'designer' goods. Illumination was from Italian Murano glass light fittings. The four penthouse and executive suites were individually themed, one being decorated in Louis XV style, another 'with the dignified and restrained features of an English gentlemen's club', the third in the manner of a country house and the fourth with 'ultra-modern trappings that anticipate the 2001 era, including a water bed.'[400] Just as at the Glasgow Albany's suites, the idea was clearly to give those who booked it a taste of the Playboy lifestyle.

Before the end of 1972, the Esso Motor Hotels' owners, Standard Oil, had a major change of policy, deciding henceforth to concentrate on its core activities of making and selling refined oil products. It therefore agreed to sell most of the European Esso Motor Hotels chain to the Crest Hotels subsidiary of the British brewer Bass-Charrington; by this point, the Esso chain consisted of 59 properties. The Scandinavian properties were excluded from this deal as laws there prevented brewers from also owning overnight accommodation.

A consequence of this change was that the intended Esso Motor Hotel in the new town of Runcorn in north-west England was completed instead for Crest in January 1973 and named the Beechwood Motor Hotel. Architecturally, it was a very superior offering – indeed, it was among the very best British post-war hotel buildings and one of the few to win unequivocal praise from the architectural press. Although similar in concept and capacity and concept to the one at Hambrook, rather than hiring a design-and-build team here Esso worked with the Runcorn Development Corporation's Architect's Department, which was headed by R.L.E. Harrison; the project architects were Keith Smith, John Randle and N.J. Mayman. As the *Architect's Journal* observed,

'At Runcorn, Esso had one of those rare flashes of good sense and went to the Runcorn Development Corporation's architects. The result is very satisfying – a piece of architect's architecture which works.'[401] In practice, this meant that the building 'quoted' other recent examples of critically acclaimed British and international modernism, an approach architecture critics and enthusiasts find intellectually appealing, but which is of little interest or value to those who finance or operate commercial buildings (and, thus, rarely found in them).

The bedroom block was of six storeys and located on steeply sloping land beside a river. Clad in Accrington red brick and consisting of overhanging upper floors and brick buttresses articulating the lower elevations, in appearance, it was somewhat reminiscent of Leslie Martin's early 1960s Harvey Court building at Gonville and Caius College at Cambridge University. The reception and public spaces formed a separate pavilion, built on flatter land adjacent. Standing on a brick-clad plinth, its strongly horizontal projecting roof, black-painted columns, beams and facias, interspersed by large expanses of tinted glazing, appeared highly reminiscent of Ludwig Mies van der Rohe's Neue Nationalgalerie in Berlin, which had been completed in 1968. That a university and an art gallery were considered as suitable precedents for a motel is highly revealing of modernism's 'high cultural' ideals. The *Architect's Journal* records how the motel's two elements were articulated and intended to be read and appreciated:

> 'The blocks are connected by a glazed link, a neutral mass which separates the two visually while linking their circulation patterns… The stylistic discontinuity between these two styles is resolved by the continuation of the brick into the interiors and the public spaces. It is as if the solid brick mass of the bedroom block is changed at the point of the transparent link into a hollowed out set of brick volumes and the latter protected by a steel pavilion.'[402]

While the bedrooms were designed according to Esso Motor Hotels' standard specifications for all its European properties, the public rooms in the pavilion allowed the architects much greater freedom. Rather than changing the ceiling heights to create a sense of hierarchy (which would have run contrary to the logic of the pavilion's roof being its major continuous design element), the floor levels were varied slightly.

An aerial view of the Esso Motor Hotel at Hambrook near Bristol, the exterior of the Esso Motor Hotel at Wembley plus two interior views, one showing the conference foyer and the other, the restaurant.

The spaces all featured bare brickwork, stone floors with rugs and textured ceilings. Against this backdrop, the interior designers, Lucy Halford and Associates and Cope Notter Associates, produced a swish Club Bar with deep leather chairs, a restaurant furnished in light oak and a conference facility called the Cheshire Suite, also with oak-framed chairs. The *Architect's Journal* considered that:

> 'Given the obsession with the need for 'themes' in the bars and restaurants which is widespread among hoteliers and which always ends up as a collection of embarrassing little features, the architects are to be congratulated for their skills of diplomacy in steering their clients away from yet more variations on the 'baronial theme.'[403]

Although the interiors have been changed during the period since, the motel's exterior survives largely intact and the building is now known as the Holiday Inn.

Another notable exception to the general situation of mediocre hotel buildings being constructed with undue haste in the early 1970s should have been a large 215-room hotel, office and retail development in central Manchester. Located close to Piccadilly Station on Mancunian Way, the elegantly curved ten-storey structure designed by local architect J.L. Hammond was in terms of overall form a *homage* to the United Nations building in Paris by Marcel Breuer and Pier Luigi Nervi and to the newly-completed European

A sectional drawing through the bedroom block and public rooms of the Beechwood Motor Hotel at Runcorn and an image showing part of the building's exterior.

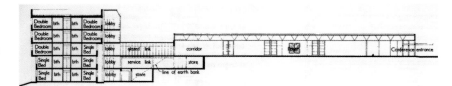

schemes were woven wool interwoven with chenille and tapestry wool in brilliant colour bands as well as loose-weave semi-sheer mohair fabric… The bed valances and bed covers have also been made for every bed in the hotel, together with all the matching cushions and special bed-head cushions wall-hung from rails…'[416] On the topmost storey were three penthouse suites, giving 'superb views over Hyde Park… They each comprise a large sitting room with bathroom and small kitchen with adjoining bedrooms on either side…'[417] Staff uniforms were by Cecil Gee, a fashionable London tailor.

The Seifert firm's design for the very large London Penta Hotel on Cromwell Road utilised what Seifert described as 'corkscrew twist planning' in a vain attempt to lessen the structure's considerable mass. The Penta was London's biggest post-war hotel to date with 27 storeys, containing 914 rooms. Developed by European Hotel Corporation and operated by Grand Metropolitan Hotels, it aimed to serve the mid-market and to provide only a basic level of service. Even though its immediate environs already were characterised by 'high, chasm-like streets… running at unexpected angles', the *Architectural Review* found it a 'terrible interruption of the weave' of that part of the city. Passers-by would perceive a 'chaotic pile, forcing its way upwards through successive layers of low-level impediments', the two-storey podium at the base being 'like some hoarding put up to mask the early beginnings of a monster apparition.'[418]

The hotel's communal facilities consisted of a large coffee shop and pub, but only a small grill restaurant, cocktail bar and conference area. The interior design was by Henry End & Associates, the California-headquartered designers whose earlier work in London included the swish Carlton Tower Hotel in Cadogan Square. The London Penta's extensive foyer had a polished white terrazzo floor, above which was suspended a series of large 'golf ball' chandeliers. Both the cocktail bar and the grill room had 'island' counters, accessible from all four sides and thereby allowing the maximum number of guests to be served using a minimum of labour. The Four Seasons Coffee Shop was brightly coloured with red and green carpet and orange pedestal chairs. The Pub of

The London Penta Hotel's exterior, foyer and coffee shop; the latter's relatively basic furnishings reflected the level of comfort and service to be provided to a predominantly tourist clientele.

Pubs, by contrast, sought to evoke 'a nostalgic Victorian setting and is panelled throughout with a mahogany veneer treated to comply with very stringent fire regulations and inset with acid etched mirrors.' Its Ceiling had 'moulded beams and decorative acrylic vacuum moulded panels' while the two bar counters were 'traditional polished brass fitments.'[419] It is indeed intriguing that Grand Metropolitan withdrew from the upmarket Park Tower project in favour of the mass-market London Penta; presumably its resources could not be stretched to two such large hotels and, with high-throughput employing fewer staff in facilities such as the Pub of Pubs, the Penta may have promised the better yield.

Next to Kensington High Street Station, Aer Lingus, Ireland's national airline, built the very large London Tara, which was designed by Farrington, Dennys, Fisher & Associates (formerly known as Cassidy, Farrington, Dennys, who had been the co-ordinating architects of the Royal Lancaster Hotel interiors, described above). The firm was chosen on account of having previously prepared several speculative designs for the site for other clients, including a design for a 2,000-room hotel, offices and a shopping centre – but none of these had come to fruition. The London Tara had 850 rooms, contained in a monolithic 14-storey accommodation block with the reception and other facilities in a lower entrance block in front. As Nigel Farrington recalled, the entire scheme was a 'dirty rush' as it had to be:

> '...Designed and built in just 27 months for £5,000 per bedroom. Time was so short that the detailed drawings were evolved as the building went up. A design that was structurally simple was therefore developed and refined as the process proceeded. Throughout the process, the architects and other consultants worked from an office on the building site so that decisions involving the contractor could be taken as quickly as possible...'[420]

The exterior, the foyer and a suite in the London Tara Hotel, another very large West London hotel developed primarily to accommodate tourists, but also offering a small proportion of more expensive and luxurious accommodation.

The foyer's finishes somewhat resembled those of a London Underground station with tiled columns and bare brickwork selected for cheapness and resilience. There were even built-in vending machines for food and drink. Otherwise, the hotel's facilities consisted of a cocktail bar, the Ormonde Restaurant (seating just 80 as most guests wanting a meal were expected to eat out) and a Coffee Shop. The Dublin Bar was intended as the hotel's 'social centre', an early example of the type of capacious pastiche Irish pub so popular with tourists in cities all over the world.[421]

Reviewing the London Tara for *Interior Design* magazine, the architect and critic Peter J. Lord observed:

> 'Perhaps it is from this organisational background that the consistency on approach and detailing, which is one of the scheme's strongest characteristics, derives... Even so the rash of ill-considered major buildings created by the artificial hotel property boom can hardly claim this example to totally redress the balance. Its massing is unfortunate and

no amount of justification can justify the stack-a-guest bedroom block's overbearing and unhappy relationship to the mass containing the main public areas… What of the interiors? I regret to say I found them adequate but dull…'[422]

Of other buildings critiqued by Lance Wright in the *Architectural Review*, the West Centre Hotel in West Brompton by Raymond Spratley possessed 'the harsh, coarse contrasts of some little factory, run up at great speed in some unfavoured part of Slough.'[423] (Suggesting that a building was fit only for Slough was a major insult; the *AR*'s famous inter-war era contributor, John Betjeman, had written a notorious poem inviting 'friendly bombs' to fall on that maligned railway town.) The hotel's owner, Centre Hotels, was a newly-formed subsidiary of the long-established Glaswegian provider of temperance hospitality, Cranstons Ltd. In the early twentieth century, Cranston's had been a well-known patron of progressive architecture and design, having employed Charles Rennie

Centre Hotels' West Centre Hotel, Bloomsbury Centre Hotel, Regent Centre Hotel and Heathrow Centre Hotel.

Mackintosh (among others) to design its Glasgow tea room premises. Now, half a century later, its management evidently decided that investing in high quality architecture was unimportant as a prerequisite for maximising profitability. In a sense, Centre Hotels' approach prefaced that of chains such as Travelodge or Premier Inn in more recent times. Of the company's other London premises, the 240-room Bloomsbury Centre Hotel was built adjacent to the eponymous residential and shopping development which had a distinctive terraced design. Unfortunately, the hotel's drearily repetitive bands of brick and glazing did nothing to emulate this. The 350-room Regent Centre Hotel in Carburton Street was faced in moulded concrete panels with the lower storeys in dark engineering brick, making it hardly any more appealing. Worst of all aesthetically was the Centre Hotel at Heathrow Airport, consisting of a series of two-storey units, punctured with narrow windows. Centre Hotels soon announced plans for numerous further similar hotels elsewhere in the capital and in the provinces.[424]

The ongoing development of Heathrow Airport into a sprawling complex of shopping, catering and hotel facilities, serving the new high-capacity Boeing 747s and other types of wide-bodied jets actually required the building of a number of large, new hotels. As the *Caterer and Hotel Keeper* pointed out 'a delayed or cancelled Jumbo Jet could result in 400 passengers needing to be accommodated at short notice.'[425] With this potential problem in mind, the airport's owner, the government-owned British Airports Authority, decided to build a hotel on its own land within the airport's boundary, directly adjacent to the main runway. Leased to the Hotel Corporation of America, the Heathrow Hotel had 700 rooms and was yet another design by the prolific Richard Seifert & Partners.

To speed up the hotel's construction, which took place in less than a year, a system of prefabricated units was used; both the manufacture of these and their assembly on site were the responsibility of the contractor, Cementation Building Ltd.

Although nearly all of recent Seifert designs made a virtue of repetitive concrete elements, the Heathrow Hotel's appearance of stacked boxes, each containing a bedroom, was the most extreme and utilitarian example of this approach. Given its runway-side location, the structure was heavily sound-proofed with triple-glazed windows. The *Caterer and Hotel Keeper* reported that, from its rooms, '...the uncanny feeling of seeing a jumbo jet roar off down the runway and not hearing a sound is quite remarkable.'[426] The hotel's prefabricated design was, however, appropriate in the context of a rapidly-growing airport complex where the idea of new elements being 'plugged in' to existing infrastructure – or stacked like shipping containers – was fairly typical, particularly airside.

Within the concrete boxes lay a different world, characterised by white marble flooring, glitzy brass chandeliers, shag-pile carpeting and leisure facilities, including an indoor pool, sauna and gymnasium. As at Hotel Corporation of America's Carlton Tower in Cadogan Square, the dining facilities included a 'Rib Room' serving steaks. Adjacent, the Sir Frances Drake Lounge had a Tudor theme, while the 'Flying Machine Bar told 'the history of aviation with Royal Air Force memorabilia decorating the walls.' There was also a 24-hour coffee shop, the York Theatre for Conferences and the Wessex Ballroom with space for 750.[427]

On a green field site further away from the airport complex, but reachable by car or shuttle bus, Trust Houses Forte commissioned Nelson Foley to design a new 600-room Post House for completion in April 1973. At Charles Forte's insistence, the cost-effective cruciform plan of the Excelsior Hotel at Glasgow Airport was replicated, albeit in greatly enlarged form. The *AR* grudgingly conceded that Foley had faced a nigh-impossible task and that:

'The real failure of this honest and rather pedestrian form of architecture lies in

Images showing the Heathrow Hotel's modular shell, its reception with glitzy polished brass light fittings and its Sir Frances Drake Lounge.

the fact that the human realities it must express are in themselves ugly… A rack containing bedrooms for 500 overnight visitors on expenses accounts, rising suddenly out of a field of kale is in itself an unattractive social proposition.'[428] The Heathrow Post House's public rooms were by the noted London-based 'society' interior designer, decorator and design educator, Michael Inchbald, while the bedrooms were by Valerie Toegal, Trust Houses Forte's own décor consultant. At that time, Inchbald was at the height of his powers, having recently designed the 'space age' Queens Room on the liner *Queen Elizabeth 2*, which was widely acclaimed as being among the vessel's greatest design successes. Perhaps due to time pressure, or having identified a less discerning clientele, his hotel interiors lacked the finesse of his *QE2* design work. The T-shaped entrance hall and reception spaces were certainly commodious and, there, Inchbald produced an eye-popping scheme in orange, red and dark brown. The carpet featured a repeat pattern of large orange and red 'targets' while the walls were a rich orange. In the centre was a 'spray' light with numerous small bulbs illuminating the ends of its many aluminium stalks. In complete contrast to the foyer's trendy 'pop' design, the Great Britain Grill, Buttery and Brunel Bar had themed décor and colouration suggestive of nineteenth century industrial heritage, combining dark green, red and black shades with the hard textures of grey brick and dark wood. The carpeting, designed by Inchbald, had a pattern of crossed spanners.

The *Architectural Review* blamed the large sizes of recent hotels such as this on the fact that 'we seem to be going through an unattractive "managerial" phase in our society which operates equally in public and private sectors. Hospitals, schools, factories – all are on average much bigger than they used to be. This arises because administrators… are deeply impressed by the apparent advantages of scale…'[429] Yet, hoteliers would have countered this argument by pointing out that increasing business and tourist traffic meant more demand, equating to bigger hotels, while better off-setting construction and operational costs. The *AR* optimistically suggested that 'architects…should on principle react against their clients' bias in favour of great size' – naively implying that individual members of the profession might be able to exercise such a level of control over hoteliers' wishes and over the realities of the political and economic contexts in which they were operating.[430] The *AR* predicted that the outcome of not taking a firmer stance would be system-built 'hotels which will last two generations and took perhaps two years to build' looking 'as if they had taken about two hours to design.'[431]

The *AR*'s next target – the commercial property developers who commissioned hotels for 'third party' occupiers – was perhaps a fairer one. The archetypal developer was characterised as:

'The man who nips in simply and solely to make money… He is a scourge because, by getting between the architect and the man who is to own and use the building, he frustrates the ordinary processes of design. Architecture… can't happen when the real client is some third party who has no real interest in, or knowledge of, the enterprise he is endeavouring to house… The buildings which result… – whether they are office blocks, city centre developments or hotels – have the same overall character; at once faceless, thoughtlessly standardised and brash.'[432]

Although the *AR* might justifiably have blamed the architecture profession too for its part in this 'disaster in the annals of British architecture', perhaps wisely, it chose to skirt around antagonising its core readership.[433] Only those working directly for hotel chains

The large Post House at Heathrow Airport was built on a green field site, further away from the terminals than any of the existing hotels. The exterior was clad in pre-cast concrete panels but, in contrast, the interior designs by Michael Inchbald, shown in (2) and (4), varied between the vividly-coloured 'pop'-style of the foyer and Victoriana in the Brunel Bar, the ceiling of which had lighting recesses in the form of spoked wheels.

– such as Trust Houses Forte's Nelson Foley, who had earlier on produced several superior buildings – were rather unkindly singled out as 'the men who go far this sort of job tend not to be the men of firm architectural convictions; and apart from this, the chains who have tied architects tend to treat them like dogs.' However, such relationships also had the potential to give rise to fine buildings, as other commercial sectors had often demonstrated.

Most significantly, and perhaps without full consideration of the implications, the *AR* began to suggest, albeit obliquely, that perhaps the Modern Movement itself might be partly to blame for the paucity of attractive hotel designs. For the past half-century, modernist dogma had been obsessed with designing buildings to appear radically different from anything that had existed beforehand, invariably emphasising the universal over specificities of context. Now that British cities were encumbered with large numbers of its commercial manifestations, the atmosphere they engendered perhaps inevitably felt rather anonymous. Both locals and visiting tourists, however, apparently still wanted to experience a distinctive sense of place. As the *AR* put it, 'ideally, a hotel is a social building in which, above all, it is a pleasure to be… In an all too real sense, a modern hotel fulfils the Corbusian dictum and has become a "machine for staying the night in."'[434] But, having diagnosed this problem, the *AR* then deflected most of the blame for this situation upon to the tourist industry itself, citing its apparent desire to massify and standardise experiences as the prime factors encouraging ugly and repetitive design solutions. Yet, in reality, it was surely architects who had learned, then inflicted, such design approaches on the tourist industry and not the other way around.

An alternative to the international style that had never fully disappeared was revived period décor. But, as the *AR* put it, 'the regurgitation of the past involving no creative act' was likely to result in a mere 'stage set' being produced which would be 'in no sense unique… not a place, only a shadow of a place.'[435] Furthermore, 'the wider spans and lower ceilings engendered by air conditioning, coupled with 'the client's meanness, which aims at keeping the proportion of room heights to room widths as low as possible resulted only in pastiche interiors with all the wrong proportions.'[436] In addition, such interiors clashed incongruously with the modernist shells in which they were invariably inserted. A recent redecoration of the five-year-old Royal Lancaster Hotel was a case-in-point, Gordon Bowyer's modernist foyer there having been overlaid with ornate cornices, columns and door pediments, all squeezed in beneath the existing suspended ceiling. Such effects were:

> 'Hilarious; for here the dire effects of modern economy extend not merely to the room shape, but also to the trim. Mouldings which should be of wood and several inches thick are reproduced in plastic a few millimetres thick. As they are constantly peeling, the effect is hardly more convincing than that produced by a cheap period wallpaper.'[437]

The *AR* concluded that the problems of low-quality finishes were 'attributable to our dislocated society… No buildings in previous history have been subject to quite this degree of financial duress as those built by commerce in the '60s and '70s. Is it therefore surprising that none before have been quite so shoddy?'[438] Gordon Bowyer recalls ruefully that Rank's management had hated his design for the Royal Lancaster as they found it insufficiently luxurious – which points to a wide divergence in taste between the architecture profession's more critically acclaimed practitioners, such as Bowyer, and that of business leaders in the commercial leisure sector.[439]

While one might have expected the architectural press to retain its traditional snobbery about hotels and the compromises their design apparently so often entailed, the *Caterer and Hotel Keeper* too published stark criticisms of some of the examples recently completed under the auspices of the Hotel Development Incentives Scheme. Hugh Wontner, the Chairman and Managing Director of the Savoy Hotel Group, wrote scathingly of the economic realities underpinning the mass market hotel operators' decisions and their consequences for the character of their premises:

> 'They really have no alternative but to build what amounts to an ant heap, with every cubicle the same and the service cut to the barest minimum… Such hotels, offer a visitor tiny bathrooms and baths too short for anyone of average length, where a linen sheet has never been heard of and where it is very doubtful if the sheets are changed every day…'[440]

The Savoy Hotel Group therefore decided on a different approach when commissioning a design for its New Berkeley Hotel, to be built in Wilton Place off Knightsbridge. In replaced the existing Berkeley Hotel with a new one of three times the capacity, Savoy decided to eschew modernism altogether in favour of a neo-Georgian approach. The resulting six-storey structure – symmetrical with projecting wings at either end – was an intriguing but remarkably convincing throw-back to the 1920s, or even earlier. The greater surprise was that its architect was Brian O'Rorke, a London-based New Zealander who had first attracted widespread attention in the mid-1930s when commissioned by the Orient Line to produce interiors for its new UK-Australia liner *Orion* that were positively avant garde by the standards of the day. O'Rorke had subsequently been involved in designing interiors for all of Orient Line's subsequent vessels, culminating with the *Oriana* of 1961, in which he worked alongside Misha Black and Ian Hodgson of Russell, Hodgson & Leigh, both of whom had also recently designed interiors for London hotels. So far as critics were concerned, O'Rorke's sudden reversion to traditionalism divided opinion; the *Caterer and Hotel Keeper* was full of praise:

> 'Take a look at the impressive Clipsham stone clad exterior pictured above… a truly de luxe hotel. Neither time nor cost have been spared… Larger than the old Berkeley to be sure, 300 sleepers as opposed to just over 100, but so carefully designed in the manner of a country house as not to suggest a bigger hotel at all. Everything about it must be described – and judged – by the superlative…'[441]

The New Berkeley Hotel in Wilton Place in London represented a return to tradition.

The *Architectural Review*, on the other hand, found little to comment upon positively. While it had disliked the unsatisfactory proportions and inattention to the coherence of the cityscape of other recent London hotels, it found that the New Berkeley's 'sins' represented:

> 'A wholly different case… it does not sin notably against townscape. It is not built for tourists, but for a known, pre-existing and conservative clientele. It was subject to a set of financial circumstances which were hardly of this age; and if it shows much pastiche indoors, this is not to entertain the under educated and feeble minded, but because the customers are used to it and expect it… The fault of the New Berkeley is not that its designer has gone for the fine materials and craftsmanship of an earlier period and has re-used some of its proportions and decorative trim. It is that he has done these things while forgetting the important lessons that have been learned since…'[442]

That one such 'important lesson' might have been the limitations of the 'international style' was inadmissible – and so instead the *AR* resorted to mild insult:

'This building is in fact a very expensive version of a nurses home of circa 1935: it has the same equal floor-to-ceiling heights, the same general massing, the same degree of repetition of its parts… This sort of architecture was abandoned for this sort of problem, not because architects were led off by some delusive fancy, but because, for good aesthetic reasons, it didn't work. Classical design is deeply hierarchic. It simply does not permit the piling of similar units one above the other… The New Berkeley certainly does not rape its neighbourhood in the way Colonel Seifert's buildings often do, but it is a lugubrious and pudding pile.'[443]

Yet, as we have seen, back in the 1920s, several large Mayfair hotels did indeed use neo-Classical aesthetics, as did a great many public buildings of the inter-war era whose contents were indeed highly repetitive. It seems that, although the *AR*'s critic could not have condoned the thought, the New Berkeley's real 'crime' was to demonstrate that, so far as well-educated sections of the public were concerned, modernism was failing and any alternative showing an application of craft skill was welcome.

Although the vast majority of new hotels developed using Hotel Development Incentives Scheme subsidies related poorly to their contexts, there were a very few exceptions, with moderation either forced upon their developers by planners or by architects genuinely concerned about issues of townscape and urbanity.

Since the mid-1960s, Hilton had wished to develop a new hotel in the centre of Stratford-on-Avon, a tourist destination very popular with American visitors to Britain who wished to enjoy 'Shakespearian' experiences. These attempts had all been rebuffed and it took the Hotel Development Incentives Scheme's loosening of planning strictures to enable progress to be made. Hilton's favoured site covered five acres on the bank of the River Avon, close to the Royal Shakespeare Theatre.

Doubtless wishing to avoid causing unnecessary controversy, Hilton's architects Sidney Kaye, Eric Firmin & Partners, who had designed the London Hilton a decade before, took a cautious approach, producing plans for a fairly unobtrusive four-storey hotel, consisting of three co-joined wings, altogether containing 261 rooms. The exterior was faced in local brick with lead sheeting cladding the top floor (thereby disguising it as roofing to lessen the building's appearance of mass).

Within, Hilton's American-based in-house interior designers David T. Williams and Inge Bech sought to combine modernist elements with those of Elizabethan England. The foyer was lined with locally-quarried Hornton stone and had an open fireplace. The adjacent lounge sought to 'emulate the charm of a stately English home, accentuated by additional 'period pieces.' An internal mall containing gift and souvenir shops was

The Actor's Bar and Warwick Grill in the Hilton at Stratford-on-Avon.

designed to 'simulate bow-window-fronted shops in the 17th century Tudor style as found in Stratford-upon-Avon's own shopping centre.' Projecting at ground floor level from the main accommodation block, The Actor's Bar was a free-standing, octagonal-shaped cocktail lounge with a wavy cast concrete roof, the interior of which was reminiscent of stage scenery. Its hand-painted ceiling was executed according to the instruction of Christopher Morley, the Design Director of the Royal Shakespeare Theatre. The Warwick Grill, adjacent, had 'a stone-walled grill at one end where all the boiled meats are prepared…' while the Tavern Restaurant and Tavern Bar were 'decorated and furnished to represent an old English tavern.'[444]

Although aimed at a wealthier and more international clientele than Trust Houses Forte's Post Houses, for example, the Stratford-on-Avon Hilton's exterior and interior design strategies were actually remarkably similar. The Hilton, however, provided much more extensive facilities and a far higher standard of cuisine and service at much greater cost to guests.

While the Stratford-on-Avon Hilton was forced to defer to its historic surroundings, in London's East End, another much larger new hotel was under construction on a new type of British leisure site – post-industrial dockland. Among the final major hotels to be completed during the early 1970s building boom, the 826-room Tower Hotel was built adjacent to St Katherine's Dock on the River Thames, close to Tower Bridge. The dock had closed in 1968, one of the first in the Port of London to be mothballed as cargo-handling activities began to move to new roll-on, roll-off and container-handling facilities much further downriver. The site was then purchased by the Greater London Council, who leased it to the developer, Taylor Woodrow, who in turn negotiated an agreement with J. Lyons' Strand Hotels to be the Tower Hotel's eventual operator.

The idea of building a large tourist-orientated hotel on post-industrial land in London's East End was a radical departure from the existing practice of constructing such properties to the west in Mayfair, Kensington and Westminster. Just a decade before, the East End would have been considered too polluted and industrial for tourism development – but the Clean Air Act of 1956 had rapidly transformed the situation.

Designed by Renton Howard Wood Partnership and completed in September 1973, the Tower Hotel simultaneously reflected the end of an era and the beginning of a new one. Its concrete modernist facings represented an architectural aesthetic by then falling gradually out of fashion, while its stepped upper floors sought to achieve a better than usual relation to context, in line with emerging approaches to 'locale' that were to become increasingly commonplace in subsequent decades. The *Architect's Journal*'s critic, Lance Wright, approvingly observed:

> '…The big difference between this hotel and the others of the same order of size and housing the same sort of accommodation. While the others rise out of their sites like complete strangers and deploy their grotesque bulk to the utmost, this one pays serious respect to its locality and with its stepped profile comes down as near as it can to the scale of the structures next door. It is too big – no architectural skill could ever quite conceal this fact: but all that architecture can do has been done.'[445]

Wright also wrote a more fulsome critique in the *Architectural Review*, in which he commented that when 'seen at a distance and from certain viewpoints, you get the impression not of a single building, but of a cluster… a piece of 'built landscape.' This resulted in part from the hotel's 'windmill' plan with a series of offset wings emanating

The exterior of the Tower Hotel by St Katherine's Dock and two views of its well-articulated reception and foyer space.

from a central core (this was a successful variation of the cruciform arrangement favoured for several recent large hotels, such as the Heathrow Post House and Glasgow Excelsior). The offsets, however, gave a clustered effect, rather than that of a monolith.

The hotel's public rooms, the interior design of which was by Glyn Smith Associates, formed a two-storey complex along the length of the building facing Tower Bridge, while the Carvery restaurant and two conference rooms overlooked the dock basin. The reception foyer was of double-height with a dog-leg staircase accessing a wide gallery, connecting together the first floor public rooms. Wright considered this space 'a great architectural achievement...very large...but also intimate.' He went on to criticise other recent hotels' use of extreme open planning at the expense of human-scale, finding that the Tower Hotel's foyer was much the better for this latter quality. Yet, despite these commendable efforts, the hotel's exterior appeared as an institutional expanse of grey, punctuated by repetitive, slit-like windows. There was nothing about its external design to suggest pleasure and an enjoyable experience.

By the mid-1970s, however, J. Lyons & Co, was in decline. Notwithstanding heavy ongoing investment in new business areas (including computer electronics), its core Lyons Corner Houses were falling rapidly out of fashion, superseded by newer generations of coffee shop and cafeteria. In 1976, Strand Hotels was sold to Trust Houses Forte and, two years thereafter, what remained of J. Lyons was acquired by Allied Breweries.

Back in London's more familiar West End tourist territory, two new hotels were built on sites adjacent to Park Lane, each of which attempted to blend much more discreetly into this admittedly somewhat fragmented context than the London Hilton had done. The Inn on Park Lane was a late project by Michael Rosenauer in his typically understated, yet precisely detailed idiom. Its eight-storey tower, clad in Portland stone, rose from a two-storey public room block, which followed the lines of the surrounding streets. In some respects, the overall approach was a smaller version of Rosenauer's

The Inn on Park Lane, a late work by Michael Rosenauer and designed with his customary attention to detail.

much earlier Carlton Tower project. Rather than repeating its flat frontages and recessed fenestration, however, Rosenauer instead used chamfered corners and vertically-stacked bay windows. These features helped to break up the building's mass while also making oblique references to the forms of older neighbouring properties. At ground and first floor levels, very large expanses of glazing were used to lessen further the building's apparent mass, while also enabling views outward to Hyde Park.

The hotel's interior was, by complete contrast, an ostentatious neo-Regency affair by the American designer Tom Lee. His choice of dark woodwork, marble slabs and pilasters, ornate chandeliers, open fireplaces and buttoned velvet-upholstered chairs clashed with Rosenauer's modernist stairways with their open treads and rather minimalistic balustrading. Quite what he made of Lee's interior decorations is unrecorded, but the hotel's owner and its guests were apparently very satisfied. Indeed, most unusually, significant elements of the hotel's original interior design have survived to the present in fairly intact condition (the building is now known as the Four Seasons).

Almost adjacent, on a site close to the corner of Piccadilly and Park Lane, a new 825-room hotel was developed by a consortium of InterContinental Hotels (which was a subsidiary of the Pan American Airline Corporation, better known as PanAm) and the construction firm, Sir Robert McAlpine & Sons, who set up a joint company, Apsley Park Hotel Co Ltd, to manage the project. Back in the USA, PanAm was well-known as a progressive patron of modern architecture and design. For the London InterContinental project, the very prominent and well-established firm of Sir Frederick Gibberd & Partners was selected as architects. Having been in practice since 1930, Gibberd had become one of the most respected 'grandees' of British modernism, a serious figure whose major architecture and planning projects encompassed numerous blocks of modern flats, the layout of Harlow New Town and Liverpool's Metropolitan Cathedral. In addition, Gibberd was highly considered as a theoretician, educator and architectural writer.

The InterContinental's project architects were Gibberd's assistants, Richard S. Smith and G.W. Dunton. Rather than challenge the Greater London Council eight-storey height limitation, Gibberd and his team decided to use an even more contextually respectful design approach to that of Rosenauer. They chose to dissipate, rather than concentrate the hotel's potential bulk by designing three linked blocks, running along the sides and rear of the site with the space between, facing Park Lane, filled by a lower structure of only two-storeys. On the exterior façades, combinations of projecting bays, cutbacks at roof level and double-storey windows made the building less assertive, as did its curved north and south elevations which additionally enabled the bedrooms' bay windows to give oblique views towards Knightsbridge and Marble Arch. As Lance Wright observed in the *Architect's Journal*:

> 'By design, the newcomer was conceived more as a work of 'townscape' than as a work of 'architecture', as something you take in at a flash, as an acceptable part of a larger whole, rather than as something you gaze at for minutes on end. This, surely, was the correct decision. To measure Sir Frederick's achievement you have

only to recall what the client would have really liked: something manifestly bigger and taller and more aggressively different from its neighbours and which would have 'stood out': in a word, something much more like the Hilton.'[446]

Gibberd, Wright suggested, was an unexpected choice as architect; his typically 'pristine and puritan' approach certainly contrasted with the profit-centred vulgarity of most American hoteliers. As Wright put it, 'To have a man like this working for an American hotel chain is rather like asking John Bunyan to write a little skit for a pornographic review.'[447] Wright saw the approach as both a welcome moderation of the international style's worst excesses and a return to certain aspects of classical hierarchy and proportion:

> 'At the time when the modern idiom was first framed this was not thought to be a problem. Size and repetition, it was thought, could look after themselves; and the elaborate manipulation of façades used by the historical styles to cope with this problem was thought to be so much dispensible flummery… But was it? We seem now on the way back to a recantation… A classical façade is inflected to offset the oppressiveness which comes from too much repetition… the InterContinental has been inflected in the traditional sense.'[448]

The InterContinental Hotel's stepped exterior and a detail of an Art Deco-style balustrade in the foyer.

The interior design of the public rooms, which were located on the ground and first floors, was by InterContinental's in-house consultant Neal A. Prince and the bedrooms were by the Walter M. Ballard Corporation (whose previous British work consisted of the considerably less glamorous Esso Motor Hotel at South Mimms). Throughout, the problem of low ceiling heights was overcome by modelling them with a variety of levels to give an illusion of there being greater height.

Most significantly, the interior design represented an early example of revived Art Deco. In 1968, Bevis Hillier's book 'Art Deco of the 20s and 30s' had been published, defining the style and giving rise to a major re-evaluation. Subsequently, the fashion retailer Biba's new store on Kensington High Street, which opened in early 1973, had an Art Deco interior theme, evoking 'the golden age of Hollywood.' More generally, in the second half of the 1960s, early twentieth century decorative modern styles – such as Art Nouveau and jazz moderne – had been revisited by the era's counter culture, their potentially subversive bohemian associations, psychedelic colours and patterns being in contrast to modernism's rather straight-laced 'mainstream' (as represented by Gibberd's architectural output, for example). At the more conservative upper end of the wealth spectrum, meanwhile, Art Deco of the kind found in 1930s first class hotel and ocean liner interiors continued to represent the epitome of luxury. Lance Wright summarised this problem succinctly in his critique of the InterContinental's interiors:

> 'At the best of times the Modern Movement has never been very successful in producing an equivalent for the lush social interiors of the preceding age… Hoteliers… want warmth and atmosphere: they want 'character.' In this difficulty, they have gone for pastiche. This is

what has happened to most (but not all) of the public spaces in the InterContinental... Art Deco was, of course, vulgar from start to finish. It shared the Modern Movement's passion for new materials like chromium, stainless steel and the first of the plastic coverings, but used them in the most un-modern way possible... Yet Art Deco has crossed the threshold between tradition and modernity: it is a style of revolt which flew in the face of taste. Also, it is the only phase of the Modern Movement which has a popular following. As the waitresses and shop girls of c1920 said "it's ever so nice". And they were right... So too is this reincarnation of it.'[449]

As Wright records, the InterContinental's foyer and ballroom entrance featured decorative railings:

'...One directly above the other, which criss-crosses with a vertical pilaster and end up in a grotesque newel, square topped, formed like a square of stacked sugar lumps. This is indeed of an "architecture of incident" reminiscent of a time when the Modern Movement was not so weighed down with social purpose.'[450]

Coffered ceilings had clustered suspended Art deco-style cut-glass pendant lights, rather than the concealed troughs more conventionally used by modernist architects and interior designers. Wright, to his own surprise, considered these to be 'so satisfying' in their effect. He concluded that:

'There is, about this building, a curious paradox. It is, in a sense, a pristine example of High Modern Movement practice: the rules are followed scrupulously and this gives to the whole a force and conviction... But on the other hand, these rules are applied in a very unmodern way, to achieve a traditional effect... gives the impression that the idiom is somehow replaying its early development in reverse, is feeling its way back to the wisdom that was so gaily discarded; and that in the InterContinental Hotel is back in the stage represented by the middle works of Charles Holden.'[451]

Wright might also have observed that, in some senses, the InterContinental also represented a reversion to the design approach first found in nearby early 1930s hotels such as the Dorchester and the Cumberland. In general, the hotel's conscious following of modernist 'rules', while also twisting them to acknowledge history and context, were to become characteristics of post-modernism, the term applied to the multiplicity of knowing, ironic, critical and conceptual design approaches to visual culture applied from the mid-1970s onward. So far as the Modern Movement in British hotel architecture was concerned, therefore, the InterContinental not only represented the end of one era but also the beginning of another.

In the early 1970s, Gibberd was commissioned to produce another London hotel, named the Howard, and located at Temple, adjacent to the River Thames, where it replaced an existing property of the same name. The project formed part of a wider comprehensive redevelopment by Capital & Counties Properties, named Arundel Great Court, which Gibberd's practice designed almost in its entirety. The site was a deep rectangle, stretching back from Temple Place to the Strand. As with the recent InterContinental Hotel, Gibberd decided to build around the site's perimeter with the hotel forming a ten-storey block with 171 rooms, facing the Thames. Offices occupied the three sides to the rear with a terraced walled garden in the centre. This formal layout far more reflected those of eighteenth century city squares than it did the spatial dynamics of orthodox modernism. The external design of both the hotel and office blocks was again understated with Portland stone facings and bronzed windows, forming slim horizontal strips on the lower bedroom storeys, the top two floors being recessed.[452] Although the materials used were of high quality, the façade composition was actually very similar to that of the Tower Hotel and many other hotel, office, hospital and university buildings of the period. Late corporate modernism had, it appeared, become highly circumscribed and, consequently, rather derivative and dull. Acknowledging that public confidence in British architecture was not high, The *Architect's Journal*'s critic, Sutherland Lyall, observed:

> 'Unlike the shiny mini skyscrapers which the City has put up recently, [Arundel Great Court] attempts the difficult balance between fitting into an historic environment and at the same time making a well-bred reticent show of modern architecture. If anything, it is probably overbalanced on the side of conservatism; it is the sort of thing that somebody like Sir Reginald Blomfield might have done had he been fifty years younger. It lacks decorative gimmicks, it pays respect to its surroundings, as far as that is possible, by its very unassertiveness.'[453]

Within, the Howard Hotel was decorated according to the wishes of its operator, Barclay Hotels Ltd, owned by the up-and-coming business entrepreneurs, David and Frederick Barclay. They employed the long-established London craft interior decorators George Jackson & Sons to produce a flamboyant and expensive mix of palatial eighteenth century styles. This specialist company had been founded in the 1760s and had indeed been responsible for several of the finest neo-classical interiors in late Georgian London. Lyall summarised the outcome of their efforts in the hotel as 'Adamesque pastiche in the foyer and what seems to be a gloss on a distant cousin to the Brighton Pavilion in the bar…' Yet, he grudgingly admired the fact that:

> 'This lavish assemblage… has been put together with tremendous care and first class workmanship. So well finished are the solid (genuine) marble columns that they look on first inspection exactly like plastic… It is all rather bright and, given the available ceiling heights, diminutive. Meantime, the managers and their business clients rather like it.'[454]

In the early 1970s, the muscular alternative to Gibberd's restrained corporate modernism remained brutalism. A new London Central YMCA (Young Men's Christian Association) building, containing a hostel, hotel and other facilities, was a notable very late example of this idiom. Its construction was spurred by London's on-going hotel-building boom, leading the YMCA to fear that its existing premises, which were of Edwardian vintage, would no longer be able to compete with the many large, new,

The Howard Hotel at Temple, showing the slick exterior and the remarkable miniaturised neo-Georgian interior; note how tall the table in the middle of the foyer is relative to the door frames.

tourist-orientated hotels under construction. The YMCA occupied a large, approximately rectangular site next to Tottenham Court Road between Great Russell Street and Bedford Avenue which was viewed as offering considerable scope for more efficient and lucrative high-density usage. Not only would a new edifice provide fully *en suite* YMCA accommodation, more in character with hotels in the vicinity, but part of it would be run by a commercial hotel operator as a separate business known as the St Giles Hotel.[455]

The project's architects were the Elsworth Sykes Partnership, which had been founded in the early 1920s in Hull by Wilfred Elsworth Sykes. Following his death in 1966, his son, Ronald, became the senior partner. The YMCA project was carried out by project architects Michael Mulchinock, Philip Little and R. J. Peto. The design solution was for a concrete megastructure, the construction of which lasted for five years between 1971 and 1977. As the new YMCA needed to make best use of its costly location, the site was excavated five-storeys-deep, with two levels of parking, sports facilities and a multi-purpose hall for religious meetings, film shows and other activities all below ground. Above the surface, a two-storey podium contained perimeter shop units with the YMCA and hotel receptions and communal facilities accessed from opposite sides of the block. Rising above this were four inter-connected towers, all of which were slightly hexagonal in plan but of unequal height (ranging from seven to thirteen storeys; altogether, these contained 670 rooms. The tapering external walls enabled all of the bedrooms to have oblique views outward, a simple but ingenious variation of the well-established 'Statler plan'.[456] The towers were held high above the street on chunky-looking concrete piers, projecting outward and faced in vertically-ribbed rough-textured concrete panels. The composition was boldly expressive and wilfully intimidating. By the time that the project was finally completed, however, brutalism had fallen from grace and so, far from being a vision of the future, the structure instead represented the very end of an era.

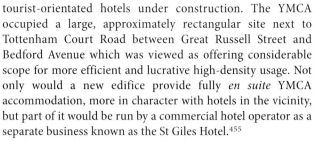

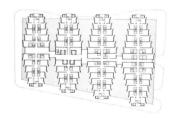

The London Central YMCA and St Giles Hotel, the accommodation blocks of which tapered to allow each room an oblique view outward.

Conclusion

When the construction of new hotels subsidised under the Hotel Development Incentives Scheme was at its peak at the beginning of 1973, Britain officially became a member of the European Economic Community. This development was warmly welcomed by the British hotel industry, which saw an even brighter future with increased business trade and, especially, larger numbers of visiting foreign tourists. In terms of repositioning the country to take advantage of growth in tourism, the many new hotels were judged by the British Tourist Authority's Chairman, Sir Alexander Glen, to be both timely and necessary. As he told an audience of hoteliers at a dinner at the Dorchester in London, 'Tourism has become one of Britain's four major export earners'; this was, he believed, thanks in large part to the country's 'tremendously increased stock of new hotels coming into operation over the whole of England, Scotland and Wales… We can now truly succeed in achieving this much wider spread of visitors over Britain as a whole.'[457]

In Northern Ireland, meanwhile, the Irish Republican Army commenced a vigorous terrorist campaign which targeted hotels, killing and injuring guests and causing substantial damage. Simultaneously, in the in the Middle East, Arab nations in the Organization of Petroleum Exporting Countries (OPEC) decided to retaliate against the United States and its allies to punish them for supporting Israel in the Yom Kippur War. In 1973 they slashed oil production by between 5 and 10 per cent per month, hoping that resulting political pressure would force Israel to withdraw from the areas it had occupied. Since the Second World War, oil prices had remained more or less stable at around ten dollars a barrel but during the latter part of 1973 they quadrupled, precipitating a global downturn and an end to the steady growth experienced in the western world since the mid-1940s. This made travel much more expensive and also greatly increased hoteliers' overheads, leading to tighter margins, cost-cutting and a phase of consolidation during which the larger hotel chains absorbed smaller ones. By the 1980s, Trust Houses Forte had gained a substantial lead, having absorbed Strand and Crest, among other hotel brands.

Looking back upon Britain's post-war hotel architecture, it seems unfortunate that the country never produced a specialist hotel architect matching – or even coming close to – the calibre and enthusiasm of Americans such as Morris Lapidus and William B. Tabler, whose modernist hotels were just as grandly proportioned and elaborately equipped as the best examples of previous eras. Yet, in the USA of the 1950s, just as in Britain, narrower and ever more utilitarian readings of modernist ideals within the architecture profession and among architectural critics made it difficult for even these architects to have their works fairly assessed by peers. Indeed it is only posthumously that Lapidus' Miami hotels have come to develop a cult following among architecture enthusiasts. In Britain, where the cultural climate was calibrated by the experience of rationing and where existing cityscapes tended to be insufficiently spacious to accommodate such grand architectural gestures as Lapidus and Tabler preferred, the situation was even more constricting – theoretically, economically and physically. Planners, on the one hand, typically demanded moderation of scale while developers and hotel operators, on the other, insisted upon the highest possible building density. Above all, the naïve belief then held by many architects that façades would somehow 'design themselves' from plans, coupled with mercenary commercial demands for speed and simplicity, led to too many hotels of the 1960s lacking sufficient finesse in proportion, materiality and detail. Exceptions – such the Carlton Tower in London, the Ariel at Heathrow Airport, the Atlantic in Liverpool and the InterContinental (also in London) – demonstrated that, when greater care was expended, results could be achieved equal to be the best internationally.

Although many hotel buildings of the post-war era were felt to be deleterious to the British streetscape and urbanity, with hindsight, one can judge that their interior design was often far superior to the edifices in which it was housed and, at best, represented the epitome of fashionable taste at particular moments. This ranged from the mid-1950s Festival of Britain-style of the Hotel Leofric in Coventry to the louche 'space age rococo' of the early-1970s in the Park Tower in London. Interiors, however, were the aspects of hotels least likely to survive in the longer term. Partly, this was due to wear and tear and to the fact that large numbers of hotel guests were smokers, resulting in a frequent need to refresh furnishings and paintwork. Yet, the fact that so many hotels of the 1960s were so quickly refitted in the 1970s and 80s with eighteenth and nineteenth century 'retro' styles, rather than with finishes complementary to their modernist exteriors, suggests that neither operators nor a majority of guests perceived modernism to be sufficiently grand, luxurious or reflective of 'locale', 'history' and 'tradition'. Even the Carlton Tower's beautiful original interiors by Henry End were destroyed in this way and, with them, Feliks Topolski's foyer bas relief was removed too. The Modern Movement's aim of achieving greater egalitarianism though standardised and minimalistic aesthetics was arguably contrary to commercial hoteliers' instinct towards palatial excess to make their guests feel 'special' and that they were receiving 'good value for money'. Many of those who had not received an architecture or design education never understood why 'less' should be considered as 'more'.

The problems created by the manner in which a majority of hotels were procured under the Hotel Development Incentives Scheme raises important wider issues about British architecture and urbanity in general. Hotels are prominent buildings which could potentially exemplify 'good design' but, during the period of the Incentives Scheme, such high design ambitions as there may have been were too often thwarted by greedy developers representing remote financiers with little motivation to take pride in the appearance of the buildings they procured. As the architecture critic Owen Hatherley has shown in *The New Ruins of Britain*, this situation continues today. Whereas in 1972 the *AR* singled out hotels for criticism, Hatherley makes remarkably similar comments about the design of recent student accommodation which, according to him, represents a current nadir of design imagination and quality:

> 'With university accommodation now defined by the developers' desire to cram students in as densely as possible, high-quality design may be too much to ask… There is justified outrage that something so transparently barbaric can be perpetuated on any social group, and long overdue calls for the imposition of standards and regulation. How did this toxic combination of ruthlessly stripped-down existenz-minimum, system-building and stunning formal ineptitude come to be the norm for student housing?'[458]

Hatherley might equally have applied the same criticisms to the current generation of suburban budget hotel – comprising Travelodges, Premier Inns, Holiday Inn Expresses and Ibises – most of which are banally faced in breeze block or rain-screen cladding, just like so many blocks of student flats. While offering clean and comfortable beds, decent food and warm showers, these generic buildings arguably fail to contribute in any positive way to the making of distinctive or even coherent townscapes.

The design historian and theorist Guy Julier, meanwhile, has arrived at the concept of the 'neo-liberal object' to describe condominiums, shopping malls, offices, hotels and other pieces of commercial infrastructure that are owned by remote investors, such as pension funds or venture capital firms, with no connection other than a share of profits in the properties belonging to them.[459] According to Julier, the chains of causation identified by the *Architectural Review* in 1972 with regard to hotels have only intensified since the 1980s.

Since the period for study, architecture historians and conservationists appear to have treated hotels differently from other types of qualitatively variable mid-twentieth century commercial leisure building – such as cinemas, theatres, pubs or sports venues, for which thematic studies and selective listing have been carried out by English Heritage/Historic England and Historic Scotland/Historic Environment Scotland. Furthermore, whereas these other types of premises have developed considerable enthusiast followings, for hotels, there is no equivalent of the Cinema Theatre Association or the Pub History Society. In part, this is arguably due to social and political factors. Whereas these other popular commercial building types were aimed at very broad audiences including the working class, hotels were more likely to be associated with bourgeois and conservative aspirations and with a desire by their guests to leave 'the masses' behind outside (the design of hotels' approaches and entrance areas makes this clear). Thus, while an old Granada cinema with a moderne façade and a neo-Gothic interior will be listed at a high level, the remarkable Howard Hotel in London, in which Frederick Gibberd's international modernism was fused with a very ornate neo-Georgian interior, was demolished in 2015 without a backward glance. When I told a friend engaged in architectural conservation about the hotel's remarkable design and recent demise, his first reaction was to say that he had only ever been in it once and the thing he most remembered was that, in the dining room, he was seated at a table beside that of the then Conservative Chancellor of the Exchequer, Nigel Lawson; this alone caused him to hate the place.

The hotels cited in this work that continue to serve their original purposes nowadays mostly are operated under the brands of large international chains, such as Holiday Inn (which acquired the Trust Houses Forte chain, incorporating the Albany chain) or Marriott – or by British chains, such as Thistle. Typically, the buildings belong to remote capital funds with operators merely applying a temporary brand colour scheme and graphic identity to their interiors. This approach has led them to be justifiably criticised for their anonymous and mundane atmospheres – as Marc Augé would observe in *Non Places*.[460] Yet, in the years towards the end of the period covered by this book, hotels with remote corporate owners appear to have had at least one positive virtue. Not only has the 1925-1975 timespan covered that of modernism's rise and decline but also that of the disintegration of the British Empire and its replacement by a Commonwealth. During this process, Britain became truly multi-cultural and, as émigrés from Africa, Asia and the Caribbean arrived to begin new lives, unfortunately large numbers of privately-owned hotels became notorious for their racial discrimination against non-whites.

In 1943, Imperial London Hotels' owner, Harold Walduck, personally intervened to insist that a famous West Indian cricketer, Learie Constantine, be moved from his flagship hotel, the Imperial, to a smaller one because guests of the first had objected to his presence on account of his colour.[461] This incident made national newspaper headlines, the irony of a hotel named the Imperial refusing to accommodate a subject of empire leading to a vigorous debate which showed that Constantine's experience typified a much wider problem. There is, however, no evidence that any 'corporate' Hilton, Albany, Trust Houses, Forte or brewery-owned hotels ever were anything other than welcoming to guests of whatever background. The large organisations owning them were entirely disinterested in their guests' ethnicity, only in making as much money as possible to please their shareholders and so, as long as one could pay, one was welcome. Thus, such hotels were early and important sites of cosmopolitanism in British cities – albeit ones serving relatively wealthy and well-travelled core clienteles. Cosmopolitanism also extended to hotel ownership and operation. Charles Forte was the most famous and successful of several prominent British hospitality entrepreneurs to have migrated from overseas. Immigrant staff employed in hotels, meanwhile, tended to be more prepared to work for longer hours for relatively low pay than much of the indigenous population and to behave in an obligingly servile manner towards guests.

Today, only a small number of Art Deco hotel interiors from the 1930s survive and are much-cherished – such as at Claridge's and at the Park Lane Hotel in London, as well as the simpler decoration of Burgh Island Hotel and the foyer of the renovated Midland Hotel in Morecambe. No post-war British modernist hotel interior remains intact. Had any of the more stylish examples avoided destruction, however, they would have by now become highly fashionable again as the 'cycle of taste' has come full-circle with 'sixties aesthetics being appreciated by a younger generation. The exteriors of many of the buildings have often been modified too through the retro-fitting of rain-screen cladding (the need for this may reflect the inadequate quality of their original construction). Other hotels built in the 1960s have fallen on hard times or closed altogether since the 2008 economic downturn. Abandoned hotels that half-a-century before were considered the last word in modern glamour soon appear particularly abject. Their empty shells are often irresistible targets for vandals to attack or, more benignly, for urban explorers to scrutinise. It seems that the passage of time is particularly unforgiving of the modern hotel.

The derelict shell of the Hallam Tower Hotel in Sheffield – once glamorous, now only accommodating vagrants and pigeons.

Endnotes

1. Hotels: The Immediate Prospect, *Architectural Review*, 1 October 1960, p. 297.
2. Franziska Bollerey, Beyond the lobby: Setting the stage for modernity – the cosmos of the hotel in Tom Avermaete and Anne Massey (eds), Hotel Lobbies and Lounges, Abingdon: Routledge, 2013, pp. 6-7.
3. Tom Avermaete and Anne Massey (eds), Hotel Lobbies and Lounges, Abingdon: Routledge, 2013, p. 2.
4. Tom Avermaete and Anne Massey (eds), Hotel Lobbies and Lounges, Abingdon: Routledge, 2013, p. 2.
5. Julian Leathart, Dorchester Hotel, Park Lane, W, W. Curtis Green A.R.A. and Partners, Architects, *Architects' Journal*, 22 April 1931, pp. 577-582.
6. A. L. Chapman and R. Knight, Wages and Salaries in the United Kingdom, 1920–38 Cambridge: Cambridge University Press, 1953, pp. 26–30, 154, 201–202; J. Burnett, A History of the Cost of Living London: Harmondsworth, 1969, pp. 297–310; G. Routh, Occupation and Pay in Great Britain, 1906–79 Cambridge, Cambridge University Press, 1980, pp. 120–121.
7. R. Stone and D. A. Rowe, The Measurement of Consumer Behaviour in the United Kingdom, 1920–38, Cambridge: Cambridge University Press, 1966, p. 92.
8. John Carey, The Intellectuals and the Masses, London: Faber & Faber, 1992.
9. Henry End, The Interiors Book of Hotel & Motor Hotels, New York: Whitney Library of Design, p. 14.
10. Raymond Loewy, Industrial Design, London: Laurence King, 1979, pp. 74-76.
11. In Soviet Russia, a resort hotel at Sochi, completed in 1928, also appears to have been a very early exemplar of modernism within the hotel genre, but it was never published in the British architectural press.
12. See Erli, Doswell, Copp, Beavis, Campbell-Smith and Lawson, Principles of Hotel Design (1970), Fred Lawson, Hotels, Motels and Condominiums: Design, Planning and Maintenance (1976) and Douglas Smith, Hotel and Restaurant Design (1978).
13. Elain Harwood, Space, Hope and Brutalism, New Haven and London: Yale University Press, 2015, p. 411.
14. Henry End, The Interiors Book of Hotel & Motor Hotels, New York: Whitney Library of Design, 1963, p. 4.
15. Barnabas Calder, Raw Concrete: The Beauty of Brutalism, London: William Heinemann, 2016, p. 7 and p. 17.
16. Henri Lefebvre, The Production of Space, London: Wiley-Blackwell, 1991.
17. John Urry, The Tourist Gaze: Leisure and Travel in Contemporary Societies, London: Sage, 2002, p19.
18. John Urry, The Tourist Gaze: Leisure and Travel in Contemporary Societies, London: Sage, 2002, p129.
19. Rob Shields, Places on the Margin: The Alternative Geographies of Modernity, London: Routledge, 1991, p3.
20. Rob Shields, Places on the Margin: The Alternative Geographies of Modernity, London: Routledge, 1991, p4.
21. Marc Augé, Non-places: An introduction to the anthropology of supermodernity, London: Verso, 1993.
22. The concept of 'aura' in responses to visual culture was most famously delineated by the German philosopher and cultural theorist, Walter Benjamin, in his 193? Essay 'The World of Art in the Age of Mechanical Reproduction'. Benjamin argues that, with the passage of time, cultural artefacts accumulate aura as they stand witness to history and develop patina. Thus a newly-made or 'reproduced' object or environment will lack the auratic quality of an authentic original.
23. Sir Francis Towle, The Full Story of the May Fair Hotel, *Caterer and Hotel Keeper*, 15 February 1927, pp. 122-123.
24. Sir Francis Towle, The Full Story of the May Fair Hotel, *Caterer and Hotel Keeper*, 15 February 1927, pp. 122-123.
25. Sir Francis Towle, The Full Story of the May Fair Hotel, *Caterer and Hotel Keeper*, 15 February 1927, pp. 122-123.
26. Faye Hammill, Sophistication: A literary and cultural history, Liverpool: Liverpool University Press, 2010.
27. *Architect and Building News*, 1 April 1927, p. 578.
28. *The Times*, 5 April 1928, p. 8. See also Christopher Hussey, The Great Estates of London and Their Development: The Grosvenor Estate, *Country Life*, 21 April 1928, p. 565.
29. Andrew Saint, Evolution of a Hotel Interior, Country Life, 2 July 1981, p. 40.
30. Death of Britain's Most Eminent Hotelier, *Caterer and Hotel Keeper*, 20 January 1966, p. 39.
31. Park Lane Hotel Piccadilly Extension, *Architects' Journal*, 8 July 1931, pp. 39-40.
32. Park Lane Hotel Piccadilly Extension, *Architects' Journal*, 8 July 1931, pp. 39-40.

33. Julian Leathart, Dorchester Hotel, Park Lane, W, W. Curtis Green A.R.A. and Partners, Architects, *Architects' Journal*, 22 April 1931, p. 57.

34. Julian Leathart, Dorchester Hotel, Park Lane, W, W. Curtis Green A.R.A. and Partners, Architects, *Architects' Journal*, 22 April 1931, pp. 582.

35. Alan Powers, Modern: The Modern Movement in Britain, London: Merrell, 2005, p. 220.

36. Julian Leathart, Dorchester Hotel, Park Lane, W, W. Curtis Green A.R.A. and Partners, Architects, *Architects' Journal*, 22 April 1931, p. 577.

37. Julian Leathart, Dorchester Hotel, Park Lane, W, W. Curtis Green A.R.A. and Partners, Architects, *Architects' Journal*, 22 April 1931, 579.

38. Julian Leathart, Dorchester Hotel, Park Lane, W, W. Curtis Green A.R.A. and Partners, Architects, *Architects' Journal*, 22 April 1931, pp. 580.

39. M.H. Baillie Scott, Dorchester Hotel, *Architects' Journal*, 13 May 1931, p. 689.

40. See John K. Galbraith, The Great Crash 1929, London: Penguin, 1954 for a detailed description of the circumstances leading to and consequences of the Wall Street Crash.

41. E. Maxwell Fry, Cumberland Hotel, *Architectural Review*, January 1934, p. 13.

42. J. Lyons had progressively purchased the Cumberland Hotel's site from 1901 onwards but had encountered numerous difficulties with the result that development could not begin until the early-1930s. In the interim, the Strand Palace and Regent Palace hotels were completed elsewhere in Central London.

43. E. Maxwell Fry, Cumberland Hotel, *Architectural Review*, January 1934, p. 13.

44. E. Maxwell Fry, Cumberland Hotel, *Architectural Review*, January 1934, p. 13.

45. E. Maxwell Fry, Cumberland Hotel, *Architectural Review*, January 1934, p. 13.

46. Cumberland Marks and Epoch In History of Industry, *Caterer and Hotel Keeper*, December 1933, p. 1180.

47. Maurizio Eliseo and Paolo Piccione Transatlantici: The History of the Great Italian Liners on the Atlantic, Genoa: Tormena, 2001, pp. 246-7.

48. Gustavo Pulitzer Finali, Navi e Case: Architetture Interni 1930-1935, Milan: Hoepli, 1935, pp. 183-191.

49. £1,000,000 'Flatels' Scheme: Mount Royal nearly ready, Caterer and Hotel Keeper, 17 August 1934, p. 331.

50. £1,000,000 'Flatels' Scheme: Mount Royal nearly ready, Caterer and Hotel Keeper, 17 August 1934, p. 331.

51. Mr T.C. Gordon's Affairs: Adverse World Conditions, *The Times*, 14 July 1939, p. 4.

52. J. Ernest Franck, Matthew J. Dawson, *Journal of the Royal Institute of British Architects*, February 1944, pp. 94-95.

53. I am grateful to Anthony Orchard, the owner of Burgh Island Hotel, for assisting me with detailed information about its history and for showing me around the property on 2 September 2016.

54. I am grateful to Deborah Tritton and Alison Spence of Cornwall Archives for their assistance in helping to research the history of the Seacroft Hotel.

55. Rex Pope, Railway companies and resort hotels between the wars, *Journal of Transport History*, March 2001, pp. 63-65.

56. Rex Pope, Railway companies and resort hotels between the wars, *Journal of Transport History*, March 2001, p. 67.

57. Alan Powers, Oliver Hill: Architect and Lover of Life, London: Mouton Publications, 1989, p. 34.

58. Alan Powers, Oliver Hill: Architect and Lover of Life, London: Mouton Publications, 1989, pp. 5-27.

59. Alan Powers, Oliver Hill: Architect and Lover of Life, London: Mouton Publications, 1989, pp. 24-25.

60. Barry Guise and Pam Brook, The Midland Hotel: Morecambe's White Hope, Lancaster: Palatine Books, 2007, p. 15.

61. RAIL 418/29, LMS HCC, 26 November 1930, 20 May 1931; AN 109/636, Memos by A. E. Towle, 1 and 21 April 1927; Glynn to Stockton, 18 May 1931, Public Records Office, Kew.

62. Barry Guise and Pam Brook, The Midland Hotel: Morecambe's White Hope, Lancaster: Palatine Books, 2007, p. 16

63. Barry Guise and Pam Brook, The Midland Hotel: Morecambe's White Hope, Lancaster: Palatine Books, 2007, p. 29.

64. Hotel That Looks Like a 'Great White Ship', *Caterer and Hotel Keeper*, 15 July 1933, p. 106.

65. Alan Powers, Oliver Hill: Architect and Lover of Life, London: Mouton Publications, 1989, p. 34.

66. Albert L. Louis, The Hotel of the Future: looking 50 years ahead, *Caterer and Hotel Keeper*, 31 March 1934, p. 628.

67. Saunton Sands Hotel is Ready: Luxury building in Devon: Bookings already heavy, *Caterer and Hotel Keeper*, 14 June 1935, p. 15.

68. New Clacton Hotel: Association pays visit to Oulton Hall, *Caterer and Hotel Keeper*, 12 July 1935, p. 13.

69. New £200,000 Hotel for Bournemouth: Palace Court nearly ready to open, *Caterer and Hotel Keeper*, 27 September 1935, p. 15.

70. New £200,000 Hotel for Bournemouth: Palace Court nearly ready to open, *Caterer and Hotel Keeper*, 27 September 1935, p. 15.

71. Obituary for A.E.O. Geens, *Building*, 17 March 1972, p. 91.

72. RIBA Elections, *Architects' Journal*, 2 June 1938, p. 936.

73. The Newcastle Competition, *Architects' Journal*, 23 February 1939, p. 321.

74. Hotel Planned with an Eye on the Future: Every bedroom has bathroom at new Green Park, Bournemouth, *Caterer and Hotel Keeper*, 19 November 1937, p. 20.

75. Hotel Planned with an Eye on the Future: Every bedroom has bathroom at new Green Park, Bournemouth, *Caterer and Hotel Keeper*, 19 November 1937, p. 20.

76. Novel Ideas in New Luxury Hotel: Cumberland, Bournemouth opens this week-end, *Caterer and Hotel Keeper*, 11 February 1938, p. 13.

77. Obituary of Willie Richard Halstone Gardner, *The Builder*, February 1962, p. 253.

78.

79. Bruce Peter, Form Follows Fun: Modernism and modernity in British pleasure architecture 1925-1940, Abingdon: Routledge, 2007, pp. 114-115.

80. Lavish Décor in Butlin's £50,000 Hotel, *Caterer and Hotel Keeper*, 25 August 1938, p. 10.

81. Lavish Décor in Butlin's £50,000 Hotel, *Caterer and Hotel Keeper*, 25 August 1938, p. 10.

82. Lavish Décor in Butlin's £50,000 Hotel, *Caterer and Hotel Keeper*, 25 August 1938, p. 10.

83. Lavish Décor in Butlin's £50,000 Hotel, *Caterer and Hotel Keeper*, 25 August 1938, p. 10.

84. New Holiday Lido at the edge of the sea, *Caterer and Hotel Keeper*, 14 August 1936, p. 20.

85. Shell of £200,000 hotel nearly ready, *Caterer and Hotel Keeper*, 11 March 1938, p. 30.

86. 400-room hotel on South Coast, *Caterer and Hotel Keeper*, 1 July 1938, p. 15.

87. The Ocean Hotel, Saltdean, Brighton, *Architect and Building News*, 12 August 1938, pp. 175-178. See also The Ocean Hotel, Saltdean, Sussex, *The Builder*, 5 August 1938, pp. 249-253.

88. Seven single houses, now one hotel, *Caterer and Hotel Keeper*, 10 January 1936, p22.

89. Reconstruction of Carlton, Blackpool: 'Virtually a new hotel', *Caterer and Hotel Keeper*, 3 September 1937, p. 12.

90. Reconstruction of Carlton, Blackpool: 'Virtually a new hotel', *Caterer and Hotel Keeper*, 3 September 1937, p. 12.

91. Passenger Travel News, *Commercial Motor*, 13 March 1928, p. 16.

92. Famous LMS Hotel to Close?, *Caterer and Hotel Keeper*, 21 December 1934, p. 1182.

93. LMS Restaurant to 'Go Overseas': From Gleneagles to South Africa, *Caterer and Hotel Keeper*, 15 November 1935, p. 15.

94. Transforming Famous Railway Hotel: Great Western Royal at Paddington on Third Stage of Modernisation, *Caterer and Hotel Keeper*, 4 June 1937, p. 14.

95. Transforming Famous Railway Hotel: Great Western Royal at Paddington on Third Stage of Modernisation, *Caterer and Hotel Keeper*, 4 June 1937, p. 14.

96. Transforming Famous Railway Hotel: Great Western Royal at Paddington on Third Stage of Modernisation, *Caterer and Hotel Keeper*, 4 June 1937, p. 14.

97. Modernisation at Paddington: Great Western Royal Hotel, *The Times*, 6 May 1937, p. 12.

98. Courage, Barclay and Simmonds (Brewers) files ACC/2305/01/1004 and ACC/2305/01/1005 in the London Metropolitan Archives. I am grateful to David Trevor-Jones for examining these items on my behalf and to Elain Harwood for supplying additional information about Major Henry Oliver.

99. New Hotel on North Circular Road, *Caterer and Hotel Keeper*, 17 June 1938 p. 22.

100. *Blackpool Gazette*, 30 May 1936, p. 12, information courtesy of Anne Cameron, Blackpool Archives.

101. To Manage Aerodrome Hotel, *Caterer and Hotel Keeper*, 29 April 1938, p. 6.

102. Law Report, *Architects' Journal*, 1 April 1937, p. 382.

103. Elmdon Airport, Birmingham, *Architect and Building News*, 18 August 1939, p. 187.

104. A.H. Jones, The Hotel of the Future: A forecast for the next 60 years, *Caterer and Hotel Keeper*, 29 July 1938, pp. 33-35.

105. Charles McKean, The Scottish Thirties: An Architectural Introduction, Edinburgh: Scottish Academic Press, 1987, p. 197.

106. Charles McKean, The Scottish Thirties: An Architectural Introduction, Edinburgh: Scottish Academic Press, 1987, pp. 54-58.

107. Bruce Peter, Form Follows Fun: Modernism and Modernity in British Pleasure Architecture 1925-1940, Abingdon: Routledge, 2007, pp. 146-147.

108. Opening date for Beresford in Glasgow, *Caterer and Hotel Keeper*, 4 March 1938, p. 13.

109. Glasgow's First 'Skyscraper' Hotel, *Caterer and Hotel Keeper*, 29 April 1938, p. 13.

110. Glasgow's First 'Skyscraper' Hotel, *Caterer and Hotel Keeper*, 29 April 1938, p. 13.

111. Glasgow's First 'Skyscraper' Hotel, *Caterer and Hotel Keeper*, 29 April 1938, p. 13.

112. Glasgow's First 'Skyscraper' Hotel, *Caterer and Hotel Keeper*, 29 April 1938, p. 13.

113. Glasgow's First 'Skyscraper' Hotel, *Caterer and Hotel Keeper*, 29 April 1938, p. 13.

114. 50,000 Guests in Six Months, *Caterer and Hotel Keeper*, 14 October 1938, p. 26.

115. New £40,000 Scottish Hotel, *Caterer and Hotel Keeper*, 22 July 1938, p. 15.

116. New £40,000 Scottish Hotel, *Caterer and Hotel Keeper*, 22 July 1938, p. 15.

117. Charles McKean, The Scottish Thirties: An Architectural Introduction, Edinburgh: Scottish Academic Press, 1987, pp. 57.

118. I am grateful to Debbie Potter of Highland Archives for her assistance in researching the circumstances of the completion of the Drumossie Hotel.

119. I am grateful to Colin Waller of Highland Archives for his assistance in researching the circumstances of the completion of the Grampian Hotel.

120. Elain Harwood, White Light/White Heat: rebuilding England's Provincial Towns and Cities in the Sixties in Elain Harwood and Alan Powers (eds), Twentieth Century Architecture 6: The Sixties: Life, Style, Architecture, London: Twentieth Century Society, 2002, p. 58.

121. Tourists: Million Mark in Sight, *Caterer and Hotel Keeper*, 8 January 1955, p. 19.

122. Britain's first American hotel opens in London, *Caterer and Hotel Keeper*, 19 March 1955, pp45-53.

123. Walter Stanley Hattrell (1900-1977) was the son of Coventry architect Walter Herbert Hattrell. Educated at Oundle School and articled to his father, he became senior partner in 1925 following the latter's death. In 1938, the year he designed the new Coventry Theatre, Hattrell became Chairman of the Coventry Society of Architects. The year after, he was elected FRIBA. The assistant in charge of the Hotel Leofric project was G.W. Hammond, assisted by F.R. Mutch, J. Siedlecki, J.A. Metcalf, R.E. Eckersley. From Ind Coope's in-house Architects' Department A.G. Drew, B.R. Davis, D.M. Rickard and R.L.G. Carter were involved. See Hotel at Coventry, *Architectural Review*, September 1955, p. 195.

124. Ind Coope & Co was founded in Romford, Essex in 1845, through a merger of the brewing interests of Edward Ind and those of Octavius Edward and George Coope. Their Burton-on-Trent brewery opened in 1856. In 1961, Ind Coope merged with Ansells and Tetley Walker to form Allied Breweries.

125. Hotel at Coventry, *Architectural Review*, September 1955, pp. 195-199.

126. Christina Savvas, Sadness as Coventry's Leofric Hotel Closes, Coventry News, 2 June 2008.

127. Interview with Ray Leigh, former partner in Russell, Hodgson & Leigh, by Bruce Peter by telephone on 19 July 2016.

128. Interview with Ray Leigh, former partner in Russell, Hodgson & Leigh, by Bruce Peter by telephone on 19 July 2016.

129. Neil Gregory, Monro and Partners: Shopping in Scotland with Marks & Spencer, Architectural Heritage XIV, 2003, p. 75.

130. Neil Gregory, Monro and Partners: Shopping in Scotland with Marks & Spencer, Architectural Heritage XIV, 2003, pp. 75-76.

131. See Annabel Jane Wharton, Building the Cold War; Hilton International Hotels and Modern Architecture, Chicago: The University of Chicago Press, 2001, pp. 19-22 for a detailed description of this project.

132. Hotel in Istanbul, *Architectural Review*, November 1955, pp. 291-296.

133. U.S. Hotel Architect States Six Basic Rules for New Hotel Design, *Caterer and Hotel Keeper*, 24 August 1957, p. 17.

134. Hotels: Inquest on a Defeat, *Architectural Review*, September 1972, pp. 131-412.

135. Rob Harris, Evolution in the Supply of Commercial Real Estate: The emergence of a new relationship between suppliers and occupiers of real estate, Simon Guy and John Hanneberry (eds), Developers and Development: Perspectives on Property, London: Blackwell, 2002, p. 206.

136. Raymond Fitzwalter and David Taylor, Web of Corruption, Granada Publishing, St Albans, 1981, p. 51.

137. Raymond Fitzwalter and David Taylor, Web of Corruption, Granada Publishing, St Albans, 1981, p. 52.

138. J.M. Richards, Buildings of the Year: 1954, *Architects' Journal*, 20 January 1955, p. 86.

139. Built Environment, October 1972, p. 448, cited in Elain Harwood, White Light/White Heat: rebuilding England's Provincial Towns and Cities in the Sixties in Elain Harwood and Alan Powers (eds), Twentieth Century Architecture 6: The Sixties: Life, Style, Architecture, London: Twentieth Century Society, 2002, p. 58.

140. G. Charlesworth, A History of British Motorways, London: Thomas Telford Ltd, 1984, pp. 25-8.

141. John Carter, Technical Study: Integrated design and construction Esso Motor Hotel at Bristol, *Architects' Journal*, 21 March 1973, p. 707.

142. John Carter, Technical Study: Integrated design and construction Esso Motor Hotel at Bristol, *Architects' Journal*, 21 March 1973, p. 712.

143. Interview with Ronald Rabson, Louis Erdi's former architectural partner, by Bruce Peter by telephone on 18 January 2016.

144. Interview with Ronald Rabson, Louis Erdi's former architectural partner, by Bruce Peter by telephone on 18 January 2016.

145. The Royal Oak Motor Hotel, *Caterer and Hotel Keeper*, 3 July 1955, p. 24.

146. Interview with Ronald Rabson by Bruce Peter by telephone on 18 January 2016.

147. Continental Holidays by Car, *The Times*, 14 February 1956, p. 7.

148. Striking Design of New Coachotel at Dover, *Caterer and Hotel Keeper*, 18 May 1957, p. 25.

149. Unique Hotel for Coach Tourists Costs Under £1,700 a Bedroom, *Caterer and Hotel Keeper*, 1 June 1957, p. 39.

150. Interview with Ronald Rabson by Bruce Peter by telephone on 18 January 2016.

151. Motel at Epping in Essex, *Architect and Building News*, 17 October 1962, pp. 579-582.

152. Interview with Ronald Rabson by Bruce Peter by telephone on 18 January 2016.

153. Scotland's Greatest Tourist Lure Means Prosperity for Hotels, *Caterer and Hotel Keeper*, 18 February 1965, p. 75.

154. The Falcon Hotel, Stratford-upon-Avon, *Architect and Surveyor*, May-June 1968, pp. 3-7.

155. Esso open first Scottish motor hotel, *Glasgow Herald*, 22 May 1970, p. 14.

156. Esso open first Scottish motor hotel, *Glasgow Herald*, 22 May 1970, p. 14.

157. Henry End, Interiors Book of Hotels and Motor Hotels, New York: Whitney Library of Design, 1963, p. 79.

158. Henry End, The Interiors Book of Hotel & Motor Hotels, New York: Whitney Library of Design, 1963, p. 84.

159. Henry End, The Interiors Book of Hotel & Motor Hotels, New York: Whitney Library of Design, 1963, p. 84.

160. Henry End, The Interiors Book of Hotel & Motor Hotels, New York: Whitney Library of Design, 1963, p. 84.

161. Henry End, The Interiors Book of Hotel & Motor Hotels, New York: Whitney Library of Design, 1963, p. 84.

162. Henry End, The Interiors Book of Hotel & Motor Hotels, New York: Whitney Library of Design, 1963, p. 84.

163. 1960 Sees Opening of London Airport's First Hotel, *Caterer and Hotel Keeper*, 16 January 1960, p. 53.

164. 1960 Sees Opening of London Airport's First Hotel, *Caterer and Hotel Keeper*, 16 January 1960, p. 54.

165. Rival Hotel Plans in Jermyn Street, *Caterer and Hotel Keeper*, 14 May 1960, p. 25.

166. Ambitious Scheme for New Hotel at Hastings, *Caterer and Hotel Keeper*, 24 June 1961, p. 37.

167. Hotels Prepare for 30 Million Guests, *Caterer and Hotel Keeper*, 28 May 1960, p. 23.

168. London Airport's Circular hotel to be Known as 'The Ariel', *Caterer and Hotel Keeper*, 26 March 1960, p. 22.

169. Ariel Hotel, London Airport, *Architect and Building News*, March 1961, pp. 379-386.

170. Britain's First Circular Hotel Opens, *Caterer and Hotel Keeper*, 14 January 1961, p. 19 and pp. 26-27.

171. Dolphin leaps into Swansea's Banquet Life, *Caterer and Hotel Keeper*, 26 January 1963, pp. 41-43.

172. Hotel, London Airport, *Architect and Building News*, 8 April 1964, pp. 623-628.

173. Interviews with Michael Lyell's former architectural partners John Knight by Bruce Peter by telephone on 22 May 2016 and with Clive Sturley by Bruce Peter by telephone on 30 May 2016.

174. 'Caterer' Preview of Forte's New Hotel at London Airport, *Caterer and Hotel Keeper*, 23 January 1964, p. 38.

175. Hotel, London Airport, Architect and Building News, 8 April 1964, pp. 623-628. See also *Architects' Journal*, 17 October 1962, p. 918.

176. New Forte Motor Lodge opens next month, *Caterer and Hotel Keeper*, 28 May 1964, p. 34.

177. Interview with Michael Lyell's former architectural partner Clive Sturley by Bruce Peter by telephone on 30 May 2016.

178. Skyway Hotels' £450,000 Plan in Southampton, *Caterer and Hotel Keeper*, 11 February 1965, p. 35.

179. 1961 Advertisement for the Skyway Hotel in Southampton, purchased by the author from eBay.

180. Polynesian Room at New Skyway Hotel, *Caterer and Hotel Keeper*, 21 July 1966, p. 34.

181. Forte treatment for Airport Hotel, *Caterer and Hotel Keeper*, 9 January 1969, p. 11.

182. Design supplement, *Caterer and Hotel Keeper*, 25 November 1971, p. 12.

183. Park-Eat-Sleep hotel Planned – No Extras, *Caterer and Hotel Keeper*, 21 November 1963, p. 17. See also Signing Agreement, *Caterer and Hotel Keeper*, 4 June 1964, p. 15.

184. Top Rank plan 150-bedroom hotel in Gibraltar.

185. *Caterer and Hotel Keeper*, 3 September 1964, p. 34. See also *Caterer and Hotel Keeper*, 17 November 1966, p. 39.

186. Hotel for Bournemouth, *Caterer and Hotel Keeper*, 10 March 1966, p. 34.

187. Motel idea became high class hotel, *Caterer and Hotel Keeper*, 24 April 1969, p. 19.

188. English Traditions the Aim of New American Hotel in London, *Caterer and Hotel Keeper*, 4 June 1960, p. 21.

189. Henry End, The Interiors Book of Hotel & Motor Hotels, New York: Whitney Library of Design, 1963, p. 86.

190. London's First Skyscraper Hotel, *Caterer and Hotel Keeper*, 7 January 1961, p. 21.

191. Brochure from the inauguration of the Carlton Tower Hotel, author's collection.

192. Carlton Tower Hotel is Dedicated to the Highest Standards, *Caterer and Hotel Keeper*, 21 January 1961, pp. 32-33.

193. Brochure from the inauguration of the Carlton Tower Hotel, author's collection.

194. 450-Room skyscraper in Hammersmith Scheme, *Caterer and Hotel Keeper*, 29 October 1960, p. 24.

195. Hotels Prominent in Piccadilly Plans, *Caterer and Hotel Keeper*, 18 February 1961, p. 27.

196. Annabel Jane Wharton, Building the Cold War: Hilton International Hotels and Modern Architecture, Chicago: The University of Chicago Press, 2001, pp. 19-87.

197. Annabel Jane Wharton, Building the Cold War: Hilton International Hotels and Modern Architecture, Chicago: The University of Chicago Press, 2001, p. 33

198. Annabel Jane Wharton, Building the Cold War: Hilton International Hotels and Modern Architecture, Chicago: The University of Chicago Press, 2001, pp. 98-99.

199. The New York Times, 5 October 1953, p. 29.

200. David Clutterbuck and Marion Devine, Clore: The Man and his Millions, London: George Weidenfeld & Nicholson Ltd, 1987, pp. 60-61.

201. David Clutterbuck and Marion Devine, Clore: The Man and his Millions, London: George Weidenfeld & Nicholson Ltd, 1987, pp. 57-58.

202. David Clutterbuck and Marion Devine, Clore: The Man and his Millions, London: George Weidenfeld & Nicholson Ltd, 1987, pp. 118-119.

203. Annabel Jane Wharton, Building the Cold War: Hilton International Hotels and Modern Architecture, Chicago: The University of Chicago Press, 2001, p. 99.

204. Skyscraper Hotel Inquiry Opens, *Caterer and Hotel Keeper*, 9 November 1957, p. 21.

205. David Clutterbuck and Marion Devine, Clore: The Man and his Millions, London: George Weidenfeld & Nicholson Ltd, 1987, p. 111.

206. David Clutterbuck and Marion Devine, Clore: The Man and his Millions, London: George Weidenfeld & Nicholson Ltd, 1987, p. 110.

207. Kate Wharton: Talking to Sidney Kaye, *Architect and Building News*, December 3, 1970, pp. 50-51.

208. Eric Firman, Obituary: Sidney Kaye, *Royal Institute of British Architects Journal*, September 1992, p. 69.

209. Mr Clore and Mr Hilton Sign Contract to Build Skyscraper Hotel, *Caterer and Hotel Keeper*, 2 April 1960, p. 27.

210. David Clutterbuck and Marion Devine, Clore: The Man and his Millions, London: George Weidenfeld & Nicholson Ltd, 1987, pp. 119-120.

211. David Clutterbuck and Marion Devine, Clore: The Man and his Millions, London: George Weidenfeld & Nicholson Ltd, 1987, p. 120.

212. Visit by the author to the London Hilton on 4 May 2013. Information from the hotel's assistant manager.

213. Annabel Jane Wharton, Building the Cold War: Hilton International Hotels and Modern Architecture, Chicago: The University of Chicago Press, 2001, p. 98.

214. Scottish Tapestry for Ballroom Stairway Wall, *Caterer and Hotel Keeper*, 20 April 1963, p. 75.

215. The London Hilton Opens New Vista for West End Hotels, *Caterer and Hotel Keeper*, 20 April 1963, pp. 42-45.

216. Easter Debut for London Hilton, *Caterer and Hotel Keeper*, 23 February 1963, p. 41.

217. Easter Debut for London Hilton, *Caterer and Hotel Keeper*, 23 February 1963, p. 41.

218. Charles Gordon, The Two Tycoons: A personal memoir of Charles Clore and Jack Cotton, London: Hamish Hamilton, 1984, p. 133.

219. Elain Harwood, Space, Hope and Brutalism, New Haven and London: Yale University Press, 2015, p. 401.

220. Richard Seifert in conversation with Martin Pawley, Building Design, February 1970, p. 6.

221. Elain Harwood, Space, Hope and Brutalism, New Haven and London: Yale University Press, 2015, p. 401.

222. Everything in the 'Garden', *Architect and Building News*, 1 December 1965, p. 1020.

223. Charles Gordon, The Two Tycoons: A personal memoir of Charles Clore and Jack Cotton, London: Hamish Hamilton, 1984, pp. 126-145.

224. Everything in the 'Garden', *Architect and Building News*, 1 December 1965, p. 1020.

225. A Showcase for Today's Artists, *Caterer and Hotel Keeper*, 5 August 1965, p. 47.

226. Brochure for the Royal Garden Hotel, author's collection.

227. A Showcase for Today's Artists, *Caterer and Hotel Keeper*, 5 August 1965, p. 47.

228. Towards the Rocket Age, Caterer and Hotel Keeper, 5 August 1965, p. 29.

229. Everything in the 'Garden', *Architect and Building News*, 1 December 1965, p. 1020.

230. Elain Harwood, Space, Hope and Brutalism, New Haven and London: Yale University Press, 2015, p. 401.

231. Alexander Koch, Hotelbauten, Stuttgart: Verlaganstalt Alexander Koch GmbH, 1958, p. 3

232. Alexander Koch, Hotelbauten, Stuttgart: Verlaganstalt Alexander Koch GmbH, 1958, p. 19, p. 21 and p. 25.

233. Alexander Koch, Hotelbauten, Stuttgart: Verlaganstalt Alexander Koch GmbH, 1958, p. 35

234. W.S. Hattrell and Partners, Hotels Restaurants, London: B.T. Batsford Ltd, 1962, p

235. W.S. Hattrell and Partners, Hotels Restaurants, London: B.T. Batsford Ltd, 1962, p

236. W.S. Hattrell and Partners, Hotels Restaurants, London: B.T. Batsford Ltd, 1962, p. 18.

237. W.S. Hattrell and Partners, Hotels Restaurants, London: B.T. Batsford Ltd, 1962, p. 42.

238. W.S. Hattrell and Partners, Hotels Restaurants, London: B.T. Batsford Ltd, 1962, pp. 58-59.

239. Charles Forte, Forte: The Autobiography of Charles Forte, London: Pan Books, 1997, p. 89.

240. Escoffier and the Deep-Freeze, *Caterer and Hotel Keeper*, 12 January 1967, p. 1.

241. New Bedford will give 184 more rooms, *Caterer and Hotel Keeper*, 16 January 1964, p. 51.

242. Television and Stereo Music for Guests in New 450-Room London Hotel, *Caterer and Hotel Keeper*, 14 May 1960, p. 21.

243. Hotels: The immediate present, *Architectural Review*, 1 October 1960, p. 303

244. Mary Cathcart Borer, The British Hotel Through the Ages, Guildford and London: Lutterworth Press, 1972, p. 237-244

245. Trust Houses Plan £2 Million Expansion, *Caterer and Hotel Keeper*, 14 January 1961, p. 21.

246. Trust Houses' 'Dragon' in Swansea will be the next new hotel to Open, *Caterer and Hotel Keeper*, 28 January 1961, p. 17.

247. Trust Houses open new Dragon Hotel in Swansea, *Caterer and Hotel Keeper*, 20 May 1961, p. 33 and p. 37.

248. Another Trust House in London, *Caterer and Hotel Keeper*, 24 December 1960, p. 11.

249. Trust Houses Commemorate County of their Birth, *Caterer and Hotel Keeper*, 16 September 1961, pp. 49-53.

250. Trust Houses Plan 'Hotel in the Sky' on Site of Old Queen's Hall, *Caterer and Hotel Keeper*, 19 August 1961, p. 25.

251. Interview with Brian Beardsmore at his home in London by Bruce Peter on 20 February 2012.

252. Trust Houses Chairman Reveals Plans for Vast Developments, *Caterer and Hotel Keeper*, 15 July 1961, p. 29.

253. Interview with Nelson Foley's son, Professor Robert Foley of Cambridge University, by Bruce Peter by telephone on 26 May 2016.

254. Palisadoes Airport, *Architect and Building News*, 12 February 1958, pp. 219-221. Foley worked on this project with Michael Manser and Hugh Laing Davis.

255. Buildings in the News, *Architects' Journal*, 23 April 1953, p. 517. See also *Architects' Journal*, 9 February 1961, p. 232.

256. Interview with Nelson Foley's son, Professor Robert Foley of Cambridge University, by Bruce Peter by telephone on 26 May 2016.

257. 400-year-old 'Ship' to become Motor Hotel, *Caterer and Hotel Keeper*, 22 July 1961, p. 26.

258. The Lincoln Handicap, *Architects' Journal*, 12 May 1965, p. 1104.

259. The Lincoln Handicap, *Architects' Journal*, 12 May 1965, p. 1104.

260. The Lincoln Handicap, *Architects' Journal*, 12 May 1965, p. 1104.

261. Hallam Tower Hotel, Sheffield, *The Builder*, 2 April 1965, pp. 719-722.

262. The Hallam Tower Hotel, *Architect and Building News*, 17 November 1965, p. 924.

263. Interview with Nelson Foley's son, Professor Robert Foley of Cambridge University, by Bruce Peter by telephone on 26 May 2016.

264. The Hallam Tower Hotel, *Architect and Building News*, 17 November 1965, pp. 921-924.

265. Inaugural press brochure for the Hallam Tower Hotel, author's collection.

266. Breakspear Motor Hotel, Hemel Hempstead, *Caterer and Hotel Keeper*, 4 February 1965, p . 27 and p. 38.

267. Breakspear Motor Hotel, Hemel Hempstead, *Caterer and Hotel Keeper*, 4 February 1965, p. 38.

268. Contrasting styles of two recently-completed hotels, *Architect and Building News*, 24 February 1965, p. 347.

269. Breakspear Motor Hotel, Hemel Hempstead, *Caterer and Hotel Keeper*, 4 February 1965, p. 38.

270. Trust Houses extract from the annual report and statement of accounts, *Caterer and Hotel Keeper*, 10 March 1966, p. 91.

271. Grosvenor House, Sheffield, will have 118 rooms, *Caterer and Hotel Keeper*, 1963, 1 June 1963, p. 34.

272. Design for a luxury hotel: why furniture was exclusively produced for the Grosvenor House in Sheffield, *Caterer and Hotel Keeper*, 10 March 1966, pp. 44-45.

273. Cavendish Strikes New Hotel Formula, *Caterer and Hotel Keeper*, 7 July 1966, p. 37.

274. Cavendish Strikes New Hotel Formula, *Caterer and Hotel Keeper*, 7 July 1966, p. 37.

275. Cavendish Strikes New Hotel Formula, *Caterer and Hotel Keeper*, 7 July 1966, p. 37.

276. Inside the New Cavendish, *Caterer and Hotel Keeper*, 7 July 1966, p. 21

277. Trust Houses to shelve Long-Term Projects, *Caterer and Hotel Keeper*, 11 August 1966, p. 21.

278. Richard Binstead, The new-look Trust Houses, *Caterer and Hotel Keeper*, 7 September 1967, p. 43.

279. £300,000 motor hotel for Trust Houses, *Caterer and Hotel Keeper*, 11 July 1968, p. 11.

280. £300,000 motor hotel for Trust Houses, *Caterer and Hotel Keeper*, 11 July 1968, p. 11.

281. Elain Harwood, White Light/White Heat: rebuilding England's Provincial Towns and Cities in the Sixties in Elain Harwood and Alan Powers (eds), Twentieth Century Architecture 6: The Sixties: Life, Style, Architecture, London: Twentieth Century Society, 2002, p. 62.

282. Interview with Brian Beardsmore at his home in London by Bruce Peter on 20 February 2012.

283. David Lawrence, Food on the Move: The extraordinary world of the motorway service area, London: Donlon Books, 2010, p. 50.

284. Rank move into North-East, *Caterer and Hotel Keeper*, 22 October 1964, p. 37.

285. Ann Glen, The Cairngorm Gateway, Dalkeith: Scottish Cultural Press, 2002, pp. 253-254.

286. Interview with Ray Leigh, former partner in Russell, Hodgson & Leigh, by Bruce Peter by telephone on 19 July 2016.

287. Interview with Ray Leigh, former partner in Russell, Hodgson & Leigh, by Bruce Peter by telephone on 19 July 2016.

288. Coylumbridge Hotel, Speyside – where Ranks have combined hotel-keeping and entertainment, *Caterer and Hotel Keeper*, 20 January 1966, pp. 85-87.

289. Coylumbridge Hotel, Speyside – where Ranks have combined hotel-keeping and entertainment, *Caterer and Hotel Keeper*, 20 January 1966, p. 87.

290. Coylumbridge Hotel, Interior Design, May 1966, p. 243.

291. Rank Give Tyneside New 108-Bedroom Hotel, *Caterer and Hotel Keeper*, 26 May 1966, p. 37.

292. Microwave Ovens in Rank's 'Office Block' Hotel, *Caterer and Hotel Keeper*, 30 June 1966, p. 23.

293. Microwave Ovens in Rank's 'Office Block' Hotel, *Caterer and Hotel Keeper*, 30 June 1966, p. 23.

294. *Caterer and Hotel Keeper*, 27 October 1966, p. 35.

295. Rank Open Their Fourth New Hotel This Year, *Caterer and Hotel Keeper*, 8 December 1966, p. 27.

296. Marketing Expert Takes Over Rank Hotel Division, *Caterer and Hotel Keeper*, 7 July 1966, p. 35.

297. *Caterer and Hotel Keeper*, Royal Lancaster Hotel Supplement, 3 august 1967, pp. 5-8.

298. Interview with Sarah Evelegh, formerly of Cassidy, Farrington and Dennys, by Bruce Peter by telephone on 30 January 2016, interview with Nigel Farrington by Bruce Peter by telephone on 1 February 2016 and interview with John Rhodes, formerly of Cassidy, Farrington and Dennys, by Bruce Peter by telephone on 1 February 2016.

299. Interview with Sarah Evelegh, formerly of Cassidy, Farrington and Dennys by Bruce Peter by telephone on 30 January 2016.

300. The Royal Lancaster Hotel, Bayswater, London, *Architectural Review*, February 1968, p. 119.

301. The Royal Lancaster Hotel, Bayswater, London, *Architectural Review*, February 1968, p. 122.

302. The Royal Lancaster Hotel, Bayswater, London, *Architectural Review*, February 1968, p. 122.

303. The Royal Lancaster Hotel, Bayswater, London, *Architectural Review*, February 1968, p. 121.

304. The Royal Lancaster Hotel, Bayswater, London, *Architectural Review*, February 1968, p. 121.

305. 'Height of Luxury': the new London Hilton roof restaurant, *Caterer and Hotel Keeper*, 18 May 1967, p. 62.

306. Design Problems at the Falkirk Met, *Caterer and Hotel Keeper*, 17 March 1966, p. 37.

307. New £250,000 Hotel Opens Next Week in Burnley, *Caterer and Hotel Keeper*, 23 April 1960, p. 22.

308. Britain's Newest Hotel Opens This Week, *Caterer and Hotel Keeper*, 30 April 1960, p. 31.

309. Interview with Enrico de Pierro by Jim Donaldson, McGill University School of Architecture website, https://www.mcgill.ca/architecture/aluminterviews/depierro

310. 40-bedroomed Garrion Hotel at Motherwell Costs £200,000, *Caterer and Hotel Keeper*, 5 January 1963, pp. 38-39.

311. New hotels planned for Glasgow but few are under way, *Caterer and Hotel Keeper*, 12 January 1963, p. 41.

312. Tower of Strength for Glasgow Tourism, *Caterer and Hotel Keeper*, 25 February 1965, p. 43.

313. Gosforth Park Hotel, *Building*, 7 April 1967, pp. 89-93.

314. Thistle's £1 m. Hotel Opens To-day, *Caterer and Hotel Keeper*, 6 October 1966, p. 37.

315. Thistle Pacesetter, *Caterer and Hotel Keeper*, 13 October 1966, p. 27.

316. Gosforth Park Hotel, *Building*, 7 April 1967, pp. 89-93.

317. Thistle Pacesetter, *Caterer and Hotel Keeper*, 13 October 1966, p. 27.

318. Scandinavian touch at York's new hotel, *Caterer and Hotel Keeper*, 14 November 1968, pp. 73-75.

319. The Bruce – More than a luxury hotel, *Caterer and Hotel Keeper*, 24 October 1968, p. 51.

320. The Bruce – More than a luxury hotel, *Caterer and Hotel Keeper*, 24 October 1968, p. 51.

321. 1963 will see the opening of this new hotel in Manchester, *Caterer and Hotel Keeper*, 30 December 1961, p. 13.

322. Ann Satchell, Manchester's Hotel Piccadilly, *Caterer and Hotel Keeper*, 22 April 1965, p. 57.

323. Elain Harwood, White Light/White Heat: Rebuilding England's Provincial Towns and Cities in Elain Harwood and Alan Powers (eds), The Sixties, Twentieth Century Architecture Six: The Sixties, London: The Twentieth Century Society, 2002, p. 64.

324. *Architect and Building News*, 17 November 1965, p. 15.

325. http://www.scotsman.com/news/obituaries/michael-demarco-1-631667

326. Anne Satchell, Manchester's Hotel Piccadilly, *Caterer and Hotel Keeper*, 22 April 1965, p. 57.

327. Brewers open Elegant New Hotel in Dundee, *Caterer and Hotel Keeper*, 12 March 1964, p. 93.

328. New Hotel Planned in Falkirk Scheme, *Caterer and Hotel Keeper*, 14 May 1960, p. 51.

329. Opening Next Week, *Caterer and Hotel Keeper*, 3 March 1966, p. 37.

330. Design Problems at the Falkirk Met, *Caterer and Hotel Keeper*, 17 March 1966, p. 37.

331. Design Problems at the Falkirk Met, *Caterer and Hotel Keeper*, 17 March 1966, p. 37.

332. £2m Grand Met. Hotel for Glasgow, *Caterer and Hotel Keeper*, 27 January 1966, p. 38.

333. Thornaby new town centre, *The Times*, 12 May 1967, p. 6.

334. New Hotel for New Town, *Caterer and Hotel Keeper*, 11 August 1966, p. 27.

335. Scottish hotels are being built just to get a licence – claim, *Caterer and Hotel Keeper*, 9 September 1971, p. 2.

336. Corporation may buy hotel and then have it demolished, *Glasgow Herald*, 23 November 1981, p. 5.

337. Ann Glen, The Cairngorm Gateway, Dalkeith: Scottish Cultural Press, 2002, pp. 259-260.

338. Ann Glen, The Cairngorm Gateway, Dalkeith: Scottish Cultural Press, 2002, pp. 259-260.

339. Raymond Fitzwalter and David Taylor, Web of Corruption, St Albans: Granada Publishing, 1981, p. 92.

340. Aviemore Centre brochure, 1968.

341. Ann Glen, The Cairngorm Gateway, Dalkeith: Scottish Cultural Press, 2002, p. 262.

342. Ann Glen, The Cairngorm Gateway, Dalkeith: Scottish Cultural Press, 2002, p. 262.

343. See Raymond Fitzwalter and David Taylor, Web of Corruption, St Albans: Granada Publishing, 1981 for a detailed description of Poulson's illegal activities and downfall.

344. Kjeld Vindum and Carsten Thau, Jacobsen, Copenhagen: The Danish Architectural Press, 2001, p. 167.

345. *Newcastle Evening Chronicle*, 17 August 1968, p. 5.

346. What State Aid Will Do, *Caterer and Hotel Keeper*, 23 June 1966, p. 49.

347. A Hotel Victory – But Commons Hurdle Stays, *Caterer and Hotel Keeper*, 11 August 1966, p. 19.

348. Hotels: Indictment, *Architectural Review*, 1 September 1972, p. 134.

349. £320 m. invested in new hotel beds, *Caterer and Hotel Keeper*, 15 April 1971, p. 3.

350. 235 new hotel bedrooms every week, *Caterer and Hotel Keeper*, 15 October 1970, p. 5.

351. Wanted: 40,000 staff for new hotels by 1973, *Caterer and Hotel Keeper*, 6 May 1971, p. 1.

352. Trust Houses advertisement, *Caterer and Hotel Keeper*, 11 July 1968, p. 11.

353. £800,000 150-Bed Hotel Planned for Plymouth Hoe, *Caterer and Hotel Keeper*, 19 March 1960, p. 35.

354. Michael Blee, Building Study: Hotel: Architect's Account, *Architects' Journal*, 29 July 1970, p. 239 (pp. 239-252).

355. Michael Blee, Building Study: Hotel: Architect's Account, *Architects' Journal*, 29 July 1970, p. 242 (pp. 239-252).

356. Michael Blee, Building Study: Hotel: Architect's Account, *Architects' Journal*, 29 July 1970, p. 239 (pp. 239-252).

357. Michael Blee, Building Study: Hotel: Architect's Account, *Architects' Journal*, 29 July 1970, p. 239 (pp. 239-252).

358. The Leicester Post House, *Caterer and Hotel Keeper*, 17 September 1970, p. 41.

359. The Leicester Post House, *Caterer and Hotel Keeper*, 17 September 1970, p. 41. The Bell Hotel was a Georgian coaching inn, operated by Trust Houses and demolished as part of the redevelopment of Leicester's Haymarket.

360. Trust Houses pull off the double, *Caterer and Hotel Keeper*, 23 September 1971, p. 11.

361. Aviemore Post House gets breathing space after hectic start, *Caterer and Hotel Keeper*, 10 December 1971, p. 13.

362. Charles Forte, Forte: The Autobiography of Charles Forte, London: Pan Books, 1997, p. 120-146.

363. Interview with Michael Lyell's former architectural partner Clive Sturley by Bruce Peter by telephone on 30 May 2016.

364. Advertisement for the Excelsior Hotel, Seeing Glasgow: the official guide book, The Corporation of Glasgow, 1971.

365. Historic changes for Trust Houses Forte Hotels, *Caterer and Hotel Keeper*, February 1972, p. 35.

366. T.H.F. opens 19th Post House at Norwich, *Caterer and Hotel Keeper*, 15 June 1972, p. 21.

367. Post House number 20 opens in Ipswich, *Caterer and Hotel Keeper*, 20 July 1972, p. 71.

368. Interview with Brian Beardsmore at his home in London by Bruce Peter on 20 February 2012.

369. 1972 brochure for the Albany Hotel, Glasgow.

370. Albany Hotel, Glasgow, Architect: Dennis Lennon, *Architectural Review*, June 1973, pp. 375-380

The moderne-style Bewdley Hotel in Newquay demonstrates typical rectilinear and symmetrical design of the mid-1930s.

371. Thistle in Birmingham, *Caterer and Hotel Keeper*, 2 March 1972,

372. Lenin plaque unveiled at new Royal Scot, *Caterer and Hotel Keeper*, 10 September 1972 p. 8.

373. Thistle to open Luton's largest hotel, *Caterer and Hotel Keeper*, 10 September 1972, p. 8.

374. Dan Cruikshank, Edinburgh: the image crumbles, *Architects' Journal*, 16 January 1974, p. 101.

375. Dan Cruikshank, Edinburgh: the image crumbles, *Architects' Journal*, 16 January 1974, p. 102.

376. Thistle's flagship launched at Liverpool, *Caterer and Hotel Keeper*, 2 July 1973, p. 68.

377. Thistle's flagship launched at Liverpool, *Caterer and Hotel Keeper*, 2 July 1973, pp. 68-69.

378. Thistle's flagship launched at Liverpool, *Caterer and Hotel Keeper*, 2 July 1973, p. 71.

379. Thistle's flagship launched at Liverpool, *Caterer and Hotel Keeper*, 2 July 1973, p. 71.

380. Thistle's flagship launched at Liverpool, *Caterer and Hotel Keeper*, 2 July 1973, p. 72.

381. Ladbroke's Dragonara Hotels off to a flying start, *Caterer and Hotel Keeper*, 12 April 1973, p. 4.

382. Ladbroke's Dragonara Hotels off to a flying start, *Caterer and Hotel Keeper*, 12 April 1973, p. 4.

383. https://www.questia.com/newspaper/1G1-433364950/digging-into-past-life-of-dragonara

384. Michael Forsyth, Pevsner Architectural Guides: Bath, New Haven and London: Yale University Press, 2003, p223. Somewhat unfairly, Forsyth describes it as 'the most reviled building in Bath.'

385. The Holiday inns Story – How it all works, *Caterer and Hotel Keeper*, 20 May 1971, p. 43.

386. Alan Sutton, The Holiday Inn invasion begins, *Caterer and Hotel Keeper*, 7 January 1971, p. 11.

387. Patricia Wilkins, Holiday Inn comes to Leicester, *Caterer and Hotel Keeper*, 16 September 1971, p. 11.

388. John V. Punter, Design Control in Bristol 1940-1990, Bristol: Redcliffe Press, 2001, p. 88.

389. Bristol Holiday Inn started, *Caterer and Hotel Keeper*, 25 March 1971, p. 13.

390. Skyline: Access All Areas, *Caterer and Hotel Keeper*, 14 October 1971, p. 72.

391. Skyline food service, *Caterer and Hotel Keeper*, 14 October 1971, p. 79.

392. Skyline bedrooms, *Caterer and Hotel Keeper*, 14 October 1971, p. 72.

393. Esso open first Scottish motor hotel, *Glasgow Herald*, 22 May 1970, p. 14.

394. New hotel in progress near Erskine Bridge, *Glasgow Herald*, 10 January 1972, p. 6.

395. New hotel in progress near Erskine Bridge, *Glasgow Herald*, 10 January 1972, p. 6.

396. John Carter, Technical Study: Integrated design and construction Esso Motor Hotel at Bristol, *Architects' Journal*, 21 March 1973, p. 707.

397. John Carter, Technical Study: Integrated design and construction Esso Motor Hotel at Bristol, *Architects' Journal*, 21 March 1973, p. 712.

398. John Carter, Technical Study: Integrated design and construction Esso Motor Hotel at Bristol, *Architects' Journal*, 21 March 1973, p. 712.

The Tides Reach Hotel near Salcombe on the Kingsbridge Estuary was one of many new holiday hotels completed in the late-1930s in south-west England.

399. Esso open Bristol hotel, *Caterer and Hotel Keeper*, 20 July 1972, p. 4.

400. The Esso Motor Hotel, Wembley, *Interior Design*, August 1973, p. 518.

401. Beechwood Motor Hotel, Runcorn, *Architects' Journal*, 7 August 1974, p. 321.

402. Beechwood Motor Hotel Runcorn, *Architects' Journal*, 7 August 1974, p. 321.

403. Topping out at Runcorn, *Caterer and Hotel Keeper*, 27 July 1972, p. 9.

404. Hotels: Indictment, Architectural Review, 1 September 1972, p. 133.

405. Hotels: Indictment, Architectural Review, 1 September 1972, p. 133.

406. Hotels: Indictment, Architectural Review, 1 September 1972, p. 133.

407. Hotels: Indictment, *Architectural Review*, 1 September 1972, p. 134.

408. William Wilkins, High Visual Illiteracy, *The Spectator*, 11 May 1973, p. 7.

409. William Wilkins, High Visual Illiteracy, *The Spectator*, 11 May 1973, p. 7.

410. Trafalgar House's first flagship, *Caterer and Hotel Keeper*, 3 September 1970, p. 27.

411. Hotels: Indictment, *Architectural Review*, 1 September 1972, p. 136.

412. Introducing the Park Tower, *Caterer and Hotel Keeper*, 21 June 1973, p. 39.

413. The Park Tower hotel reception, *Caterer and Hotel Keeper*, 21 June 1973, p. 41.

414. The Park Tower restaurants, *Caterer and Hotel Keeper*, 21 June 1973, p. 41.

415. The Park Tower restaurants, *Caterer and Hotel Keeper*, 21 June 1973, p. 41.

416. The Park Tower bedrooms, *Caterer and Hotel Keeper*, 21 June 1973, p. 53.

417. The Park Tower bedrooms, *Caterer and Hotel Keeper*, 21 June 1973, p. 53.

418. Hotels: Indictment, *Architectural Review*, 1 September 1972, p. 137.

419. The London Penta Hotel, *Interior Design*, August 1973, p. 524.

420. Interview with Nigel Farrington by Bruce Peter by telephone on 1 February 2016.

421. London's largest 'sleeper' opens, *Caterer and Hotel Keeper*, 8 March 1973, p. 6.

422. Peter J. Lord, Comment on the Tara Hotel, *Interior Design*, August 1973, p. 514.

423. Hotels: Indictment, *Architectural Review*, 1 September 1972, p. 134.

424. New Centre Hotel for London, *Caterer and Hotel Keeper*, 15 October 1970, p. 5.

425. It's quiet at the new Heathrow Hotel, *Caterer and Hotel Keeper*, 28 June 1973, p. 47.

426. It's quiet at the new Heathrow Hotel, *Caterer and Hotel Keeper*, 28 June 1973, p. 47.

427. It's quiet at the new Heathrow Hotel, *Caterer and Hotel Keeper*, 28 June 1973, p. 47.

428. Hotels: Indictment, Architectural Review, 1 September 1972, p. 138.

429. Hotels: Indictment, Architectural Review, 1 September 1972, p. 134.

430. Hotels: Indictment, Architectural Review, 1 September 1972, p. 134.

431. Hotels: Indictment, Architectural Review, 1 September 1972, p. 134.

432. Hotels: Indictment, Architectural Review, 1 September 1972, p. 139.

433. Hotels: Indictment, Architectural Review, 1 September 1972, p. 142.

434. Hotels: Indictment, Architectural Review, 1 September 1972, p. 139.

435. Hotels: Indictment, *Architectural Review*, 1 September 1972, p. 141.

436. Hotels: Indictment, *Architectural Review*, 1 September 1972, p. 142.

437. Hotels: Indictment, *Architectural Review*, 1 September 1972, p. 142.

438. Hotels: Indictment, *Architectural Review*, 1 September 1972, p. 142.

439. Interview with Gordon Bowyer by Bruce Peter by telephone on 20 January 2016.

440. No choice but to build an expensive ant heap, *Caterer and Hotel Keeper*, 15 April 1971, p. 1.

441. London's latest – and last? – de luxe hotel, *Caterer and Hotel Keeper*, 2 March 1972, p. 27.

442. Hotels: Indictment, *Architectural Review*, 1 September 1972, p. 139.

443. Hotels: Indictment, Architectural Review, 1 September 1972, p. 139.

444. The Hilton, Stratford-upon-Avon, *Interior Design*, August 1973, p. 523.

445. Townscape with hotel, *Architects' Journal*, 8 August 1979, p. 283.

446. Lance Wright, Hotel, Hyde Park Corner, London, *Architects' Journal*, December 1975, p. 343.

447. Lance Wright, Hotel, Hyde Park Corner, London, *Architects' Journal*, December 1975, p. 343.

448. Lance Wright, Hotel, Hyde Park Corner, London, *Architects' Journal*, December 1975, p. 344.

449. Lance Wright, Hotel, Hyde Park Corner, London, *Architects' Journal*, December 1975, p. 344.

450. Lance Wright, Hotel, Hyde Park Corner, London, *Architects' Journal*, December 1975, p. 344.

451. Lance Wright, Hotel, Hyde Park Corner, London, *Architects' Journal*, December 1975, p. 344.

452. Georgian elegance revived: the Howard Hotel, London; Architects: Frederick Gibberd & Partners, *Interior Design*, August 1976, pp. 370-371.

453. Sutherland Lyall, Building Study: Arundel Great Court, *Architects' Journal*, 3 November 1976, p. 844.

454. Sutherland Lyall, Building Study: Arundel Great Court, *Architects' Journal*, 3 November 1976, p. 838-839. See also Georgian elegance revived: the Howard Hotel, London; Architects: Frederick Gibberd & Partners, *Interior Design*, August 1976, pp. 370-371.

455. London Central YMCA, *Building*, December 1977, pp. 75-82.

456. London Central YMCA, *Building*, December 1977, pp. 75-82.

457. British tourism – the world's great success story, *Caterer and Hotel Keeper*, 1 June 1972, p. 4.

458. Building Design, 7 November 2013, http://www.bdonline.co.uk/whatever-happened-to-student-housing?/5063213.article

459. Guy Julier, The Neo-Liberal Object (conference paper), Material Culture in Action, The Glasgow School of Art, 7 September 2015.

460. Marc Augé, Non-places: An introduction to the anthropology of supermodernity, London: Verso, 1993.

461. See The Spectator, 9 September 1943, Page 13, http://archive.spectator.co.uk/article/10th-september-1943/13/coloured-british-citizens Subsequently, Walduck is reported to have stated in the Manchester Guardian 'for myself, I don't care whether they are black or white or green or yellow, I only carry on the hotel to meet the requirements of the patrons.'

An early-1960s advertisement for the Ariel Hotel at London Airport makes a virtue of its high degree of sound-proofing. The image shows the importance of night illumination on buildings such as this, where guests might be checking in 24 hours a day.

The first thing you notice inside the **ARIEL** is the quiet

Bibliography and source list

Interviews

Interview with Brian Beardsmore at his home in London by Bruce Peter on 20 February 2012.

Interview with Gordon Bowyer by Bruce Peter by telephone on 20 January 2016.

Interview with Sarah Evelegh by Bruce Peter by telephone on 30 January 2016.

Interview with Nigel Farrington by Bruce Peter by telephone on 1 February 2016.

Interview with Robert Foley by Bruce Peter by telephone on 26 May 2016.

Interview with John Knight by Bruce Peter by telephone on 22 May 2016.

Interview with Ray Leigh by Bruce Peter by telephone on 19 July 2016.

Interview with Ronald Rabson, by Bruce Peter by telephone on 18 January 2016.

Interview with John Rhodes by Bruce Peter by telephone on 1 February 2016.

Interview with Clive Sturley by Bruce Peter by telephone on 30 May 2016.

Books

Augé, M., Non-places: An introduction to the anthropology of supermodernity, London: Verso, 1993.

Avermaete, T. and Massey, A. (eds), Hotel Lobbies and Lounges, Abingdon: Routledge, 2013.

Borer, M.C., The British Hotel Through the Ages, Guildford and London: Lutterworth Press, 1972.

Calder, B., Raw Concrete: The Beauty of Brutalism,London: William Heinemann, 2016.

Carey, J., The Intellectuals and the Masses, London: Faber & Faber, 1992.

Chapman, A. L. and Knight, R., Wages and Salaries in the United Kingdom, 1920–38 Cambridge: Cambridge University Press, 1953.

Charlesworth, G., A History of British Motorways, London: Thomas Telford Ltd, 1984.

Clutterbuck, D. and Devine, M., Clore: The Man and his Millions, London: George Weidenfeld & Nicholson Ltd, 1987

Eliseo, M. and Piccione, P., Transatlantici: The History of the Great Italian Liners on the Atlantic, Genoa: Tormena, 2001.

End, H., The Interiors Book of Hotel & Motor Hotels, New York: Whitney Library of Design, 1963.

Erdi, L., Doswell, R., Copp, B. and Lawson, F., 'Principles of Hotel Design', London: The Architectural Press, 1970.

Fitzwalter, R. and Taylor, D., Web of Corruption, St albans: Granada Publishing, 1981.

Forsyth, M., Pevsner Architectural Guides: Bath, New haven and London: Yale University Press, 2003.

Forte, C., Forte: The Autobiography of Charles Forte, London: Pan Books, 1997

Galbraith, J.K., The Great Crash 1929, London: Penguin, 1954.

Glen, A., The Cairngorm Gateway, Dalkeith: Scottish Cultural Press, 2002.

Gordon, C., The Two Tycoons: A personal memoir of Charles Clore and Jack Cotton, London: Hamish Hamilton, 1984.

Guise, B. and Brook, P., The Midland Hotel: Morecambe's White Hope, Lancaster: Palatine Books, 2007.

Guy, S. and Hanneberry J. (eds), Developers and Development: Perspectives on Property, London: Blackwell, 2002.

Hammill, F., Sophistication: A Literary and Cultural History, Liverpool: Liverpool University Press, 2010.

Harwood, E., Space, Hope and Brutalism, New Haven and London: Yale University Press, 2015.

Hattrell, W.S. and Partners, Hotels Restaurants, London: B.T. Batsford Ltd, 1962.

Koch, A., Hotelbauten, Stuttgart: Verlaganstalt Alexander Koch GmbH, 1958.

Lawrence, D., Food on the Move: The extraordinary world of the motorway service area, London: Donlon Books, 2010.

Lawson, F., 'Hotels, Motels and Condominiums: Design, Planning and Maintenance', London: The Architectural Press, 1976.

Lefebvre, H., The Production of Space, London: Wiley-Blackwell, 1991.

Loewy, R., Industrial Design, London: Laurence King, 1979.

McKean, C., The Scottish Thirties: An Architectural Introduction, Edinburgh: Scottish Academic Press, 1987.

Peter, B., Form Follows Fun: Modernism and modernity in British pleasure architecture 1925-1940, Abingdon: Routledge, 2007.

Powers, A., Oliver Hill: Architect and Lover of Life, London: Mouton Publications, 1989.

Pulitzer Finali, G., Navi e Case: Architetture Interni 1930-1935, Milan: Hoepli, 1935.

Punter, J.V., Design Control in Bristol 1940-1990, Bristol: Redcliffe Press, 2001.

Routh, G. Occupation and Pay in Great Britain, 1906–79. Cambridge: Cambridge University Press, 1980.

Shields, R., Places on the Margin: The Alternative Geographies of Modernity, London: Routledge, 1991.

Smith, D., Hotel and Restaurant Design, London: Design Council, 1978.

Stone, R. and Rowe, D.A. The Measurement of Consumer Behaviour in the United Kingdom, 1920–38, Cambridge: Cambridge University Press, 1966.

Urry, J., The Tourist Gaze: Leisure and Travel in Contemporary Societies, London: Sage, 2002.

Vindum, K., and Thau, C., Jacobsen, Copenhagen: The Danish Architectural Press, 2001.

Wharton, A.J., Building the Cold War; Hilton International Hotels and Modern Architecture, Chicago: The University of Chicago Press, 2001.

Journals

Architect and Building News

The Grosvenor House Hotel, 1 April 1927, p.578.

The Ocean Hotel, Saltdean, Brighton, 12 August 1938, pp.175-178.

Elmdon Airport, Birmingham, 18 August 1939, p.187.

Palisadoes Airport, 12 February 1958, pp.219-221.

Ariel Hotel, London Airport, Architect and Building News, March 1961, pp.379-386.

Motel at Epping in Essex, 17 October 1962, pp.579-582.

Hotel, London Airport, 8 April 1964, pp.623-628.

Contrasting styles of two recently-completed hotels, 24 February 1965, p.347.

The Hallam Tower Hotel, 17 November 1965, p.924.

Everything in the 'Garden', 1 December 1965, p.1020.

Wharton, K., Talking to Sidney Kaye, 3 December 1970, pp.50-51.

Architect and Surveyor

The Falcon Hotel, Stratford-upon-Avon, May-June 1968, pp.3-7.

Architects' Journal

Leathart, J., Dorchester Hotel, Park Lane, W, W. Curtis Green A.R.A. and Partners, Architects, 22 April 1931, pp.577-582.

Baillie Scott, M.H., Dorchester Hotel, 13 May 1931, p.689.

Park Lane Hotel Piccadilly Extension, 8 July 1931, pp.39-40.

RIBA Elections, 2 June 1938, p.936.

Law Report, 1 April 1937, p.382.

The Newcastle Competition, 23 February 1939, p.321.

Buildings in the News, 23 April 1953, p.517.

Richards, J.M., Buildings of the Year: 1954, 20 January 1955, p.86.

Crawley New Town, 9 February 1961, p.232.

Hotel, London Airport, 17 October 1962, p.918.

The Lincoln Handicap, 12 May 1965, p.1104.

Blee, M., Building Study: Hotel: Architect's Account, 29 July 1970, pp.239-252.

Carter, J., Technical Study: Integrated design and construction Esso Motor Hotel at Bristol, 21 March 1973, pp.707-712.

Cruikshank, D., Edinburgh: the image crumbles, The Architect's Journal, 16 January 1974, p.101.

Beechwood Motor Hotel, Runcorn, 7 August 1974, p.321.

Wright, L., Hotel, Hyde Park Corner, London, December 1975, pp.343-344.

Lyall, S., Building Study: Arundel Great Court, 3 November 1976, p.844.

Townscape with hotel, 8 August 1979, p.283.

Architectural Heritage

Neil Gregory, Monro and Partners: Shopping in Scotland with Marks & Spencer, Architectural Heritage XIV, 2003, p.75.

Architectural Review

Fry, E.M., Cumberland Hotel, January 1934, p.13.
Hotel at Coventry, September 1955, pp.195-199.
Hotel in Istanbul, November 1955, pp.291-296.
Hotels: The Immediate Prospect, October 1960, p.297-303.
The Royal Lancaster Hotel, Bayswater, LondonFebruary 1968, pp.119-121.
Hotels: Inquest on a Defeat, September 1972, pp.131-412.
Albany Hotel, Glasgow, Architect: Dennis Lennon, June 1973, pp.375-380.

Blackpool Gazette

The Manchester Hotel, 30 May 1936, p.12.

The Builder

The Ocean Hotel, Saltdean, Sussex, 5 August 1938, pp.249-253.
Obituary of Willie Richard Halstone Gardner, February 1962, p.253.
Hallam Tower Hotel, Sheffield, 2 April 1965, pp.719-722.

Building

Gosforth Park Hotel, 7 April 1967, pp.89-93.
Obituary for A.E.O. Geens, 17 March 1972, p.91.
London Central YMCA, December 1977, pp.75-82.

Building Design

Richard Seifert in conversation with Martin Pawley, February 1970, p.6.

Built Environment

Lord Holford on property development, October 1972, p.448.

Caterer and Hotel Keeper

Sir Francis Towle, The Full Story of the Mayfair Hotel, 15 February 1927, pp.122-123.
Hotel That Looks Like a 'Great White Ship', 15 July 1933, p.106.
Cumberland marks an epoch in history of Industry, December 1933, p.1180.
Louis, A.L., The Hotel of the Future: looking 50 years ahead, 31 March 1934, p.628.
£1,000,000 'Flatels' Scheme: Mount Royal nearly ready, 17 August 1934, p.331.
Famous LMS Hotel to Close?, 21 December 1934, p.1182.
Saunton Sands Hotel is Ready: Luxury building in Devon: Bookings already heavy, 14 June 1935, p.15.
New Clacton Hotel: Association pays visit to Oulton Hall, 12 July 1935, p.13.
New £200,000 Hotel for Bournemouth: Palace Court nearly ready to open, 27 September 1935, p.15.
LMS Restaurant to 'Go Overseas': From Gleneagles to South Africa, 15 November 1935, p.15.
Seven single houses, now one hotel, 10 January 1936, p22.
New Holiday Lido at the edge of the sea, 14 August 1936, p.20.
Transforming Famous Railway Hotel: Great Western Royal at Paddington on Third Stage of Modernisation, 4 June 1937, p.14.
Reconstruction of Carlton, Blackpool: 'Virtually a new hotel', 3 September 1937, p.12.
Hotel Planned with an Eye on the Future: Every bedroom has bathroom at new Green Park, Bournemouth, 19 November 1937, p.20.
Novel Ideas in New Luxury Hotel: Cumberland, Bournemouth opens this week-end, 11 February 1938, p.13.
Opening date for Beresford in Glasgow, 4 March 1938, p.13.
Shell of £200,000 hotel nearly ready, 11 March 1938, p.30.
Glasgow's First 'Skyscraper' Hotel29 April 1938, p.13.
New Hotel on North Circular Road, 17 June 1938 p.22.
To Manage Aerodrome Hotel, 29 April 1938, p.6.
400-room hotel on South Coast, 1 July 1938, p.15.

New £40,000 Scottish Hotel, 22 July 1938, p.15.

A.H. Jones, The Hotel of the Future: A forecast for the next 60 years, 29 July 1938, pp.33-35.

Lavish Décor in Butlin's £50,000 Hotel, 25 August 1938, p.10.

50,000 Guests in Six Months, 14 October 1938, p.26.

Tourists: Million Mark in Sight, 8 January 1955, p.19.

Britain's first American hotel opens in London, 19 March 1955, pp45-53.

The Royal Oak Motor Hotel, 3 July 1955, p.24.

Striking Design of New Coachotel at Dover, 18 May 1957, p.25.

Unique Hotel for Coach Tourists Costs Under £1,700 a Bedroom, The Caterer and Hotel-Keeper, 1 June 1957, p.39.

U.S. Hotel Architect States Six Basic Rules for New Hotel Design, 24 August 1957, p.17.

Skyscraper Hotel Inquiry Opens, 9 November 1957, p.21.

1960 Sees Opening of London Airport's First Hotel, 16 January 1960, p.53-54.

£800,000 150-Bed Hotel Planned for Plymouth Hoe, 19 March 1960, p.35.

London Airport's Circular hotel to be Known as 'The Ariel', 26 March 1960, p.22.

Mr Clore and Mr Hilton Sign Contract to Build Skyscraper Hotel, 2 April 1960, p.27.

New £250,000 Hotel Opens Next Week in Burnley, 23 April 1960, pp.22 and 31.

Television and Stereo Music for Guests in New 450-Room London Hotel, 14 May 1960, p.21.

Hotels Prepare for 30 Million Guests, 28 May 1960, p.23.

Rival Hotel Plans in Jermyn Street, 14 May 1960, p.25.

New Hotel Planned in Falkirk Scheme, 14 May 1960, p.51.

English Traditions the Aim of New American Hotel in London, 4 June 1960, p.21.

400-year-old 'Ship' to become Motor Hotel, 22 July 1961, p.26.

450-Room skyscraper in Hammersmith Scheme, 29 October 1960, p.24.

Another Trust House in London, 24 December 1960, p.11.

London's First Skyscraper Hotel7 January 1961, p.21.

Trust Houses Plan £2 Million Expansion, 14 January 1961, p.21.

Britain's First Circular Hotel Opens, 14 January 1961, p.19 and pp.26-27.

Carlton Tower Hotel is Dedicated to the Highest Standards, 21 January 1961, pp.32-33.

Trust Houses' 'Dragon' in Swansea will be the Next New Hotel to Open, 28 January 1961, p.17.

Hotels Prominent in Piccadilly Plans, 18 February 1961, p.27.

Trust Houses open new Dragon Hotel in Swansea, 20 May 1961, p.33 and p.37.

Ambitious Scheme for New Hotel at Hastings, 24 June 1961, p.37.

Trust Houses Chairman Reveals Plans for Vast Developments, 15 July 1961, p.29.

Trust Houses Plan 'Hotel in the Sky' on Site of Old Queen's Hall, 19 August 1961, p.25.

Trust Houses Commemorate County of their Birth16 September 1961, pp.49-53.

1963 will see the opening of this new hotel in Manchester, 30 December 1961, p.13.

40-bedroomed Garrion Hotel at Motherwell Costs £200,000, 5 January 1963, pp.38-39.

New hotels planned for Glasgow but few are under way, 12 January 1963, p.41.

Dolphin leaps into Swansea's Banquet Life, 26 January 1963, pp.41-43.

Easter Debut for London Hilton, 23 February 1963, p.41.

The London Hilton Opens New Vista for West End Hotels, The Caterer and Hotel-Keeper, 20 April 1963, pp.42-45.

Scottish Tapestry for Ballroom Stairway Wall, 20 April 1963, p.75.

Grosvenor House, Sheffield, will have 118 rooms, 1 June 1963, p.34.

Park-Eat-Sleep hotel Planned – No Extras, 21 November 1963, p.17.

New Bedford will give 184 more rooms, 16 January 1964, p.51.

'Caterer' Preview of Forte's New Hotel at London Airport, 23 January 1964, p.38.

Brewers open Elegant New Hotel in Dundee, 12 March 1964, p.93.

Forte Motor Lodge opens next month, 28 May 1964, p.34.

Signing Agreement, 4 June 1964, p.15.

Top Rank plan 150-bedroom hotel in Gibraltar, 3 September 1964, p.34.

Rank move into North-East, 22 October 1964, p.37.

Tower of Strength for Glasgow Tourism, 25 February 1965, p.43.

Breakspear Motor Hotel, Hemel Hempstead, 4 February 1965, p.27 and p.38.

New Skyway Hotels' £450,000 Plan in Southampton, 11 February 1965, p.35.

Scotland's Greatest Tourist Lure Means Prosperity for Hotels, 18 February 1965, p.75.

Satchell, A., Manchester's Hotel Piccadilly, 22 April 1965, p.57.

Towards the Rocket Age, 5 August 1965, p.29.

A Showcase for Today's Artists, 5 August 1965, p.47.

Death of Britain's Most Eminent Hotelier, 20 January 1966, p.39.

Coylumbridge Hotel, Speyside – where Ranks have combined hotel-keeping and entertainment, 20 January 1966, pp.85-87.

£2m Grand Met. Hotel for Glasgow, 27 January 1966, p.38.

Opening Next Week, 3 March 1966, p.37.

Hotel for Bournemouth, 10 March 1966, p.34.

Design for a luxury hotel: why furniture was exclusively produced for the Grosvenor House in Sheffield, 10 March 1966, pp.44-45.

Trust Houses extract from the annual report and statement of accounts, 10 March 1966, p.91.

Design Problems at the Falkirk Met, 17 March 1966, p.37.

Rank Give Tyneside New 108-Bedroom Hotel, 26 May 1966, p.37.

What State Aid Will Do, 23 June 1966, p.49.

Microwave Ovens in Rank's 'Office Block' Hotel, 30 June 1966, p.23

Inside the New Cavendish, 7 July 1966, p.21.

Marketing Expert Takes Over Rank Hotel Division7 July 1966, p.35.

Cavendish Strikes New Hotel Formula, 7 July 1966, p.37.

Polynesian Room at New Skyway Hotel, 21 July 1966, p.34.

A Hotel Victory – but Commons Hurdle Stays, 11 August 1966, p.19.

Trust Houses to shelve Long-Term Projects, 11 August 1966, p.21.

New Hotel for New Town, 11 August 1966, p.27.

Thistle's £1 m. Hotel Opens To-day, 6 October 1966, p.37.

Thistle Pacesetter, 13 October 1966, p.27.

Rank open their fourth new hotel this year, 8 December 1966, p.27.

Escoffier and the Deep-Freeze, 12 January 1967, p.1.

'Height of Luxury': the new London Hilton roof restaurant, 18 May 1967, p.62.

Royal Lancaster Hotel Supplement, 3 August 1967, pp.5-8.

Binstead, R., The new-look Trust Houses, 7 September 1967, p.43.

£300,000 motor hotel for Trust Houses, 11 July 1968, p.11.

Trust Houses advertisement, 11 July 1968, p.11

The Bruce – More than a luxury hotel, 24 October 1968, p.51.

Scandinavian touch at York's new hotel, 14 November 1968, pp.73-75.

Forte treatment for Airport Hotel, 9 January 1969, p.11.

Motel idea became high class hotel, 24 April 1969, p.19.

Trafalgar House's first flagship, 3 September 1970, p.27.

The Leicester Post House, 17 September 1970, p.41.

235 new hotel bedrooms every week, 15 October 1970, p.5.

New Centre Hotel for London, 15 October 1970, p.5.

Sutton, A., The Holiday Inn invasion begins, 7 January 1971, p.11.

No Choice but to build an expensive ant heap, 15 April 1971, p.1.

Patricia Wilkins, Holiday Inn comes to Leicester, 16 September 1971, p.11.

Trust Houses pull off the double, 23 September 1971, p.11.

Bristol Holiday Inn started, 25 March 1971, p.13.

£320 m. invested in new hotel beds, 15 April 1971, p.3.

Wanted: 40,000 staff for new hotels by 1973, 6 May 1971, p.1.

The Holiday Inns Story – How it all works, 20 May 1971, p.43.

Scottish hotels are being built just to get a licence – claim, 9 September 1971, p.2.

Skyline: Access All Areas, 14 October 1971, pp.72-79.

Design supplement, 25 November 1971, p.12.

Aviemore Post House gets breathing space after hectic start, 10 December 1971, p.13.

Historic changes for Trust Houses Forte Hotels, 12 February 1972, p.35.

Thistle in Birmingham, 2 March 1972, p.12.

London's latest – and last? – de luxe hotel, 2 March 1972, p.27.

British tourism – the world's great success story, 1 June 1972, p.4.

T.H.F. opens 19th Post House at Norwich, 15 June 1972, p.21.

Esso open Bristol hotel, 20 July 1972, p.4.

Post House number 20 opens in Ipswich, 20 July 1972, p.71.

Topping out at Runcorn, 27 July 1972, p.9.

Lenin plaque unveiled at new Royal Scot, 10 September 1972 p.8.

Thistle to open Luton's largest hotel, 10 September 1972, p.8.

London's largest 'sleeper' opens, 8 March 1973, p.6.

Ladbroke's Dragonara Hotels off to a flying start, 12 April 1973, p.4.

Introducing the Park Tower, 21 June 1973, p.39.

The Park Tower Hotel Reception, 21 June 1973, p.41.

The Park Tower Restaurants, 21 June 1973, p.41.

The Park Tower Bedrooms, 21 June 1973, p.53.

It's quiet at the new Heathrow Hotel, 28 June 1973, p.47.

Thistle's flagship launched at Liverpool, 2 July 1973, pp.68-72.

Commercial Motor

Passenger Travel News, 13 March 1928, p.16.

Country Life

Hussey, C., The Great Estates of London and Their Development: The Grosvenor Estate, 21 April 1928, p.565.

Saint, A. Evolution of a Hotel Interior, 2 July 1981, p.40.

Coventry News

Christina Savvas, Sadness as Coventry's Leofric Hotel Closes, 2 June 2008.

Glasgow Herald

Esso open first Scottish motor hotel, 22 May 1970, p.14.

New hotel in progress near Erskine Bridge, 10 January 1972, p.6.

Corporation may buy hotel and then have it demolished, 23 November 1981, p.5.

Interior Design

Coylumbridge Hotel, May 1966, p.243.

The Esso Motor Hotel, Wembley, August 1973, p.518.

Lord, P.J., Comment on the Tara Hotel, August 1973, p.514.

The Hilton, Stratford-upon-Avon, August 1973, p.523.

The London Penta Hotel, August 1973, p.524.

Georgian elegance revived: the Howard Hotel, London; Architects: Frederick Gibberd & Partners, August 1976, pp.370-371.

Journal of the Royal Institute of British Architects

Franck, J.E., Matthew J. Dawson, February 1944, pp.94-95.

Firman, E., Obituary: Sidney Kaye, September 1992, p.69.

Journal of Transport History

Pope, R., Railway companies and resort hotels between the wars, March 2001, pp.63-67.

Newcastle Evening Chronicle

Hotel for Eldon Square, 17 August 1968, p.5.

New York Times

Conrad Hilton Hotel in London, 5 October 1953, p.29.

The Spectator

Coloured British Citizens, 9 September 1943, p.13.

Wilkins, W., High Visual Illiteracy, The Spectator, 11 May 1973, p.7.

The Times

The Grosvenor House Hotel, 5 April 1928, p.8.

Modernisation at Paddington: Great Western Royal Hotel, 6 May 1937, p.12.

Mr T.C. Gordon's Affairs: Adverse World Conditions, 14 July 1939, p.4.

Continental Holidays by Car, 14 February 1956, p.7.

Thornaby new town centre, 12 May 1967, p.6.

Twentieth Century Architecture

Elain Harwood, White Light/White Heat: rebuilding England's Provincial Towns and Cities in the Sixties in Elain Harwood and Alan Powers (eds), Twentieth Century Architecture 6: The Sixties: Life, Style, Architecture, London: Twentieth Century Society, 2002, p.58.

Archival sources

Public Records Office, Kew

RAIL 418/29, LMS HCC, 26 November 1930, 20 May 1931; AN 109/636, Memos by A. E. Towle, 1 and 21 April 1927; Glynn to Stockton, 18 May 1931.

Web sources

http://www.scotsman.com/news/obituaries/michael-demarco-1-631667

Interview with Enrico de Pierro by Jim Donaldson, McGill University School of Architecture website, https://www.mcgill.ca/architecture/aluminterviews/depierro

https://www.questia.com/newspaper/1G1-433364950/digging-into-past-life-of-dragonara

Building Design, 7 November 2013, http://www.bdonline.co.uk/whatever-happened-to-student-housing?/5063213.article

Other items

1961 Advertisement for the Skyway Hotel in Southampton, author's collection.

Brochure from the inauguration of the Carlton Tower Hotel, author's collection.

Inaugural press brochure for the Hallam Tower Hotel, author's collection.

1966 brochure for the Royal Garden Hotel, author's collection.

1968 brochure for the Aviemore Centre, author's collection.

Guy Julier, The Neo-Liberal Object (conference paper), Material Culture in Action, The Glasgow School of Art, 7 September 2015.

Advertisement for the Excelsior Hotel in 'Seeing Glasgow: the official guide book', The Corporation of Glasgow, 1971.

1972 brochure for the Albany Hotel, Glasgow, author's collection.

Thanks:

The author and publisher extend their especial thanks to Ian Smith of Camrose Media for designing the book, to Elain Harwood for reading and correcting the manuscript, to Anthony Cooke for copy-editing the manuscript, to Ken Neil, Julie Ramage and Alison Hay of The Glasgow School of Art Research Office and to David Buri, Rebecca Olivia and Duncan Chappell of The Glasgow School of Art Library. In addition, the author wishes to thank the following for their assistance with the research: Joe Baldwin of Southampton City Archives, Susan Bennett, Gordon Bowyer, Robyne Calvert, Anne Cameron of Blackpool Archives, Paul Cleave, David Cornforth, Dawn Dyer of Bristol Central Library, Sarah Evelegh, Nigel Farrington, Anna Ferrari, Robert Foley, Thom Gorst, Theresa Gorst, David A. Hail of Glamorgan Archives, Ann Haynes, Ivan Jordan, Ceri Joseph of Porthcawl Museum, John Knight, Ray Leigh, Jonathan Makepeace of the British Architectural Library, RIBA, Darren Marsh, the staff of the General Services Department of the Mitchell Library in Glasgow, Catherine Moriarty, Theresa Oakley, Anthony Orchard of Burgh Island Hotel, Debbie Potter of Highland Archives, Robert Proctor, Olga Polizzi of Rocco Forte Hotels Ltd, Peter Quartermaine, Ronald Rabson, John Rhodes, Alison Spence of Cornwall Archives, Caroline Stockdale of Explore York Archives, Clive Sturley, Vicky Sutherland of Bristol Central Library, David Trevor-Jones, Deborah Tritton of Cornwall Archives, Colin Waller of Highland Archives.

Photo credits:

Brian Beardsmore collection: 28, 166, 167, 168, 169, 215, 216, Creative Commons/David Dixon: P233, Robert Foley collection: 24 bottom, 155, 157, 158, Anthony Orchard collection: 52, Ronald Rabson collection: 22 top left, 25, 104 centre, 108, 110. RIBA/British Architectural Library Photographs Collection: 37, 38 top, 58, 79 bottom, 80 bottom, 95, 107, 114, 124 top, 153, 175, 207, 211, 232, 236. David Trevor-Jones: 244, 249 bottom. All other illustrations are from the author's collection.

The Dover Stage Coachotel, occupying a commanding position on Dover's promenade.

Index

The De Montfort Hotel in Kenilworth was built in the late-1960s for the De Vere chain.

The Golden Acorn Hotel in the Scottish new town of Glenrothes.